T0271275

Mighty Microeconomics

Economics helps us to understand that certain slick mechanisms are operating beyond what we see in our daily economic lives. To fully understand and appreciate these mechanisms, we need to master the core mathematical theories, some of which are highly advanced and typically covered in a graduate course. This textbook presents those theories without compromising rigor, but, at the same time, the author offers a number of innovative pedagogical twists that make the difficult materials completely accessible to undergraduate students, and even to general readers. Written in a chatty, colloquial style, the author explains basic messages and core insights that are usually hidden between the lines. The usefulness of these theories is shown through a number of real-life examples, and, in the end, the readers can see that the mathematical models provide deep insights into social justice and philosophy. This book helps readers to think like an economist.

Michihiro Kandori is Professor of Economics at University of Tokyo. He was former Assistant Professor at the University of Pennsylvania and Princeton University, and Taussig Visiting Professor at Harvard University. He is the president of the Game Theory Society (2022–2024) and was a former associate editor of *Econometrica*, and fellow of the Econometric Society. He has published numerous articles in high-impact journals. He received his PhD from Stanford University under the supervision of Nobel laureate, Paul Milgrom. He has consistently received high ratings for his "Welcome to Game Theory" course on Coursera (more than 85,000 learners since 2015).

Mighty Microeconomics
A Guide to Thinking Like An Economist

Michihiro Kandori
University of Tokyo

CAMBRIDGE
UNIVERSITY PRESS

CAMBRIDGE
UNIVERSITY PRESS

Shaftesbury Road, Cambridge CB2 8EA, United Kingdom

One Liberty Plaza, 20th Floor, New York, NY 10006, USA

477 Williamstown Road, Port Melbourne, VIC 3207, Australia

314–321, 3rd Floor, Plot 3, Splendor Forum, Jasola District Centre, New Delhi – 110025, India

103 Penang Road, #05–06/07, Visioncrest Commercial, Singapore 238467

Cambridge University Press is part of Cambridge University Press & Assessment,
a department of the University of Cambridge.

We share the University's mission to contribute to society through the pursuit of
education, learning and research at the highest international levels of excellence.

www.cambridge.org
Information on this title: www.cambridge.org/highereducation/isbn/9781009161077

DOI: 10.1017/9781009161091

First published 2023

A catalogue record for this publication is available from the British Library.

Library of Congress Cataloging-in-Publication Data
Names: Kandori, Michihiro, author.
Title: Mighty microeconomics : a guide to thinking like an economist / Michihiro Kandori, University of Tokyo.
Other titles: Mikuro keizaigaku no chikara. English Description: Cambridge, United Kingdom ; New York, NY :
    Cambridge University Press, 2023. | Includes bibliographical references and index.
Identifiers: LCCN 2022049023 (print) | LCCN 2022049024 (ebook) | ISBN 9781009161077 (hardback) | ISBN
    9781009161084 (paperback) | ISBN 9781009161091 (epub)
Subjects: LCSH: Microeconomics.
Classification: LCC HB172 .K35713 2023 (print) | LCC HB172 (ebook) | DDC 338.5–dc23/eng/20221013
LC record available at https://lccn.loc.gov/2022049023
LC ebook record available at https://lccn.loc.gov/2022049024

ISBN 978-1-009-16107-7 Hardback
ISBN 978-1-009-16108-4 Paperback

Additional resources for this publication at www.cambridge.org/kandori

I dedicate this book to my wife, Sanae, and my sons, Kosei and Daichi.

They have been always with me, rain or shine, to make my academic and personal life full of joy.

Contents

Case Studies

Preface

Let's talk about the economy: prices, profits, taxes, and insurance, and so on. If I say that, your reaction might be, *"Oh no! I do not want to hear anything about dirty and boring money-making!"* Your point is well taken, because that was exactly what I felt when I started to study economics. But later, as I went on with my further studies, I was pleasantly surprised that economics showed me **a truly amazing mechanism** operating behind all those seemingly "boring" things, a magical mechanism that makes sure that we can get what we need in our society. Don't you want to see what that is?

According to a poll that asked which subjects businesspeople regretted not studying in school, economics came second, after national history.[1] This means that those businesspeople who, every day, face the economy, prices, profits, and so on found that there must be something, "secrets" of some kind, beyond what they see in their daily business lives, and, as a result, they are eager to understand what they are. If you hear that, aren't you now a bit more tempted to study economics?

If that is what you think, you have come to the right place, because this is a somewhat unusual and ambitious textbook. *It is completely self-contained, meaning that no prior knowledge of economics is required, which starts at the very basic level and guides you step by step to make sure you understand all the important topics in economics, including fairly advanced though vastly important materials that are typically taught in first-year graduate courses.* This book is for you if you are:

- an undergraduate or graduate student in economics;
- an economic policy-maker who needs to understand the basic principles of economics and economic policies;
- a person working for media in charge of economic news and reports;
- a businessperson who regrets not having studied economics;
- a person who likes to argue about how to make our society better and is keen to see the big picture of how our economy works;
- an economist in a think tank who needs a handbook of all essential tools of economics;
- a non-economics major student who is curious to see what economics is all about; or
- an ambitious high school student.

Although this book is readable for this general audience, it is quite different from the usual "introduction to economics" textbooks, which narrowly focus only on the very basic,

---

[1] As reported in a Japanese magazine, *Nikkei Business Associé*, February 2013.

easy-to-understand stuff; nor is it similar to popular "how to" books on economy and economics, which are targeted at busy businesspeople. Instead, this book squarely covers all standard academic topics taught in any economics department, starting from the first-year undergraduate economics up to the graduate core course in microeconomics. The book is based on my long teaching experience at the University of Tokyo, the University of Pennsylvania, Princeton University, London School of Economics and Political Science, and the École Polytechnique.

This textbook is unique in the following respects. First, *it does not shy away from the fact that the discipline of economics is built upon mathematical models and theories*. In my long teaching experience, I have found that a majority of significant findings in economics, something truly intellectually stimulating, can be presented and appreciated only with reference to mathematical models and theories, and teaching these at relatively early stages is quite effective to spur the interest of students. That is exactly what this book intends to do.

Second, the book is *nevertheless accessible not only to students with strong mathematical background but also to average undergraduate students, and even to a general audience* with the right mindset not to be scared by seemingly frightening mathematical ideas and symbols. Mathematical concepts and tools are explained "on the spot" where they are used, without assuming much prior knowledge of mathematics.[2] I know this works fine because I have been successfully teaching these things to second-year undergraduate students, in a large class that accommodates all economics major students, and I made liberal use of a number of pedagogical tips I have obtained in that course to make the mathematical models accessible without compromising rigor.

Third, I made sure that the ultimate goal of the book is not to understand economics *per se* but to understand how our economy works. To this end, I have incorporated *many real-life cases and examples that convincingly match the (highly stylized and seemingly "unrealistic") mathematical models and theories*. They include the average and marginal cost curves of a real-life firm, London congestion charge as a real-life example of Pigovian tax, traffic allocation that is close to a Nash equilibrium, mixed strategy in a professional sport, and MBA programs in the light of signaling. You can see the list of these real-life cases at the end of the Contents section. I have also tried to convince the reader that the mathematical models and theories in economics provide us with deep insights into how our society works. For example, "globalism" is one of the most talked-about issues on the world economy, which refers to the fact that all areas around the world are incorporated into global markets; but why does this happen, and is it good or bad for us? The book offers an answer based on a highly mathematical concept and theory.[3] In the last section, I show that the theory of competitive markets and game theory provide unifying insights into the problem of how to make our society better and various issues in social justice and philosophy.

Fourth, the text is written in a chatty and colloquial style, and I *have tried to "tell stories" about, for example, why we need this concept and how that result is useful*, and so on. These

---

[2] If you have taken a high school mathematics course about differentiation and vaguely remember how to differentiate x^2, that will be enough.

[3] What is known as the concept and theory of the "core" of resource allocation.

things are usually hidden between the lines of most textbooks, and the teacher teaches the class how to read between the lines. In this textbook, I fully incorporated what I tell my students in my class, and therefore this book may be regarded as a live recording of my lectures. I hope that makes this book fun to read.

I would like to invite you on a the journey to discover the amazing mechanisms underlying our daily economic activities. In the end, you can gain "economic literacy," an essential art of understanding how our economy works, and not only will you be able to "think like an economist" but also, I promise you, you will gain a completely new perspective on our society.

A few words for the instructors (and for students who would like to know how this book fits in to the courses they plan to take).

In a typical economics program, students first take a principles of economics course, which offers a very basic economic analysis based on demand and supply. This is followed by an intermediate microeconomics course, which introduces some of the mathematical models and theories. Intermediate microeconomics usually comes with two versions: with or without the use of calculus. For some advanced students, an honors course may be offered, covering more advanced materials and selected topics. Finally, the full-fledged mathematical models and theories are taught at graduate core courses in microeconomics.

This book may be used as a main textbook for *intermediate microeconomics with calculus* in top-notch departments and for honors courses. However, it can also be used as *side reading* in any other course. Because of the self-contained nature of this textbook, it can be read by *highly motivated first-year students in the principles courses*, who are eager to learn more advanced materials. It is also suitable for *first-year graduate students who need some guidance as to how to "read between the lines"* of standard graduate-level textbooks that are highly mathematical. Anyone who is eager to understand the moral of the story told by the mathematical models may be able to find the answers in this book. The book covers the majority of materials in a graduate microeconomics course, including duality in consumer theory, the complete proof of the first and second welfare theorems, and the proof of existence of general market equilibrium by a fixed-point theorem. At the same time, the book omits some of the advanced materials for professional economists, materials that might not directly appeal to a general audience (such as indirect utility function and the axioms for expected utility maximization). Game theory as covered in this book focuses on the basic concepts of the Nash equilibrium and subgame-perfect equilibrium, and I have made sure that students get a thorough understanding about why and how the concept of Nash equilibrium is useful and how strategies in dynamic games should be formulated and analyzed. This part can be used in game theory courses.

I originally thought that this book was only for a handful of truly advanced students because it covers such advanced materials, but in the end my efforts to make it readable bore fruit, and the Japanese edition of the book was welcomed by a surprisingly wide range of readers. Given that, I am confident to recommend this book to all levels of students, ranging from ambitious freshmen to first-year graduate students in doctoral or masters programs. I hope that this book is a good read for anyone who is eager to learn how our economy works.

Acknowledgments

This is an English translation of the textbook published in Japan in 2014. Chapters 1, 2, and 6 to 10 and all the Appendices were translated by a team consisting of Yuichiro Kamada and Will Sandholtz at the University of California, Berkeley. The Introduction and Chapters 3, 4, and 5 were translated by Murdoch MacPhee. Figures and tables were formatted by Yusuke Iwase. I would like to thank all of them for their great efforts to convert the chatty colloquial style of my original text into something accessible to the international audience. Financial support for the translation of Chapters 1 to 10 was provided by the International Publication Initiative (IPI) at the University of Tokyo. James Babb at IPI worked hard to help me out to make the translation possible, and I am most grateful to him for his continuous help and invaluable advice. Cambridge University Press kindly supported the rest of the translation, the Introduction, and the Appendices.

Publisher's Acknowledgements

The Press has made every effort to contact the copyright holders of materials reprinted in *Mighty Microeconomics*. It has not been possible in every case, however, and we would welcome correspondence from individual or companies we have been unable to trace. We will undertake to rectify errors or omissions in future editions of the book. We would like to thank all the authors as well as the following publishers and institutions for the permission to reprint their material:

Figure 0.2: Reproduced with permission from Japan Oil, Gas and Metals National Corporation.

Figure 1.11: Reproduced with permission from The Institute of International Relations and Area Studies, Ritsumeikan University, Japan in Jin Xiangdong, (2006) "An examination of the controversy regarding North Korea's economic growth: mainly from 1965 to 80s," *Ritsumeikan Journal of International Relations and Area Studies*, 24, 131–141.

Table 2.1: Reproduced with permission from the Agency for Natural Resources and Energy, "Summary of Demand and Supply for Electric Power," in *Annual Securities Report* (Tokyo: Agency for Natural Resources and Energy, 2002).

Figure 2.10 (formula): Reproduced with permission from IEEE for Tomomichi Sugihara (2010) "Consistent Biped Step Control with COM-ZMP Oscillation Based on Successive Phase Estimation in Dynamics Morphing," 2010 IEEE International Conference on Robotics and Automation, Anchorage, AK, USA, pp. 4224-4229, https://doi.org/10.1109/ROBOT.2010.5509270.

Figure 2.10 (picture): Reproduced with permission from Associate Professor Eishi Hirasaki, Primate Research Institute, Kyoto University, Japan.

Figure 2.49: Reproduced with permission from Elsevier for Kathryn G. Marshall (2012) "International Productivity and Factor Price Comparisons," *Journal of International Economics*, 87(2), pp.386–390, Table 3. https://doi.org/10.1016/j.jinteco.2012.01.003.

Figure 2.61: Reproduced with permission from the Ministry of Health, Welfare and Labor (Japan), "Summary of Comprehensive Survey of Living Conditions, 2011".

Figure 2.62: Reproduced with permission from the Ministry of Finance, *Statistics on Corporations and Firms* (Tokyo: Ministry of Finance, 2018).

Figure 3.22 (a): Reproduced with permission from the Ministry of Agriculture, Forestry and Fisheries, *Report on Results of 2010 World Census of Agriculture and Forestry in Japan* (Tokyo: MAFF, 2011).

Figure 3.22 (b): Reproduced with permission from the Ministry of Health, Labour and Welfare, "Comprehensive Survey of Living Conditions" (Tokyo: Ministry of Health, Labour and Welfare, 2006).

Figures 6.7, 6.8 and 6.9: Reproduced with permission from the Traffic Demand Forecast Technology Review Subcommittee, Committee of Infrastructure and Management (editor), "Theory and Application of Road Traffic Demand Forecasting: Toward the Application of Equal Distribution of Users," Japan Society of Civil Engineers, August 2003.

Figure 10.5: Reproduced with permission from Play Guide Journal Sha for "Baito-kun", copyright Hasaichi Ishii.

Figure 10.9: Reproduced with permission from Elsevier for Peter H. Lindert and Jeffrey G. Williamson (1985) "Growth, Equality, and History," *Explorations in Economic History*, 22, 341–377, Figure 1 (p.344). https://doi.org/10.1016/0014-4983(85)90001-4

Figure 10.10: Reproduced with permission from Yasuyuki Sawada (2003) "Kokusai Keizaigaku" Kiso Kosu Keizaigaku 7, Shinseisha.

Figure 10.11: Reproduced with permission from Springer Nature for David Dollar and Aart Kraay, (2002) "Growth is Good for the Poor." *Journal of Economic Growth*, 7, 195–225. https://doi.org/10.1023/A:1020139631000

Introduction
Why and How We Use Microeconomics

Each and every society will inevitably need to solve basic problems, such as these.

(1) Who makes (2) how much of (3) what? And (4) how?
(5) Who receives (6) how much of (7) what?

Economists call (1) to (7) **resource allocation** issues. More specifically, (5) to (7) are called **distribution** issues. Each society resolves these issues with its own institutions and rules, which have historically included feudal systems, planned economies, and market economy mechanisms.

For any given set of society-specific institutional arrangements, we will need to consider:

(i) what outcome is realized; and
(ii) whether that outcome is "good" or "bad."

(i) is a **positive question** (a question about facts), whereas (ii) is a **normative question** (a question about value judgments). Microeconomics offers the following very specific framework for answering these questions (Figure 0.1).

(1) The **technology** available to the society needs to be formally described in order to determine which resource allocations are physically possible.
(2) The "interests" of each and every individual in the society need to be described. Different people will tend to have different needs and desires, which, for the purposes of microeconomic analysis, are called **preferences**.
(3) The rules that determine resource allocations need to be clearly stated.[1]

---

[1] The horizontal arrow corresponding to "Institutions and rules" may be a little difficult to understand without a concrete example. "Institutions and rules" essentially outline what sort of behavior is permissible for each individual and what sort of resource allocation will result from that behavior. For example, in a market economy individuals are offered "freedom of choice," meaning that they can buy whatever they wish provided that their budgets are not exceeded. In contrast, consumption in a planned economy will be determined by behavior such as "responding to government surveys" and "lobbying politicians."

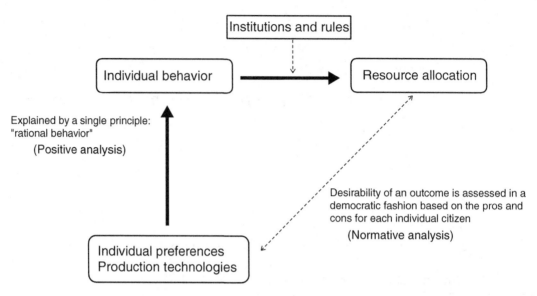

Figure 0.1 The microeconomic methodology

(4) How do individuals behave under these rules? This is explained in terms of **rational behavior**, a single principle capturing the central driving force of economic decision-making.

(5) How "good" or "bad" is the resulting outcome? This question needs to be answered in a democratic fashion, based on the preferences of each and every individual in the society.

This might all seem a bit abstract, so let us now sketch out how this microeconomic methodology can be used to answer the specific question of whether a country should liberalize its imports of agricultural products (such as sugar in the United States and rice in Japan). This question has both "positive" and "normative" dimensions.

Positive: what will happen if imports are liberalized?

Normative: will that outcome be "good" or "bad"?

The positive question deals solely with objective truth, and therefore we can agree on what the "right" answer is. However, the normative question will necessarily entail some sort of subjective value judgment, which means that the answer might differ from one individual to the next. Breaking down questions into these two – positive and normative – dimensions can prove very useful in facilitating constructive debate on a social problem between people who have competing interests.

Positive questions and microeconomics: liberalization would be likely to alter both the price of the agricultural product and its domestic production. It could also be expected to generate various spillovers to other industries (whether positive or negative). *Instead of applying "common sense" on an ad hoc basis* by saying things such as "liberalization will lower sugar prices" or "cheaper sugar will boost cake sales," *microeconomics provides a unified framework for explaining outcomes in terms of rational behavior* – in this case, on the part of farmers, consumers, and other producers – subject to a given technology. (How does it work? Well, we see the answers in Section 3.2.) "Rational behavior" might sound somewhat "mechanical" or "unrealistic," but, basically, it boils down to each and every individual acting in his or her own best interest, which is the main driving force of economic decision-making. This point of view also helps us to recognize the importance of each and every individual being provided with *appropriate incentives* in order for an economy to function smoothly.

Many of the conclusions arrived at using microeconomic analysis – by applying mathematical models as well as the principle of rational behavior – turn out to be consistent with our common sense, such as "supply will increase when prices rise." Those hoping for somewhat more surprising results – such as the finding in theoretical physics that time slows down if you travel on a rocket at close to the speed of light – may therefore be disappointed. So why don't we just rely on our common sense to begin with? The short answer is that the formal analysis in microeconomics helps us to avoid overlooking important aspects of the problem and ensure that our reasoning is not flawed or incomplete.

"Common sense" unfortunately tends to be quite patchy and vague, and "common-sense" arguments may sometimes lead to entirely different conclusions. Let us illustrate this with an example.

Case Study 0.1 Price Pass-Through and Problems with the "Common-Sense Approach" to Analysis

Oil prices have fluctuated a lot in recent years (Figure 0.2). Particularly sharp rises were seen in 2005/2006, at which point many people started to ask who was capable of **passing through** higher fuel costs to the end consumer.

The majority view, as expressed in the media and on the Internet, was essentially as follows.

Big firms have greater power and are able to raise their prices in order to pass through higher fuel costs to the end consumer.
Smaller firms face fiercer competition and are unable to raise their prices, meaning that their profits are squeezed.

However, there were also some (minority) opinions to the contrary. For example, a newspaper article reported price hikes by 35 local gas stations and explained that fierce competition made it impossible for the small and weak gas stations to absorb cost increases, leaving them with no option but to raise their retail prices.

Case Study 0.1 (cont.)

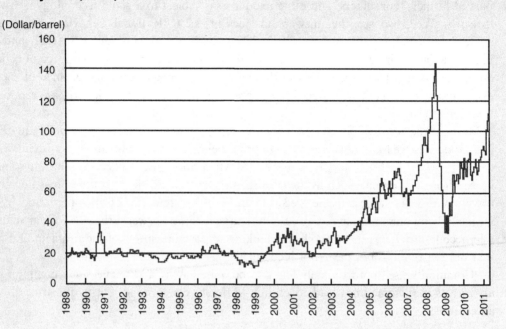

Figure 0.2 The price of oil, 1989–2011
Source: Japan Oil, Gas and Metals National Corporation.

This example illustrates two points.

(1) Whatever we say can sound "right" or "obvious" when we apply common sense to social problems
Some might consider it "obvious" that smaller firms will have no power to pass cost increases
through to end consumers. Others might see no other option for smaller firms but to hike their retail
prices. But both cannot be simultaneously true, which leads us to the second point.

(2) Common sense can sometimes lead to conclusions that are completely contradictory.

Debate often heats up when common sense is applied to "high stakes" economic issues, and
may sometimes descend into an emotionally charged shouting match. However, discussions
should be more productive if couched in terms of a theoretical framework that (a) is based on
the uncontroversial assumption that each and every individual in an economic problem acts
in accordance with his or her own best interest and (b) ensures careful reasoning without any
logical flaws. It is for this very reason that microeconomics relies so heavily on mathematical
models along with the principle of rational behavior. It should be clear from the above
example that "common-sense" arguments will in many cases – perhaps 90 out of 100? – lead

to conclusions that are flawed. One of the most important roles of microeconomics is to provide a set of tools for identifying those remaining – 10 out of 100? – conclusions that are indeed valid.

Comment 0.1

Of the above two opinions pertaining to price pass-through, which is correct? All should become clear as you read ahead (see Section 5.2).

Case Study 1.1 in Chapter 1, Section 3, offers a further example of how microeconomics can be used to identify which "common-sense" arguments are reasonable and legitimate.

Normative questions and microeconomics: once we are in agreement as to the impact of liberalization, the next step is to ask whether that outcome is desirable or otherwise. To highlight the unique way in which microeconomics answers this normative question, let me contrast it with outdated economic doctrines. For example, advocates of the mercantile doctrine would likely argue that running a trade surplus is in a nation's best interest (as was indeed argued when US–China trade friction became an issue around 2020) and that liberalization is best avoided if it wishes to reduce the trade deficit. Advocates of physiocracy (from the Greek for "government of nature," an eighteenth-century school of thought contending that agriculture is the basis of the economy) would oppose liberalization as an existential threat to domestic farmers. But microeconomics takes a different perspective, arguing that assessments of any proposed policy *should be based on the well-being of individual citizens* – those who constitute society – *without invoking sweeping value judgments such as "trade surpluses are good" or "agriculture is the heart and soul of the nation."* In other words, microeconomics focuses on who stands to benefit from trade liberalization, who will lose out, and whether it might be possible for the former to adequately compensate the latter (how this works is explained in detail in Section 3.2).

The basic structure of this book is as follows. In Part I we examine **perfectly competitive markets**. This treatment of so-called "price theory" is the core of traditional microeconomics. But wait, there's more! Part II builds on recent advances in the field of "economics of information and **game theory**" by introducing various tools that can be used to analyze economic issues that fall outside the perfectly competitive market framework.

As should soon become apparent, our discussion becomes quite "technical" at times and features copious use of graphs and equations. But this approach is vital: by carefully framing the issues and defining important concepts, we can promote productive discussions and avoid the emotionally charged debates that, unfortunately, surround so many important social and economic problems. Please don't let the thought of "mathematics" discourage you, since I will explain the basic toolkit as we go along. I know some of you are not fond of math, but I will show you how mathematical models can beautifully capture what is going on in many social and economic problems.

Part I

Price Theory: Merits and Limitations of the Market Mechanism

In modern society, everything – including food, housing, and music – is traded with a number called "price." We usually don't give this much thought, but isn't it puzzling, if you stop to think about it? The objective of Part I is to understand the basic function of a market and its limitations. To this end, we first try to understand consumer behavior and firm behavior, and then analyze what happens if they interact in a market.

1   Theory of Consumer Behavior

As we have seen in the Preface, in microeconomics we explain economic phenomena using "rational behavior," the idea that all individuals behave in the most beneficial way possible for themselves, and then decide whether the consequences are good or bad based on each citizen's interest. This is necessary (i) to understand the incentives that govern economic behavior and (ii) to be able to make policy that pays attention to every citizen's well-being. In this chapter, we formally define each individual's needs or interest (which we call an individual's "preferences") and rational behavior, which are the basis for such economic analysis. We then apply this to consumer behavior and reveal how demand for various goods is determined.

1.1   Rational Behavior: Preferences and the Utility Function

First, let's consider how we can express each individual's "preferences." As a concrete example, consider (a glass of) sparkling water, beer, and wine. If an individual "prefers sparkling water to beer," we write

$$\text{sparkling water} \succ \text{beer},$$

and we say that "sparkling water **is preferred to** beer." The symbol $\succ$ looks like the math symbol $>$ for inequality, but, whereas $>$ is used to compare the size of numbers, $\succ$ *is used to compare an individual's preferences for two things.* We use the curved symbol $\succ$ to make this distinction.

If an individual "thinks beer is just as good as wine," we write:

$$\text{beer} \sim \text{wine},$$

and we say that "beer **is indifferent to** wine."

Moreover, it will be useful to create notation for "is preferred to or is indifferent to" by combining the notations above. That is, for two options (*a*) and (*b*), if

$$a \succ b \quad (a \text{ is preferred to } b)$$

or

$$a \sim b \quad (a \text{ is indifferent to } b)$$

holds,

$$a \gtrsim b,$$

and we say that "*a* **is weakly preferred to** *b*." You can think of this as analogous to the weak inequality $\geq$ in math.

There is a reason for introducing the notation $\gtrsim$ even if intuitively it might seem easier to use $\succ$ and $\sim$. The reason is that *it is sufficient to only consider $\gtrsim$ in order to express an individual's preferences.*

In fact, "$\succ$ (is preferred to)" and "$\sim$ (is indifferent to)" can be derived from $\gtrsim$ in the following manner:

 (i) $a \sim b$ if both $a \gtrsim b$ and $b \gtrsim a$ hold;
 (ii) $a \succ b$ if $a \gtrsim b$ holds but $b \gtrsim a$ does not hold.[1]

The individual's preferences that we expressed above by the notation $\gtrsim$ are called, unsurprisingly, "**preferences**" in economics.

Individuals have various preferences, but, whatever they are, it seems reasonable to suppose that they are consistent to some degree. In order to explain this consistency, we will denote by X "the set of everything that is being compared" – that is, the domain over which the preferences $\gtrsim$ are defined. X varies depending on the problem at hand.

Example 1.1

In the example we discussed before, we can think of everything that is being compared as the items on the drink menu of a restaurant. So

$$X = \{\text{sparkling water, beer, wine}\}.$$

For an individual's preferences to be "consistent," the following two conditions should be satisfied.

Conditions for an Individual's Preferences to Be Consistent

Condition 1: for any two available items x and y (that is, for any x and y that belong to the set X), at least one of $x \gtrsim y$ or $y \gtrsim x$ holds. This condition is called **completeness**.

This may look complicated at first glance, but all this is saying is that "everything can be compared." In the above example, this condition means that if the individual were asked *"Do you prefer sparkling water or beer?"* then she would answer *"I prefer this"* or *"I like both equally."* She would not say: *"I don't know."*

---

[1] This can be understood as follows. If "both $a \gtrsim b$ and $b \gtrsim a$ hold," then (i) implies that $a \sim b$. Thus, "$a \gtrsim b$ holds but $b \gtrsim a$ does not hold" means that $a \gtrsim b$ but not $b \sim a$, so $a \succ b$ holds.

Condition 2: if $x \succsim y$ and $y \succsim x$, then $x \succsim z$ holds. This condition is called **transitivity**.

This condition also has a simple explanation. All this is saying is that if an individual likes sparkling water at least as much as beer, and likes beer at least as much as wine, then of course she should like sparkling water at least as much as wine.

In a nutshell, these two conditions mean (when there are a finite number of available items) that *you can rank the available items from best to worst, allowing for ties.*

An individual who has preferences that are "consistent" in the above sense can make clear decisions in various situations. First, recall that we denoted by X the set of everything that is compared. Usually it is rare that one can choose anything from X freely; the range of what is available to pick is typically narrower. Let's denote such a set of available options by S. For example, we can think of X as all the drinks on the menu at a restaurant and S as the drinks on the menu that can be bought within your budget. What exactly S is depends on the circumstances, but, once an individual knows what S is, she will:

$$\text{Choose the best item from } S \text{ given her preferences.} \tag{1}$$
$$\text{That is, she chooses } x^* \text{ such that } x^* \succsim x \text{ for all } x \text{ in } S.$$

We call this "rational behavior."

Example 1.2

Continuing with the previous example, suppose that you have the preferences "sparkling water $\succ$ beer" and "beer $\sim$ wine", and suppose that your budget permits you to buy only sparkling water or beer. That is, $S = \{$sparkling water, beer$\}$. In this case, rational behavior dictates that you choose the better item from S, so $x^* =$ sparkling water.

To summarize our discussion so far, we have the following: **rational behavior** means that one always *chooses the better or best item according to preferences that are consistent (i.e. preferences $\succsim$ that satisfy Condition 1 (completeness) and Condition 2 (transitivity)).*

Comment 1.1

How was that? In order to clearly express the most important principle of behavior in economics – that individuals choose the most beneficial option possible – and capture the notion of an individual's interest, both of which are necessary for evaluating economic problems, we made use of formal notation. But don't you think: *"Frankly speaking, this is too abstract and hard to digest! Aren't there any ways to make this easier to understand?"* The "utility function" is a tool for economic analysis that fits the bill.

Utility Functions

The basic idea of utility functions is to express the preference relation $\succsim$ in an easy-to-understand manner using numbers. Let's assign to each option x a number $u(x)$, so that *more desirable options have higher numbers.* (Note that we can make such assignments due to Conditions 1 and 2, completeness and transitivity!)[2] That is,

> $x \succsim y$ implies $u(x) \geq u(y)$.
>
> Such a function u is called a **utility function** *representing the preferences* $\succsim$.

Since any assignment of number is fine as long as more desirable options are assigned higher numbers, *there can be many utility functions that represent an individual's preferences.* For example, the utility function of the individual we discussed before, whose preferences are "sparkling water $\succ$ beer" and "beer $\sim$ wine," can be

$$u(\text{sparkling water}) = 10,$$
$$u(\text{beer}) = u(\text{wine}) = 5,$$

or

$$u(\text{sparkling water}) = 100,$$
$$u(\text{beer}) = u(\text{wine}) = 0.$$

More generally, *any assignment of numbers works as long as we assign the same number for beer and wine, for which she is indifferent, and assign a higher number for sparkling water, which she prefers to both beer and wine.*[3] You might wonder which utility function should be used, but in microeconomics we use utility functions in such a way that whichever function is used does not affect the result. I explain why this is the case below.

Using utility functions, we have a clear way of expressing rational behavior:

rational behavior = behavior that maximizes utility.

In our example of drinks at a restaurant, if we let S be the set of drinks that can be afforded, behaving rationally amounts to

---

[2] If Conditions 1 and 2 (completeness and transitivity) hold and the number of options is finite, then we can rank the options from best to worst (allowing for ties), which means that we can assign a higher number to a more desirable option (and assign the same number to equally desirable options). However, if there are infinitely many options, we could construct a weird example in which such an assignment is impossible even if Conditions 1 and 2 hold. I explain a condition that rules out such a pathological example in the next section, Section 1.2 (see Footnote 4).

[3] For a utility function $u(x)$ that represents an individual's preferences, we can transform it by an increasing function f (that is, $f(a) > f(b)$ holds for any $a > b$) to construct a new function $v(x) = f(u(x))$. Then this function v also assigns a higher number for a more desirable option, so it is also a utility function representing the individual's preferences. Therefore, *a function that is obtained by an increasing transformation of a utility function representing an individual's preferences is itself a utility function representing the same individual's preferences.*

choosing the drink x^* that maximizes utility $u(x)$ among the set of affordable drinks S. (2)

Comparing with (1), you can see that this is much easier to understand. There are many functions that represent an individual's preferences $\succsim$, but every one of these functions *assigns a higher number to a more desirable option*. Thus, regardless of which specific utility function we use, the element that maximizes the utility function, x^*, is the most desirable option according to $\succsim$. This is the reason we said earlier that whichever particular utility function we use does not matter. *There are many utility functions representing an individual's preferences, but which specific utility function is used does not affect the outcome determined by rational behavior, since each function will be maximized by the same element.*

Comment 1.2 A Common Misunderstanding

Suppose that a customer at a restaurant is drinking sparkling water because he prefers sparkling water to beer. Imagine that an economist walks up to him and says, *"Your utility from sparkling water is two and your utility from beer is one. Therefore, you are maximizing utility."* Most likely, the customer would respond, *"I don't know what you mean! I've never heard of utility and I'm not maximizing any such thing!"* However, don't let this make you think that economics is detached from reality. Instead, what the economist really means is this: *"In order to record that you prefer sparkling water to beer and use this for future discussions, I assigned sparkling water the number "2" and beer the number "1," since two is bigger than one. These numbers are called "utilities," and, when I say you maximize utility, I don't mean that you consciously think about these numbers, only that I as an economist am using these numbers to represent the fact that you are drinking sparkling water, which you like more."* Please don't misunderstand this important point.

Comment 1.3 History of Economics (continued from the discussion in Comment 1.2)

Given that the customer likes sparkling water more than beer, any function that assigns a higher number to sparkling water is a utility function representing this customer's preferences. This means that *what is important is the ordering of the numbers, and not the size of the numbers.* For instance, if an economist says

$$u(\text{sparkling water}) = 2,$$
$$u(\text{beer}) = 1,$$

as in Comment 1.2, *this does not mean that the satisfaction from drinking sparkling water is twice as much as the satisfaction from drinking a beer! All it means is that the individual prefers sparkling water to beer.* It would be fine to write:

$$u(\text{sparkling water}) = 1,000,000,000,000,000,$$
$$u(\text{beer}) = 1.$$

Comment 1.3 (cont.)

I want you to understand that utility functions do not tell you the amount of "satisfaction" that two things provide the consumer; they can show only which of the two things the consumer views as better. The idea of using utility functions as a convenient tool to represent people's preferences $\succsim$ (which in principle we can measure, either by asking them or actually observing their choices) is called **ordinal utility theory**, and most modern economic theory uses this idea.

By contrast, economic theory in the nineteenth century regarded utilities as the degree of satisfaction, and believed there was meaning not only to the order of the utility values but also the magnitude of the values (which of course we cannot observe). This way of thinking, called **cardinal utility theory**, is now obsolete.

Comment 1.4 Measurement of Preferences: Seeing Is Believing

In order to measure a consumer's preferences $\succsim$, it would be more accurate to actually observe what the consumer chooses instead of asking her which she prefers. Suppose that there are bowls of food on a table: a salad with lots of raw vegetables and an ice cream sundae. If you ask a young child which she prefers to eat, she might answer: *"Well, ice cream is nice and sweet, but the salad is also good because it's nutritious and healthy."* This leaves you without a clear idea of which she actually prefers to eat. However, if you were to just watch which bowl she picks up, you would probably observe her immediately choosing the sundae. In this case, it would be reasonable to believe that the child prefers the ice cream sundae after all.

To give you another example, if a stock trader says *"This stock will surely turn a profit!"* but does not actually buy it himself, then it would be wise not to buy this stock. In this sense, economists often believe that actual behavior gives us a more accurate picture of consumers' preferences than we would get by asking them to report their preferences. This "seeing is believing" way of thinking – that actual choice behavior reveals a consumer's preferences, which otherwise are unobservable – is an important tool for economic analysis. The area of economics that tries to systematically estimate the preferences that are behind a consumer's observable behavior is called the theory of **revealed preferences**.

1.2   Consumer Preferences and Indifference Curves

Let's analyze consumer behavior using the idea of rational behavior that we defined above. First things first: we'll define some terminology. Among the things that are bought and sold in a market, those that are intangible are called "services" and those that are tangible are called "goods." But, in most cases, we'll just call general commodities "goods." Suppose now that there are N different goods available to the consumer. We can describe the consumer's consumption choices as

$$x = (x_1, x_2, \ldots, x_N)$$

where x_i is the amount of the ith good the consumer chooses. We call this the consumer's **consumption bundle**. The consumer will have preferences over various consumption bundles, which we'll use to understand how the consumer's demand is determined.[4] It is valuable to consider *all bundles that give the same utility* in order to understand consumer behavior. Using the terminology we defined in Section 1.1, if two consumption bundles give the same utility, it means the consumer is indifferent between them. A set of consumption bundles that the consumer is indifferent to usually has the shape of a curve, so we call this set an **indifference curve**. Just as the contours on maps represent the collection of all points that have the same elevation, indifference curves represent the collection of all consumption bundles that give the same utility.

This is a concept that many people (especially those who don't really like mathematical models) are puzzled about, because they may be thinking, *"I've never thought about anything like indifference curves when I make a consumption decision!"* Let me start with some special cases in which you can clearly see that indifference curves do indeed exist, and, hopefully, I can convince you that indifference curves actually are a useful way of thinking about some properties of the goods we are considering.

Example 1.3

Suppose that there's a customer at a bar who doesn't care whether he drinks Coors or Budweiser. If we denote the amount of Coors and Budweiser consumed by x_1 and x_2 respectively, then the customer gets the same utility from any combination of Coors and Budweiser as long as he drinks the same total amount of beer – that is, for any values of x_1 and x_2, the customer will get the same utility as long as $x_1 + x_2$ is the same. Assuming that the customer is happier when he drinks more beer, his utility increases as the total amount of beer consumed, $x_1 + x_2$, increases. Therefore, we can write an indifference curve as a downward-sloping line such that $x_1 + x_2 = c$, where c is a constant. The utility is larger for the line that is above the other (see Figure 1.1). In this case, Coors and Budweiser are called **perfect substitutes**.

---

[4] A rather minor note for readers who care about mathematical details: the amount of consumption x_i can take continuous values, such as the amount of gasoline purchased, or discrete values, such as the number of hamburgers ordered. In price theory, in order to make the analysis easier, we assume that the consumption of each good takes continuous values. This means that there are infinitely many possible consumption bundles for the consumer to choose from. For the consumer's preferences to be represented by a utility function in such a situation, it is sufficient if, in addition to the two consistency conditions (completeness and transitivity) we discussed before, the following condition holds: "**continuity**." For any consumption bundle, the set of consumption bundles that are at least as good and the set of consumption bundles that are at most as good are closed sets (i.e. the sets contain their boundary).

The proof of this can be found in Gerard Debreu, *Theory of Value* (New Haven, CT: Yale University Press, 1972), sect. 4.6 (1).

Example 1.3 (cont.)

Figure 1.1 The indifference curves of perfect substitutes

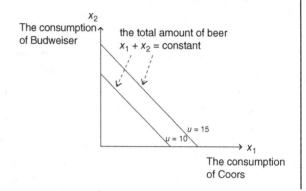

Example 1.4

Consider disposable contact lenses for a patient whose prescriptions are different for her right eye and her left eye. Since her prescriptions are different, she can't use her left lenses in her right eye, and vice versa. Therefore, it's necessary for her to buy left lenses and right lenses in a 1:1 ratio. In this case, the indifference curves have an L shape, as in Figure 1.2. The dashed line indicates situations in which the left and right lenses are bought in a 1:1 ratio. The reason the indifference curves are L-shaped with the kink occurring at the dotted line can be understood if you think carefully about it in the following way. If the consumer does not buy left and right lenses in a 1:1 ratio – for instance, at point B (which is to the right of point A) – she has no use for the leftover right lenses, since she needs only one lens in her eye at a time. *If we assume that the leftover lenses aren't used*, the utility the consumer receives at point B is the same as at point A. Therefore, the indifference curves have an L shape.

   The goods that are used with some constant ratio, such as contact lenses in this example, are called perfect complements. Left shoes and right shoes, or a computer and an operating system, are other examples of **perfect complements**.

Figure 1.2 The indifference curves of perfect complements

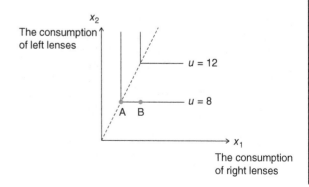

In general, indifference curves will be something in between these two extreme cases. Most goods will be somewhat substitutable and somewhat complementary. Considering the consumption of bread and water, the indifference curves of a person who doesn't care whether she eats bread or drinks water as long as her stomach is full will be linear, as in Figure 1.1. Conversely, a person who is not satisfied unless she consumes bread and water in a 1:1 ratio would have L-shaped indifference curves, as in Figure 1.2. In reality, though, most people will have indifference curves that are somewhere in the middle. In other words, most people would like to consume bread and water together, even if they don't have a fixed ratio for their consumption, as in the contact lens example. Moreover, most people would also choose to drink water to fill their stomach if there's no bread, as in the beer example. Based on these observations, it seems reasonable to assume that indifference curves are somewhere in between (see Figure 1.3) those shown in Figure 1.1 and Figure 1.2.

Now, let's consider more carefully why we might think that indifference curves for a wide variety of goods will be shaped like those shown in Figure 1.3. Under normal circumstances, *it's natural to think that the desirability of a good decreases as its consumption increases.* For example, on a hot day, the first cup of water is extremely refreshing, the second is less so, and the third is even less tasty than the second. In fact, indifference curves that are bowed toward the origin, as in Figure 1.3, express the general idea that the desirability of goods decreases as the quantity consumed gets larger. Let me explain why this is so.

Take a look at the indifference curve in Figure 1.4, which is bowed toward the origin. Starting from point A, at which no water is drunk, we move to point B if the consumer is given a cup of water and eats 500 g less bread. The consumer's utility remains the same, because both A and B are on the same indifference curve. That is, the consumer's degree of satisfaction does not change if he is given a cup of water but given 500 g less bread to eat. In other words, these statements are true.

- To get the first cup of water, the consumer is willing to give up 500 g of bread. The first cup is precious, so he is willing to give away a lot of bread.
- To get the second cup of water, the consumer is willing to give up 200 g of bread. The second cup is not as refreshing as the first, so the amount of bread that he's willing to give away decreases.
- To get the third cup of water, the consumer is willing to give up only 10 g of bread. Once he already has two cups of water, having a third cup isn't very valuable.

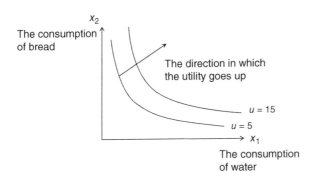

Figure 1.3 General indifference curves

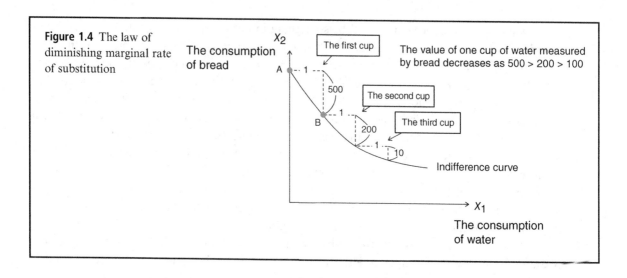

Figure 1.4 The law of diminishing marginal rate of substitution

We can see that the amount of bread the consumer is willing to give up to get an additional cup of water decreases as the consumption of water increases. *In other words, the value of an extra cup of water, measured in terms of bread, decreases as consumption of water gets larger.* This is the intuition behind the bowed shape of indifference curves.

Let's generalize this observation. *The slope of an indifference curve represents the maximum amount of the second good (bread) that the consumer is willing to give up in order to increase consumption of the first good (water) by one unit.* Roughly speaking, this amounts to the value of the first good measured in units of the second good. *This is VERY IMPORTANT, so make sure you understand it well by studying Figure 1.4!*

We call the "value" of the first good in terms of the second good the **marginal rate of substitution** of the first good for the second good, and we denote it by MRS_{12}. The fact that the desirability of a cup of water gradually fades can be represented by the slope of the indifference curve (the marginal rate of substitution) becoming smaller as we move to the right. We call this the **law of diminishing marginal rate of substitution**. This creates the bowed shape of the indifference curve. A more formal discussion of the marginal rate of substitution is provided later.

Comment 1.5

It is therefore reasonable that indifference curves are bowed toward the origin; but can we really assume that they are *always* like this? Microeconomics textbooks consider such a case only when studying consumer behavior, but is it really okay to ignore other cases? We discuss this point in detail in the Appendix of Section 1.6. (To give you the conclusion in advance, surprisingly, it really is okay.)

Now let's try to summarize the discussion above by using an elegant mathematical concept. The law of diminishing marginal rate of substitution means that indifference curves are bowed toward the origin. So, in general, it's convenient to formally define "bowed toward to origin" as follows.

A Math Toolkit for Economists

Convex set: this is a very useful concept for understanding the behavior of an economic agent through optimization (i.e. utility maximization or profit maximization). Informally, a set A is convex if it doesn't have any "dents." To make this more precise, we say that a set A is convex if, for any two points a and b in A, all points in between them are also contained in A. Without a picture, this might be difficult to understand, so take a look at Figure 1.5.

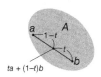

Figure 1.5 What is a convex set?

A is a convex set   A set that is not convex

Figure 1.5 depicts a convex set and a set that is not convex, and indeed we can see that the condition we just gave will ensure that a set does not have any "dents." In general, "points in between a and b" can be written, using a parameter t satisfying $0 \leq t \leq 1$, as a weighted average:

$$ta + (1 - t)b.$$

For example, $t = 1/2$ represents the point that is exactly midway between a and b. A higher value of t represents a point closer to a, and a lower value of t represents a point that is closer to b. Using this formalization, we say that a set A is a **convex set** if

for all $a, b \in A$ and all $0 \leq t \leq 1$
$ta + (1 - t)b \in A$ holds. [5]

Using the concept of convex sets, we can restate the law of diminishing marginal rate of substitution as saying that the areas above the indifference curves are convex sets.

---

[5] $x \in A$ is mathematical notation that means "x is contained in the set A."

This is sometimes called **convexity of preferences**.

Convex sets may seem exotic at the first glance, but I want you to note that this very effectively represents the following characteristic of many consumption goods:

The desirability of a good gradually fades when a lot of it is consumed.

Economics, in its long history, has discovered that important aspects of various economic phenomena can be succinctly described by various mathematical concepts. Convexity is one such mathematical concept. As we will see from here on, the concept of convexity plays a key role in the theory of production and the proof that markets are efficient.

1.3   Optimal Consumption: Analysis with a Diagram

Next, let's consider how the optimal consumption bundle is determined. First, for simplicity, we'll consider the case where there are only two goods, which can be analyzed by a figure. Let I denote a consumer's income and let p_1 and p_2 denote the prices of the first good and second good respectively. Combining these two prices, we write

$$p = (p_1, p_2).$$

In this book, we call this p a **price profile**. If a consumer buys the consumption bundle $x = (x_1, x_2)$ under this price profile, since x_i represents the amount of good i that is consumed, she pays $p_1 x_1 + p_2 x_2$ dollars in total. Thus, the set of consumption bundles that the consumer can buy if she uses all of her income are those bundles (x_1, x_2) satisfying

$$p_1 x_1 + p_2 x_2 = I.$$

This expression is called the **budget constraint**. In order to simplify this expression, let's introduce some notation. Given a price profile $p = (p_1, p_2)$ and a consumption bundle (x_1, x_2), we will write $p_1 x_1 + p_2 x_2$ as px.[6]

Now, the consumption behavior of a rational consumer can be stated as:

> Among the consumption bundles x that satisfy the budget constraint $px = I$, choose the one that maximizes utility $u(x)$.

---

[6] We use analogous notation even when there are many goods. For instance, given $p = (p_1, \ldots, p_N)$ and $x = (x_1, \ldots, x_N)$, we write

$$px = p_1 x_1 + \cdots + p_N x_N.$$

(A comment for those who like math: in math, px is called the "inner product" of the two vectors p and x.)

It would be tedious to write this every time we need to, so we simplify it by writing

$$\max_x u(x)$$

$$\text{s.t. } px = I$$

the optimal consumption problem

Here,

$$\max_x u(x)$$

means "maximize the function $u(x)$ by choosing the appropriate x" and "s.t." is an abbreviation for "subject to," which means "under the constraint that..."

Next, let's solve this optimal consumption problem using a figure. First, the various consumption bundles satisfying the budget constraint can be described by the straight line $p_1x_1 + p_2x_2 = I$. This is called the **budget line**. Since rearranging this expression gives us

$$x_2 = -\underbrace{\left|\frac{p_1}{p_2}\right|}_{\text{slope}} x_1 + \frac{1}{p_2},$$

the slope of the budget line is the price ratio p_1/p_2. This fact will play a key role from here on, so make sure you understand it well.

The optimal consumption problem is to find the point on the budget line that maximizes utility. This is depicted in Figure 1.6.

There are two indifference curves in this figure. Note that the curve that is above the other one gives higher utility (the utility on the bottom-left curve is $u = 5$ and the utility on the top-right curve is $u = 8$). The budget line and bottom indifference curve cross at point x^0. By moving in the direction of the arrow, you will see that it is possible to achieve higher utility while remaining on the budget line. Utility increases from 5 to 8 by moving from x^0 toward x^*.

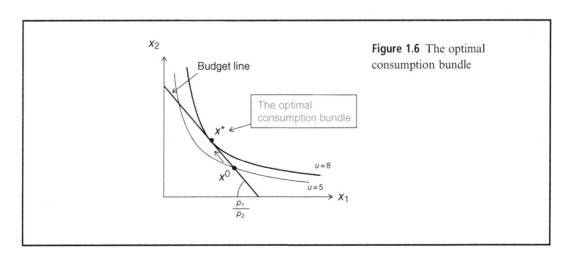

Figure 1.6 The optimal consumption bundle

By contrast, *at x*, the budget line and indifference curve are touching each other, and there is no way to increase utility by moving from x* in either direction.* Therefore, we see that optimal consumption is determined in the following manner:

The optimal consumption bundle x^* is a point at which the budget line and the indifference curve are touching (tangent to each other).

1.4   Important Digression: The Relationship between Mathematical Models and Reality and Thinking like an Economist

If I tell you that this is the great theory of optimal consumption, most likely your reaction would be: *"That's it?! This is just a bunch of nonsense and garbage!"* Your point is well taken, because you may well think that the theory of consumption should give deep insights into the psychology of a consumer. In contrast, what we have seen is just saying that the consumer chooses what she likes, using fancy-looking concepts such as indifference curves and utility to cover up its meager contents. However, using the very simple tool summarized in Figure 1.6, we are actually able to do economic analysis and evaluate policies. The following example will show you the meaning and power of rigorously modeling the most important principle of economic choice: *everyone makes choices that are most beneficial to him- or herself.*

From now on, you'll see a number of analyses using mathematical models, but I don't want you to miss the true meaning of such analyses while you are busy turning the pages. So let me carefully explain, by means of one example, the power of mathematical models to understand the real world and highlight several principal features of economic analysis. This is an important part, so don't skip this section. Read it!

Case Study 1.1 Policy Evaluation: The Problem with Subsidizing Old-Age Medical Bills

As of 2022, in Japan the average co-pay of the medical bill of a person 75 or older was 10 percent of the total cost (see Figure 1.7). The remaining 90 percent was paid for by Japanese taxpayers.

Figure 1.7 The co-payment share of medical bills, 2022

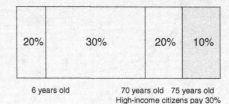

6 years old   70 years old   75 years old
High-income citizens pay 30%

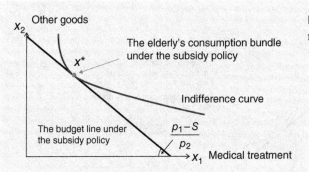

Figure 1.8 The elderly's consumption under the medical subsidy policy

In order to evaluate this policy, let's denote by x_1 the amount of medical care consumed and summarize by x_2 the consumption of other goods. Supposing that the Japanese government pays a subsidy of S dollars for each unit of medical care consumed, the budget constraint of an elderly person is

$$(p_1 - S)x_1 + p_2x_2 = I.$$

Note that, because of the subsidy, the price of the medical care is $(p_1 - S)$, which is cheaper by the amount of the subsidy S. Then optimal consumption of the elderly under the subsidy policy becomes x^* in Figure 1.8.

The optimal consumption bundle x^* satisfies the budget constraint, so, necessarily,

$$(p_1 - S)x_1^* + p_2x_2^* = I \tag{3}$$

holds. Now, let's suppose that the government decides to abandon the subsidy policy. Then the elderly would need more money in order to continue to consume x^*. Denoting by Y the income needed to consume x^* without the government subsidy, we see that Y is determined by

$$p_1x_1^* + p_2x_2^* = I + Y. \tag{4}$$

By moving Sx_1^* to the right-hand side in the initial expression (3) and comparing it with Equation (4), you will notice that $Y = Sx_1^*$ holds. This means that, *if the government abandons the subsidy policy and instead provides the elderly with a pension increase of the same amount of money, Sx_1^*, as the total healthcare subsidy, then the elderly could continue to consume x^*.* What happens in this case?

The budget constraint when the subsidy policy is abandoned in favor of the pension increase is

$$p_1x_1 + p_2x_2 = I + Sx_1^*.$$

If we depict this new budget constraint graphically, it will be a straight line such that the slope is the post-subsidy price ratio, p_1/p_2, and such that it passes through the previous optimal consumption bundle x^*. The reason the new budget line passes through the previous consumption bundle x^*, as we saw above, is that the previous optimal bundle x^* can still be afforded under the new policy. Therefore, the optimal consumption bundle x^{**} under the new policy is shown in Figure 1.9.

Case Study 1.1 (cont.)

Figure 1.9 If the government abandons the subsidy and increases the pension...

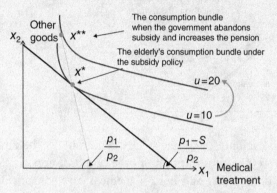

Note that the optimal consumption bundle moves to x^{**}, meaning that the elderly spend less on medical care and achieve a higher utility. In other words, *if the government abandons the subsidy policy and increases pensions by the same amount as it provided as a healthcare subsidy, the satisfaction of the elderly increases even though the cost to the government stays the same.* In this sense, the subsidy policy is inefficient.[7]

Comment 1.6 Models and Reality

Since a mathematical model is an abstraction of reality, some parts of it are realistic, but others are not. Consequently, any analysis derived from a model will be partly accurate and partly inaccurate. In order to check whether the results you derive from a model actually capture important aspects of reality, *it is helpful to rephrase the results in everyday language.*

Tips for Economic Analysis: Not only should you master the technical skills to understand and use mathematical models, but you should also be able to digest the central messages derived from the model in everyday language.

In fact, being able to do this is what separates the best economists from the rest. In our profession, we call this "**nurturing economic intuition**." This would be difficult to grasp in the

---

[7] If a subsidy policy is inefficient, then why have a medical subsidy policy? Obviously, the goal of a healthcare subsidy policy is to help those who are struggling with illness. In our example, we made the assumption that the consumer's pension was increased by exactly the amount that the government spending on subsidizing that individual's healthcare. However, in practice, if we don't implement a subsidy plan, we don't observe how much subsidized healthcare an elderly person consumes, so it's impossible to know exactly who needs the pension increase and how much the increase should be for each person! If the government gives the money as a healthcare subsidy, in contrast, it at least ensures that people who badly need medical care automatically receive it. This is the reason a healthcare subsidy policy is used in reality, but our example does illustrate that subsidy policies can entail some inefficiencies. Designing good policy requires balancing such advantages and disadvantages.

abstract, so let's use the preceding case study to practice. If we restate in everyday language what we found using theoretical model of indifference curves, we have:

(1) if the government abandons the medical subsidy and increases the pension by the same amount,
(2) the elderly can afford just as much healthcare as they consumed before, but
(3) they can save a large amount on their medical bills by reducing the amount of medical care they consume, so
(4) they choose to decrease their spending on healthcare;
(5) since they could still afford to buy the same amount of medical care as they did under the subsidy policy, but they choose not to, they must be better off than they were beforehand.[8]

Points (3) to (5) might be a bit too abstract to understand, so let's consider concrete numbers. If an elderly person has a 10 percent co-pay, that means that, if a person is paying $10 for each visit to the doctor's office, then the total bill is $100. If the pension is increased instead of continuing the medical subsidy, the elderly person can still go see the doctor as many times as before, but can save as much as $100 by forgoing a visit. Since $100 is a considerable amount of money, an elderly person might think:

(4') I'll skip a visit to the doctor's office and use the money I save to dine at a nice restaurant.
(5') I'm better off because I got to treat myself to a night out and a $100 meal.

Although total government expenditure does not change at all, if the government increases pensions instead of subsidizing medical care, the elderly will think, *"I'm better off, because now I can treat myself to a fancy dinner."* This means that the subsidy policy was wasteful in the sense that it prevents the nice outing. Given that the $100 treat is substantial, isn't that a remarkably big inefficiency?

What do you think? Don't you think that the effect of the policy change as described in points (1) to (5) is realistic and makes much sense, even though we arrived at this conclusion by analyzing indifference curves? Do you still think indifference curves are so detached from reality? Here I want you to note the following point.

> *When we restate the results of our mathematical model in everyday language, as we have seen, they look so convincing that you could in principle reach them by using your common sense. However, the point is that it would have been nearly impossible to arrive at these conclusions directly without using a formal model.*

---

[8] This is based on the important principle in microeconomics that, if one observes an individual's behavior, one can infer what his or her preferences must be. This is the idea of revealed preferences, which we discussed in Comment 1.4.

In the Preface, I explained that arguments that rely only on common sense can be ambiguous and can easily be tweaked to provide very different, oftentimes conflicting conclusions. One of the purposes of microeconomic analysis is to select the right one from among all those plausible explanations. I hope this case study illustrates this point.

Let's also examine the (reasonable) criticisms of microeconomics that might arise from this case study. Many people might feel uncomfortable with the conclusions of Figure 1.9, and think the following.

(Criticism 1) It isn't good to impose so many unrealistic assumptions.

(Criticism 2) We can't trust the conclusion because it might change a lot if the assumptions are slightly altered.

(Criticism 3) It doesn't make sense to use the model if we can't actually measure each elderly person's indifference curves and prove with high precision (as in physics) that the elderly's behavior exactly matches the prediction of the model.

Nonetheless, our analysis of the mathematical model yielded our conclusions (1) to (5), which can be understood in plain English and are highly realistic and reasonable. By rereading our rephrased conclusions, you will notice that they don't hinge on some fine details, such as

- the assumption that there are only two goods;
- the assumption that the indifference curve has a nice (convex) shape; or
- the assumption that the elderly perfectly maximize utility.

The main point I want to impart to you is this.

The Meaning of a Mathematical Model

Although microeconomic models do not describe human behavior with the same precision that mathematical models describe the laws of physics, *they are useful for capturing the essential aspects of real-world problems in a clear-cut way*.

The paragraph above may seem overly abstract and may not sound compelling, but, if you think about it in the context of the medical subsidy case study presented above, I hope you will find it makes good sense. Because of this, *at least in the context of this case study*, I think that Criticisms 1 to 3 of microeconomics are not really valid. Of course, there will be results derived from microeconomics to which these criticisms absolutely apply. However, I would be happy if this case study helps you understand that mathematical models and microeconomics can capture important aspects of reality, despite the fact that Criticisms 1 to 3 may look convincing.

Comment 1.7 The Market Mechanism and the Size of the Pie

Hidden in Case Study 1.1 is an important theme that you will see microeconomics uncover. By abandoning the subsidy policy, the government was able to raise the well-being of the elderly without increasing the burden on taxpayers – that is, by abandoning the subsidy policy, the "size of the pie" (i.e. total welfare) for society increases.

Viewing this from the opposite angle, if the government uses a policy that artificially reduces the market price, then the size of the pie for society shrinks. This is an important principle of microeconomics: *the market mechanism makes the size of the pie as big as possible.* If one distorts the price determined by the market mechanism, then the size of the pie shrinks. We will see that this claim is applicable not only in this particular case study but also under very general circumstances.

Increasing the satisfaction of the elderly without increasing the burden on the taxpayers means that we have made at least one person better off without making anyone worse off. This is called **Pareto improvement**. (The concept is named after Italian civil engineer and economist Vilfredo Pareto (1848–1923), who came up with this notion, and we explain Pareto improvement in more detail in Section 3.3: "Market Equilibrium.") *Note that, when the size of the pie for society is increased, then, by appropriately cutting the pie, we can achieve a Pareto improvement.* Examining if it is possible to increase the size of the pie (i.e. whether or not a Pareto improvement is possible) is called the **problem of efficiency** in economics. Promoting efficiency and achieving Pareto improvements are, admittedly, a particular value judgment. However, it makes good sense, because what it means is that we should effect changes that all members of society unanimously agree on.

Another major issue that we have to consider alongside the efficiency problem is how we should divide the pie. How should we divide the expanded pie, shown in Figure 1.10, between the elderly and the taxpayers? This is **the problem of fairness**, and we might have very different opinions about this issue. *Microeconomics primarily deals with solving the efficiency problem, leaving it to each individual's value judgment how best to solve the fairness problem.*

Now, which is more important, the problem of efficiency or the problem of fairness? Where should the tradeoff between the two take place? Abandoning the subsidy policy would indeed expand the pie to some extent, but don't you think what is really important is how to divide the pie? We especially want to support the most vulnerable in the society, don't we? This appears to make good sense, and consequently, when critics and the media discuss economic policies, they tend to focus intensely on issues of fairness and economic justice, and focus less on how much the size of the pie increases. However, if we look at the history of the twentieth century, we can see

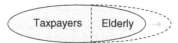

Figure 1.10 The pie for society

that the efficiency problem, which is often overlooked by those who do not understand economics, is extremely important over the long run. Figure 1.11 shows how the size of the pie per citizen (i.e. gross national product [GNP] per capita) has changed over time in South Korea and North Korea, which employ two different economic systems: the market economy and the planned economy. Although the two countries have almost identical geographical and demographic features, they have had dramatically different economic outcomes.

If you look at this comparison, it's hard to ignore how powerful the market mechanism is. Whatever your stance on the value judgment is, it should be clear that we need to rely on the market mechanism to some extent. By increasing the size of the pie, the market mechanism can vastly improve citizens' standard of living. This is one of the key lessons we learned in the twentieth century. Learning about how markets function is the central problem of microeconomics.

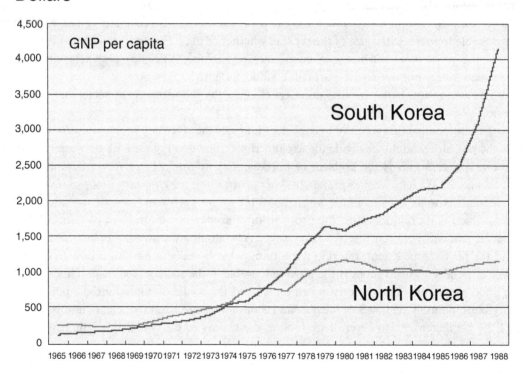

Figure 1.11 The market mechanism and the size of the pie

Source: Jin Xiangdong "An examination of the controversy regarding North Korea"s economic growth: mainly from 1965 to 80s," *Ritsumeikan Journal of International Relations and Area Studies*, March 2006, 131–41.

Comment 1.8 Institutional Knowledge versus Theoretical Understanding

Facts such as "The co-pay for medical bills is 10 percent for citizens over the age of 75, but high-income citizens pay 30 percent…" are examples of **institutional knowledge**. Some parts of your high school education may seem like memorization of those facts, and you might think that the university's economics department (or economics textbooks) would just teach you such institutional facts that are directly useful in business and everyday life. If you study (micro)economics expecting only to learn such facts, you might be disappointed. Of course, institutional knowledge is important, but the most important contribution of economics and other quantitative social sciences is that they allow us to understand the mechanisms behind real-world phenomena, using theoretical models such as the one we explored earlier. The case study should show you how important it is to have both institutional knowledge (such as the amount of the healthcare subsidy) and theoretical understanding of how policies may affect peoples' decisions (such as how the elderly will skip a trip to the doctor's office). Practical institutional knowledge can be picked up on the job or in your daily life. However, it's crucial that you build theoretical understanding now, since it's difficult to learn by yourself later on after you graduate. This is why microeconomics textbooks put so much weight on imparting theoretical understanding developed by earlier scholars.

1.5   Introduction to Marginal Analysis

In Section 1.3 we studied the case where there are only two goods. But the real economy has tons of different goods, and it's no longer possible to draw a picture in such a case. In order to understand more realistic situations, we can turn to mathematical analysis. In particular, as you will see, it is crucial to study whether consumers are able to improve their satisfaction (i.e. increase their utility) by "fine-tuning" their consumption, or making *slight adjustments* to the amounts of the different goods they consume. In economics, these slight adjustments are referred to as **marginal changes** or adjustments. The reason we use the rather strange word "marginal" is that, as economists, we often consider changes "at the margin," which means "at the boundary." For example, the "marginal" rate of substitution of water for bread refers to the case where we slightly adjust the last cup of water consumed (i.e. at the margin), which lies at the boundary that separates the amount of water that is consumed and the amount of water that is not consumed.

Mathematically, the effects of slight adjustments can be studied by "differentiating" functions, and the art of analyzing the rational behavior of consumers and producers is called marginal analysis. In this section, we will learn the basic ideas and methods behind marginal analysis. The prerequisite math for this section is some basic calculus. If you (at least vaguely) remember things such as

- differentiation is about the slope of the tangent line of a graph, or
- the derivative of x^2 is $2x$,

then you have enough knowledge of calculus to follow my explanations. If you want to briefly review the math materials, check out Appendix A.

(a)   Marginal Utility

The **marginal utility** of a good represents the change in satisfaction the consumer receives from slightly adjusting his or her consumption of that good. It will be the central component of the marginal analysis we are going to do. Suppose that there are N goods in total, and define the marginal utility of good i (for $i = 1, \ldots, N$) as in Figure 1.12. We denote the marginal utility of good i by MU_i. In the left panel you see that

the marginal utility of good i, MU_i = the amount that utility increases when consumption of good i increases by 1 unit.

This is the intuitive definition of marginal utility, which you'll see in many introductory textbooks. However, the more mathematical definition that most working economists (and more advanced textbooks like this one) use is the one in the right panel of Figure 1.12.

Note that Figure 1.12 has graphs for the case in which *only consumption good i is changed, while consumption of other goods remains the same.* The slope of the tangent line to this graph is equal to marginal utility MU_i, and, since differentiation captures "the slope of the tangent line of a graph," the derivative of the utility function gives us the marginal utility MU_i. Although the utility function $u(x_1, \ldots, x_i, \ldots, x_N)$ is a function of the consumption of various goods, *we fix (meaning "hold constant") the consumption of other goods and differentiate it assuming that it is only a function of good i.*

Figure 1.12 The definition of marginal utility MU_i

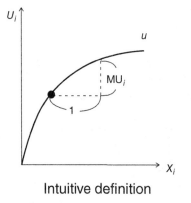

Intuitive definition

(The increment of utility when the consumption of good *i* increases by one unit)

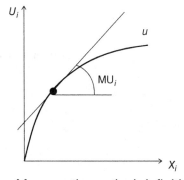

More mathematical definition

(The slope of this graph)

In mathematics this is called a "partial derivative," and is denoted

$$\frac{\partial u}{\partial x_i}.$$

In advanced textbooks, this is the definition of the marginal utility of good i:

$$\text{marginal utility of good } i = \frac{\partial u}{\partial x_i}.$$

Comment 1.9

Phrases such as "partial derivative" and symbols such as ∂ (read as "round d") may be intimidating and make marginal analysis seem like an extraordinarily difficult task, but this is just an extension of the basic calculus that you might learn in high school.

Example of a calculation: for a utility function $u = x_1^2 x_2^3$, the marginal utility of good 1 is $MU_1 = \partial u / \partial x_1$, which is the derivative of u with respect to x_1 when we regard x_2^3 as a constant. The derivative of x_1^2 is $2x_1$, so the marginal utility of good i is

$$MU_1 = \frac{\partial u}{\partial x_1} = 2x_1 \boxed{x_2^3}. \quad \text{(regard this part as a constant)}$$

If you recall differentiation from high school, there's no need to be afraid of partial derivatives.

Conducting Analysis Using Partial Derivatives

Many of you may be feeling that the book has suddenly become cryptic at this moment. Perhaps you're thinking, *"I'm a consumer, but I've never partially differentiated my utility. Therefore, analysis that uses partial derivatives is completely unrealistic and can't be trusted. (And I don't like math.)"*

The math might intimidate you, but all it does is capture and express your guiding principles when you shop, such as *"I want to buy things I like at the lowest possible price."* Microeconomics does *not* claim that *people literally use differentiation* to determine their consumption. Rather, the mathematics merely presents a tractable *model* that captures the intuition and guiding principles that people use when making decisions. Just as a map captures the essential features of a geographic region, our mathematical model captures the essence of economic behavior. And, as you will see, we can understand the main functions of the market mechanism by using mathematical models that capture the major principle of economic behavior: people do things to make themselves as happy as possible.

For the mathematical expressions that you find unfamiliar, I will explain them carefully so that you can understand if you make an effort to read the text closely. So, don't stop reading when you encounter strange mathematical expressions; keep reading!

Why do we use such a fancy definition of marginal utility? The answer is that this concept borrowed from math clearly shows the effects of "fine-tuning" consumption of various goods. Let me explain.

(b)   How Utility Responds to Small Changes in Consumption

First, let's try to rigorously understand the relationship between marginal utility and how utility responds when the consumption of a good is changed slightly.

(i) How Utility Responds to a Small Change in the Consumption of a Single Good

Suppose that the consumption x_i of good i has changed slightly. We denote the amount of this change by Δx_i. For example, if $\Delta x_i = 2$, that means that the consumption of good i has increased by two. If we denote the resulting change in utility Δu, the relationship between these two amounts is shown in Figure 1.13.

First, if you look at the grey triangle in the figure, its height is (the slope of the tangent line $\times \Delta x_i$). Moreover, since the slope of the tangent line is equal to the marginal utility $\partial u/\partial x_i$, the height of the triangle is ($\partial u/\partial x_i \times \Delta x_i$). If you visually compare this with the actual change in utility, Δu, there is a small gap between them; Δu is slightly smaller. But you can see that this gap becomes "vanishingly" small (compared to Δx_i) as we decrease Δx_i. We now can see the following.

If the change in consumption, Δx_i, is small, the change in utility, Δu, is *approximately*

$$\Delta u = \frac{\partial u}{\partial x_i} \Delta x_i.$$

Let us denote the above statement by (*).

It is bothersome to write all of this every time, so we introduce more notation, du and dx_i, which represent very small changes in the utility and consumption of good i respectively, and we write

$$du = \frac{\partial u}{\partial x_i} dx_i.$$

The meaning of this expression is the same as the phrase marked by the (*). This is an important point, so let's rephrase (*) in a way that's more easily understood. The equality in

Figure 1.13 Marginal utility and the change in utility

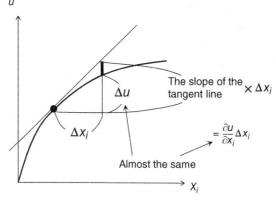

the statement (*) approximately holds when the change in consumption of good i, Δx_i, is small. By taking the unit of measurement of good i to be arbitrarily small (for instance, measuring gasoline not by the gallon but by the fluid ounce), a "one unit" change in consumption becomes very small. Thus, we can restate (*) as follows:

$$\begin{array}{c} du/dx_i \\ \text{(marginal utility of good } i) \end{array} = \begin{array}{l} \text{how much utility changes for an additional unit} \\ \text{of consumption of good } i, \text{when the unit of} \\ \text{measurement of good } i \text{ is sufficiently small } (*) \end{array}$$

Saying this every time is cumbersome, so let's agree that, when we say we **marginally increase** consumption of good i we mean that *for a unit of measurement that is sufficiently small*, we *increase* consumption of good i *by one unit*.

Using this terminology, the meaning of marginal utility can be rewritten in a simple form:

$$\begin{array}{c} \partial u/\partial x_i \\ \text{(marginal utility of good } i) \end{array} = \begin{array}{l} \text{how much utility changes for } a \text{ marginal} \\ \text{increase in consumption of good } i \end{array}$$

The meaning of this is the same as (*). The terminology "a marginal increase" or "to marginally increase" will be extremely useful, because it will enable you to interpret various mathematical expressions that you encounter from here on.

(ii) How Utility Responds to Small Changes in the Consumption of Multiple Goods

What if consumption of all goods is changed at the same time? This is a very complicated problem in general, but, if utility is given by the simple linear equation

$$u = a_1 x_1 + \cdots + a_N x_N + c,$$

then we can easily analyze the change in utility. There might not be many people whose preferences are represented by such an odd utility function, but it will give some intuition for analyzing more general and realistic cases, so let's study it carefully. If utility is given by a linear equation as above, then what does the graph of this utility function look like? We can draw a picture if we consider the case where there are two goods, and, as you can see (Figure 1.14), the graph is a plane.

In addition, *if the utility function is linear*, then the change in utility when consumption of each good changes simultaneously by $\Delta x_1, \ldots, \Delta x_N$, is given by

$$\Delta u = a_1 \Delta x_1 + \cdots + a_N \Delta x_N$$
$$= \text{the effect of changing } only \ x_1 + \cdots + \text{the effect of changing } only \ x_N,$$

which takes the form of the sum of the individual effects. In this sense, linear equations are very easy to handle. This is an important point, so make sure you understand this before moving on.

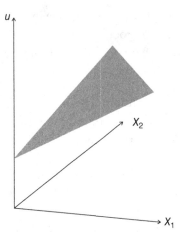

Figure 1.14 The graph of a linear utility function is a plane

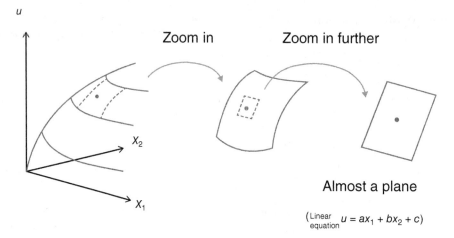

Figure 1.15 If you zoom into the graph of a utility function, it is almost a plane (i.e. a linear equation)

Now, consider a general (nonlinear) utility function. If you zoom into a part of the graph of the utility function, usually it will be almost flat, or look almost like a plane, as in Figure 1.15.[9] If you recall that the graph of a linear function is a plane, *for any (smooth) utility function we can regard it as being almost linear if we consider a small portion of its graph.*

Since for a linear equation the change in utility is given by the sum of the individual effects, we can say:

When the changes in consumption for each good, $\Delta x_1, \ldots, \Delta x_N$, are small, the utility change Δu is *approximately given by*

---

[9] By "usually," I mean the cases in which the graph is not jagged or sharp, but is smooth. It is of course possible that a utility function has a jagged part, but we don't see a reason for such a case to be particularly important, so we consider the smooth case, which is easier to analyze.

$$\Delta u = \text{the effect of changing } \textit{only } x_1 + \cdots + \text{the effect of changing } \textit{only } x_N$$

$$= \frac{\partial u}{\partial x_1} \Delta x_1 + \cdots + \frac{\partial u}{\partial x_N} \Delta x_N$$

which is the sum of the individual effects. Let us call this "statement (**)".

As in Part (i), let's represent this formula by

$$du = \frac{\partial u}{\partial x_1} dx_1 + \cdots + \frac{\partial u}{\partial x_N} dx_N.^{10}$$

The meaning of this formula is (**), which we stated above. In this way, we can use a simple sum to express the total effect on utility of simultaneously changing the consumption of many goods. *This illustrates why differentiation is useful in analyzing microeconomic models: we can, essentially, approximate small regions of complicated functions by linear functions, which are much easier to deal with.* This will be a very useful technique to have in our toolkit when we consider the issues of the production and consumption of multiple goods.

(c)   The Relationship between the Marginal Rate of Substitution and Marginal Utility

Using the method we learned above, let's consider the relationship between the marginal rate of substitution and marginal utility. This will be useful later when we derive the general condition for optimal consumption.

In the example of bread and water from Section 1.2, the marginal rate of substitution was defined to be "the amount of bread the consumer is willing to give up in order to consume an additional cup of water." In Figure 1.16, we consider a more mathematically formal definition of the marginal rate of substitution.

In the plot on the right, the marginal rate of substitution is shown as *the slope of the tangent line to the indifference curve*. However, since the slope is negative, we define the marginal rate of substitution to be the absolute value of the slope. This is the definition of the marginal rate of substitution that is given in advanced textbooks. In order to calculate this value, we'll use the method we learned in Part (b). Suppose that the consumer increases consumption of the first good (water) by a little bit ($dx_1 > 0$) and decreases consumption of the second good (bread) by a little ($dx_2 < 0$). The change in utility is, as seen in Part (b),

$$du = \frac{\partial u}{\partial x_1} dx_1 + \frac{\partial u}{\partial x_N} dx_2,$$

which is the sum of the individual effects. The situation in which the two effects cancel each other out (i.e. moving along an indifference curve, where utility stays constant) is described by

$$0 = \frac{\partial u}{\partial x_1} dx_1 + \frac{\partial u}{\partial x_2} dx_2.$$

---

[10] This is sometimes called the formula for a **total derivative**.

Figure 1.16 The definition of the marginal rate of substitution MRS_{12}

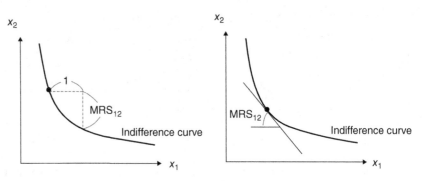

Intuitive definition

(The amount of the second good that the consumer is willing to give up in order to increase consumption of the first good by one unit)

More mathematical definition

(The slope of the tangent line to the indifference curve)

Manipulating this expression, we get

$$\frac{dx_2}{dx_1} = -\frac{\partial u/dx_1}{\partial u/dx_2}.$$

Since dx_2/dx_1 is the ratio between dx_1 and dx_2 such that utility is held constant, let's denote this using the notation

$$\left.\frac{dx_2}{dx_1}\right|_{u\,=\,\text{constant}}.$$

In other words, the ratio between dx_1 and dx_2 such that utility is held constant is the (absolute value of the) slope of the tangent line to the indifference curve. Putting everything together, we obtain

$$
\mathrm{MRS}_{12} \qquad = \quad -\left.\frac{dx_2}{dx_1}\right|_{u\,=\,\text{constant}} \qquad = \quad \frac{\partial u/\partial x_1}{\partial u/\partial x_2}
$$

the marginal rate of substitution of the first good for the second good[11]   the slope of the tangent line to the indifference curve   the ratio of marginal utilities

(5)

This is the mathematical definition of the marginal rate of substitution, and the one that more advanced textbooks use.

---

[11] It's always confusing whether to call this the marginal rate of substitution "of good 1 for good 2" or "of good 2 for good 1." I remember it in the following way: the general rule is that the "marginal X of Y" is the derivative of X with respect to Y. For example, the marginal utility of water is the derivative of the utility function with respect to the amount of water consumed. In Equation (5), since it is the derivative of the amount of good 2 with respect to the amount of good 1, we call it "the marginal rate of substitution of good 1 for good 2."

(d)   Condition for Optimal Consumption

Using the preparation we did in Parts (a) through (c), let's use our mathematical toolkit to solve for the general condition for optimal consumption. As we saw in Section 1.3, the optimal consumption bundle in the two-good case was determined by the point at which the indifference curve and the budget line touch each other, as in Figure 1.16.

If the indifference curve and the budget line are exactly touching each other, it means that the slopes of the two lines are equal to each other at the point where they are touching. Since the slopes of the indifference curve and the budget line are "the marginal rate of substitution MRS_{12}" and "the price ratio p_1/p_2" respectively, the condition for the optimal bundle can be written as follows:

$$\underset{\substack{\text{marginal rate of} \\ \text{substitution}}}{MRS_{12}} \quad = \quad \underset{\text{price ratio}}{\frac{p_1}{p_2}} \tag{6}$$

Condition 1 for Optimal Consumption

If we depict this graphically, it will be as in Figure 1.17.

As we found in Part (c), the marginal rate of substitution is equal to the ratio of the marginal utilities (see Equation (5)). That is, $MRS_{12} = (\partial u/\partial x_1)/(\partial u/\partial x_2)$, so, if we rewrite the optimality condition above, we get

$$\frac{\partial u/\partial x_1}{p_1} = \frac{\partial u/\partial x_2}{p_2} \tag{7}$$

Let's try to understand what this equation says.

The $\frac{\partial u/\partial x_1}{p_1}$ that appears in Equation (7) is (almost) equal to the change in utility that comes from increasing consumption by 1¢'s worth of good 1. To see this, assume that prices are expressed in cents and first note that the amount of good 1 that can be bought with 1¢ is $1/p_1$,

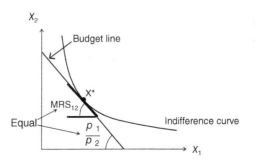

Figure 1.17 The condition for optimal consumption

because $(1/p_1) \times p_1 = 1$ cent. Therefore, if the consumer increases or decreases her expenditure on good 1 by 1¢, her utility increases or decreases by (almost)

$$\frac{\partial u}{\partial x_i} \times \boxed{\frac{1}{p_i}}.$$

(the amount of good i
that can be bought with 1¢).

Based on this observation, let's consider what happens if Equation (7) does not hold. For example, if

$$\frac{\partial u / \partial x_1}{p_1} > \frac{\partial u / \partial x_2}{p_2},$$

then decreasing her expenditure on good 2 by 1¢ reduces the consumer's utility by the amount on the right-hand side. If the consumer subsequently uses that 1¢ to buy more of good 1, then her utility increases by the amount on the left-hand side. In total, this means that utility increases by

left-hand side − right-hand side > 0.

Looking back at Equation (7), we see that it represents the situation where it is not possible to increase utility by slightly adjusting expenditure on goods 1 and 2. Thus, Equation (7) holds at the optimal consumption bundle. If we were to put this condition into words, we would say:

The consumer's degree of satisfaction does not change regardless of which good she spends her last cent of income on.

We call this the **law of equi-marginal utility** (per 1¢).

The above claim holds for any number of goods. Even if there are 100 goods, if the consumer is choosing her consumption bundle optimally, the above condition should be satisfied for any pair of goods. Otherwise, she could increase her utility by reducing her spending on one good and using that money to buy a different good that would give her more utility than she gave up when she reduced consumption of the original good. To summarize, the optimality condition for the case with many (N) goods is as follows:

$$\frac{\partial u / \partial x_1}{p_1} = \cdots = \frac{\partial u / \partial x_N}{p_N}$$
Condition 2 for Optimal Consumption
The Law of Equi-Marginal Utility (per 1¢)

(8)

This condition says that *marginal utility divided by price is the same for each good*. Let's call this number λ, so we have

$$\frac{\partial u / \partial x_1}{p_1} = \cdots = \frac{\partial u / \partial x_N}{p_N} = \lambda.$$

The symbol λ is a Greek letter called "lambda," and it represents *the amount of additional utility the consumer gets when income is increased by 1¢*. Therefore, this λ is sometimes called the **marginal utility of income**. Using this notation, we can rewrite the condition for optimal consumption as

$$
\begin{cases}
\dfrac{\partial u}{\partial x_1} = \lambda p_1 \\
\quad \vdots \\
\dfrac{\partial u}{\partial x_N} = \lambda p_N
\end{cases}
\tag{9}
$$

Now I'll explain *how to quickly derive this optimality condition by following a simple procedure. Once you know this method, you can apply it to quickly and effortlessly solve similar problems.* This is an alternative (and more mathematical) method to derive *the same thing as we did earlier*, so you won't miss anything crucial by skipping this portion, especially if you aren't interested in math. However, if you are interested in math or want to become a professional who does economic analysis using models, it's best if you understand this portion, since it is a commonly used method to solve economic models.

Since optimal consumption means maximizing utility subject to a budget constraint, we can solve for the optimal consumption bundle with a very easy procedure, if we use *the general mathematical method for solving a constrained optimization problem*. A constrained optimization problem is the problem of maximizing a function $f(x_1, \ldots, x_N)$ subject to a constraint $g(x_1, \ldots, x_N) = 0$. Now, denoting $(x_1, \ldots, x_N)$ by x, we can write a constrained optimization problem as

$$
\max_{x} f(x)
$$

$$
\text{s.t. } g(x) = 0.
$$

In order to solve this, we construct a new function:

$$
L(x) = f(x) + \lambda g(x).
$$

We call the coefficient λ the **Lagrange multiplier**. Under certain conditions,[12] the solution for the constrained optimization problem is given by

$$
\begin{cases}
\dfrac{\partial L}{\partial x_1} = 0 \\
\quad \vdots \\
\dfrac{\partial L}{\partial x_N} = 0
\end{cases}
\tag{10}
$$

---

[12] If the area above the indifference curve (i.e. the set of consumption bundles that gives at least as much utility) is a convex set, and a strictly positive amount of each good is consumed, then the solution will satisfy these equations.

With these N equations and the constraint $g(x_1, \ldots, x_N) = 0$, we have $N + 1$ equations, which we can use to determine the $N + 1$ unknowns $x_1, \ldots, x_N, \lambda$. This method of solving a general constrained optimization problem is called the **method of Lagrange multipliers**. If you want more details, refer to Appendix B.

Now let's confirm that this method does indeed give us the condition for optimal consumption that we derived before. In order to maximize $u(x_1, \ldots, x_N)$ under the constraint $I - p_1 x_1 - \ldots - p_N x_N = 0$, we construct a new function,

$$L = u + \lambda(I - p_1 x_1 - \ldots - p_N x_N),$$

and compute Equation (10) to get

$$\begin{cases} \dfrac{\partial L}{\partial x_1} = \dfrac{\partial u}{\partial x_1} - \lambda p_1 = 0 \\ \qquad\vdots \\ \dfrac{\partial L}{\partial x_N} = \dfrac{\partial u}{\partial x_N} - \lambda p_N = 0 \end{cases}.$$

It's clear now that this will give us the same condition as the system of equations (9).

At the end of Chapter 1, I'll walk you through an example that demonstrates how to calculate the optimal consumption by applying this technique (see Problem Session 1).

1.6   Properties of Optimal Consumption

The optimal consumption bundle x^* depends on the price profile p and income I. The dependence of x^* on p and I is expressed as $x^* = x(p, I)$, and we say that x^* is a function of p and I. In this book, we call $x(p, I)$ a **demand function**. How does the optimal consumption bundle x^* change if the price profile p and income I change?

First, let's consider the case where income changes. Since the consumer can buy more if her income increases, the budget line moves outward, away from the origin. Since the slope of the budget line is the price ratio, the new budget line and the original budget line have the same slope if prices don't change – that is, the new budget line is a *parallel translation* away from the origin. The new optimal consumption bundle x^{**} (the point where the indifference curve and the new budget line are tangent to each other) is depicted in Figure 1.18.

In Figure 1.18, consumption of good 1 increases when income increases. Goods such as good 1 that are consumed in higher quantity when income increases are called **normal goods** or **superior goods**. However, it's not necessarily the case that consumption of a good increases when income increases. In some cases, consumption of a good might decrease when income increases, as in Figure 1.19.

Goods that are consumed in lower quantity when income increases are called inferior goods. For example, second-hand clothing might be an inferior good. If an individual's income increases, she might shop for her clothes at a department store such as Macy's instead of a consignment store such as GoodWill.

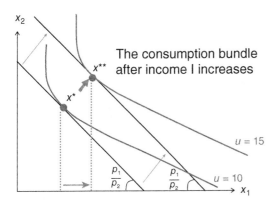

Figure 1.18 Change in income and change in consumption

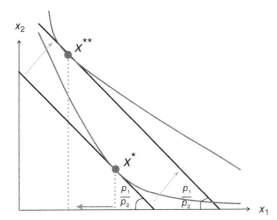

Figure 1.19 The case in which good 1 is an inferior good

Now let's consider the case in which prices change. It is easy to understand what happens to the budget line when the price of the first good is increased, if we note the following.

- Since the slope of the budget line is the price ratio p_1/p_2, *the slope of the budget line becomes steeper if p_1 increases.*
- The point at which the budget line crosses the vertical axis represents the amount of the second good the consumer can afford if she spends all her income I on it. This amount is I/p_2, so it does not change even if p_1 changes. Therefore, *even if the price of the first good increases, the point at which the budget line crosses the vertical axis does not change.*

Using these observations, I draw the change in the budget line when the price of the first good, p_1, increases. Figure 1.20 shows how the optimal consumption bundle changes in this situation.

In Figure 1.20, you can see that consumption of good 1 decreases. In this way, we can determine the new optimal consumption bundle when the price of good 1 changes in various ways. If we plot the relationship between the quantity of good 1 in the optimal consumption

Figure 1.20 Change in price and change of the consumption bundle

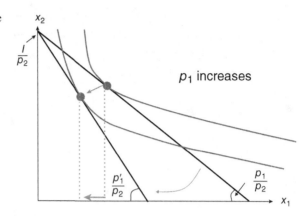

Figure 1.21 The demand curve derived from the indifference curves in Figure 1.20

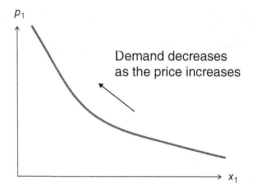

bundle and the price of good 1, we have the "**demand curve** of good 1." Figure 1.21 shows an example of a demand curve.

Deriving demand curves from indifference curves/utility maximization is the main objective of consumer theory. Most high-school-level or introductory textbooks in economics do analysis only with demand curves. By contrast, in intermediate and advanced microeconomics, we *derive* demand curves from consumers' optimal behavior. This is useful, because it enables us to analyse the welfare (utility) of a consumer. For example, as we will see, this model enables us to rigorously examine how much a consumer gains from market transactions.

In Figure 1.21 we see that demand for good 1 decreases as the price of good 1 increases. The property that demand for a good decreases as its price increases is called the **law of demand**, and it holds for almost all goods we observe in reality. However, theoretically speaking, it is not necessarily the case. We can construct an example in which demand for a good actually increases as the price of the good increases, as in Figure 1.22.

Goods that are demanded at higher quantities when their prices increase are called **Giffen goods**.

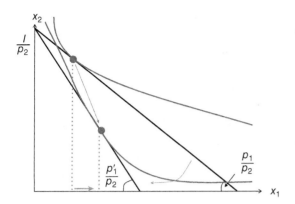

Figure 1.22 The case in which demand increases as the price increases

---

Comment 1.10 Is a Louis Vuitton Handbag a Giffen Good?

Some brand-name goods are valuable to consumers precisely *because* they are expensive. You might think that people want designer handbags to flaunt how much money they have, and if a handbag was less expensive it wouldn't be as desirable since it's no longer a status symbol. This line of thinking might lead you to believe that luxury goods such as Louis Vuitton handbags are Giffen goods, but, technically, this is incorrect.

Supposing that good 1 is a Louis Vuitton handbag, consider whether the plot in Figure 1.22 captures the idea that a Louis Vuitton handbag "sells more when it's expensive." If the Louis Vuitton handbag is valuable to the consumer because it's expensive, then the consumer's utility depends directly on the price, and we can write the consumer's utility as

$$u = u(x_1, x_2, p_1).$$

For any given quantity x_1 of Louis Vuitton handbags a consumer owns, the amount of satisfaction she gets from her bag(s) changes depending on the current price p_1 of the bags. Therefore, the reason demand for a luxury item is high when the price is high is not because consumers' indifference curves are like those in Figure 1.22 but because the price of the good enters directly into the utility function.

Giffen goods are those goods that have upward-sloping demand curves even when the price of the good does not enter into consumers' utility functions. Giffen goods are theoretically possible, but we rarely observe them in the real world.

Appendix: Is It Safe to Assume that Indifference Curves Are Bowed Toward the Origin?

One thing that might be nagging at you as you study microeconomics is the assumption that indifference curves are bowed toward the origin. It might feel as if we're making an unreasonably strong assumption just to derive "nice" results. As we saw in Section 1.2, indifference curves being bowed toward the origin captures the intuitive idea that the desirability of a good decreases as it becomes more abundant. We called this the law of diminishing marginal rate of substitution, and it makes good sense. However, you might doubt that this *always* holds, so let's carefully examine this assumption.

What happens if indifference curves are not bowed toward the origin? Figure 1.23 describes how optimal consumption changes when the price of the first good changes for the case where indifference curves are not bowed toward the origin. If we draw the demand curve for good 1 based on Figure 1.23, we see that demand for good 1 jumps at a certain price, as in Figure 1.24.

The price at which demand jumps is the price that brings about the situation shown in Figure 1.23 (b). Thus, *microeconomics' assumption that indifference curves are bowed toward the origin implies that demand does not jump discontinuously when there's a slight change in price.* If there is a real-life situation in which demand jumps dramatically when there are small price changes, and this phenomenon occurs frequently, we would need to consider modeling this situation with indifference curves that are not bowed toward the origin. Conversely, if demand does not jump dramatically when the price of the good changes slightly, then models with indifference curves that are bowed toward the origin are a reasonably good approximation of reality.

Even with this explanation, *you may still be feeling that you're being tricked* (and even I feel this way). Let's try to think about this issue in greater depth. If we consider a model in which the indifference curves seen in Figure 1.23 are modified so that they are bowed toward the origin, how does demand change? Figure 1.25 shows what happens to demand.

As you can see, *the demand curve induced by the modified indifference curves is almost the same as the demand curve induced by the original indifference curves that were not bowed toward*

Figure 1.23 Indifference curves that are not bowed toward the origin

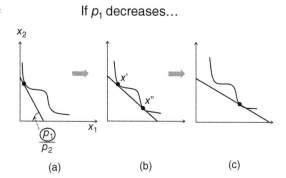

Figure 1.24 Demand may jump if the indifference curves are not bowed toward the origin

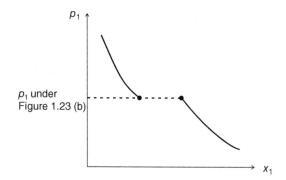

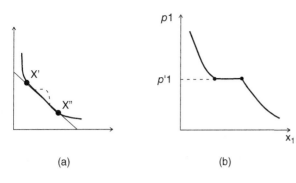

Figure 1.25 The case in which the indifference curves are modified to be bowed toward the origin

(a)   (b)

the origin. The only difference is that the part where the original demand curve jumps is now connected by a straight line segment. This comes from the fact that all the points between x' and x'' in Figure 1.25 (a) are optimal consumption bundles. Note that the price levels where demand jumps are only a tiny fraction of all possible price levels, so we can describe almost all cases that arise in the real world using models with indifference curves that are bowed toward the origin.

The takeaway from this is that, even though indifference curves may not always be bowed toward the origin, we can approximate these cases quite well using a model with indifference curves that are bowed toward the origin.

1.7 A Tool for Measuring the Degrees of Substitution and Complementarity: The Compensated Demand Function

Recall that in Section 1.2, when we were learning about indifference curves, we discussed perfect substitutes and perfect complements. We gave the example of Coors and Budweiser being perfect substitutes for a consumer who just wants beer and doesn't care about the brand. In essence, the consumer views these two goods as being the same, and we saw that the indifference curves for such a case are straight lines. We also gave the example of left and right contact lenses being perfect complements, since they must necessarily be consumed in a certain ratio (a 1:1 ratio in the example of left and right contact lenses). The consumer views one good as being useless without also having some of the other, and we saw that the indifference curves for such a case are L-shaped. In reality, most situations will be somewhere in between these two extreme cases. Intuitively speaking, the goods are highly complementary if the indifference curves are very curved and the goods are highly substitutable if the indifference curves are not very curved (see Figure 1.26).

Therefore, it seems *that the substitutability or complementarity of various goods is related to the curvature of the indifference curves.* But how can we measure the curvature of indifference curves? We could use a purely mathematical definition of curvature, but it will be more insightful to use a concept of curvature that has more economic meaning. We use the following concept, called a **compensated demand function**, which is:

The cheapest consumption bundle that achieves *a* certain utility level.

Figure 1.26 The curvature of indifference curves and substitutability/complementarity

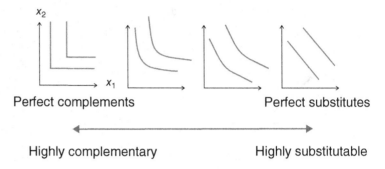

Perfect complements   Perfect substitutes

Highly complementary   Highly substitutable

Figure 1.27 Consumption bundles for constant expenditure

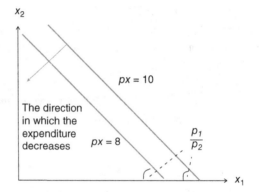

From the definition, it's not clear why compensated demand functions will be a useful tool for measuring the curvature of indifference curves (which tells us about the substitutability and complementarity of the goods). I now explain in detail how exactly they will help us.

In formal mathematical language, the compensated demand function $\bar{x}(p, u)$ is the solution to the following expenditure minimization problem:

$$\min_x px$$
$$\text{s.t.} \quad u(x) = u$$

The expenditure minimization problem is to find the consumption bundle that minimizes total expenditure $px = p_1 x_1 + \cdots + p_N x_N$ from among the consumption bundles that provide a certain utility level u.

Let's solve this problem for the two-good case by analyzing figures. The consumption bundles (x_1, x_2) such that total expenditure is constant $(= c)$ satisfy the condition

$$p_1 x_1 + p_2 x_2 = c.$$

Drawing this set of consumption bundles in a figure, it is a downward-sloping line with slope equal to the price ratio p_1/p_2 (see Figure 1.27).

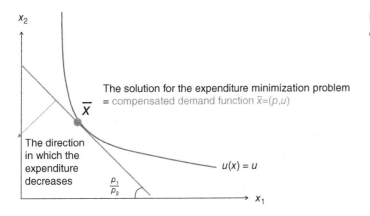

Figure 1.28 Compensated demand function

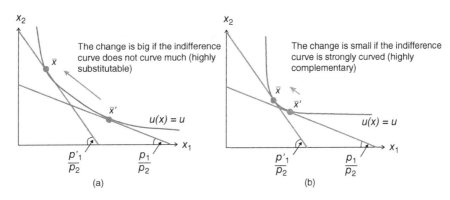

Figure 1.29 The response of compensated demand to a change in price

As this line moves toward the origin – i.e. as the consumer decreases consumption of all goods – total expenditure decreases. Using this observation, we know that the solution $\bar{x}$ for the expenditure minimization problem is determined as shown in Figure 1.28.

The expenditure minimizer $\bar{x}$ depends on the utility level u that must be achieved and on the price profile p. This relationship is written as $\bar{x} = \bar{x}(p,u)$, and we call $\bar{x}(p,u)$ the compensated demand function.

The curvature of the indifference curves can be measured by how responsive the compensated demand function is to price changes. Figure 1.29 (a) shows the case in which the indifference curve is not very curved (so the goods are highly substitutable) and compensated demand changes drastically when prices change slightly. In contrast, Figure 1.29 (b) shows the case in which the indifference curve is very curved (so the goods are highly complementary) and compensated demand does not change much when prices change slightly.

This discussion should make clear that how the compensated demand (i.e. the cheapest consumption bundle that achieves a certain utility) reveals the curvature of indifference curves, which in turn tells us about the substitutability/complementarity of the goods. We can represent the change in compensated demand of good i due to a small change in the price of good j with the (partial) derivative

$$\frac{\partial \overline{x}_i}{\partial p_j}.$$

In microeconomics, we define substitutability and complementarity in this way.[13]

The arrow in Figure 1.29 represents the direction of the change in compensated demand when the price of good 1 increases. As you can see from the figure, in the two-good case the compensated demand for good 1 decreases as the price of good 1 increases. Does a similar conclusion hold when there are more than two goods? If there are three goods, we would have to visualize a three-dimensional version of Figure 1.29, which is rather tricky. And if there are even more goods, say 20, then it's impossible to visualize, so we can't do the analysis using figures. It seems as if it would be very difficult to show that, when there are many goods,

If the price of a good increases, then compensated demand for that good decreases. (More precisely, the compensated demand for that good does not increase.) (*)

However, with a clever use of simple math, this claim can be proved fairly easily.

Proving (*)

Let the number of goods be arbitrary. Now, consider two arbitrary price profiles p^0 and p^1 and let $\overline{x}^0$ and $\overline{x}^1$ be the cheapest consumption bundles that achieve utility u under prices p^0 and p^1 respectively.

Price profile	p^0	p^1
	↓	↓
Compensated Demand	$\overline{x}^0$	$\overline{x}^1$

(the cheapest bundle that achieves utility u)

Note that both $\overline{x}^0$ and $\overline{x}^1$ achieve the same level of utility. What if the consumer purchases $\overline{x}^0$ and $\overline{x}^1$ (which both achieve utility u) under prices p^1? If

$$p^1 \overline{x}^0 < p^1 \overline{x}^1$$

then, in order to achieve utility u under p^1, it's cheaper to choose $\overline{x}^0$ than $\overline{x}^1$. But this contradicts that $\overline{x}^1$ is the cheapest consumption bundle that achieves utility u under prices p^1. Therefore, it must be that

$$p^1 \overline{x}^1 \leq p^1 \overline{x}^0. \tag{11}$$

This is an easy concept once you understand it, but it may take a while for many people to grasp it. I want you to read the explanation above one more time and try to understand it well.

---

[13] While it is the size of $\frac{\partial \overline{x}_i}{\partial p_j}$ that represents the degree of substitutability/complementarity in the two-good case, it is actually the sign of $\frac{\partial \overline{x}_i}{\partial p_j}$ that represents the degree of substitutability/complementarity if there are many goods. The details are explained below.

(Close the book and try to explain it to yourself by writing the inequality. If you can do it without looking, then you are on the right track!)

Using a similar line of reasoning, it must be that

$$p^0 \bar{x}^1 \geq p^0 \bar{x}^0. \tag{12}$$

Subtracting each side of (12) from the corresponding side of (11), we have

$$(p^1 - p^0)\bar{x}^1 \leq (p^1 - p^0)\bar{x}^0.$$

The direction of the inequality in (11) is preserved because we subtracted the bigger amount from the smaller amount in the left-hand side and subtracted the smaller amount from the bigger amount in the right-hand side. Rearranging this inequality, we get

$$(p^1 - p^0)(\bar{x}^1 - \bar{x}^0) \leq 0, \tag{13}$$

which is a *very important* inequality. Recall that p is a price profile $p = (p_1, \ldots, p_N)$, x is a consumption bundle $x = (x_1, \ldots, x_N)$, and px is not a product of two numbers but is given by $px = p_1 x_1 + \cdots + p_N x_N$. Using this observation, we can rewrite Inequality (13) as

$$(p_1^1 - p_1^0)(\bar{x}_1^1 - \bar{x}_1^0) + \cdots + (p_1^1 - p_1^0)(\bar{x}_1^1 - \bar{x}_1^0) \leq 0.$$

Now consider a special case where p^1 is the same as p^0 except that the price of good i has increased. Then all but the ith term on the left-hand side become 0, and we get

$$(p_i^1 - p_i^0)(\bar{x}_i^1 - \bar{x}_i^0) \leq 0 \tag{14}$$

$$\underset{\text{positive}}{\uparrow} \qquad \underset{\text{negative or zero}}{\uparrow}$$

This implies that, if the price of good i increases, then the compensated demand for that good decreases $((\bar{x}_i^1 - \bar{x}_i^0) < 0)$ or stays the same $((\bar{x}_i^1 - \bar{x}_i^0) = 0)$.

We can restate the meaning of (14) by using derivatives. Doing so, we obtain

$$\frac{\partial \bar{x}_i}{\partial p_i} \leq 0 \tag{15}$$

The self-substitution effect is non-positive.[14]

Inequalities (14) and (15) are very important. They show that *the compensated demand for a good never increases if the price of that good increases. In this case, we say that the self-substitution effect is non-positive.*[15]

---

[14] Mathematically, letting $\Delta p_i = p_i^1 - p_i^0$, $\Delta \bar{x}_i = \bar{x}_i^1 - \bar{x}_i^0$, (14) implies $\frac{\Delta \bar{x}_i}{\Delta p_i} \leq 0$, and by letting $\Delta p_i \to 0$ we obtain (15).

[15] We saw in the previous section that there is a possibility that the demand for a good actually increases when the price of that good increases. We call such goods "Giffen goods." However, for *compensated* demand functions, which give the cheapest consumption bundle that achieves some fixed utility level, this does not happen.

Based on this fact, we can now precisely define the substitutability and complementarity of goods. We first consider the case in which the compensated demand for a good decreases when the price of that good increases – i.e. $\left(\frac{\partial \overline{x}_i}{\partial p_i} < 0\right)$. In order to understand the definitions we will give, let's work through a simple example.

Example 1.5

Let's consider the compensated demand (which is the cheapest consumption bundle that achieves a fixed utility level) when there are three goods: pasta (good 1), pasta sauce (good 2), and bread (good 3). If the price of pasta increases, since the self-substitution effect is always non-positive, the compensated demand for pasta does not increase. In particular, if we consider the case in which compensated demand for pasta decreases, the consumption of pasta sauce or bread needs to be increased in order to maintain the fixed utility level. (If compensated demand for pasta decreases and consumption of pasta sauce and bread do not increase, then utility will decrease, and so utility will fall short of the required level.) In this case, it would be natural to suppose that consumption of pasta sauce decreases $\left(\frac{\partial \overline{x}_2}{\partial p_1} < 0\right)$ and consumption of bread increases $\left(\frac{\partial \overline{x}_3}{\partial p_1} > 0\right)$ as consumption of pasta decreases. We then say that pasta and pasta sauce are **complements** and pasta and bread are **substitutes**.

Let's summarize what we've discussed above. The consumption bundle that achieves a fixed utility level in the cheapest manner is called compensated demand, and we denote it by $\overline{x} = (\overline{x}_1, \ldots, \overline{x}_N)$ We know that, if the price of good i is increased, the compensated demand $\overline{x}_i$ for good i either decreases or stays the same. In many cases it decreases (i.e. $\frac{\partial \overline{x}_i}{\partial p_i} < 0$), and in this case substitutes and complements are defined as follows.

The Definition of Substitutes and Complements (when the self-substitution effect is negative $\frac{\partial \overline{x}_i}{\partial p_i} < 0$)

If $\frac{\partial \overline{x}_j}{\partial p_i} > 0$ then good i and good j are substitutes.

If $\frac{\partial \overline{x}_j}{\partial p_i} < 0$ then good i and good j are complements.

Comment 1.11 Complements in the Two-Good Case

In the two-good case, if the self-substitution effect is strictly negative, then by definition the two goods will be substitutes. This is because, when the price of one good increases, the compensated demand for that good decreases, and the compensated demand for the other good must increase to keep the same level of utility. Therefore, the two goods are substitutes. The case of perfect complements in the two-good case (such as our example with left and right contact lenses) is not covered by the above definition, since the self-substitution effect is zero. In this case, the indifference curves are L-shaped, so, even if the price of the first good (right lenses) increases, the cheapest consumption bundle that achieves the necessary utility level (i.e. compensated demand) does not change. To be more precise, since compensated demand for the first good does not change, the self-substitution effect is zero $\left(\frac{\partial \overline{x}_i}{\partial p_i} = 0\right)$. Moreover, it is the case that compensated demand for the second good (left lenses) does not change. In general, it seems natural to define complements to be goods for which, when the price of good i changes, compensated demand moves *in the same direction* as good i's compensated demand. *If we decide that, when* $\frac{\partial \overline{x}_j}{\partial p_i} = 0$ *and* $\frac{\partial \overline{x}_i}{\partial p_i} = 0$, *we say goods i and j are complements*, then we can incorporate the notion of (perfect) complements for the two-good case.

1.8   The Expenditure Function

The compensated demand function $\overline{x}(p,u)$ gives the cheapest consumption bundle that achieves the fixed utility level u given prices p. Therefore, $p\overline{x}(p,u)$ is the least amount of money that is needed to achieve utility u given prices p. This is written as

$$I(p, u) = p\overline{x}(p, u),$$

where $I(p,u)$ is called the **(minimum) expenditure function**. Before delving into the properties of the expenditure function, let's look at a case study that will illustrate why the expenditure function is a useful concept.

Case Study 1.2 TPP and Income Compensation for Farmers

In anticipation of participating in the Trans-Pacific Partnership (TPP), the Japanese government is considering direct compensation for farmers. TPP aims for participating countries to eliminate tariffs on agricultural products. (We call this the "liberalization" of agricultural products.) If liberalization is achieved, then the market prices of agricultural products will fall, so Japanese farmers will lose revenue while Japanese consumers save money. What is the maximum compensation a consumer would be willing to give farmers for the losses they incur under TPP?

Let p denote the price profile and let u denote a consumer's utility level before liberalization. Suppose that the value of the consumer's expenditure function I(p,u) decreases by $800 after the prices of agricultural products go down due to liberalization. This means that, even if the consumer has to give up $800 after liberalization, she is still able to achieve the utility level u that she had before liberalization took effect. Therefore, *if the compensation that the consumer pays to farmers is less than $800, then the consumer is still benefiting from liberalization, even though she has to pay compensation to farmers.*

As this example shows, *the expenditure function expresses, in units of money, the gains and losses that a consumer faces as a result of price changes.* It plays a key role in the analysis of the economic welfare of citizens. However, one issue is that the utility level u is not usually observable, so, unless we relate $I(p,u)$ to something observable, it is difficult to use the expenditure function in practice. In this section and the next, we will see some mathematical analysis that is an important step toward *relating the expenditure function with observable consumption levels.* To this end, let's analyze how the expenditure function $I(p,u)$ changes when prices change.

How does the expenditure function I(p,u) change when prices change?

Take any price profile p^0. The expenditure function that achieves utility level u is, by definition,

$$I(p^0, u) = p^0 \overline{x}(p^0, u). \tag{16}$$

Moreover, for any price profile p that is different from p^0, we will see

$$I(p, u) \leq p\overline{x}(p^0, u). \tag{17}$$

This follows from the definition of the expenditure function through the following line of reasoning. Recall from the definition of the compensated demand function that $\overline{x}(p^0, u)$ is the cheapest way to achieve utility *u under prices p^0, but, after prices change to p, there may be an alternative consumption bundle that achieves utility level u at a lower cost.* The cost of the new cheapest consumption bundle giving utility u is, by definition, $I(p,u)$. Therefore, we have Inequality (17).

Now, let's consider the situation where only good 1's price has changed, from p_1^0 to p_1, and depict these observations in a figure. Plotting the new prices p_1 on the horizontal axis and expenditure on the vertical axis, let's first depict the right-hand side of (17), which is the consumer's expenditure when she continues to consume $\overline{x}(p^0,u)$ even after the prices change. Note that

$$p\overline{x}(p^0, u) = p_1 \boxed{\overline{x}_1(p^0, u)} + \boxed{p_2^0 \overline{x}_2(p^0, u) + \cdots + p_I^0 \overline{x}_I(p^0, u),}$$

$$\underbrace{\phantom{p_1 \overline{x}_1(p^0,u)}}_{\text{slope}} \qquad \underbrace{\phantom{p_2^0 \overline{x}_2(p^0, u) + \cdots + p_I^0 \overline{x}_I}}_{\text{part that is unrelated to } p_1 \text{(constant)}}$$

In other words, "no adjustment expenditure," which is equal to $p\overline{x}(p^0, u)$, is given by this equation,

$$\text{No adjustment expenditure} = (\text{slope})p_1 + (\text{constant}),$$

which is the equation for a line. The slope of this line is the compensated demand of good 1, $\overline{x}_1(p^0, u)$. Figure 1.30 shows the graph of this line, which we call L.

At the same time, if we look at how the expenditure function $I(p,u)$ changes in response to the price change, Equation (16) implies that it passes through the same point as L at p_1^0 and Inequality (17) implies that it lies below L at all other prices of good 1. In other words,

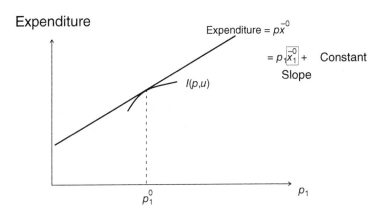

Figure 1.30 The slope of the expenditure function

the graph of the expenditure function is tangent to the straight line L at p_1^0. From these observations, we conclude:

The slope of the tangent line to $I(p,u)$ at p_1^0 = the slope of $L = \overline{x}_1\left(p^0, u\right)$.

Since the slope of the tangent line to a graph can be represented by a (partial) derivative, the above relationship implies that

$$\frac{\partial I\left(p^0, u\right)}{\partial p_1} = \overline{x}_1\left(p^0, u\right). \tag{18}$$

The above equation (18) holds for every good, not just for good 1, and at every point p^0. Summarizing our discussion above, we have

$$\underbrace{\frac{\partial I\left(p, u\right)}{\partial p_i}}_{\substack{\text{the derivative of the expenditure} \\ \text{function with respect to the} \\ \text{price of good } i}} = \underbrace{\overline{x}_i(p, u).}_{\text{compensated demand for good } i} \tag{19}$$

The fact that compensated demand of a good is obtained by differentiating the expenditure function with respect to the price of that good is called **Shephard's lemma**. This is the first step in connecting the expenditure function, which is difficult to observe, to observable demand behavior. In the next section, Section 1.9, we relate the right-hand side of Equation (19) to real demand.

1.9   Income Effects and Substitution Effects

In this section, I'll finally explain the most important part of consumer theory. So far, we've learned about the compensated demand function, substitutability and complementarity, the expenditure function, and more. Everything we've learned up to this point is actually a tool for understanding the income effect and the substitution effect, which I discuss in this section.

The key to understanding a person's consumption behavior is knowing what the effect of a price change is on his or her consumption of that good. When the price of a good increases, a consumer might consume more of a similar, substitutable good that can replace the original. The closer the substitute is to the original, the more the consumer will shift consumption from the original good to the substitute. For example, if the price of butter increases, then the consumer might switch to margarine, a close substitute for butter. This type of effect is called the substitution effect, and the compensated demand function (which we saw contains information on the substitutability and complementarity of goods) will be useful for studying this.

At the same time, when the price of a good increases, then a consumer can no longer purchase as much as she used to be able to purchase. In effect, it feels as though she has less income, even though the nominal value of her income is unchanged. Therefore, when the price of a good increases, her income is effectively reduced, and this will have an effect on what consumption bundle she chooses. We call this the income effect. In order to understand the implications of a price change on the demand for various goods, it's useful to decompose the total effect into the income effect and substitution effect.

Before learning in Part (c) exactly what the income effect and the substitution effect are, we'll do some preparation in Parts (a) and (b).

(a)   Duality of Consumption

First, take a look at Figure 1.31. What do you think this figure shows?

Of course, this looks like an illustration of the optimal consumption bundle given by utility maximization. However, if we recall Section 1.7, this could also be seen as the outcome of an expenditure minimization problem – that is, it shows the cheapest consumption bundle among all those that achieve a target level of utility. In other words, if the consumer behaves rationally, the chosen consumption bundle (x in the figure) can be interpreted in the following two ways. By denoting income, prices, and utility at a certain point in time (here, we'll say the "current" time) by I, p, and u respectively, we have

Figure 1.31 Duality of consumption

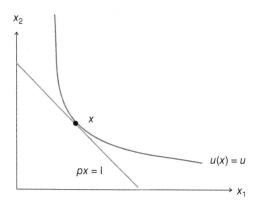

$$
\begin{array}{ccccc}
x(p, I) & = & x & = & \overline{x}(p, u).
\end{array}
$$

the utility–maximizing bundle under current income I and current prices p the observed consumption bundle   the cheapest bundle under prices p that achieves the current utility level   (20)

(*duality of consumption*)

The fact that *observed consumption can be seen as the solution to the utility maximization problem and as the solution to the expenditure minimization problem* is called **duality**.

(b)   The "Effective Decrease" in Income due to a Price Increase

Let x_i be the consumption of good i before the price of good i increases and let u be the utility level before the price of good i increases. When the price of good i increases slightly, how much additional money is needed to be able to achieve the same level of utility from before the price change? By combining Shephard's lemma (which we saw in Section 1.8) with the duality of consumption (which we have just seen in Part (a)), we find that the necessary amount of money is

$$
\frac{\partial I(p, u)}{\partial p_i} = x_i.
$$

how much extra money is needed in order to maintain utility level u when the price of good i increases slightly   the consumption of good i before the price increase   (21)

There are two reasons why this holds.

- By Shephard's lemma (Equation (19)), the left-hand side of the equation is equal to compensated demand $\overline{x}_i(p, u)$.
- Moreover, by the duality of consumption that we saw in Part (a), the compensated demand $\overline{x}_i(p, u)$ (under price and utility levels before the price increase) is equal to the actual consumption x_i from before the price increase.

In Equation (20), you may think that it's weird that the left-hand side appears to involve terms that give amounts of money, but the right-hand side is an amount of consumption. However, it's easy to understand if you rewrite the equation in the following way. Suppose that the price of good i has increased by Δp_i. Equation (21) says that (if this price increase is small) the additional money ΔI needed to maintain the same level of utility from before the price increase approximately satisfies $\Delta I / \Delta p_i = x_i$. Rewriting this equation, we have the following.

If the price increase Δp_i of good i is small, then the following approximately holds:

$$\underset{\substack{\text{the additional money that is needed} \\ \text{to keep the same utility level } u \\ \text{after the price of good } i \text{ has increased}}}{\Delta I} = \underset{\substack{\text{consumption of good } i \\ \text{before the price increase}}}{x_i} \times \underset{\substack{\text{the price increase} \\ \text{for good } i}}{\Delta p_i} \quad (22)$$

In other words, *income effectively decreases when the price of good i increases, and we can think of this "decrease" in income as* $x_i \Delta p_i$.

Example 1.6

Consider a consumer who drinks four cans of beer per month ($x_i = 4$), and suppose that the price of a can of beer is increased by 25¢. Then, in order to keep the same utility as before, the consumer needs almost

$$x_i \Delta p_i = 4 \times 25 \text{ cents} = 1 \text{ dollar}$$

of additional money. This is what Equation (21) is saying. If the consumer is given an additional dollar, she can consume the same amount as she could before the price was increased – i.e. she can still afford to drink four cans of beer. Therefore, if she is given an extra dollar, she can still achieve the same utility level that she had before the price was increased. Moreover, suppose that after the price increase there is a possibility to

decrease her consumption of beer (which is now 25¢ more expensive) and instead consume more of other goods, which would give her a higher level of utility.   (*)

Then, if the consumer were actually given an extra dollar, she might be able to achieve a utility greater than what she could achieve by spending the extra dollar on continuing to consume four cans of beer. Therefore, it's actually possible that she needs less than $1 to achieve the same level of utility that she had before the price of beer increased. However, Equations (21) and (22) show that the additional effect (*) is small, and almost negligible if the size of the price increase Δp_i is small.

(c)   Price Change and Demand Change (the Slutsky Decomposition)

Using our observations above, we now analyze in detail how demand responds to price changes. Let's carefully look at the duality of consumption that we studied in Part (a). Denoting current income, prices, and utility by I, p, and u respectively, we have

$$\overline{x}(p,u) \qquad = \qquad x \qquad = \qquad x(p,I)$$

| the cheapest way to achieve the current utility under the current prices p | the observed consumption bundle | the way to maximize the utility under income I and prices p |

This shows the duality of consumption that we first saw in Equation (19). Let's look at Figure 1.32, which illustrates this property.

In particular, if we view the consumption bundle x in this figure as the solution to the expenditure minimization problem, then we know that *the current income I is the least amount of money needed to achieve current utility u under the current prices p* – that is, $I = I(p,u)$. By substituting this relationship into the equation above, we get

$$\overline{x}(p,u) = x(p, I(p,u)). \tag{23}$$

In particular, if we look at demand for good i, we obtain

$$\overline{x}_i(p,u) = x_i(p, I(p,u)). \tag{24}$$

What does this equation mean? If the price of a good increases, then, if her income I does not change, the consumer cannot keep the same utility level she had previously. In order to keep the same utility, it is necessary to increase her income, which has, effectively, been reduced by the price increase. The expenditure function $I(p,u)$ will tell us how much additional income the consumer needs to maintain her old utility level u. In other words, Equation (24) tells us this.

Compensated demand $\overline{x}_i(p,u)$ represents what the consumer would choose if she were given a higher income to compensate for the price increase.

This is the reason why we call $\overline{x}_i(p,u)$, the cheapest consumption bundle that achieves a fixed utility level, the "*compensated*" demand function.

Using the above relationship, we can easily study the response of compensated demand to a price change. Equation (24) holds for all p, so the derivative of the left-hand side with respect to p_i must be equal to the derivative of the right-hand side with respect to p_i. Let's do the differentiation. If you don't know how to differentiate these functions, I want you to read

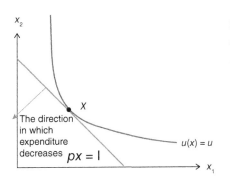

Figure 1.32 Duality of consumption and income

Comment 1.12. Those who already know how to differentiate these functions can skip this comment.

Comment 1.12 The Formula for Differentiation

Let me introduce the formula we can use to differentiate Equation (23). Consider differentiating the function $a(y) = x(y, z(y))$ with respect to y. The following formula holds:

$$\frac{da}{dy} = \underbrace{\frac{\partial x}{\partial y}}_{\text{the direct effect of } y} + \underbrace{\frac{\partial x}{\partial z}\frac{dz}{dy}}_{\text{the indirect effect through } z}.$$

That is, how much $a = x(y, z(y))$ increases when y increases slightly (i.e. da/dy) is the sum of the "direct effect" $(\partial x/\partial y)$ of the change in y through x and the "indirect effect" $\left(\frac{\partial x}{\partial z}\frac{dz}{dy}\right)$ of the change in y through z. This "indirect effect" is the idea that z responds to the change in y, (dz/dy), and x responds to the change in z, $(\partial x/\partial z)$, which occurs because of the change in y.

Now, substituting

- p_i for y
- I for z
- $\overline{x}_i$ for a

we can differentiate Equation (24) following the formula we just learned. You will see that the result is Equation (25), which we state next.

Differentiating Equation (24), we obtain

$$\frac{\partial \overline{x}_i}{\partial p_i} = \frac{\partial x_i}{\partial p_i} + \frac{\partial x_i}{\partial I}\frac{\partial I}{\partial p_i}. \tag{25}$$

Recalling Equation (21), which follows from Shephard's lemma and the duality, we know that $\partial I/\partial p_i = x_i$. Substituting this into Equation (25) and rearranging, we obtain the following equation, which we call the **Slutsky decomposition**:[16]

---

[16] This expresses how a change in the price of good i affects the demand for good i itself, but we can also use the Slutsky decomposition to express how a change in the price of good j affects the demand for good i. Partially differentiating Equation (23) with respect to p_j, we obtain a Slutsky decomposition that expresses how a change in the price of good j affects the demand of good i:

$$\frac{\partial x_i}{\partial p_j} = \frac{\partial x_i}{\partial p_j} - \frac{\partial x_i}{\partial I}x_j$$

$$
\underset{\substack{\text{how demand} \\ \text{for good } i \text{ responds to} \\ \text{the change of its price}}}{\frac{\partial x_i}{\partial p_i}} = \underset{\text{substitution effect}}{\frac{\partial \overline{x}_i}{\partial p_i}} - \underset{\text{income effect}}{\frac{\partial x_i}{\partial I} x_i.} \tag{26}
$$

This shows that the effect of a change in the price of good i on the demand for good *i* can be decomposed into two effects. The first is the effect that, due to the increase in the price of good *i*, the cheapest consumption bundle that gives the same utility as before changes. This is captured by the response of the compensated demand function, $\frac{\partial \overline{x}_i}{\partial p_i}$, which is the first term on the right-hand side of Equation (26). As we saw in Section 1.7, the way that the compensated demand function responds to prices tells us about the complementarity and substitutability of the goods. In particular, recall that, since there is a substitution away from the good whose price has increased and toward other goods, $\frac{\partial \overline{x}_i}{\partial p_i}$ is either negative or zero. (This comes from Equation (15), which says that the self-substitution effect is non-positive.). We call $\frac{\partial \overline{x}_i}{\partial p_i}$ the **substitution effect**. *The substitution effect is always negative or zero.*

The second effect is due to the consumer's feeling that her income has effectively decreased since the price of one of the goods increased. This effect is captured by the second term on the right-hand side of Equation (26), and we call it the **income effect**. It's easy to understand the income effect if you rewrite the Slutsky decomposition in the following way. Suppose that the price of good *i* has increased by Δp_i and that the demand for good *i* has changed by Δx_i in response. The Slutsky decomposition shows that the following equation approximately holds (when Δp_i is small):

$$
\Delta x_i = \frac{\partial \overline{x}_i}{\partial p_i} \Delta p_i - \frac{\partial x_i}{\partial I} (x_i \Delta p_i)
$$

The first term on the right-hand side is the substitution effect that I explained earlier. The second term is the income effect. The $(x_i \Delta p_i)$ part of the income effect represents the effective decrease in income due to the increase in the price of good *i*. Concretely, if we say good *i* is beer, then *a consumer who used to drink four cans of beer ($x_i = 4$) before the price increase of 25¢ per can ($\Delta p_i = 25$ cents) will feel as if her income has decreased by $x_i \Delta p_i = 1$ dollar.* (You may remember that I explained this in detail in Part (b).) Since goods whose consumption decreases when income increases are inferior goods and goods whose consumption increases when income increases are normal goods, *the income effect $\left(-\frac{\partial x_i}{\partial I} x_i\right)$ is negative for inferior goods and positive for normal goods.*[17]

---

[17] For normal goods, $\frac{\partial x_i}{\partial I} > 0$, and, for inferior goods, $\frac{\partial x_i}{\partial I} < 0$.

Figure 1.33 An increase in the price of electricity and the resulting change in consumption

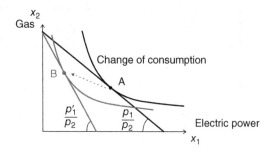

Figure 1.34 Compensation and the substitution effect

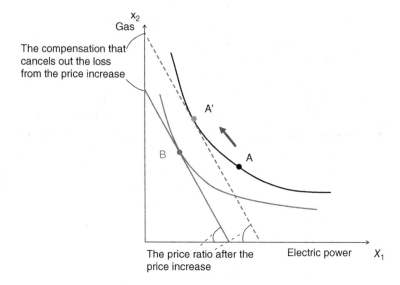

Next, let's express the Slutsky decomposition in a figure.[18] In order to help with the intuition, consider the following scenario. Suppose that a big earthquake in Japan destroys a power plant, and suddenly there's not enough electricity. In order to suppress electricity demand and try to avoid a power outage, Tokyo Electric Power decides to substantially increase the price of electricity. Then, the consumption bundle of their customers changes from point A to point B, as shown in Figure 1.33.

The customers obviously suffer a loss due to the price increase, and they argue: *"The reason the price had to increase was because the power plant wasn't prepared enough for an earthquake! Making the power plant earthquake-safe is the responsibility of the government and Tokyo Electric Power, so we want to be compensated for our losses!"* In this case, how much should the government or Tokyo Electric Power have to pay? The answer is shown in Figure 1.34. If the amount of compensation is such that the budget line becomes the dashed line in the figure, then customers can consume bundle A' and therefore achieve the same utility as before the earthquake.

---

[18] The Slutsky decomposition is an equation that uses differentiation, so what it actually represents is the case where the price change is infinitesimally small. Since we can't draw infinitesimally small price changes in a figure, the figures that follow only roughly express the Slutsky decomposition. There are several different ways to depict the Slutsky decomposition graphically; I've chosen just one of these.

Although consumption bundles A and A' give consumers the same level of utility, since electricity is now more expensive they substitute away from electricity and use more gas. Therefore, at point A' their consumption of electricity has decreased and their consumption of gas has increased. This shows that A', which is the cheapest consumption bundle that achieves their old level of utility, is not the same as their old consumption bundle A. This change from A to A' is called the substitution effect.

In reality, for most goods, when their prices increase, consumers can't receive compensation in the way they do in our story. If the customers in our story hadn't received any compensation, then they would have moved to consumption bundle B, shown in Figure 1.35. Let's compare consumption bundle A' (with compensation) to consumption bundle B (without compensation). The difference between A' and B is due to the difference in their incomes (with or without compensation) and shows the income effect. In effect, the customers' incomes have been reduced by the price increase, and, without additional money to compensate them, they can't consume consumption bundle A', which would have left them just as well off as before the earthquake. Summarizing this discussion, we can depict the Slutsky decomposition as in Figure 1.36.

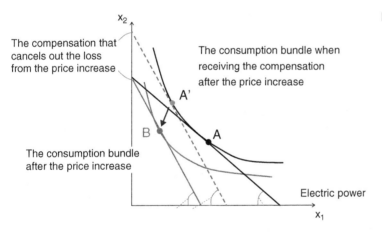

Figure 1.35 The income effect

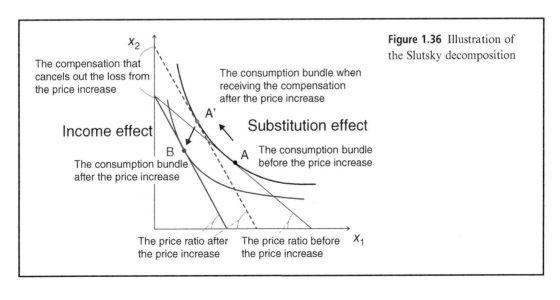

Figure 1.36 Illustration of the Slutsky decomposition

Let's now summarize the Slutsky decomposition in words.

Understanding the Slutsky Decomposition in English

After the price of electricity increases, *if the consumer receives compensation* that allows her to keep the same utility as before, then the following apply.

- Since the price of electricity has increased, there is substitution away from electricity to other goods, such as gas (substitution effect).
- Since the consumer won't actually receive compensation in reality, her true consumption is what she chooses when she does not have the additional income (income effect).

Comment 1.13 Who Wants the Slutsky Decomposition?

When learning microeconomics for the first time, the Slutsky decomposition can be especially puzzling. Someone new to economics might think, *"I have no idea why we should ever be interested in such a decomposition!"* I am happy to tell you that there are in fact three good reasons we need the Slutsky decomposition.

(1) It helps us to better understand how demand responds to prices.
(2) It can be used to test whether real-world demand data come from utility maximization.
(3) It shows how to use observable demand data to estimate the gains and losses a consumer experiences due to a price change.

Points (2) and (3) are rather advanced topics, so in the next section, Section 1.10, I explain only point (1). Point (3) is an important issue when drafting and evaluating various economic policies. This is summarized in Appendix C at the end of the book.

1.10 Price Elasticity

What's the best way to analyze how responsive demand is to price changes? Naively, it might seem that we can just look at the slope of the demand curve. For example, if Figure 1.37 shows the demand for coffee, it seems as if we can say that demand for coffee "reacts moderately" to the price.

However, the slope of the demand curve changes if the unit of measurement of coffee changes! In Figure 1.37 coffee is measured by milliliters (ml). If we depict the demand for coffee in liters, then the horizontal axis shrinks by 1/1,000, and we get the demand curve shown in Figure 1.38. This time, if we look at the slope, it appears that the demand for coffee "almost doesn't respond" to the price. This is problematic. *Is it possible to measure the responsiveness of demand to prices in a way that doesn't depend on the unit of measurement?*

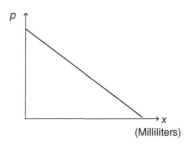

Figure 1.37 Demand curve for coffee

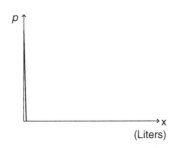

Figure 1.38 Demand curve for coffee with modified unit of measurement

Note that the percentage change (rate of change) does not depend on the unit of measurement. Suppose that we measure the demand for coffee in liters, and consumption increases from the current amount x by Δx. In this case, the *rate of change* in coffee consumption is

$$\frac{\Delta x}{x}.$$

Multiplying this ratio by 100, we get the *percentage change* that we commonly use in daily life. (For example, if $\Delta x/x = 0.5$, then we say there was a 50 percent change.) Now, suppose we measure the demand for coffee in milliliters. Then the rate of change is

$$\frac{1000\Delta x}{1000x} = \frac{\Delta x}{x},$$

which is exactly the same as when we measured coffee in liters. In other words, the *rate of change does not depend on the unit of measurement*.

Now, suppose that demand changes by $((\Delta x/x) \times 100)\%$ when the price increases by $((\Delta p/p) \times 100)\%$. Demand usually decreases when the price increases, so Δx is negative. Converting it to a positive number and considering

$$\frac{\left(\frac{-\Delta x}{x}\right)}{\left(\frac{\Delta p}{p}\right)} = -\frac{\Delta x}{\Delta p}\frac{p}{x},$$

we can see that *this represents the percentage decrease in demand when the price increases by 1 percent*. To see the effects of small price changes, we consider the value of this number as Δp approaches zero. We call this value the **price elasticity of demand**.

$$\text{Price elasticity of demand} = -\frac{dx}{dp}\frac{p}{x}$$

The price elasticity of demand is a way of measuring the responsiveness of demand to prices that is not affected by the units of measurement of demand and prices. It plays a very important role in economic analysis. Here are some estimates of the price elasticity of demand for various goods in Japan.[19]

Gas	Beef	Eating out
0.205	0.944	1.318

How to interpret these numbers? Consider the price elasticity of demand for gas. If the price elasticity of demand for gas is 0.205, it means that, when the price of gas increases by 1 percent, the demand for gas decreases by (approximately) 0.205 percent. This means that demand for gas is not very responsive to changes in the price of gas, and we say that the demand for gas is quite inelastic.

The price elasticity of demand is particularly useful when studying the effect that a price change has on revenue. Since revenue is equal to $px(p)$, we can differentiate this with respect to p to obtain[20]

$$\frac{dpx}{dp} = x + p\frac{dx}{dp} = x\left(1 - \left(\underbrace{-\frac{dx}{dp}\frac{p}{x}}_{\text{elasticity}}\right)\right).$$

If the price elasticity of demand is less than one, then $dpx/dp > 0$, so revenue increases if the price increases. We can express the relationship between the price elasticity of demand and the change in revenue as we've done below.

The Relationship between Elasticity and Revenue

Price elasticity of demand *is less than 1.*

⇒ *Revenue increases* if the price increases.

---

[19] Sources are as follows: gas: Chiharu Murakoshi, Hidetoshi Nakagami, Michiko Takano, Yasuhiro Murota, and Fumio Murazeki, "Analysis of Price Elasticity Values of Household City Gas in Tokyo," *Papers of Seminars in Energy System Economics Conference*, vol, 12 (1996); beef: Masahiko Ariji, Ryohei Yoshida, and Yoshihito Senda, "Estimate of the Economic Effect of Suspended Import of US Beefs due to BSE," Document on Press Release (Tokyo: UFJ Research Institute, 2004); eating out: Atsushi Maki, *Consumption Preferences and Demand Measurement: Approach from Linear Expenditure System including Habit Formation and Endowment Adjustment* (Tokyo: Yuhikaku Publishing, 1983).

[20] We can use the "product rule" to differentiate the product $f \times g$ of two functions f and g. Recall that $d(fg)/dx = (df/dx)g + f(dg/dx)$.

Price elasticity of demand *is 1*.

⇒ *Revenue does not change* even if the price changes.

Price elasticity of demand *is greater than 1*.

⇒ *Revenue decreases* if the price increases.

Now, if you look at the estimates of elasticities from before, we can infer the following. Since gas has an elasticity less than one, demand does not decrease much when the price increases, so revenue increases when the price increases. To try to increase revenue in this situation, it would be most effective to limit the volume of sales and increase the price. Since beef has an elasticity almost equal to one, revenue will remain roughly the same when the price increases. Last, since eating out has an elasticity greater than one, demand for eating out drops significantly when the price increases and revenue falls. In this case, if you try to increase revenue it wouldn't be wise to increase the price, as for the case of gas. Instead, it would be better to cut the price and try to increase the volume of sales.

What kinds of factors determine the price elasticity of demand? In order to understand how the price elasticity of demand is determined, it's useful to use the Slutsky decomposition. Recall that the Slutsky decomposition says

$$\underbrace{\frac{\partial x_i}{\partial p_i}}_{\substack{\text{price sensitivity of the} \\ \text{demand for good } i.}} = \underbrace{\frac{\partial \overline{x}_i}{\partial p_i}}_{\text{substitution effect}} - \underbrace{\frac{\partial x_i}{\partial I} x_i}_{\text{income effect}}.$$

In order to express the left-hand side as an elasticity, we multiply both sides by $(-p_i/x_i)$, which gives us[21]

$$\underbrace{-\frac{\partial x_i}{\partial p_i}\frac{p_i}{x_i}}_{\text{price elasticity}} = \underbrace{-\frac{\partial \overline{x}_i}{\partial p_i}\frac{p_i}{\overline{x}_i}}_{\substack{\text{price elasticity of} \\ \text{compensated demand}}} + \underbrace{\left(\frac{\partial x_i}{\partial I}\frac{I}{x_i}\right)}_{\text{income elasticity}} \underbrace{\left(\frac{p_i x_i}{I}\right)}_{\text{share of expenditure}}.$$

---

[21] When multiplying the first term on the right-hand side by $(-p_i/x_i)$, use the fact that $x_i = \overline{x}_i$ (from duality of consumption) and multiply by $(-p_i/\overline{x}_i)$.

The $\left(\frac{\partial x_i}{\partial I} \frac{I}{x_i}\right)$ in the second term of the right-hand side is called the income elasticity of demand for good i. It measures the percent increase in demand for good i when income increases by 1 percent. The share of expenditure $\left(\frac{p_i x_i}{I}\right)$ that appears next to it is the ratio of expenditure on good i, $p_i x_i$, to income, I.

From this, we know that the price elasticity of demand is high in the following cases.

- There is a close substitute for the good (so the price elasticity of compensated demand is high).
- The income elasticity of demand is high.[22]
- The money spent on the good is a large share of total spending (i.e. the good is a "big ticket" item).

Here's why these factors determine the price elasticity of demand. If there's a close substitute for a good, then, if the price of that good increases, the demand for it will decrease as people begin to consume more of the substitute. For example, if the price of Coors increases, then people will start drinking more Budweiser. Moreover, since a price increase effectively reduces consumers' incomes, if the demand for a good is very sensitive to changes in income, the demand for that good will also be sensitive to changes in prices. Last, without the Slutsky decomposition, you might not see why the price elasticity of demand is high for goods that form a large fraction of total spending. Note that, if the money a consumer spends on a good is a large fraction of that consumer's total spending, even a 1 percent increase in the price of that good means that the consumer will need to spend quite a bit more money to be able to afford a new bundle that can give her the same utility. In other words, when the price of such a good increases, even by only 1 percent, the consumer's income effectively decreases substantially. Therefore, for goods that form a large fraction of total spending, the decrease in demand is large, due to the income effect.

By checking these three factors for the examples of gas, beef, and eating out, it seems reasonable that the price elasticity of demand increases from gas to beef to eating out, as the data suggest.

Table 1.1 Factors that raise price elasticity

		There is a close substitute	Income elasticity is high (luxury good)	"Big ticket item"
Gas	0.205			✓
Beef	0.944	✓✓	✓✓	
Eating out	1.318	✓✓	✓✓	✓✓

---

[22] Goods for which income elasticity of demand is greater than one are sometimes called **luxury goods**.

Problem Session 1 Deriving Demand from Utility Maximization

Problem

Suppose that there are two goods. Consumption of the first good is given by x, and consumption of the second good is given by y. Let the prices of the goods be p_x and p_y respectively, and let the consumer's income be I. Solve for the consumer's demand for each good when she has the following utility function:

$$u(x, y) = x^a y^b$$

(a and b are positive constants).

Student: *Wait, professor! There's nobody who actually has a utility function like this! I don't want to solve this stupid problem!*

Professor: *You might feel that way, but hear me out. As I explained earlier in the book, the purpose of microeconomic models is to capture the essence of peoples' economic behavior. Obviously, nobody consciously maximizes a utility function, but this model* does *capture a certain aspect of our real-life consumption behavior.*

Student: *Is that really true, or are you just saying that?*

Professor: *Let's solve the problem. It's sufficient to solve for the optimal consumption amounts x and y that maximize the utility function $u(x, y) = x^a y^b$ under the budget constraint $p_x x + p_y y = I$. In order to solve for the optimal consumption bundle, recall the "optimality condition for consumption."*

Student: *You mean when the indifference curve and the budget line are tangent to each other?*

Professor: *That's the one! But we should first rephrase it so that we can do some calculations.*

Marginal rate of substitution $=$ **Price ratio**

the slope of (the tangent line to) the indifference curve   the slope of the budget line

Since the marginal rate of substitution is the ratio of marginal utilities (remember Section 1.5 (c)), we can rewrite the relationship above as the following equation:

$$\frac{\frac{\partial u}{\partial x}}{\frac{\partial u}{\partial y}} = \frac{p_x}{p_y}. \tag{27}$$

We need to calculate the partial derivative $\frac{\partial u}{\partial x}$ which is the derivative of $u(x, y) = x^a y^b$ with respect to x (regarding y^b as a constant). Can you do this calculation?

Student: *Ummm, I kind of remember that the derivative of x^a is ax^{a-1}. So, treating y^b as a constant we get $\frac{\partial u}{\partial x} = ax^{a-1} y^b$?*

Professor: *That's right! In exactly the same manner, we can see that $\frac{\partial u}{\partial y} = bx^a y^{b-1}$. Therefore, the left-hand side of optimality condition (27) becomes*

(cont.)

$$\frac{\frac{\partial u}{\partial x}}{\frac{\partial u}{\partial y}} = \frac{ax^{a-1}y^b}{bx^a y^{b-1}} = \frac{ay}{bx},$$

which is very simple. In this case, optimality condition (26) is just

$$\frac{ay}{bx} = \frac{p_x}{p_y}. \tag{28}$$

Student: *But how can I solve for the optimal x and y from this?*

Professor: *We have one more equation to use: the budget constraint $p_x x + p_y y = I$. With the budget constraint and Equation (27), we have two equations in two unknowns, so we can solve for x and y! We could just compute x and y using brute force, but note that we can rearrange Equation (27) to get*

$$\frac{a}{b} = \frac{p_x x}{p_y y}. \tag{29}$$

This says that the ratio of expenditure on good x, $p_x x$, to expenditure on good y, $p_y y$, is exactly $\frac{a}{b}$ *Therefore, if the consumer divides her income into pieces $\frac{a}{a+b}I$ and $\frac{b}{a+b}I$ using the ratio $\frac{a}{b}$, and allocates $\frac{a}{a+b}I$ to spend on good X and $\frac{b}{a+b}I$ to spend on good Y, then both optimality condition (28) and the budget constraint are satisfied. That is, the optimal consumption bundle (x, y) satisfies*

$$\frac{a}{a+b}I = p_x x, \quad \frac{b}{a+b}I = p_y y.$$

Then we can solve these equations for x and y to obtain the optimal consumption levels x and y as follows.

Answer:

$$x = \left(\frac{a}{a+b}\right)\frac{I}{p_x}$$

$$y = \left(\frac{a}{a+b}\right)\frac{I}{p_y}$$

Student: *But, going back to my initial question, what part of this model actually replicates real consumption behavior?*

Professor: *You probably already know how it replicates real consumption behavior, since you pay to rent an apartment. You've probably heard the rule of thumb that you should allocate 30 percent of your monthly income to your rent payments. Many people behave in such a way and allocate a certain fraction of their income to their rent payments. The consumption behavior of such people can be* approximated using our model, if we say that good X is their apartment and good Y is all other consumption. These people will approximately behave as if they are maximizing a utility function such as $u(x,y) = x^a y^b$, where the ratio of a to b is 3/7.

Student: I still feel like this is some trick... You're telling me that people don't literally solve the mathematical models in microeconomics, but their behavior can be roughly approximated by the models – right?

Professor: Right. Now, for those who like math, let's solve the same problem using the "method of Lagrange multipliers."

Student: Isn't that the method for solving constrained optimization problems? If I remember correctly, first we construct a new function by adding the function we want to maximize (in our case, the utility function) and the constraint (in our case, the budget constraint) multiplied by a constant, λ. The new function will look like

$$L = x^a y^b + \lambda \left(I - p_x x - p_y y \right).$$

Professor: Correct. Then we differentiate this new equation with respect to x and y and set the derivatives equal to zero, which gives us

$$\frac{\partial L}{\partial x} = a x^{a-1} y^b - \lambda p_x = 0,$$
$$\frac{\partial L}{\partial y} = b x^{a-1} y^{b-1} - \lambda p_y = 0.$$

Rearranging these two equations, we get

$$a x^{a-1} y^b = \lambda p_x,$$
$$b x^a y^{b-1} = \lambda p_y.$$

Last, dividing both sides we have

$$\frac{ay}{bx} = \frac{p_x}{p_y},$$

which is the same as Equation (27). The rest of the calculation is the same as before.

2 Theory of Firm Behavior

2.1 What Is a "Firm" in Economics?

In the United States, some firms are just small-scale enterprises with a few employees, and some are huge companies with several thousand employees. Firms might have various departments, such as accounting or sales. Manufacturing firms have many factories. In order to understand the central role these firms play in markets, *traditional microeconomics (price theory) makes a dramatic simplification and treats firms like "black boxes" that output goods using production inputs* (see Figure 2.1). Details about what exactly is happening inside firms are ignored.

Various economic activities (resource allocation) happen within firms, but note that these activities do not use the price mechanism. For instance, when Apple uses parts made in factory A to produce iPhones in factory B, factory A does not directly sell the parts to factory B at the market price. Rather, agreements negotiated by the bosses determine how many parts must be delivered at what time. In this way, economic activities within firms take place under institutional policies, rules, and conventions, which are all inherently different forces from the price mechanism. Analysis of these forces and how they shape economic activities within firms is traditionally done by researchers in management science. However, in recent years economists have used game theory and information economics to make progress in this area. The basic tools for analyzing economic activities within institutions, game theory, and information economics are considered in Part II.

The fact that some economic activities take place within firms raises an interesting question regarding the functioning of market economies. In highly developed market economies – where everything from cars to food to music is traded at a market price – it may seem as if all resource allocations are determined by the market alone. However, this is not the case. A significant portion of resource allocation is done inside organizations (i.e. firms) in ways other than the market mechanism. The economist Ronald Coase, who first observed this fact, posed the following question in his famous 1937 paper, "The Nature of the Firm":[1]

---

[1] Ronald Coase, "The Nature of the Firm," *Economica*, n.s. 4 (1937), 386–405.

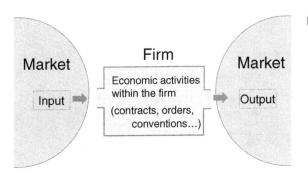

Figure 2.1 What are firms?

Why are some parts of resource allocation done in the market, while others are done within firms through non-market activities?

To rephrase, this asks, "Where can we draw the boundary between firms and the market, and where can we draw the boundary between one firm and another?" This is a very important question, which concerns subjects fundamental to the study of economics. Coase gave the following tentative answer to his question. Resource allocation takes place in the market when transaction costs are lower in the market, and resource allocation takes place within firms when transaction costs are lower within firms. This explanation based on **transaction costs** gives us a valuable insight into how resource allocation is actually implemented, but, unless we clarify exactly what we mean by a "transaction cost," it's not a totally satisfactory answer. Although the development of game theory and information economics has made it possible to partially study the optimal design of resource allocation mechanisms, defining the true meaning and importance of "transaction costs" and explaining what part of resource allocation is done within a single firm are major unsolved problems in economics. If you feel as if you're the one to solve these problems, go ahead! If you are successful, you'll surely get a Nobel Prize.

2.2 Firm Behavior in the One-Input (Labor) Case

In general, many inputs are needed to produce a good. As preparation for analyzing the general case in which there are many inputs to production, we'll first consider the case in which there is a single input, labor. Then we'll gradually work toward the more general case. In order to get a sense of how we can use mathematical models to analyze firm behavior, let's examine the following simple (but realistic) example.

Case Study 2.1 Assembly Factory

Consider the owner/manager of a small firm with an assembly factory that contracts with another company. The parts are provided by the company, which pays 25¢ for every product assembled.

Case Study 2.1 (cont.)

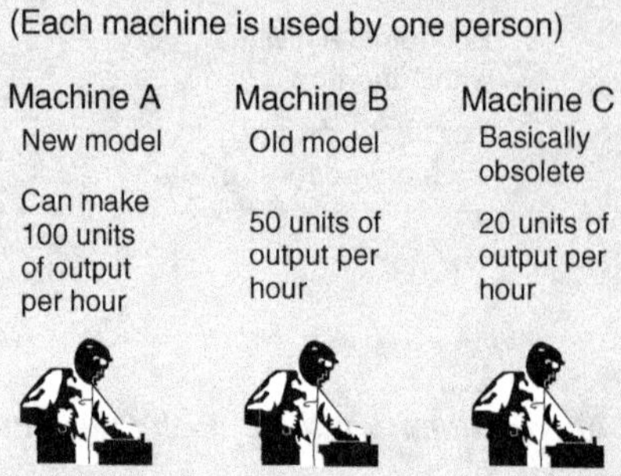

Figure 2.2 Assembly factory

(Each machine is used by one person)

Machine A	Machine B	Machine C
New model	Old model	Basically obsolete
Can make 100 units of output per hour	50 units of output per hour	20 units of output per hour

The factory simply provides the labor to assemble the products. In the factory, there are three machines, which differ in how many products they can make in one hour (see Figure 2.2).

Each machine is operated by one worker, and each worker's hourly wage is $20. By law, workers can't work more than eight hours each day. In this case, how many workers should be hired and how many hours should the factory president make them work?

First, let's consider using machine A, which is the most efficient. If this is used for one hour, then 100 products are assembled, and the factory receives $25 from the company. Since each worker is paid $20 for her hour of work, this machine makes $5 of profit every hour. Therefore, it's best to use machine A for the maximum eight hours each day.

If machine B, which is the second most efficient, is used for one hour, then 50 products are assembled and the factory receives $12.50 from the company. However, this is less than the hourly wage of $20 that must be paid to the worker who operates the machine. Therefore, operating machine B actually causes the factory to lose money. Similarly, operating machine C, which is the least efficient, also causes the factory to lose money.

In this case, hiring one worker to work eight hours per day and use machine A to assemble products is the optimal choice for the factory. With this case study in mind, let's study the theory of production.

(a)   Production Function

Let's consider a firm that produces output y using only labor L. For this firm, there must be a limit to what it's possible to produce using current technology. Let's examine all possible combinations of input L and output y that this firm can feasibly achieve and depict them in a figure. The exact shape of this set of combinations depends on the specific example, but let's consider the case in which it takes the clean shape shown in grey in Figure 2.3. The set of all combinations of input and output that the firm can achieve, which is the grey area in the figure, is called the **production possibility set**.

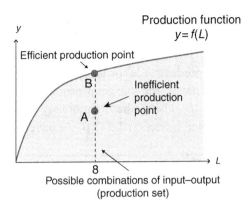

Figure 2.3 Production function

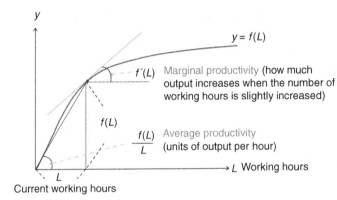

Figure 2.4 Productivity of labor

In this figure, point A, for example, is a point at which the worker is inefficient during her eight-hour workday. Maybe she checks her phone a lot and does online shopping. If she was more focused during her shift, she could produce more output, even while working eight hours. By contrast, point B is a point at which the worker is totally focused and diligent during her shift. As long as she works for only eight hours, there's no way she could possibly produce more output. In this sense, the boundary of this set represents the points at which the inputs are being used in a totally efficient manner. The function representing this boundary, $y = f(L)$, is called the **production function**. The production function $f(L)$ gives the maximum amount of output that can be produced using the amount L of labor input, and it represents the technology that's available to the firm. As I said in Section 2.1, for the sake of simplicity, traditional microeconomics (price theory) regards the firm as a black box that transforms inputs into outputs. *In other words, we represent a firm as a production function.*

Using the production function, we can measure the productivity of labor in the following way. People who work in business usually use the **average productivity of labor**, $f(L)/L$, as their measure of labor productivity. That is, they divide the total amount of output by the amount of labor needed to produce that output, which gives the amount of output that can be produced by one unit of labor (in one working hour). The angle in the bottom-left section of Figure 2.4 represents the average productivity of labor.

However, in microeconomics, it's more helpful to use a slightly different measure of labor productivity. We use a measure called the **marginal productivity of labor**, which captures how much output increases when the amount of labor is *slightly increased* (perhaps by one additional unit). Mathematically, the marginal product of labor is represented by the slope of the (tangent line to) the production function. That is, the marginal product of labor is given by $f'(L)$, the derivative of f with respect to L. Using the terminology that we learned in "Introduction to Marginal Analysis" (Chapter 1, Section 1.5 (b)), we have:

Marginal productivity of labor $= f'(L) =$ the increase in output when labor is marginally increased.

To "marginally increase labor" means that, by taking the unit of measurement of labor to be sufficiently small, we increase labor by one unit – that is, we increase labor ever so slightly. (Look back at Chapter 1, Section 1.5 (b).)

Often it's the case that the marginal productivity of labor is large when the amount of labor being used is small, but, as the amount of labor being used increases more and more, efficiency declines and the marginal productivity of labor decreases. In other words, marginal productivity decreases as the quantities of inputs increase. We call this the **law of diminishing marginal productivity** (see Figure 2.5).

There are two ways we could interpret a production function such as $y = f(L)$:

(1) labor truly is the only input necessary for production;
(2) there are other inputs to production (such as machines) besides labor, but the quantities of these other inputs are fixed in the short run.

In microeconomics the following is true.

The Short Run and Long Run in Microeconomics

The period in which the amounts of all inputs can be changed is called the **long run**, and the period in which the amounts of some inputs are fixed is called the **short run**.

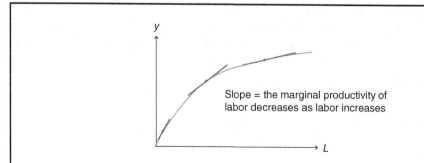

Figure 2.5 Law of diminishing marginal productivity

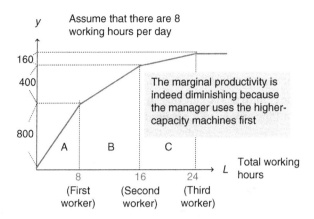

Figure 2.6 The production function of the assembly factory

Therefore, one interpretation of the production function $y = f(L)$ is that it is the firm's **short-run production function**, and that the amounts of other inputs (such as machines) cannot be changed.

A production function like the one in Figure 2.3 appears frequently in microeconomics textbooks, but is this a realistic model? To explore this question, let's return to our assembly factory, which was very simple but not so far-fetched (Case Study 2.1), and consider a period of only one day. First, note that, *since the number of machines in the factory is fixed in a single day, we are dealing with the factory's short-run production function.* We can depict this short-run production function graphically, as in Figure 2.6, where the horizontal axis shows input of labor hours, and the vertical axis shows output.

Why does the factory's short-run production function look this way?

- The first worker hired by the factory should use machine A, since it is the most efficient machine. The worker is limited to working eight hours in a single day, so, for the first eight hours of labor input ($L \leq 8$), the assembly factory can produce 100 units of output per hour.
- If the factory hires a second worker for that day, it's best to have him work on machine B, which is the second most efficient. (He can't use machine A because the first worker is already using it.). Using machine B, the worker can produce 50 units of output per hour. Therefore, for the next eight hours of labor input ($8 < L \leq 16$), the assembly factory can produce 50 units of output per hour, which is half the rate for the first eight hours of labor input.
- If the factory hires a third worker for that day ($16 < L \leq 24$), that worker has to use machine C, which is the least efficient, since machines A and B are being used by the first two workers the factory hired.
- If the factory hires even more workers, there are no machines for the workers to use, so productivity does not increase at all. Therefore, the production function after the first three workers work full shifts ($L > 24$) is flat.

Therefore, the manager of the factory will use the highest-efficiency machines first, in the order $A \rightarrow B \rightarrow C$, so marginal productivity will indeed diminish in the example of the assembly factory.

(b)   Profit Maximization

Next, let's consider how production can be chosen to maximize profits. First, we consider the case in which each producer is small relative to the size of the entire market. In this case, even if a producer changes its amount of labor input and its amount of output, the price of the output, p, and the wage given to labor, w, do not change. We call this situation **perfect competition**. The phrase "perfect competition" is used differently in various contexts, but in microeconomics it has a single, clear meaning.

The Definition of Perfect Competition

Perfect competition is the situation in which, if a single producer changes its production or a single consumer changes her consumption, the price determined by the market does not change, since there are many producers and consumers.

The assumption that each producer and consumer behaves as if the market price is fixed (i.e. their choices will not affect the market price) is sometimes called the **price-taking assumption**. Under this assumption, we say that producers and consumers are price-takers. Therefore, we can restate the definition of perfect competition as the situation in which all producers and consumers are price-takers.[2] It follows that, under perfect competition, the profit maximization problem of the firm is

$$\max_{L} pf(L) - wL.$$

Note that profit is maximized taking price p and wage w to be constants (i.e. under the price-taking assumption).

How can we find the profit-maximizing amounts of labor and output? To lay the groundwork for answering this question, let's first graphically depict the combinations of input L and output y that give a fixed amount of profit π. We can express these combinations as pairs (L,y) satisfying

$$\pi = py - wL.$$

This equation defines a straight line, which we call the iso-profit line. Rewriting this equation as

$$y = \underbrace{\boxed{\frac{w}{p}}}_{\text{slope}} L + \underbrace{\boxed{\frac{\pi}{p}}}_{\text{intercept}},$$

---

[2] Later, we'll consider the theory of monopolies and oligopolies, which covers the case in which firms are large and have market power – that is, firms' behavior can alter market prices.

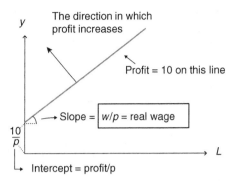

Figure 2.7 Iso-profit line

it's clear that the graph of the iso-profit line is a line with intercept and slope as shown in Figure 2.7. Note also that profit increases as we shift the iso-profit line upward and leftward (i.e. as output increases and/or labor decreases).

The fact that the slope of the iso-profit line is w/p will be important in the analysis that follows, so make sure you commit this to memory. In microeconomics, w/p is called the real wage.

Example 2.1

Consider a part-time job at McDonald's. If the price of the output (a hamburger) is \$5 and the hourly wage is \$15, then the real wage is $w/p = 15/5 = 3$. That is, *the real wage is the wage measured in units of output*. In this example, the fact that the real wage is 3 means the hourly wage is worth three hamburgers.

Since the iso-profit line corresponds to a higher profit as it moves upward and leftward, the point in the graph at which the firm's profit is highest is the point at which the iso-profit line is tangent to the production function, as in Figure 2.8. This point is the profit-maximizing point.

Since the slope of the production function is the marginal productivity of labor and the slope of the iso-profit line is the real wage w/p, at the profit-maximizing point (where the lines have the same slope) the marginal productivity of labor and the real wage are equal. This gives us the following condition for profit maximization:

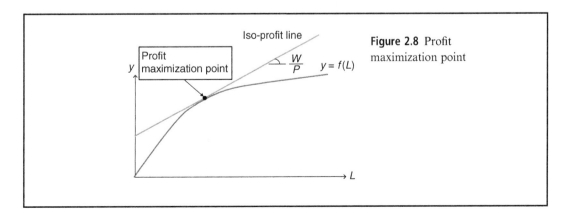

Figure 2.8 Profit maximization point

$$f'(L) \qquad = \qquad \frac{w}{p}$$

Marginal productivity of labor　　　real wage

Profit maximization condition (1)

Now, let's use a figure to analyze where the profit-maximizing point is in our (realistic) assembly factory example (see Figure 2.9). In order to describe an example with a figure, it's sufficient to incorporate the following.

- The real wage, which is the slope of the iso-profit line, is $w/p = 20/0.25 = 80$.
- The slope of the production function is
  - initially 100 (which is the productivity of machine A),
  - then 50 (which is the productivity of machine B),
  - then 20 (which is the productivity of machine C).

Therefore, the graph of the production function and the iso-profit line are tangent to each other at point x in Figure 2.9. *Note that this is indeed the optimal production plan that we solved for in Case Study 2.1: a single worker operates machine A for eight hours.*

Even though the example of production technology in Case Study 2.1 is quite realistic and intuitive, don't you think it still feels a bit messy and clunky? (It's odd for me to say this, since I came up with the example, but even I can't help thinking so). By contrast, studying the theory of producer behavior with smooth production functions (such as the profit maximization condition (1), shown graphically in Figure 2.8) feels much cleaner and more elegant, but feels somewhat unrealistic. What's the relationship between these two types of production functions?

In the assembly factory example, the production function has a kink at the profit maximization point, so it can't be differentiated. This means that the profit maximization condition (1), which uses a derivative of the production function, does not apply. However, if we slightly

Figure 2.9 Profit maximization point of the assembly factory

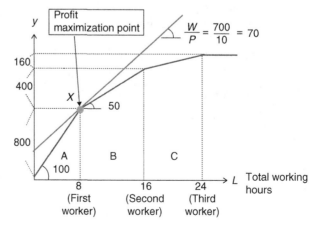

modify Figure 2.9, which shows the production function of the assembly factory, and make the kinked parts of the production function more rounded, then the profit maximization condition ($f'(L) = w/p$) will indeed hold. In other words, *we can use smooth production functions to approximate production functions with kinks*, such as the realistic production function (Figure 2.9) of the assembly factory in Case Study 2.1. In order to analyze more complicated cases, it's necessary to approximate complicated production functions with more tractable production functions. Microeconomic models of production will help us with this challenge.

Comment 2.1 The Microeconomic Model and Decision-Making in Real Life

To most practitioners, the theory of production used in microeconomics would seem bizarre. Managers of firms might think that the profit maximization condition (1), which uses a derivative, bears no resemblance to reality. For instance, our manager of the assembly factory in Case Study 2.1 would immediately know, from her years of experience, which machine she should use given the hourly wage and the price of the output. She doesn't look at the graph of her factory's production function or take a derivative. Nonetheless, the manager of the assembly factory is actually choosing the point at which the graphs of the production function and iso-profit line are exactly touching. In production theory, we approximate this slightly unwieldy production function with a more tractable (i.e. differentiable) model. To be clear, the microeconomic model of production does not literally describe the mental procedure that the manager uses to determine levels of production. It is a convenient (and, in this example, quite accurate) way of describing her behavior.

Maybe a metaphor will help you to understand. Monkeys can learn to walk on two legs. However, if we were to write a program for a robot to walk on two legs, it would be a very complicated control problem, as bipedal walking requires delicate balance and coordination. Figure 2.10 describes a formula for a robot to walk on two legs. Monkeys appear to be following this formula (or something similar to the formula).[3]

Clearly, monkeys do not actually walk by solving these equations; they use their accumulated intuition and experience. Rather, this formula is just a tool that researchers use to mathematically describe monkeys' behavior. Analogously, the production model in microeconomics, which uses mathematics such as differentiation, is just a tool that economists use to describe the behavior of the boss of the assembly factory. In reality, the boss runs the machines using the intuition and experience she has gathered over time, not using a mathematical model from microeconomics. The point is, she still behaves *as if* she were solving such a model. If you think about this abstractly, you may feel that you're being fooled, but let's return to the example of the assembly factory that we discussed in Case Study 2.1. If the boss correctly chooses how much to produce given that the hourly wage is

---

[3] There's no universally agreed-upon approach to modeling bipedal walking. Each approach will accurately capture some aspects of bipedal walking, but will fall short in other ways.

Figure 2.10 Models and reality
Source: Tomomichi Sugihara (2010) "Consistent Biped Step Control with COM-ZMP Oscillation Based on Successive Phase Estimation in Dynamics Morphing," *2010 IEEE International Conference on Robotics and Automation*, Anchorage, AK, USA, pp. 4224–4229, https://doi.org/10.1109/ROBOT.2010.5509270.

Picture: Provided by Eishi Hirasaki, Primate Research Institute, Kyoto University.

$$b_2 = S^T q$$

$$\ddot{b}_2 = S^T \ddot{q}$$
$$= S^T M(q)^{-1}(Su - h(q, \dot{q}))$$
$$= S^T M(q)^{-1}Su - S^T M(q)^{-1}h(q, \dot{q})$$

$$u = (S^T M^{-1} S)^{-1} (\varepsilon + S^T M^{-1} h)$$
$$\bar{\varepsilon} = \ddot{b}_{2d} + k_d(\dot{b}_{2d} - \dot{b}_2) + k_P(b_{2d} - b_2)$$

Program for two-leg walking

$20 and the price of a unit of output is 25¢, she unconsciously behaves as if she is computing the point at which the production function and iso-profit line are tangent to each other, as in Figure 2.9. I hope you can see that, at least in this example, a human being who does not solve the theoretical model actually behaves as if she were solving it.

What's important to understand is that models that do not look "realistic" sometimes describe economic behavior well. Of course, unrealistic models often (or most of the time) do not describe economic behavior at all. I want you to be able to critically evaluate whether the various microeconomic models you are going to see actually describe real-life economic behavior or not, but please do not immediately assume that, just because a model seems "unrealistic," it is useless.

Let's rewrite profit maximization condition (1). Note that, by multiplying both sides by p, we obtain the following condition.

$$pf'(L) = w$$

The value of the marginal product of labor   wage

Profit maximization condition $(1)'$

Writing the profit-maximizing condition in this way makes it easier to understand. The left-hand side of the equation represents how much revenue increases if labor is increased marginally, and it is called the **value of the marginal product of labor**. The right-hand side is the cost of marginally increasing labor by one unit. If the left-hand side is larger than the right-hand side, then, by slightly increasing labor L, the additional revenue exceeds the cost of the additional labor, so total profit increases. By contrast, if the right-hand side is larger than the left-hand side, then, by slightly decreasing labor L, total profit increases. At the optimal point, profit cannot be increased by slightly adjusting labor L, so the equality $pf'(L) = w$ (profit maximization condition $(1)'$) must hold.

(c)   The Cost Function and the Supply Curve

Now we introduce the notion of a firm's cost of production. Not only are costs of production important in practice for real-world firms but costs of production play an important role in microeconomic theory. By examining costs of production, we can gain a better understanding of how the supply curve is determined.

Let $C(y)$ denote the total cost of producing quantity y of output. We call the function C the **(total) cost function**. Total cost is comprised of two parts: the **variable cost**, which is the cost for variable inputs; and the **fixed cost**, which is the cost of fixed inputs. (Variable inputs are those inputs whose quantity the firm can choose, and fixed inputs are those inputs whose quantity is fixed.) What is considered a variable cost and a fixed cost may depend on the period of time that we are considering. For example, in the short run, the size of a factory might be fixed. Therefore, the cost of the factory itself is a fixed cost, and the cost of the labor is a variable cost, since the factory boss can choose how much labor to hire. By contrast, in the long run, the amounts of all inputs (including the size of the factory) can be freely chosen, so all costs are variable costs.

We can further decompose fixed costs. Consider a scenario in the short run, in which the size of the factory is fixed and the fixed cost is the cost of construction, F dollars. Since the factory is already built, the firm has to pay the cost of construction, whether it wants to or not. Suppose that, if the firm gives up on producing output and sells the factory, it can recover part or all of F. If the firm is unable to recover any of its fixed cost F, we say that the cost of the factory F is a sunk cost.

What Is Sunk Cost?

We say a cost is a **sunk cost** if it is unrecoverable, like a sunk ship. Even if the firm gives up on production, it firm cannot get back any of its sunk costs.

In contrast, if the firm is able to recover A dollars by selling the factory, then the sunk fixed cost is $F - A$ and the non-sunk fixed cost is A.

Using what we defined above, let's *consider the relationship between supply and the costs of production*. First, I'll explain the "benchmark case," in which the basic relationship between the two is easy to understand. Then I'll walk you through a more complicated case.

① Benchmark Case

In this book, the "benchmark case" is the case in which the graph of the production function has the shape shown in Figure 2.11 (a). In this case, the area beneath the production function, which is the production possibility set, is convex. Moreover, all fixed costs are sunk costs.

If we flip the vertical and horizontal axes, as seen in Figure 2.11 (b), the curve shows the amount of labor $L(y)$ that is needed to produce output y. If we multiply the entire curve by the wage w, the curve shows the cost of labor that is needed to produce output y. When construction costs (assumed to be sunk costs) are F, the graph of the total cost function can be obtained by "adding" the fixed sunk cost F, as in Figure 2.12.

Figure 2.11 Production technology in the benchmark case

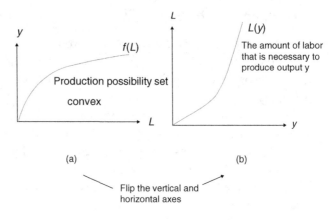

Figure 2.12 Total cost in the benchmark case

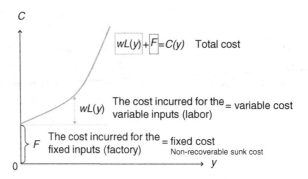

Now let's define the notions of average cost and marginal cost, which are important tools for economic analysis.

> The cost per unit of output, $C(y)/y$, is called the **average cost**. We will frequently write AC for short.
>
> *The cost of marginally increasing output is called the **marginal cost**.* We will frequently write MC for short. Note that MC $= C'(y)$. ($C'(y)$ denotes the derivative of the cost function with respect to y.)

What is the relationship between average cost and marginal cost? Using the graph of total cost, we can depict average cost and marginal cost, as shown in Figure 2.13.

Note that the slope of the tangent line of the total cost curve is $C'(y) = $ MC. When the level of output y is quite small, you can see from the figure that AC is larger than MC. What happens to this relationship when output y varies?

First, consider only the change in MC. As you can see in Figure 2.13, the total cost function is bowed toward the bottom right, so the slope of the total cost curve gets larger as the level of output increases. This means that *marginal cost, MC, increases as output increases.* This property of marginal cost comes from the assumption that the marginal productivity of labor

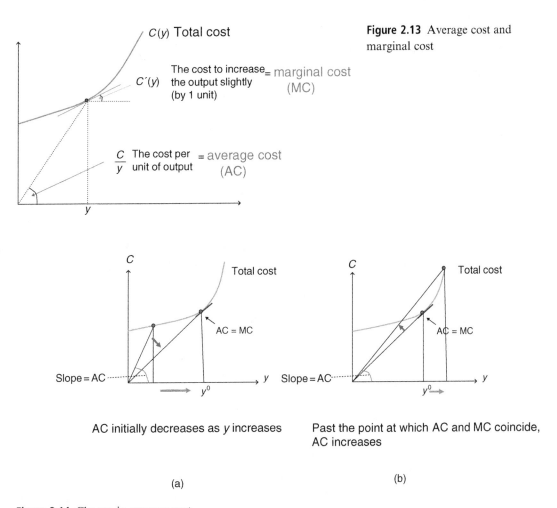

Figure 2.13 Average cost and marginal cost

Figure 2.14 Change in average cost

is diminishing, which says that, as labor input increases (and output increases), the additional productivity of labor decreases. In other words, as output increases unit by unit, the cost of the labor needed to produce that additional unit (i.e. marginal cost in this example) keeps rising.

Next, consider the change in AC and take a look at Figure 2.14 (a). As output increases from zero, we see that

(i) first, AC decreases;
(ii) at a certain level of output, y^0, *AC and MC are exactly equal.*

After output increases beyond y^0, Figure 2.14 (b) shows that

(iii) AC begins to increase.

From points (i) to (iii), we know that *the AC curve has a U shape, and its minimum intersects the MC curve.* To summarize, in the benchmark case, the average cost and marginal cost curves will look like those shown in Figure 2.15.

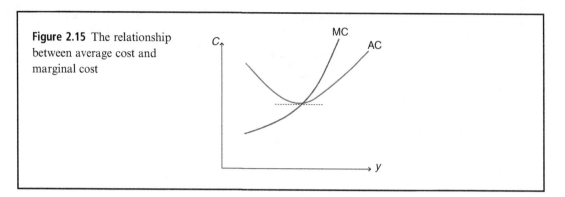

Figure 2.15 The relationship between average cost and marginal cost

Note: the shapes of the AC and MC curves depend on the shape of the production function and the presence or absence of fixed cost. Figure 2.15 shows what AC and MC curves typically look like, but they need not always look this way. Instead of just memorizing Figure 2.15, try to understand how we used the graph of the total cost curve to derive the graphs of the AC and MC curves.

Next, let's consider the shape of the supply curve. The supply curve captures the fact that firms supply more of a good when the price of the good rises. Not only does this make sense intuitively, we actually observe firms behaving like this in real markets. The objective of this part of the chapter is to understand exactly what factors determine the shape of the supply curve. First, let's represent the profit maximization problem using the cost function. Since profit is equal to revenue minus costs, we can write the profit the firm earns from producing output y as $py - C(y)$. Therefore, we can write the profit maximization problem as

$$\max_{y} py - C(y).$$

The solution y^* (the output that maximizes the firm's profit) will depend on the price of the output p. We can write this relationship between y^* and p as $y^* = S(p)$. We call $S(p)$ the **supply function**, and its graph is called the supply curve.

Now, how is the optimal level of output $y^* = S(p)$ determined? Take a look at Figure 2.16, which depicts the firm's marginal cost curve. At a level of output such as y', marginal cost is less than the price. This means that, if the firm were to marginally increase output by one unit, it would increase revenue by p and increase costs by $MC(y')$. Since $p > MC(y')$, the firm's profit would increase. By contrast, at a level of output such as y'', marginal cost is greater than the price. This means that, if the firm were to marginally decrease output by one unit, it would decrease revenue by p but decrease costs by $MC(y'')$. Since $p < MC(y'')$, the firm's profits would increase. Therefore, in the benchmark case, *the optimal level of output y^* is the amount such that price is exactly equal to marginal cost*. That is, $p = MC(y^*)$.[4]

---

[4] This can also be derived with some simple mathematics. Let $\pi(y) = py - C(y)$ be the firm's profit from producing output y. At the profit maximization point, the slope of the profit function, $\pi'(y)$, must be equal to zero. Taking the derivative of $\pi(y)$ with respect to y, and setting it equal to zero, we have $p - C'(y^*) = 0$. Since $C'(y^*) = MC(y^*)$, this implies that $p = MC(y^*)$.

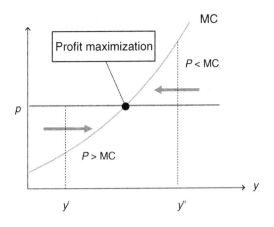

Figure 2.16 Quantity supplied (optimal output) in the benchmark case

Knowing this, if you look at Figure 2.16 again, you will see the following remarkable fact.

In the benchmark case, *the supply curve is equal to the marginal cost curve.*

So, the supply curve you saw in your high school textbooks was actually the marginal cost curve! This is one of the most important takeaways in this chapter. Now let's examine the relationship between a firm's supply curve and profit. After paying the fixed cost, in order to produce the first unit of output the firm must pay the variable cost (wages, materials, etc.). By definition, this is (approximately) equal to MC(1). Similarly, to produce the second unit of output, the firm must continue to pay the variable cost, which is approximately equal to MC(2). This is shown in Figure 2.17 (a). Therefore, the total variable cost of producing output y' can be represented by the area below the marginal cost curve, as shown in Figure 2.17 (b).[5]

Since the marginal cost curve equals the supply curve, in Figure 2.17 (b) at price p the firm supplies y', so its revenue is $p \times y'$, which is equal to the area of the shaded rectangle. Subtracting the variable cost, which is given by the lighter gray region in Figure 2.17 (b), we are left with the darker gray region to the left of the supply curve (which, as we've seen, is equal to the marginal cost curve). Recall that, in the benchmark case, there is a sunk fixed cost F. If F is equal to zero, then the area of the darker gray region gives the firm's profit. By contrast, if F is not equal to zero, then the firm's profit is just the area of the darker gray region minus F. We call this darker gray region, to the left of the supply curve and below the price, the **producer surplus**.

More generally, *the producer surplus is equal to profit before subtracting sunk fixed costs.* We can break down the firm's profit into various pieces, as shown in Figure 2.18. Whereas the firm

[5] Using equations, we can explain this point as follows. Recall that the integral of a function represents the area below that function on a graph. Therefore, the area below the marginal cost curve MC (which is the derivative of the cost function with respect to output) can be expressed as $\int_0^{y'} C'(y)dy = C(y') - C(0)$, where $C(0)$ is the cost that needs to be paid even when no output is produced. In other words, $C(0)$ is the fixed cost. The total cost of producing y', $C(y')$, minus the fixed cost, $C(0)$, gives the total variable cost of producing y'. Thus, you can see that the area below the graph of the MC curve represents the total variable cost.

Figure 2.17 Marginal cost and variable cost

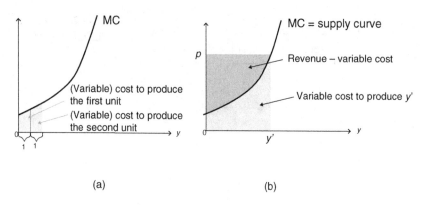

(a)   (b)

Figure 2.18 Profit and producer surplus

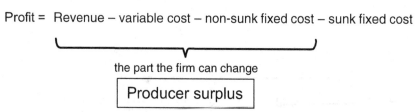

Profit =   Revenue – variable cost – non-sunk fixed cost – sunk fixed cost

the part the firm can change

Producer surplus

Figure 2.19 The supply curve and producer surplus/profit in the benchmark case

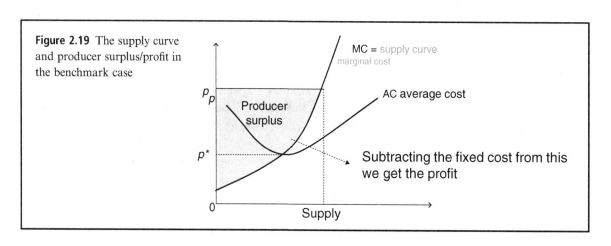

can't do anything to change its sunk fixed costs, its decisions can affect the "changeable" portion of its profits. Therefore, when we analyze a firm's gains and losses from market transactions, it's important to think about the "changeable" part of the firm's profits, which we call the producer surplus.

Let's recap what we've learned about the relationship between cost and supply.

In the benchmark case, in which the graph of the production function is bowed toward the top left (which means that the production possibility set – i.e. the area below the production function – is a convex set) and all fixed costs are sunk costs, the marginal cost curve is the supply curve (see Figure 2.19).

With a clear understanding of the benchmark case, let's consider a more complicated, and possibly more realistic, case.

Comment 2.2 Sometimes It's Better to Operate, Even When You're Going to Lose Money

When the price is below the level $p*$ shown in Figure 2.19, the average cost of production is higher than the price, no matter what level of output the firm chooses. Therefore, if the firm produces any amount of output at all, it will actually lose money. (This is because, for any level of output y, profits $= y(p - AC(y)) < 0$.) However, according to Figure 2.19, supply is not equal to zero, even when the price is less than $p*$. It seems puzzling that the firm produces anything, given that it will lose money. What is happening here? The firm's fixed costs make it inevitable that the firm will lose money, but if it produces *some* output it can actually reduce how much money it loses. The price $p*$ in Figure 2.19 (which is the smallest average cost possible) is called the **break-even price**, since it is the price at which the firm earns exactly zero profits. At prices above the break-even price the firm earns money, and at prices below the break-even price the firm loses money. As we've seen above, it's not necessarily the case that the firm should stop producing output even when the price is below the break-even price. By producing some output, the firm might be able to reduce its losses.

② **Case with "Set-Up Cost" and/or "Non-Sunk Fixed Cost"**

Let's turn to the case in which some set-up cost is required for production and/or some of the fixed costs are not sunk. For example, the firm might need to use labor to set up the factory for production, before even producing any output. In this case, the supply curve and marginal cost curve will not perfectly coincide.

Consider a scenario in which preparing the factory for production, by cleaning the floors and oiling the machines, takes five hours of labor, and production can't start until the preparation is finished. In this case, the production function will look like the one shown in Figure 2.20. Note that the production possibility set (i.e. the area below the production function) is not a convex set.

Furthermore, suppose that part of the construction cost of the factory (which is a fixed cost) can be recovered by selling the factory. In this case, part of the fixed cost is not sunk, so total cost is like that shown in Figure 2.21 (a).

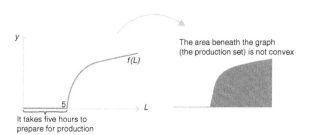

Figure 2.20 The case in which set-up is necessary

Figure 2.21 Cost in the
more complicated case

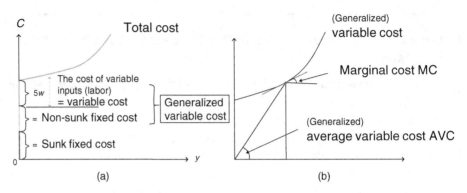

(a)

(b)

Figure 2.22 Cost curve

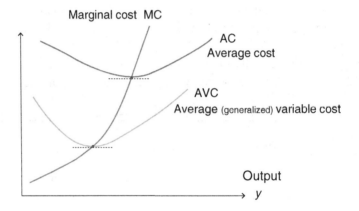

The portion of the fixed cost that is not sunk is similar to a variable cost, in the sense that the firm can change its size. In this book, we'll call the sum of the fixed costs that aren't sunk and the variable costs the **generalized variable cost**.

For the case in which there are variable costs for the set-up of the factory or there are fixed costs that are not sunk, the generalized average variable cost, defined as the generalized variable cost divided by output, plays a key role. Let's denote the generalized **average variable cost** by AVC. What shape does the AVC curve have? If you look at Figure 2.21 (b), you can see that the relationship between the AVC and MC curves is basically the same as the relationship between the AC and MC curves that we saw in part ①. That is, the AVC curve is U-shaped, like the AC curve in the benchmark case, and it intersects the MC curve at its minimum. The generalized average variable cost (AVC) is lower than the average (total) cost (AC) since it does not take the fixed cost into account. Therefore, if we put everything together, we get the graph shown in Figure 2.22.

For such cost functions, what is the shape of the supply curve? First, let's consider whether the firm should actually produce anything. Recall the decomposition of profit that we saw for the benchmark case. In this case, we can decompose the firm's profit as in Figure 2.23.

From this, it's clear that, as long as revenue minus the generalized variable cost is positive, the firm is better off if it produces output. Using the fact that revenue is equal to py, we can rewrite this condition as

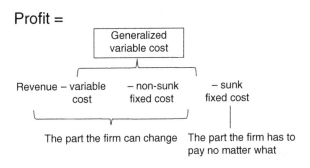

Figure 2.23 Breakdown of cost

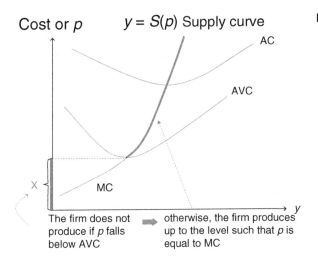

Figure 2.24 Supply curve

$$p > \text{generalized variable cost}/y = \text{AVC}(\text{average generalized variable cost}). \qquad (1)$$

Thus, *it is better for the firm to produce output as long as the price is greater than the (generalized) average variable cost.* On the other hand, if the price is less than the average variable cost, it's better for the firm to not produce any output. Using this idea, we can see that the firm's supply curve will be like the one shown in Figure 2.24. If the price is in the range X, then, no matter what the level of output is, the AVC is higher than the price. Therefore, condition (1) is not satisfied, and it's better for the firm to produce nothing. Thus, supply is zero when the price is in the range X. By contrast, if the price is above the range X, then the firm should operate and produce output. In particular, as we saw in the previous part, it's optimal for the firm to set the level of output such that the price and the marginal cost are equal. *That is, even in the presence of non-sunk fixed cost and/or set-up cost, the supply curve is basically equal to the marginal cost curve. The only difference from the benchmark case is that, if the price is too low, then this relationship no longer holds, and supply becomes zero.*

Putting everything together, for the more complicated case we can depict the relationship between the supply curve and the cost function as in Figure 2.25. The minimum value of the AC curve gives the **break-even price** that we discussed before. It separates the prices for which the firm makes negative profits and the prices for which the firm makes positive profits. On the other hand, the minimum value of the AVC curve gives the **shutdown price**, which separates the

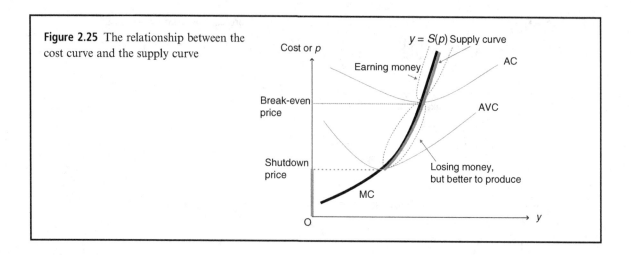

Figure 2.25 The relationship between the cost curve and the supply curve

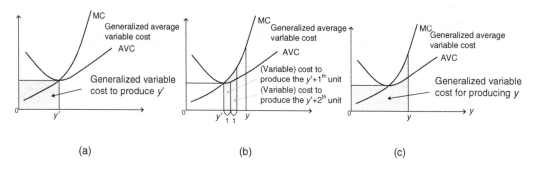

Figure 2.26 Generalized variable cost and the supply curve

prices for which the firm produces output and the prices for which the firm does not produce output. If the price is below the shutdown price, the firm will not operate at all.

Finally, let's study the relationship between the supply curve and the firm's profits in the presence of non-sunk fixed cost and/or set-up cost. First, let's look at Figure 2.26, which shows how the supply curve is related to the generalized variable cost (which, if you recall, is the variable costs plus the non-sunk fixed costs) for producing a given level of output y.

For a given output y', we can express the generalized variable cost as

$$\text{AVC} \times y' = \text{the area of the rectangle in Figure 2.26(a).}$$

As output moves from y' to y, what is the increase in the variable cost? We can solve for this amount using the fact that (for output greater than y') the supply curve is equal to the marginal cost curve. We know that, as the firm increases output from y' by one unit after another, the area beneath the marginal cost curve gives the cost of increasing output. This is shown in Figure 2.26 (b). Therefore, for a given level of output y, the generalized variable cost is given by the region shown in Figure 2.26 (c). When we subtract the generalized variable cost from revenue, we get the producer surplus, which is the area of the grey region in Figure 2.27. If we further subtract the sunk fixed costs, then we are left with the firm's profit.

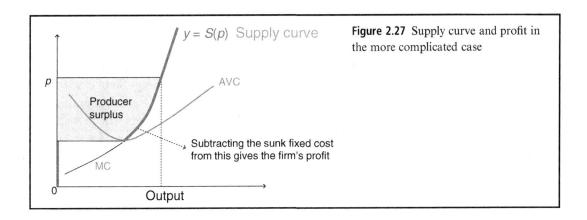

Figure 2.27 Supply curve and profit in the more complicated case

In conclusion, for the cases in which there are variable costs for set-up and for the cases in which a part of the fixed costs is not sunk, *the area to the left of the supply curve and below the price gives the producer surplus, just as in the benchmark case.*

(d)   A Real-Life Example of a Cost Curve

There are plenty of microeconomics textbooks that show the pictures of hypothetical marginal cost curves and average cost curves, but they seldom show the cost curve of a real firm. In physics textbooks, after a discussion of Newton's laws of motion, it's common to have a sequence of photos showing the path of a ball that's just been thrown. As in Newton's laws, the ball's trajectory is parabolic. Why don't we do something similar in economics? The fact that microeconomic textbooks rarely have examples showing how economic theory holds in real life is probably the reason that so many people say economics is detached from reality and useless.

Case Study 2.2 The Cost Curve of Tohoku Electric Power[6]

The short-run (say, something between several hours to several months) variable cost of an electric company is, essentially, just the company's fuel-related expenses. Other costs, such as labor, maintenance, or equipment, can be viewed as fixed costs in the short run. Tohoku Electric Power, which operates in the northern area of Japan, has many plants, and fuel expenses differ

---

[6] Deriving a marginal cost curve from plant-level data is known as the "merit order" method and has been widely used in the analysis of electricity markets. Katsuhito Hasuike at Nomura Research Institute Ltd. graciously helped me to prepare this case study for my microeconomics course in 2005, based on Katsuhito Hasuike and Yoshitsugu Kanemoto, "Policy Evaluation for Oligopolistic Markets: A Case of Wholesale Electricity Market," Discussion Paper 05-J-024 (Tokyo: Research Institute of Economy, Trade and Industry, 2005).

Case Study 2.2 (cont.)

across their plants. For hydroelectric power plants, fuel expenses (and so variable costs) are essentially zero. They simply use the flow of water to generate electricity. Similarly, for nuclear power plants, the short-run variable cost is zero, since the plant will continue to generate electricity once the nuclear reaction has begun. Conversely, at traditional power plants, where fuel is burned to create steam that turns turbines, the cost of the fuel needed to produce an additional kilowatt hour (kWh) of electricity is constant, until the plant's capacity is reached. This means that marginal cost is constant up to the factory's capacity (maximum possible production), at which point the marginal cost becomes infinite (Figure 2.28).

The fuel expenses and generating capacity per kWh can be calculated for each power plant using publicly available data. Tohoku Electric Power would use the most efficient plants first, since their cost of electricity generation is lowest. If it needs to produce more electricity, then it will begin to use the less efficient plants as well. Thus, *if we order the power plants from the one with the lowest marginal cost to the one with the highest marginal cost, then we can figure out the marginal cost curve for all of Tohoku Electric Power*. This information is summarized in Table 2.1. If you look at the utilization rate of each plant in the table, the plants with lower marginal costs do indeed have higher utilization rates.

Have you noticed that what happens at Tohoku Electric Power is the same as what happens in the assembly factory that we saw in Case Study 2.1? In our example, the assembly factory had three machines – machine A, machine B, and machine C – where machine A was the most productive and machine C was the least productive. Using a high-productivity machine means that the marginal cost of producing output is low. In our example, the first machine that the factory president puts to use is machine A, which has the lowest marginal cost. As the price of the output increases and the factory needs to produce more, the factory president will put machines B and C (which have higher marginal costs) to use. Just as the factory president uses machines A, B, and C in that order, Tohoku Electric Power uses its various power plants in ascending order of marginal cost. If you return to Table 2.1, you'll see that factories with lower marginal costs have higher utilization rates.

Figure 2.28 Marginal cost at a traditional power plant

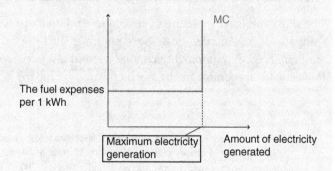

Table 2.1 Cost structure of Tohoku Electric Power, 2001

Method of power generation	Place of plant	(Thousand kWh) Generating capacity	(Thousand kWh) Cumulative generating capacity	(Yen/kWh) Marginal cost	Calendar time utilization rate (%)
Nuclear power		2,077	2,077	0	
Hydraulic power		2,896	4,973	0	
Coal-fired thermal	Haramachi	1,896	6,869	1.6	81.4
Coal-fired thermal	Noshiro	1,134	8,003	1.7	77.9
Coal-fired thermal	Sendai	476	8,479	1.8	69.5
LNG thermal	Higashi-Niigata	3,717	12,195	5.1	63.3
LNG thermal	Shin-Sendai	578	12,773	6.3	45.6
LNG thermal	Niigata	477	13,250	6.9	34.5
Thermal (petroleum, etc.)	Shin-Sendai	328	13,578	7.1	19.3
Thermal (petroleum, etc.)	Hachinohe	457	14,034	7.9	19.5
Thermal (petroleum, etc.)	Akita	1,495	15,529	8.3	10.9

Source: Agency for Natural Resources and Energy, "Summary of Demand and Supply for Electric Power," in *Annual Securities Report* (Tokyo: Agency for Natural Resources and Energy, 2002).

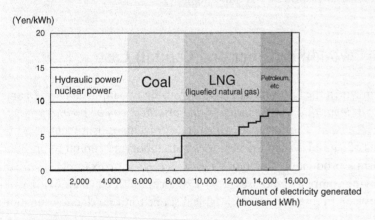

Figure 2.29 Marginal cost curve of Tohoku Electric Power

In Figure 2.29, we've taken the information in Table 2.1 and plotted Tohoku Electric Power's marginal cost curve.

Now, let's consider what Tohoku Electric Power's average cost curve looks like. In 2001 the average amount of electricity generation per hour was 8,765 thousand kWh, and the average

Case Study 2.2 (cont.)

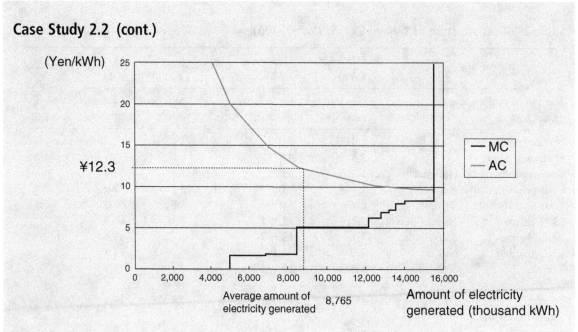

Figure 2.30 Cost curve of Tohoku Electric Power

cost per kWh of output was ¥12.3. If we use this fact to estimate the average cost curve, we get the curve shown in Figure 2.30.[7]

This is a real-world example of average cost and marginal cost. Since the fixed cost of building a power plant is so high, the average cost of production is quite high.

2.3   Firm Behavior for the Two-Input (Labor and Capital) Case

Next, let's consider the case in which the firm produces output y using two inputs: labor (L) and capital (K). **Capital** refers to an *input that, once purchased and installed, can be used to produce output for an extended period of time.* For instance, a factory, a machine, or a truck used to transport goods are examples of capital. When the firm uses both labor and capital to produce output, we can write the firm's production function as $y = F(L,K)$. For example, you can imagine that the firm is a moving company, and uses labor L and capital K (say, a moving van) to produce y (the moving service). Figure 2.31 shows a typical shape for a production function of this type.

---

[7] An especially sharp reader might notice that output at the point where the average cost curve and the marginal cost curve intersect is much larger than Tohoku Electric Power's actual average output. Thus, Tohoku Electric Power is not behaving as a perfectly competitive firm. The reason is that the electricity generation industry is regulated by the government. I talk more about regulation in Chapter 5.

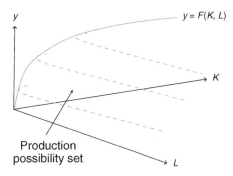

Figure 2.31 The production function for the two-input case

The area beneath the production function is called the **production possibility set**. Recall that we defined the "long run" as the period of time in which the amounts of all inputs could be freely changed, and we defined the "short run" as the period of time in which the amounts of some inputs are fixed. If the only inputs to production are L and K, then $y = F(L,K)$ represents the **long-run production function**, where the firm can freely adjust the amounts of labor and capital that it uses. By contrast, we can write the firm's **short-run production function** as $f(L) = F(L, \overline{K})$, where $\overline{K}$ is a fixed level of capital.

(a)   Returns to Scale

In the long run (when the amounts of all inputs can be adjusted), what happens when the amounts of all inputs are doubled? Will output be doubled as well? The answer depends on the characteristics of the firm's production function. To study this question, let's consider the change in output when all inputs are multiplied by some value $t > 1$. (We'll just study the case in which inputs *increase*, so we just consider values of t that are greater than one.)

When all inputs are multiplied by $t > 1$, these statements apply.

- If output increases by a factor of t, we say the production function has **constant returns to scale**.
- If output increases by more than a factor of t, we say the production function has **increasing returns to scale**.
- If output increases by less than a factor of t, we say the production function has **decreasing returns to scale**.

In order to see whether a specific production function has constant, increasing, or decreasing returns to scale, we can consider the straight line that passes through the origin in the (L,K) plane and look at the change in the production function along this line. Figure 2.32 shows exactly what I mean by this.

If all inputs enter into the production function, then decreasing returns to scale are logically impossible. For example, if a firm builds two identical factories and equips them with the same

Figure 2.32 Returns to scale

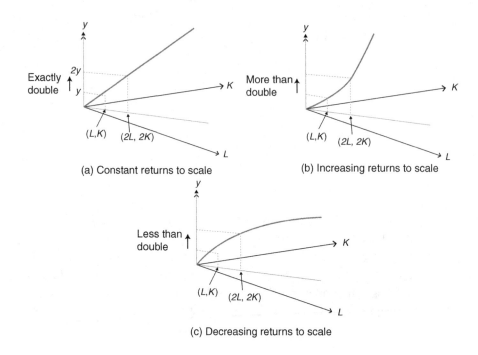

(a) Constant returns to scale

(b) Increasing returns to scale

(c) Decreasing returns to scale

number of workers, machines, and equipment, then production must be doubled. If production is not doubled, it must be because there are "hidden" inputs, such as the ability of the manager, that are not doubled. By contrast, in some cases output can be doubled even if the inputs are not doubled. For instance, if the two factories that we described are built right next to each other, and there is no need to have a wall between the two factories, then the firm can save on construction expenses. Therefore, since the firm's costs less than double even as the firm's output doubles, production has increasing returns to scale. If a firm's increasing returns to scale are sufficiently strong, the firm can continually reduce its average cost by increasing its output. This means that the firm can produce at a lower average cost by merging with its competitive rivals. The merger process will continue until there is only a single large company in the market (i.e. the market becomes monopolistic). This suggests that increasing returns to scale are incompatible with perfect competition.

(b) Substitution between Inputs and the Marginal Rate of Technical Substitution

If we look at the "contour lines" of the firm's production function, we can learn interesting properties about how the firm combines labor and capital to produce output. The lower-left graph in Figure 2.33 shows the various possible combinations of input that produce output $y = 10$. We call this curve an **isoquant**.

Returning to our example of a moving company, in order to serve $y = 10$ customers, the company could use lots of capital (moving trucks) and just a little labor, as at point A. We would call this a capital-intensive production method. On the other hand, the company could

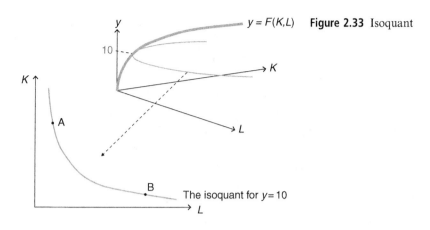

Figure 2.33 Isoquant

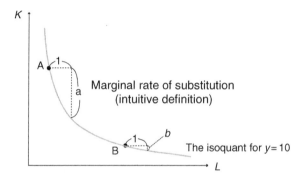

Figure 2.34 Law of diminishing marginal rate of (technical) substitution

use lots of labor and just a little bit of capital (moving trucks), as at point B. We would call this a labor-intensive production method. Changing the production method from point A to point B means that the firm increases its use of labor and decreases its use of capital. In economic terms, we say that the company "*substitutes labor for capital.*" Figure 2.34 shows a more detailed study of this relationship between labor and capital. If labor is increased by one unit from point A, as in the figure, then the company can use less capital (i.e. fewer trucks) to achieve the same output $y = 10$.[8] The amount by which the company can reduce its use of capital is denoted by a in Figure 2.34.

The size of a represents *how much the firm can reduce its use of capital by using one additional unit of labor, all while maintaining the same level y = 10 of output.* We call this the **marginal rate of (technical) substitution** of labor for capital, and denote it by MRS_{LK}.[9] The value a in

---

[8] For our example of a moving company, it might seem weird to consider a slight adjustment in the number of trucks the company uses, since the number of trucks jumps discontinuously from one to two to three, and so on. However, if you think of capital K as the total usage hours of trucks (say, if the company rents the trucks at an hourly rate), it makes more sense to consider a marginal change in the amount of capital.

[9] The word "technical" is sometimes used in order to distinguish this concept from the concept of the marginal rate of substitution in the consumer choice context, which represents the slope of a consumer's indifference curves.

Figure 2.34 is the intuitive definition of the marginal rate of substitution of labor for capital, which appears in introductory textbooks. Later I'll give a formal mathematical definition, which will be useful when we're trying to analyze mathematical models. For now, let's return to Figure 2.34. At point A, there is an abundance of moving trucks, but not enough workers. If the moving company hires one additional worker, the company is able to do its job much more efficiently, so it can reduce the number of trucks it uses by a large amount. In particular, it reduces the amount of trucks it uses by a, which we can think of as the marginal rate of substitution. By contrast, at point B, there are plenty of workers, so, even if the company hires one additional worker, it won't be able to reduce the number of trucks it uses by very much. Here, the marginal rate of substitution, b, is small. Thus, you can see that the marginal rate of substitution of labor for capital decreases as the amount of labor increases, which means that the isoquant is bowed toward the origin. We call this the **law of diminishing marginal rate of (technical) substitution**.

Next, let's redefine the marginal rate of substitution in a way that's convenient for the mathematical analysis of optimal production. Mathematically, we say this.

> *The size of the slope (of the tangent line) of the isoquant = the marginal rate of (technical) substitution.*

This is illustrated in Figure 2.35. (The slope of the tangent line is negative, but we consider only its absolute value – that is, we ignore the negative sign.)

This can be computed in the same way that we computed the marginal rate of substitution of consumption. The change in output when the firm slightly increases labor ($dL > 0$) and slightly decreases capital ($dK < 0$) is

$$dy = \frac{\partial F}{\partial L} dL + \frac{\partial F}{\partial K} dK.$$

If we consider the case in which output does not change, because the effects of the increase in labor and decrease in capital cancel each other out, we have

Figure 2.35 Mathematical definition of marginal rate of (technical) substitution

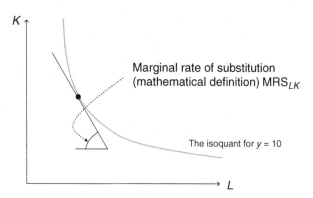

$$0 = \frac{\partial F}{\partial L} dL + \frac{\partial F}{\partial K} dK.$$

Rewriting this, we get

$$-\frac{dK}{dL} = \frac{\partial F/\partial L}{\partial F/\partial K}.$$

Since the left-hand side is the ratio of the change in K and the change in L, such that output y is constant, let's write it as

$$-\frac{dK}{dL}\bigg|_{y \,=\, \text{constant}}.$$

This is simply the slope of the isoquant, which is exactly the marginal rate of substitution. Therefore, we now know that the following relationship holds:

$$\underbrace{\mathrm{MRS}_{LK} = -\frac{dK}{dL}\bigg|_{y \,=\, \text{constant}}}_{\text{Marginal rate of (technical) substitution}} = \underbrace{\frac{\partial F/\partial L}{\partial F/\partial K}}_{\text{Ratio of marginal productivities}}$$

(c)   Profit Maximization

Let's solve for the profit maximization condition for a firm that uses labor and capital as inputs. The profit, π, in this case can be written as

$$\text{profit } \pi = py - wL - rK.$$

Here, p is the price of the output and w is the wage. What you need to be a bit careful about is r, which corresponds to the "price" of capital K. For example, if this equation represents the profits of a moving company in a day, and K gives the number of trucks it uses, then you might think that r would be the purchase price of a truck. However, you shouldn't think about r in this way. If the company purchases a truck, it can use the truck for many years, not just a single day, so it's more reasonable to think of r as the purchase price of a truck, prorated over time in some manner. A cleaner interpretation can be given in the scenario in which the firm doesn't actually own the trucks but rents them by the day. In this case, r is the rental fee the company pays each day for use of a truck.[10] Either way, *the r that we use in the calculation of profit for one*

---

[10] Alternatively, you could think of it as the rental fee the company would get by lending its truck to another company. This is called an "opportunity cost." I explain opportunity costs in detail in Chapter 3, Section 3.1 (b).

Figure 2.36 Cost minimization

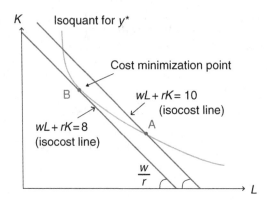

period is not the purchase price of capital per se but the cost of using capital K for one period. We call it the **rental price of capital**.

We can write the profit maximization problem of a perfectly competitive firm as

$$\max_{L,\,K} pF(L, K) - wL - rK.$$

We denote the solution for this profit maximization problem by L^*, K^*, and $y^* = F(L^*, K^*)$. Given this profit maximization problem, let's examine what the profit maximization condition is.

If profit is maximized, then (L^*, K^*) must be the cheapest way to produce output y^*. So, instead, let's consider the cost minimization problem for producing y^*. In Figure 2.36, the isoquant represents various combinations of L and K that can be combined to produce output y^*. Where is the point on the curve at which cost is lowest?

At point A, the production cost is ten. The isocost line $wL + rK = 10$ shows the various combinations of L and K that cost the firm ten to use. As you can see, we can rewrite the equation for the isocost line as

$$K = -\underbrace{\boxed{\frac{w}{r}}}_{\text{slope}} L + \frac{10}{r}.$$

Now, it's clear that the slope of the isocost line is the input price ratio w/r.

By moving from point A to point B, the cost of production falls from ten to eight. At point B, the isoquant and the isocost line are tangent to each other, so the cost cannot be decreased further by moving along the isoquant in either direction. Thus, point B is the cost minimization point. To summarize, the cost minimization condition, which is a part of the profit maximization condition, can be written as in Figure 2.37.

To fully understand the relationship between the production function and the profit maximization condition, let's introduce some mathematical concepts.

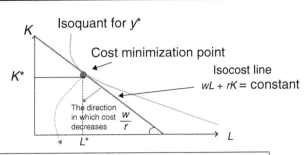

Figure 2.37 Profit maximization condition (2) (cost minimization)

The slope of the isoquant = the slope of the isocost line

$$MRS_{LK} = \frac{w}{r}$$

Marginal rate of substitution   input price ratio

‖

$$\frac{\partial F / \partial L}{\partial F / \partial K}$$ The ratio of marginal productivity

A Math Toolkit for Economists: Concave Functions and Convex Functions

In economic models, functions such as those in Figure 2.38 appear frequently. For this function, the value $f(x)$ increases dramatically as x increases. You might remember that the cost function C that we studied in Section 2.2 had this shape. *What characterizes a function of this kind is that the area above the graph of the function is a convex set.*[11] We call these functions, such as the one shown in Figure 2.38, **convex functions**. By contrast, *if the area below the graph of the function is a convex set*, such as in Figure 2.39, we call it a **concave function**. Concave functions also appear frequently in economic analysis.

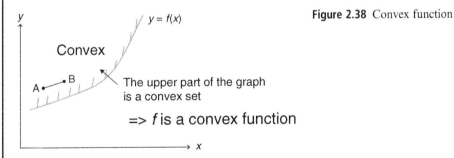

Figure 2.38 Convex function

[11] We studied convex sets in Chapter 1, but let's review what a convex set is. For any two points A and B within a set, if all the weighted averages (i.e. the points in between A and B) tA + $(1 - t)$B for $0 \le t \le 1$ are contained within the set, then we say that the set is convex. You can see that the area above the curve in Figure 2.38 satisfies this condition. (Please look at A and B in the figure.)

Figure 2.39 Concave function

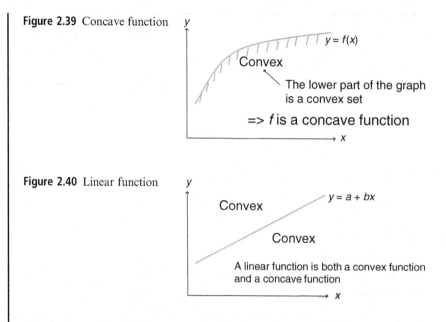

Figure 2.40 Linear function

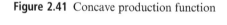

For instance, the short-run production function $y = f(L)$ that we saw in Section 2.2 had such a shape. Furthermore, by definition, a linear function is both a convex function and a concave function (see Figure 2.40). We'll use this fact later.

In microeconomics, we often assume this:

The production function is a concave function,

as in Figure 2.41. That is, *the production* possibility *set* (which is the area of the graph below the production function) *is a convex set*.

Figure 2.41 Concave production function

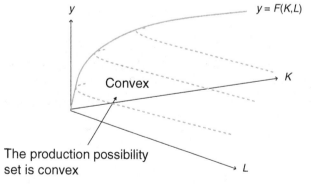

We typically assume that the production function is concave because it is a very compact and elegant way to capture the various properties of production technologies that we've discussed.

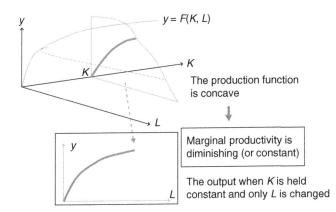

Figure 2.42 Concave production function implies the law of diminishing marginal productivity

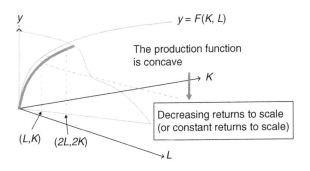

Figure 2.43 Concave production function implies constant or decreasing returns to scale

① First, if we take a "slice" of the production function along the plane parallel to the L axis, as shown in the upper part of Figure 2.42, then we have a curve that shows the relationship between L and y while holding K constant. In other words, we get the graph of the short-run production function, shown in the lower part of Figure 2.42.

If the production function is a concave function, the graph of the short-run production function is bowed toward the top left. This expresses the fact that *the marginal productivity of labor is diminishing (or constant)*.

② If we regard the production function F as a long-run production function, and we take a "slice" parallel to the output axis and passing through the origin, then the fact that the production function is concave implies that *it has decreasing or constant returns to scale* (see Figure 2.43). As we saw in Part (a), increasing returns to scale and perfect competition are incompatible, so when we are analyzing perfectly competitive markets we are dealing only with production functions that have constant or decreasing returns to scale. However, if all inputs enter into the production function, then the production function cannot have decreasing returns to scale. *Therefore, in microeconomics it is frequently assumed that the long-run production function has constant returns to scale.*

③ If we take a slice of the production function parallel to the (L,K) plane, at a height of $y = 10$, we obtain the isoquant for $y = 10$. That is, we get all combinations of L and K that can be combined to produce output of $y = 10$. If the production function is concave, then the

Figure 2.44 Concave production function implies the law of diminishing marginal rate of substitution

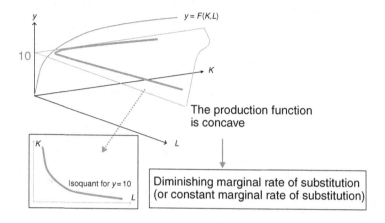

A Math Toolkit for Economists: The Mathematical Definition of a Concave Function

We defined a concave function geometrically by looking at its graph, but now let's define concave functions using mathematical expressions. This is useful in judging whether a given function is concave, without having to graph it. We will use this shortly when we discuss the profit maximization condition. If a function f is concave, then it has a rounded shape, as in Figure 2.45.

In this figure, what is written as Big is the value of f at $x = ta + (1 - t) b$. Therefore, we have

$$\boxed{\text{Big}} = f(ta + (1 - t(b))).$$

Figure 2.45 Definition of a concave function using mathematical expressions

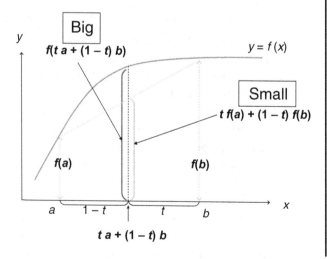

In addition, what is labeled as Small is a weighted average of $f(a)$ and $f(b)$ in the figure, so we have

$$\boxed{\text{Small}} = tf(a) + (1 - t)f(b).$$

To summarize, since $\boxed{\text{Big}} \geq \boxed{\text{Small}}$, we obtain the following.

If f is a function such that

$$f(ta + (1 - t)b) \geq tf(a) + (1 - t)f(b)$$

holds for all a, b, and t such that $0 \leq t \leq 1$, we call f a concave function.

By using this inequality, we can immediately show:

If f and g are concave functions, then $f + g$ is a concave function as well.   (2)

(It is left to you as an easy exercise.)

---

isoquant will be bowed toward the origin, as in the lower part of Figure 2.44. This captures *the law of diminishing marginal rate of substitution*.

Using our preparation above, let's solve for the profit maximization condition. If the production function is concave, then

$$\text{profit} = pF(L, K) - wL - rK$$

is a concave function. The reason is that $pF(L,K)$ is a concave function, and $-wL - rK$ is also a concave function (since it is linear). Therefore, profit, which is the sum of these two concave functions, is also concave (by (2)). This means that the graph of the firm's profit, as a function of L and K, is bowed upward, as shown in Figure 2.46.[12]

What kinds of properties does the peak of the profit function have? If we take a slice of the profit function parallel to the L axis, as in the top-right part of Figure 2.46, we obtain a curve that represents the relationship between profit π and L for a fixed level of capital K^*. At the peak of the graph the slope of the tangent line is zero, and, since the slope of the tangent line for this curve is given by the (partial) derivative $\partial\pi/\partial L$, one of the conditions for the profit-maximizing point is that $\partial\pi/\partial L = 0$. Considering an analogous argument for the curve that represents the relationship between profit π and K for a fixed level of labor L^*, we find that the

---

[12] A note about some details. If the price p of output is too high, *it is possible that profit increases without bound as more and more output is produced*. In this case, there is no profit-maximizing point. But, in such a case, since the market is in a state of excess supply, and there is too much output, eventually p decreases and the abnormal situation where profit increases without bound as more and more output is produced will cease. That is, we'll return to a situation where there is a single profit-maximizing point. In this way, in the equilibrium state, the price will adjust so that there always exists a profit-maximizing point. (In Chapter 3 I explain whether such an equilibrium price really exists or not.)

Figure 2.46 Profit maximization point

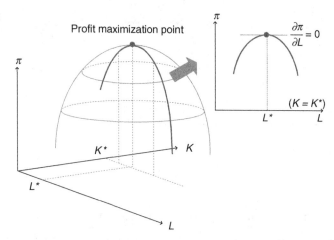

other condition for the profit-maximizing point is $\partial\pi/\partial K = 0$. Therefore, the complete condition for profit maximization is

$$\frac{\partial\pi}{\partial L} = 0 \text{ and } \frac{\partial\pi}{\partial K} = 0. \tag{3}$$

For those who care about being fully rigorous, let me make a rather detailed comment.

Comment 2.3 A Note on the Profit Maximization Condition

To better understand the profit maximization condition (3), let me make two comments on rather fine mathematical details.

① **Corner Solution.** Suppose that the rental fee is too high, and it's not optimal to use moving trucks (K). That is, $K^* = 0$. Then, the condition $\partial\pi/\partial K = 0$ will generally not hold at the optimal point. In such a case, we say that the problem has a **corner solution** (see Figure 2.47).

By contrast, if both K and L are used in positive amounts at the profit-maximizing point, then we say that the problem has an interior solution. Therefore, strictly speaking, profit maximization condition (3) is the condition for **interior solutions**.

② **Necessary Condition and Sufficient Condition**

As you can see in Figure 2.46, *if the production function F is concave*, then the profit function is also concave and has the shape of a hill. Therefore, *there is only one peak, and condition (3)*

Figure 2.47 Corner solution

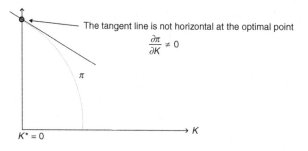

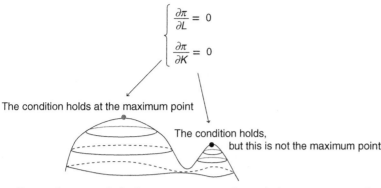

$$\begin{cases} \dfrac{\partial \pi}{\partial L} = 0 \\[2mm] \dfrac{\partial \pi}{\partial K} = 0 \end{cases}$$

Figure 2.48 The case in which profit is not a concave function

The condition holds at the maximum point

The condition holds, but this is not the maximum point

will give the point (which is an interior solution) that maximizes the profit function. Thus, for any interior point (K, L) (i.e. $K, L > 0$),

(K, L) maximizes profits. $\Leftrightarrow$ Condition (3) holds at (K, L).

When the above relationship holds, we say that condition (3) is a **necessary and sufficient condition** for an interior point to be a solution to the profit maximization problem.

However, when the production function is not concave and the graph of the profit function is not shaped like a hill, it's possible that there are multiple peaks, as in Figure 2.48. In this case, condition (3) will hold at the optimal point. However, condition (3) might also hold at points that do not maximize profits.

That is, when the production function is not concave, and so the profit function is not concave, we have it for an interior point (K, L) (i.e. $K, L > 0$) that

(K, L) maximizes profits. $\Rightarrow$ Condition (3) holds at (K, L). (A)

However, it's not necessarily the case that

(K, L) maximizes profits. $\Leftarrow$ Condition (3) holds at (K, L). (B)

When relationship (A) holds, we say that condition (3) is a **necessary condition** for an interior point to be a solution to the profit maximization problem. Conversely, when relationship (B) holds, we say that condition (3) is a **sufficient condition** for an interior point to be a solution to the profit maximization problem.

To summarize, we have this.

When the production function is concave,

$$\begin{cases} \dfrac{\partial \pi}{\partial L} = 0 \\[2mm] \dfrac{\partial \pi}{\partial K} = 0 \end{cases}$$

is a **necessary and sufficient condition** for an interior point to be a solution to the profit maximization problem.

Comment 2.3 (cont.)

When the production function is not a concave function, *the above condition is a necessary condition but not a sufficient condition* for an interior point to be a solution to the profit maximization problem.

Returning to the original discussion, if we calculate the derivatives of $\pi = pF(L, K) - wL - rK$ from condition (3), which holds at the profit-maximizing point, we get

$$\begin{cases} 0 = \dfrac{\partial \pi}{\partial L} = p \dfrac{\partial F}{\partial L} - w \\[3mm] 0 = \dfrac{\partial \pi}{\partial K} = p \dfrac{\partial F}{\partial K} - r \end{cases}$$

Rearranging this, we obtain the following profit maximization condition.

$$\begin{cases} p \dfrac{\partial F}{\partial L} \quad = \quad w \\[3mm] p \dfrac{\partial F}{\partial K} \quad = \quad r \end{cases} \tag{4}$$

value of the marginal product   input price
Profit maximization condition (3)

Let's try to understand the intuition behind this expression. If the firm increases the amount of some input, say L, marginally by one unit, then revenue increases by the value of the marginal product (i.e. $p(\partial F/\partial L)$). By marginally increasing the amount of labor by one unit, the firm's costs increase by the price of the input (which is w in this case). Therefore, if $p(\partial F/\partial L)$ is greater than w, then the firm's profits will increase if it marginally increases the amount of the input by one unit. In the opposite case, in which $p(\partial F/\partial L)$ is less than w, the firm's profits increase when it marginally decreases the amount of the input by one unit. But, at the profit-maximizing point, it can't be possible for such a marginal adjustment of inputs to increase profits. Therefore, the value of the marginal product and price of the input must be equal at the profit-maximizing point.

If we divide both sides of the upper equation in condition (3) by the respective sides of the lower equation, we get

$$\frac{\partial F / \partial L}{\partial F / \partial K} = \frac{w}{r}, \tag{5}$$

which is the same as profit maximization condition (2) (i.e. the cost minimization condition) that we saw on page 101. In other words, condition (3) captures everything about the profit maximization condition. (The cost minimization condition (2) can be derived from condition (3).) The reason for this is simple: if the firm maximizes profits, then clearly it must also be minimizing costs.

Now, what does the profit maximization condition that we have just derived tell us about the real economy? As an application, consider an international comparison of input prices.

Case Study 2.3 An International Comparison of Input Prices

According to profit maximization condition (3), and condition (5) that we derived from it, the price of an input is proportional to the marginal productivity of the input. Moreover, the marginal productivity of an input is low when it is abundant compared to other inputs. For instance, if the amount of capital is constant, the marginal productivity of labor decreases as the firm increases the amount of labor it uses. (This is the law of diminishing marginal productivity that we saw in Section 2.2.)

Consequently, in countries where labor is abundant compared to capital equipment (as in developing countries), we might expect that the wage w is low compared to the rental price of capital r. Figure 2.49 shows that, largely, this is indeed the case.[13]

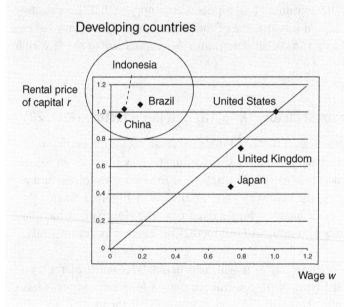

Figure 2.49 International comparison of input prices
Note: Normalized so that the United States = 1. The data are from around 2000.
Source: Kathryn G. Marshall (2012) "International Productivity and Factor Price Comparisons," *Journal of International Economics*, 87(2), pp.386–390, Table 3. https://doi.org/10.1016/j.jinteco.2012.01.003.

[13] However, input prices will be equalized across countries if there is free trade and several other conditions are satisfied. Readers who are interested should read textbooks on trade theory.

Let's generalize the profit maximization condition for the case in which there are many inputs. Besides labor and capital, things such as land or natural resources could be inputs to production. Let's denote the inputs by $x_1, \ldots, x_M$ and denote their prices by $w_1, \ldots, w_M$ respectively. Writing the production function as

$$y = F(x_1, \ldots, x_M)$$

the profit maximization condition is (similar to the two-input case) as follows.

$$\underbrace{p\,\frac{\partial F}{\partial x_m}}_{\text{Value of the marginal product}} = \underbrace{w_m}_{\text{input price}}, \quad m = 1, \ldots, M$$

Profit maximization condition (3)

As explained in Comment 2.3, when the production function F is concave, this is a necessary and sufficient condition for an interior point to be a solution to the profit maximization problem.

At the end of Chapter 2, I'll go over a detailed example to show how to calculate the profit maximization point using a production function $F(L, K)$ that uses only labor and capital.

(d)   The Long-Run Cost Function and the Supply Curve

In the long run, the firm can adjust the amounts of all inputs. Let's suppose that there's a firm that can't change the amount K of capital (i.e. the size of the factory) in the short run but can change the amount of capital in the long run. What determines *the optimal size of the factory* in the long run?

Case 1 There are only two options: a small factory ($K = 10$) or a large factory ($K = 20$)

Let r denote the unit price of factory construction. If the firm builds the small factory, then the fixed cost rK will be small. However, as output increases, the limited size of the factory becomes an issue, and the efficiency of production starts to decrease rapidly. Therefore, if the firm tries to produce a large amount of output in the small factory, the cost increases rapidly, as in Figure 2.50 (a). By contrast, if the firm builds the large factory, it incurs a larger fixed cost rK. However, it has the advantage that it can produce large amounts of output without increasing its costs as dramatically, as in Figure 2.50 (b).

If we superimpose the two graphs, as in Figure 2.51, it will help us analyze which of the two factories the firm should build. Looking at Figure 2.51, you can see that, if long-run output is less than $\bar{y}$, then it's better for the firm to build the small factory. Conversely, if long-run output is greater than $\bar{y}$, then it's better for the firm to build the large factory.

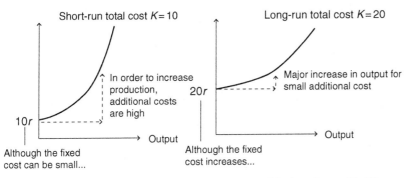

Figure 2.50 The scale of capital (factory) and the short-run total cost

(a) The case of the small factory (*K* = 10)   (b) The case of the large factory (*K* = 20)

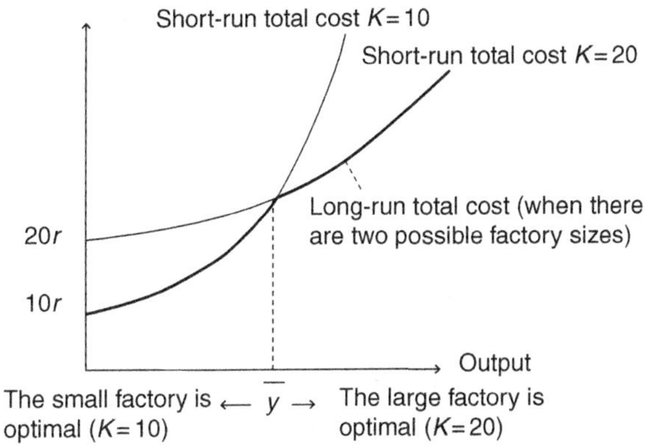

Figure 2.51 Long-run total cost when there are only two possible factory sizes

In the long run the firm can optimally choose the size of its factory, so long-run total cost is the minimum of the two short-run total cost curves, which is shown as the bold curve in Figure 2.51.

Case 2 The Firm Can Choose Any Size of the Factory

Now that we understand the case in which there are two factory sizes, let's consider the case in which the firm can freely choose the factory size K. As in the previous example, the long-run total cost function is given by the minimum of the short-run total cost functions. This is shown in Figure 2.52. In this figure, since production can't take place if the factory is too small, we assume that the smallest size of the factory is $K = 5$. The long-run total cost curve is shown in bold in Figure 2.52, and it traces out the minimum of the short-run cost curves. In this case, the long-run total cost curve is said to be the **envelope** of the short-run cost curves. Next, using Figure 2.52, let's draw a figure showing the short-run and long-run average cost curves.

Note: How to Derive the Short-Run and Long-Run Average Cost Curves from the Total Cost Curves

In order to draw a figure showing the short-run and long-run average cost curves, we just need to use the following points.

Figure 2.52 Short-run and long-run total cost

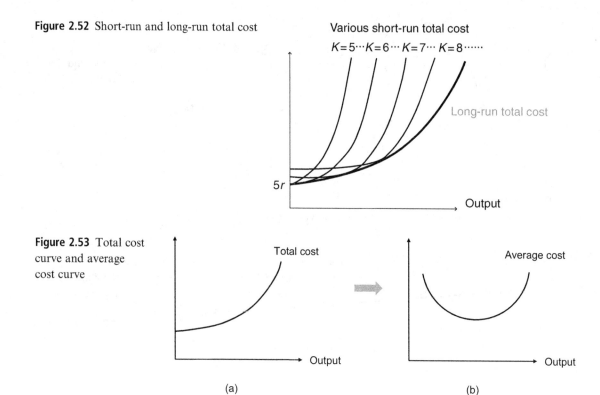

Various short-run total cost

$K=5\cdots K=6\cdots K=7\cdots K=8\cdots\cdots$

Long-run total cost

$5r$

Output

Figure 2.53 Total cost curve and average cost curve

Total cost

Output

(a)

Average cost

Output

(b)

- As we saw in Section 2.2, when I explained the cost function, when total cost has the shape shown in Figure 2.53, the average cost curve is U-shaped.

Looking back at Figure 2.52, since the total cost curve (either short-run or long-run) has the shape as in Figure 2.53, we know the following.

(i) The average cost curves in the short run and long run are U-shaped.
  ○ Moreover, since the short-run total cost is no less than the long-run total cost (cost is always lower in the long run, when the firm can optimally choose the factory size), if we divide both by output we see that the short-run average cost is no less than the long-run average cost. Therefore, the following statements hold.
(ii) The short-run average cost curves are situated above the long-run average cost curve.
(iii) In particular, for the output y at which the short-run and long-run total costs are equal, the short-run and long-run average cost curves are tangent to each other.

Therefore, if we draw a figure using points (i) to (iii) above, the relationship between the **short-run average cost (SAC)** and the **long-run average cost (LAC)** is as shown in Figure 2.54.

That is, as in the case of total cost, *the long-run average cost curve is an envelope of the short-run average cost curves.*

Next, let's examine the relationship between short-run and long-run marginal costs. First, let's try to understand what determines the shape of the marginal cost curve. As Figure 2.55

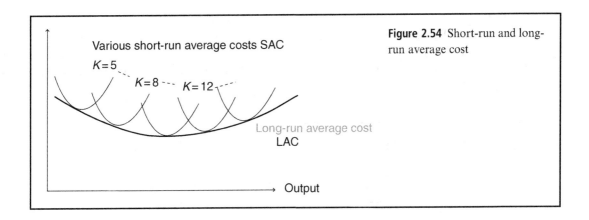

Figure 2.54 Short-run and long-run average cost

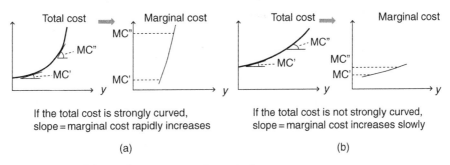

Figure 2.55 Curvature of the total cost curve and marginal cost

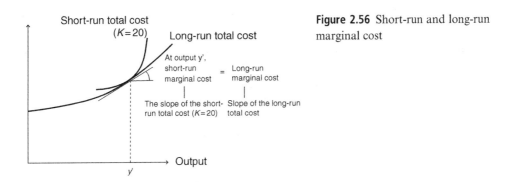

Figure 2.56 Short-run and long-run marginal cost

(a) shows, if the total cost curve is strongly curved, then the marginal cost curve (which is just the slope of the total cost curve) increases rapidly as output increases. By contrast, if the total cost curve is not strongly curved, as in Figure 2.55 (b), then the marginal cost curve is flatter.

Let's use this to examine the relationship between the long-run and short-run marginal cost curves. Figure 2.56 shows the relationship between the long-run total cost and the short-run total cost when the size of the factory is fixed at $K = 20$. You can see that the short-run total cost curve for $K = 20$ is tangent to the long-run total cost curve when output is y'. What does this mean? (This is an important point.)

This means that, when the size of the factory is $K = 20$, it's not possible to reduce the cost of producing y' even in the long run, when the firm can freely adjust the size of the factory. That is

> At output y', the short-run total cost for $K = 20$ and the long-run total cost *are equal.*
>
> $\Leftrightarrow$
>
> *The optimal factory size for producing y' is $K = 20$.*

Next, look at Figure 2.56 and note that, *at the point at which the short-run and long-run total cost curves are tangent to each other, the short-run and long-run marginal costs* (which are equal to the slopes of the curves) *are equal.* (This is another important point.) Moreover, if you carefully look at the shapes of the long-run and short-run total cost curves, you can see that the short-run total cost is more strongly curved. Therefore, as we noted in Figure 2.55, *the short-run marginal cost increases more rapidly (i.e. the slope is larger) than the long-run marginal cost does.* (This is the last important point.)

This discussion has been dense and has required patience, so let me summarize the important points.

① At the output for which the short-run total cost and the long-run total cost coincide – that is, at the output at which the short-run average cost and the long-run average cost coincide – the factory size K that is fixed in the short run is optimal in the long run in order to produce that level of output.

② At this level of output, the short-run marginal cost and the long-run marginal cost are equal to each other.

③ Moreover, the short-run marginal cost curve has a larger slope than the long-run marginal cost curve does.

Using these three observations, we can describe the relationship between the **short-run marginal cost (SMC)** and the **long-run marginal cost (LMC)** as in Figure 2.57. This is an important graph.

Furthermore, take a look at the marginal cost curves in Figure 2.57. As we saw in Section 2.2 (c), *the marginal cost curve and the supply curve are basically equal to each other.* Therefore, the two marginal cost curves, LMC and SMC, in Figure 2.57 can be regarded as the **long-run and short-run supply curves**. If we graph just the LMC and SMC curves, we get Figure 2.58.

As you can see, *the long-run supply curve is more responsive to the price (i.e. it has a smaller slope) than the short-run supply curve is.* This is called **Le Chaterier's principle**. Intuitively, since the firm can freely adjust the size of the factory (i.e. capital K) in the long run, the amount it supplies is more flexible in the long run than in the short run.

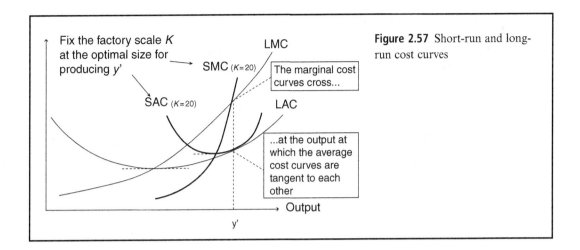

Figure 2.57 Short-run and long-run cost curves

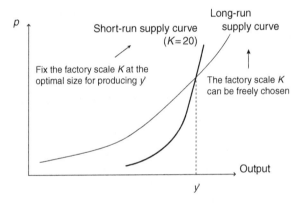

Figure 2.58 Short-run and long-run supply curves

2.4   Firm Behavior in the General Case (Many Inputs and Many Outputs)

Finally, let's analyze the most general case, in which the number of inputs is arbitrary and multiple types of goods can be produced. In this case, our analysis is clearer if we represent inputs and outputs using a **production plan**:

Production plan $y = \left(y_1, \ldots, \boxed{y_k}, \ldots, y_K \right)$

$\downarrow$

Good k is an output if y_k is positive

Good k is an input if y_k is negative

Example 2.2

Let (good 1, good 2, good 3) be (gasoline, heavy oil, crude oil). If 10 liters of gasoline and 5 liters of heavy oil can be produced from 20 liters of crude oil, then we can express this by the production plan:

$$y = (10, 5, -20).$$

Producing multiple goods at the same time, as in this example, is called **joint production**. Letting $p = (p_1, \ldots, p_N)$ be the price profile, we can write the profit that corresponds to the production plan $(y_1, \ldots, y_N)$ as

$$py = p_1 y_1 + \cdots + p_K y_K.$$

Note that py is not the product of two numbers.[14]

Example 2.3

For the oil company above, we can write profit as

$$py = \underbrace{p_1 \times 10 + p_2 \times 5}_{\text{revenue}} - \underbrace{p_3 \times 20}_{\text{cost}}.$$

In the general case, in which there can be many different types of output, it's more convenient to express the firm's production technology with production possibility sets, as I'll do, than with production functions.

> **Production Set** Y = the set of all production plans that the firm can implement.

Using this notation, we can rewrite the profit maximization problem of a perfectly competitive firm in the following manner:

> $$\max_{y} py$$
> $$\text{s.t.} \quad y \in Y.$$

Since the solution to the profit maximization problem depends on prices p, we write it as $y^*(p)$ and call it the **optimal production plan**.

Let's consider the properties of the optimal production plan. So far, we've imposed various assumptions, including:

(i) the production possibility set is convex (which implies that the law of diminishing marginal rate of substitution and the law of diminishing marginal productivity hold);
(ii) the amount of output can be changed continuously; and
(iii) the production function is differentiable.

---

[14] In fact, py represents the "inner product" of two vectors p and y.

We said that these features describe a "tractable mathematical model that captures the essential aspects of reality," though some may find these assumptions unreasonable or too strong. However, large parts of production theory still hold even if we relax or abandon these assumptions. Therefore, in what follows, *we'll derive the optimal behavior of a firm while not imposing those strong mathematical assumptions (i) to (iii). This should reassure you that the analysis in this subsection is sufficiently realistic.* Consider two arbitrary price profiles p^0 and p^1. Keep in mind that p^0 and p^1 are not numbers but, rather, denote vectors that give the price of each good. Suppose also that the optimal production plans, which maximize profits under p^0 and p^1 respectively, are y^0 and y^{1}:[15]

Price profile	p^0	p^1
	$\downarrow$	$\downarrow$
Optimal production plan	y^0	y^1

Since the production plan y^1 maximizes profits under p^1, we know that

$$p^1 y^1 \geq p^1 y^0. \tag{6}$$

Likewise, since the production plan y^0 maximizes profits under p^0, we know that

$$p^0 y^1 \leq p^0 y^0. \tag{7}$$

If we subtract each side of Inequality (7) from the corresponding side of Inequality (6), we reduce the left-hand side of (6) by a small amount $(p^0 y^1)$ and reduce the right-hand side of (7) by a large amount $(p^0 y^0)$. Therefore, the direction of the inequality $(\geq)$ in Equation (6) is preserved, and

$$(p^1 - p^0) y^1 \geq (p^1 - p^0) y^0.$$

Rearranging this expression, we obtain

$$(p^1 - p^0)(y^1 - y^0) \geq 0,$$

which is a *very important expression*. Recall that, in this setting, a price profile p is given by $p = (p_1, \ldots, p_N)$, a production plan y is given by $y = (y_1, \ldots, y_N)$, and py is given by $py = p_1 y_1 + \cdots + p_N y_N$. Therefore, we can rewrite the above inequality as

$$\left(p_1^1 - p_1^0\right)\left(y_1^1 - y_1^0\right) + \cdots + \left(p_N^1 - p_N^0\right)\left(y_N^1 - y_N^0\right) \geq 0. \tag{8}$$

---

[15] We'll proceed with our analysis in the same manner as in Chapter 1, Section 1.7, when we examined the properties of the compensated demand function.

Now, suppose that the only difference between the price profiles p^0 and p^1 is that the price of good k is higher in p^1 than in p^0. Then, all of the terms except the kth term in Inequality (8) are zero, and we get

$$\underbrace{\left(p_k^1 - p_k^0\right)}_{\text{positive}}\left(y_k^1 - y_k^0\right) \geq 0.$$

Therefore, $y_k^1 - y_k^0 \geq 0s$, which implies that

if p_k increases, then y_k increases (or is constant).

This can be interpreted in two ways, depending on whether good k is an output or an input.

① **The Case in which Good k is an Output $(y_k > 0)$**
In this case, if we depict the relationship between price and supply, as in Figure 2.59, the supply curve is necessarily upward-sloping (though there may be a part of the curve where supply is constant even if the price continues to increase). We call this the **law of supply**.

Law of Supply

The supply curve is necessarily upward-sloping. That is, if the price of an output increases, then production of that output either increases or is constant.

---

② **The Case in which Good k is an Input $(y_k < 0)$**
In this case, if we depict the relationship between price and supply, it look like the curve shown in Figure 2.60 (a). If we reflect the graph across the vertical axis, so that demand for the input is increasing in the positive direction of the horizontal axis, we obtain a downward-sloping input demand curve like that in Figure 2.60 (b). This is called the **law of factor demand**. (People often use the term "factors of production" interchangeably with the term "inputs to production.")

Figure 2.59 The supply curve is upward-sloping

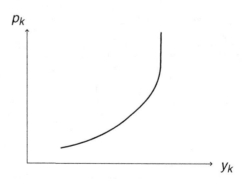

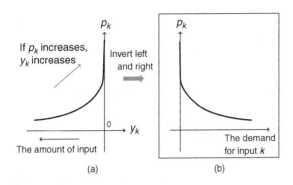

Figure 2.60 Factor demand is downward-sloping

Law of Factor Demand

The factor demand curve is necessarily downward-sloping. That is, if the price of the input increases, then the factor demand either decreases or is constant.

You might recall from the section on the theory of consumer demand that there was a possibility that, for certain goods (Giffen goods), the demand curve of a consumer is upward-sloping. However, for the factor demand of producers, this will never happen; factor demand is necessarily downward-sloping or constant.

Last, note that we don't require the assumption that the production function is differentiable or the assumption that the production possibility set is convex (i.e. diminishing marginal rate of substitution and diminishing marginal productivity) in order to derive the law of supply or the law of factor demand. Therefore, these laws apply very generally and are quite applicable to the real world.

2.5   Profit and Income Distribution: Why Is There Income Inequality?

The theory of production that we've developed up to this point can provide interesting insights into

- why and how profits are generated; and
- who earns a high income.

First, in order to study what determines the size of a firm's profit, let's consider an example in which production requires only labor and capital. In this case, the production function is

$$y = F(L, K).$$

Recall the definition of "returns to scale." When the firm multiplies the amounts of all inputs (L and K) by t, if output changes by a factor of t we say that the production function has constant returns. Likewise, if output changes by more than a factor of t we say the production function has increasing returns, and if output changes by less than a factor of t we say the production function has decreasing returns. In the case of increasing returns, cost decreases as the scale of production increases, so the market is easily monopolized. Therefore, only constant returns and decreasing returns are compatible with perfect competition. Moreover, if the only inputs that are necessary for production are truly just labor L and capital (factories) K, then there cannot be decreasing returns to scale. This is because, if the firm builds an identical factory and hires the same amount of labor, it must also double its production. If not, there must be some "hidden" inputs that do not explicitly enter into the production function, such as the ability of the manager. Here we suppose that L and K are indeed the only inputs to production, so *we're dealing with a case of constant returns*.

If we write down the definition of what it means for the production function to have constant returns (i.e. we multiply both inputs by t and multiply output by t), we have

$$F(tL^0, tK^0) = tF(L^0, K^0). \tag{9}$$

A function such that condition (9) holds is referred to as being **homogeneous of degree one**. Note that a production function that has constant returns is homogeneous of degree one. Differentiating both sides with respect to t, we can uncover some interesting insights regarding income shares and profit. Recall that the formula for differentiation says

$$\frac{d}{dt}F(L(t), K(t)) = \frac{\partial F}{\partial L}L'(t) + \frac{\partial F}{\partial K}K'(t).$$

Substituting $L(t) = tL^0$ and $K(t) = tK^0$ into this formula, and setting $t = 1$, the derivative of the left-hand side of (9) becomes

$$\frac{\partial F(L^0, K^0)}{\partial L}L^0 + \frac{\partial F(L^0, K^0)}{\partial K}K^0.$$

This is equal to the derivative of the right-hand side of (9), which is just $F(L^0, K^0)$. This holds for any (L^0, K^0), so we can remove the superscript 0. Summarizing what we've discussed so far, we have:

> The production function $y = F(L, K)$ has **constant returns to scale**.
> $\Leftrightarrow$ $F(L,K)$ is **homogeneous of degree one**.
> In this case, we have
>
> $$\frac{\partial F}{\partial L}L + \frac{\partial F}{.\partial K}K = F(L, K).$$

We call this **Euler's theorem** for homogeneous functions. Multiplying both sides of this equality by the output price p, we obtain the **product exhaustion theorem**, also called the

marginal productivity theorem of income distribution, a basic theorem about the distribution of income.

Product Exhaustion Theorem

Under constant returns,

$$\underbrace{\left(p\frac{\partial F}{\partial L}\right)L}_{\substack{\text{value of marginal.}\\\text{product of labor}}} \quad + \quad \underbrace{\left(p\frac{\partial F}{\partial K}\right)K}_{\substack{\text{value of marginal}\\\text{product of capital}}} \quad = \quad py.$$

Therefore, if

the payment for each unit of input is the value of the marginal product of that input,

then all revenue is exactly distributed among the inputs.

Let's apply the product exhaustion theorem while we consider why profits are generated. Consider the short run, in which capital K is fixed. Assuming that the firm owns the capital, and does not rent it from another party, the firm's profit is simply the firm's revenue minus the wages it pays for labor. That is,

$$\text{wages } wL + \text{profit} = \text{revenue } py. \tag{10}$$

What determines the size of the profit relative to wages? Recall that under perfect competition, at the profit-maximizing point, we know that

$$w = p\frac{\partial F}{\partial L}.$$

In other words, at the profit-maximizing point, under perfect competition, the input price is equal to the marginal product of that input. (This is just condition (3), which we learned on page 106.) Substituting this equality into Equation (10), and comparing it with the product exhaustion theorem, we discover exactly how and why profits are generated. Since

$$wL + \left(p\frac{\partial F}{\partial K}\right) = py,$$

profit $py - wL$ is equal to $\left(p\frac{\partial F}{\partial K}\right)K$. That is,

---

short-run profit = (the value of the marginal product of inputs
that are fixed in the short run) × (the amount of the fixed inputs).

Thus, profits are high if the marginal productivity of the fixed inputs that the firms owns are high, and are low otherwise.

From this discussion, we can characterize the distribution of income under the market mechanism in the following way.

Income Distribution under the Market Mechanism

In a perfectly competitive market, each individual receives a share of income according to the value of the marginal product of the input that she owns.

Thus, the wage of a worker is determined by the value of the marginal product of that worker, and the profit that the owner of the firm receives is determined by the value of the marginal product of the fixed inputs that the owner owns. Since the value of the marginal product of an input is just the price of the output × the marginal product of that input, we can say that the people who earn high incomes in the market economy

① *have inputs that are useful for producing goods that have a high market price; and*
② *are some of the few people who have that input.*

This means that, if you want to be rich in a market economy, you'd better figure out how to satisfy these conditions! By contrast, people who satisfy neither of these conditions receive little income in a market economy. Although bequests are a major factor in determining inequality, *if we were to eliminate initial differences in wealth or economic status, inequality in the market economy would be due to conditions ① and ②.*

Why is it that condition ② implies earning a high income in a market economy? Recall that most inputs obey the law of diminishing marginal productivity. That is, as the quantity of an input gets large, its marginal productivity declines. Therefore, most of the so-called "winners" of the market economy (such as lawyers, doctors, and movie stars) *own scarce resources*, for which the value of the marginal product is very high.

Case Study 2.4 The Income Distribution in Japan

Figure 2.61 shows the income distribution in Japan for 2011. According to microeconomic theory, wealth is concentrated among people who own relatively scarce resources. Therefore, we might make the following conjectures about the distribution of income. First, there is a large fraction of the population that owns only relatively abundant inputs to production. This group owns only inputs, such as manual labor, that are not scarce. Consequently, it seems reasonable to guess that, in the distribution of incomes, there will be a large mass of people around the lower incomes. Second, only a small fraction of the population owns scarce resources such as special talents or prime real estate. Therefore, we might expect that the distribution of income will have a long tail around the higher incomes. Figure 2.61 shows that the true distribution of income in Japan indeed looks like how we hypothesized. Without any intervention, market economies tend to result in a high concentration of wealth among a small fraction of people. In Chapter 3, we'll discuss what can be done to correct this extreme concentration and achieve a fairer distribution of income.

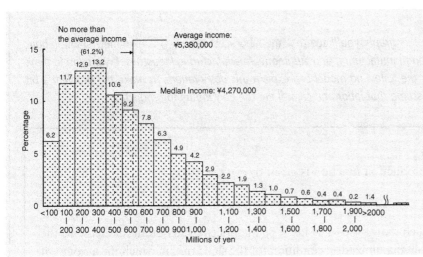

Figure 2.61 Income distribution in Japan, 2011 *Source*: Ministry of Health, Welfare and Labor (Japan), "Summary of Comprehensive Survey of Living Conditions, 2011".

Problem Session 2 The Production Function and the Workers' Share of Income

Professor: *This time, let's look at some data together before I give you a problem to work on. Figure 2.62 shows what percentages of revenue are paid to workers in various industries. This is called the "labor–cost ratio," and, written mathematically, it can be expressed as*

$$labor-cost\ ratio = \frac{wL}{py}$$

where y is output, p is the price of the output, w is the wage, and L is labor.

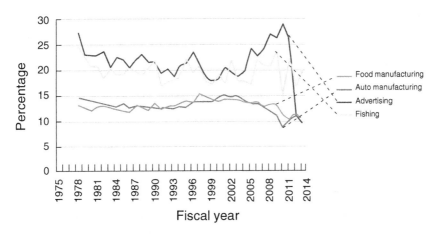

Figure 2.62 Labor–cost ratio, 1975–2014

Note: Since there are only recent data on bonuses, which are part of the wage, I did the calculations without including bonuses, even though this is slightly inaccurate.

Source: Ministry of Finance, *Statistics on Corporations and Firms* (Tokyo: Ministry of Finance, 2018).

(cont.)

If you study this graph, you'll see that the labor–cost ratio $\left(\frac{wL}{py}\right)$ is extremely stable (about 0.14) in the food-manufacturing and automotive-manufacturing industries. I want you to think about whether the following model can explain this observation. To make the problem a bit simpler, let's assume that labor and capital are the only inputs to production.

Problem

Suppose that a firm's production function is given by

$$F(L, K) = AL^a K^{1-a},$$

where a is a constant such that $0 < a < 1$. Let p be the price of the output and let w be the wage. Calculate the profit maximization condition for the short run, in which the amount of capital K is fixed and owned by the owner of the firm. Solve also for the labor–cost ratio $\frac{wL}{py}$ at the profit-maximizing point.

Student: *In the production function, there's a superscript "a" on L and a superscript "1 – a" on K. What do these mean?*

Professor: *They imply that the production function has **constant returns**.*

Student: *You mean, if labor L and capital K are both multiplied by t, then output is exactly multiplied by t?*

Professor: *That's right. If we actually write everything out, we have*

$$A(tL)^a (tK)^{1-a} = \left(t^a t^{1-a}\right) AL^a K^{1-a}$$
$$= t^{a+(1-a)} AL^a K^{1-a}$$
$$= t^1 AL^a K^{1-a}.$$

And, since $t^1 = t$, we can see that if L and K are both multiplied by t then output also changes by a factor of t.

Student: *Why do we need it to be that $0 < a < 1$?*

Professor: *This ensures that the marginal productivity of labor and the marginal productivity of capital have some sensible properties. Note that the marginal productivity of labor is*

$$\frac{\partial F(L, K)}{\partial L} = aAL^{a-1} K^{a-1}.$$

You can clearly see that, if $0 < a$, then the marginal productivity of labor is positive.

*Moreover, if the firm increases labor while holding the amount of capital fixed, then the efficiency of labor will decrease, which means that the marginal productivity of labor will decrease. This is just **the law of diminishing marginal productivity**. That is, the marginal productivity of labor $\frac{\partial F(L, K)}{\partial L}$ decreases as L increases. We can rephrase the previous statement as "the derivative of $\frac{\partial F(L, K)}{\partial L}$ with respect to L is negative." Taking this derivative, we have it that*

$$\frac{\partial^2 F(L, K)}{\partial L^2} = a(a - 1)AL^{a-2}K^{a-1}.$$

And, if $0 < a < 1$, then indeed we can see that $\frac{\partial^2 F(L, K)}{\partial L^2}$ is negative, so the marginal productivity of labor is decreasing. An analogous argument holds for the marginal productivity of capital.

Student: I see. I think now I understand why the production function could take this form. So, if I solve the short-run profit maximization problem, since K is fixed in the short run, we can choose L optimally and maximize the profit

$$\pi = py - wL = pF(L, K) - wL.$$

Is that right?

Professor: Exactly. Recall that the profit-maximizing point is the peak of the graph showing the relationship between profit π (on the vertical axis) and labor L (on the horizontal axis). At the peak of the curve, the slope of the tangent line is exactly zero. If we calculate the profit-maximizing point using this...

Student: Since the slope of the profit curve is given by the derivative of π with respect to L, I know that at the profit-maximizing point

$$\frac{\partial \pi}{\partial L} = p\frac{\partial F}{\partial L} - w = 0.$$

If I plug in $\frac{\partial F}{\partial L} = aAL^{a-1}K^{a-1}$ to this equation, I get the profit maximization condition

$$paAL^{a-1}K^{a-1} = w. \tag{11}$$

But how can I compute the labor–cost ratio, $\frac{wL}{py}$?

Professor: Isn't the left-hand side of (11) similar to $py = pAL^aK^{1-a}$, which is the denominator of the labor–cost ratio?

Student: Ah, yeah, the left-hand side of (11) looks like $py = pAL^aK^{1-a}$ divided by L... I see it now! If I divide $py = pAL^aK^{1-a}$ by L and multiply by a, then I get the left-hand side of (11). So I can rewrite (11) as

$$a\frac{py}{L} = w.$$

So the labor–cost ratio is just $\frac{wL}{py} = a$!

Answer: The profit maximization condition is

$$p\frac{\partial F}{\partial L} = paAL^{a-1}K^{1-a} = w,$$

and the labor–cost ratio is

$$\frac{wL}{py} = a.$$

(cont.)

Student: *In this model, even if the output price p and wage w change, the labor–cost ratio is always equal to the constant a – right? Going back to the data we looked at, does this mean that the behavior of food-manufacturing and auto-manufacturing firms, which have stable labor–cost ratios, can be well approximated using the production function that appeared in this problem?*

Professor: *You bet. Moreover, can't we use the data to figure out the value of the model parameter a?*

Student: *Looking back at Figure 2.62, the labor–cost ratios of the food- and auto-manufacturing industries are roughly 0.14. So, this must mean that a = 0.14!*

Professor: *Roughly speaking, that's correct.[16] The production function in this problem,*

$$F(L, K) = AL^a K^{1-a},$$

*is called the **Cobb–Douglas production function**. The coefficient A in front of $L^a K^{1-a}$ is sometimes called the total factor productivity, or TFP for short. In perfectly competitive markets, the power a on L is equal to the share of revenue that's paid to the firm's workers $\frac{wL}{py}$ and the power 1 – a on K is equal to the share of revenue that's paid to the owners of the firm's capital.[17] Since Cobb–Douglas production functions are so tractable and do a good job of capturing certain aspects of reality, they are very frequently used to do economic analysis in fields such as macroeconomics and international trade. Therefore, it's a good idea to master how to handle it. The economist Paul Douglas discovered that the ratio of labor income to gross domestic income (i.e. the **wage share**, which is the economy-wide analog of the labor cost share for the firm) in the United States is quite stable over time. This prompted Douglas to ask his colleague, the mathematician Charles Cobb, whether there was a model that could explain this fact, which resulted in the discovery of this model.*

---

[16] If we were being more rigorous about fitting the model to the data, we'd have to consider inputs other than labor and capital, such as raw materials. The point that I want to you understand from this exercise is that even simple mathematical models can do surprisingly well at replicating features of real-world data. Of course, by making models more complicated, we can always do a better job of matching the data. Hopefully you can see the potential of using mathematical models to do empirical analysis.

[17] Since a is equal to the share of revenue that is paid to the firm's workers, the remaining share $1 - a$ is the profit the owner of the firm's capital receives.

3   Market Equilibrium

3.1   Partial Equilibrium Analysis

Above we have learned about consumers and producers. What happens when they meet in the market? Let us start out by focusing on a single market under the assumption that *other things* (including other market prices and income levels) *are equal*. This sort of approach is known as **partial equilibrium analysis**. After acquiring a solid grasp of the basics, we then move on to "general equilibrium analysis" – simultaneous analysis of all markets – in Section 3.3.

(a)   Market Demand and Market Supply

In Chapter 1 we learned how demand is determined at the individual consumer level. Let us now suppose that there are I consumers in total and write Consumer i's demand for a given good as $D^i(P)(i = 1, \ldots, I)s$, where P is the price of the good in question. Demand at the market level (**market demand**) can then be expressed as

$$D(P) = D^1(P) + \cdots + D^1(P),$$

meaning that *the market demand curve is obtained as the horizontal summation of all individual demand curves* (Figure 3.1).

We similarly suppose that there are J firms in total and write Firm j's demand for a given good as $S^j(P)(j = 1, \ldots, J)$. Supply at the market level (**market supply**) can then be expressed as

$$S(P) = S^1(P) + \cdots + S^J(P),$$

meaning that *the market supply curve is obtained as the horizontal summation of all individual supply curves* (Figure 3.2).

The intersection of the market demand curve and the market supply curve constitutes the **market equilibrium**, at which quantity supplied equals quantity demanded (Figure 3.3).

In other words, the equilibrium price P^* and equilibrium quantity Q^* are – in a perfectly competitive market – determined so as to achieve a "balance" between demand and supply. This balance is achieved via the following sort of price adjustment. If the market price is higher

Figure 3.1 Market demand curve

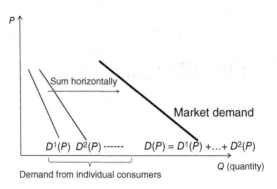

Figure 3.2 Market supply curve

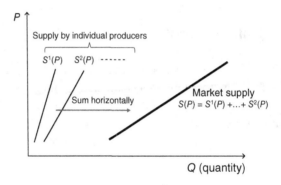

Figure 3.3 Market equilibrium

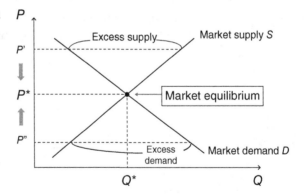

than the equilibrium price, as in the case of P' in Figure 3.3, then the market will be in a state of **excess supply** (supply > demand). Prices will then fall as a consequence of goods going unsold. Conversely, if the market price is lower than the equilibrium price, as in the case of P'' in Figure 3.3, then the market will be in a state of **excess demand** (demand > supply). Prices will then rise as a consequence of competition between buyers. This sort of price adjustment mechanism will ultimately lead the market to an equilibrium in which supply is equal to demand.

Comment 3.1 Cost-of-Production Theory of Value versus Utility Theory of Value

Back when economics was first formalized in the nineteenth century there were two competing schools of thought regarding the price determination mechanism. Economists such as David Ricardo and Karl Marx argued for the so-called "cost-of-production theory of value," or a belief that the price of a good is determined by the cost of producing it, while others such as Hermann Heinrich Gossen, William Stanley Jevons, and Léon Walras favored the "utility theory of value," or a contention that price is instead determined by the degree of desirability of the good.

These two schools of thought have been combined in modern economics, which shows that price is determined by the balance between supply (the key focus of the cost theory of value) and demand (the key focus of the utility theory of value). As was memorably explained by English economist Alfred Marshall toward the end of the nineteenth century, "We might as reasonably dispute whether it is the upper or the lower blade of a pair of scissors that cuts a piece of paper, as whether value is governed by utility or cost of production." In other words, it is pointless to focus on cost at the exclusion of utility, or vice versa; just as both scissor blades play a vital role in cutting a piece of paper, modern economics reveals that the price of a good is determined by the interaction of supply (cost) and demand (utility).

It is surprising that it ended up taking the best part of a century for the founders of economics to arrive at this basic understanding of the market mechanism, which perhaps seems almost trivially simple with the benefit of modern-day insight. As we discussed in the introduction to this book, while people are prone to believe that they fully understand the various social problems that they observe and encounter in day-to-day life, this "conventional wisdom" may at times turn out to be completely mistaken. Moreover, many may be reluctant to rethink their long-held views even when confronted with evidence to the contrary. The math models of microeconomics have been successful in overcoming those cognitive limitations. The merit of math models is the use of a massive division of labor, with a slew of contributors working to ensure that various economic phenomena are accurately captured within a shared and easy-to-understand theoretical framework.

So, what is observed in practice is the intersection between demand and supply. But care needs to be taken about this simple fact in a number of respects. Let us first consider the following two claims.

(A) Supply will increase as the price rises.

(B) The price will fall as supply increases.

Both claims might seem intuitively reasonable, but they are of course completely contradictory as stated. So which is correct, and which is wrong? Both claims are in fact correct, albeit with each needing to be considered in a different context. Figure 3.4 should help to explain what I mean.

(A) is talking about *a movement along the supply curve*, as shown in Figure 3.4 (a), with supply indeed increasing as the price rises. (B) instead refers to *a shift in the supply curve*, as shown in Figure 3.4 (b). (B) could thus be more accurately stated as "the price will fall as the

Figure 3.4 Increase in supply and change in price

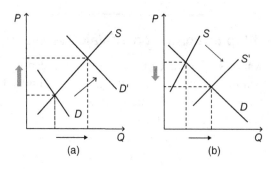

Figure 3.5 Careless estimation of the demand curve

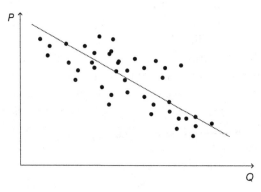

supply curve shifts to the right," thereby rendering it compatible with (A) and its reference to a movement along the supply curve.

This should illustrate the importance of distinguishing between "movements along the supply curve" and "shifts in the supply curve" when performing economic analysis. **Shift parameters** that may trigger movements in (as opposed to along) the supply curve and/or demand curve include the number of firms, factor prices, weather, income levels, and prices of other goods. **Comparative statics** entails the comparison of equilibrium price and quantity levels before and after some change in one or more shift parameters. Figure 3.4 is an example of comparative statics in its simplest form.

Distinguishing between "movements along the demand or supply curve" and "shifts in the demand or supply curve" is extremely important when using real-world data to perform empirical analysis. Suppose that Figure 3.5 is a scatter plot of price levels and quantities transacted for a given good (say, a tomato) at various points in time. The overall picture is indeed one of a downward-sloping line (to the right), but does that make it reasonable to use some sort of statistical method (such as "least squares") to fit a straight line to the data and characterize that as the "estimated demand curve"? Some may be surprised to learn that the answer is "No." Carelessly fitting a straight line as in Figure 3.5 is liable to result in something quite different from the true demand curve. This is because the scatter plot consists of *points at which the demand and supply curves intersect*. As such, the true demand curve at each given point in time (with two examples shown in Figure 3.6) could turn out to be very different from the single (carelessly) estimated demand curve shown in Figure 3.5.

So, how should we go about estimating the true demand curve? The key is to focus on data that are likely to capture movements along the demand curve. Suppose, for example, that bad

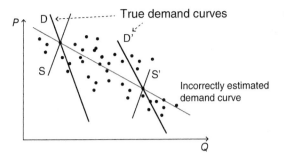

Figure 3.6 True demand and supply

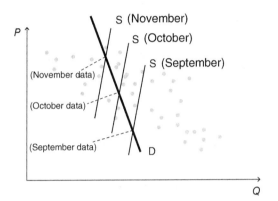

Figure 3.7 Estimating the true demand curve

weather in September, October, and November in a given year causes tomato prices to soar. A reasonable assumption would be that prices have soared due to a weather-driven decline in supply. However, it may also be reasonable to assume that we are dealing with a single demand curve for the (relatively short) period from September through November, with demand determinants such as consumer preferences and income levels unlikely to be fluctuating all that dramatically within the space of just three months. This would imply that the data for September through November are capturing movements along a (non-shifting) demand curve, thereby making it justifiable to fit a single straight line to the September–November data, as shown in Figure 3.7 (with D denoting the true demand curve).

Doing this manually would be cumbersome, if not impossible, but a somewhat more sophisticated extension of the above approach provides us with a smart technique to estimate demand and supply curves separately from real-world data in cases where (i) there are some variables that shift the supply curve only, such as weather or raw materials costs, and (ii) there are other variables that shift the demand curve only, such as income levels or population size. The field of **econometrics** involves the study of techniques for using real-world economic data to perform empirical analysis, where the aforementioned problem boils down to one of the **identification** of supply and demand.

(b)   Long-Run Equilibrium at the Industry Level

Let us next consider the attributes of a long-run market equilibrium. As readers will recall from Section 2.2 (a), the "long run" in a microeconomic context refers to a horizon over which all production factors can be considered variable. In other words, firms are assumed to have sufficient time to adjust even those factors such as plants and production equipment that must essentially be treated as "fixed" over shorter periods. Long-run equilibrium analysis *at the industry level* also assumes that:

- firms are **free to enter and exit**; and
- all firms are able to use the same technologies.

The latter assumption is equivalent to saying that the most efficient technology should become known to all firms given sufficient time.

  We begin by considering how firms decide whether to enter or exit. Firms might reasonably be expected to enter a given industry when it offers higher profits than can be earned in other industries, while the availability of higher profits elsewhere could end up triggering an exodus. The entry condition can be expressed as follows if we use the term **normal profits** to describe what can be earned in other industries over the long run:

$$\text{A given industry experiences new entry} \Leftrightarrow \text{sales} - \text{costs} > \qquad \text{normal profits} \qquad (1)$$
$$\uparrow \qquad\qquad\qquad \uparrow$$
$$\text{that industry's profits} \quad \text{profits available in other}$$
$$\text{industries}$$

  Let us take a closer look at how an entry decision is made. Entering a given industry will require the expenditure of resources such as business savvy and start-up capital. These resources could instead be used to earn normal profits elsewhere, implying that forgone normal profits need to be viewed as a form of cost. This concept of **opportunity cost** enables us to rewrite the entry condition (1) as follows:

$$\text{A given industry experiences new entry} \Leftrightarrow \text{sales} - (\text{costs} + \text{normal profits}) > 0$$
$$\uparrow$$
$$\textbf{the opportunity cost associated}$$
$$\text{with devoting resouces}$$
$$\text{industry}$$

In other words:

> A given industry experiences new entry
> $\Leftrightarrow \text{sales} - \text{costs}((\textbf{including opportunity costs}) > 0$
> (profits are positive after factoring in opportunity costs).

Long-run equilibrium analysis at the industry level thus assumes that "costs" include not only costs in the accounting sense but also the normal profits that could be earned by expending business savvy and capital elsewhere. **The entry condition then boils down to "profits are positive after factoring in opportunity costs."**

  This framework can be generalized as follows.

---

(1) The **opportunity cost** associated with using given resources for a given purpose is equal to the maximum profit that could be generated by using those resources for some other purpose.

(2) One should use given resources for a given purpose if **the benefit** of doing so **exceeds the opportunity cost** – i.e. if **profits are positive after factoring in opportunity costs**.

A concrete example should help to make this clearer.

Case Study 3.1 Running a Restaurant in One's Own Building

Suppose that Sally runs a restaurant in a building that she owns and could otherwise earn $6,000 in rental income by letting out the same space. The cost of using one's own building is zero in accounting terms, but rises to $6,000 once this opportunity cost is also factored into the equation. This implies that Sally would need to earn at least $6,000 from her restaurant in order to justify keeping it open rather than seeking a tenant. While it might be tempting to say "Well, I own the space anyway, so it doesn't matter if the restaurant isn't all that successful," in reality allowance will need to be made for the rental income that could be earned by letting that same space out to someone else (opportunity cost). An operating profit of $5,000 might appear impressive at first glance, but would actually mean that the restaurant is running at a loss after subtracting out the $6,000 in opportunity costs (forgone rental income). There is, unfortunately, a considerable body of anecdotal evidence suggesting that failure to properly account for opportunity costs may too frequently result in valuable business opportunities going unexploited.

Let us now use the above cost concept to analyze long-run equilibrium at the industry level. Dividing both sides of the entry condition (1) by output, we obtain:

$$\text{Price } p = \frac{\text{long-run costs (costs + normal profits)}}{\text{output}}$$

$$= \text{long-run average cost (LAC)}$$

Satisfying this condition – meaning that entry should occur – will require industry profits to be higher than normal profits.

Suppose that the industry in question is currently at point A in Figure 3.8 (a), and that the situation faced by individual firms is as described by Figure 3.8 (b).

Each firm will supply its output up to the point where the price is equal to long-run marginal cost (LMC) ($Q = 100$ in Figure 3.8 (b)). The difference between the price at that output level of

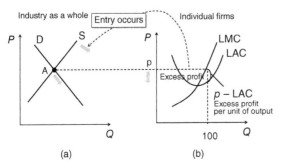

Figure 3.8 Entry and the long-run industry equilibrium

Figure 3.9 When do firms stop entering?

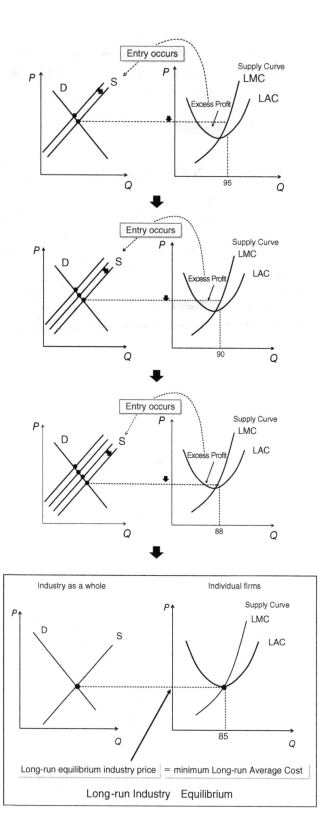

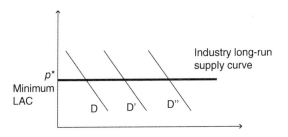

Figure 3.10 Industry long-run supply curve

100 and long-run average cost ($p - $ LAC) corresponds to **excess profit** per unit of output. This is because LAC includes normal profits. The shaded area in Figure 3.8 (b) thus corresponds to total excess profit. This availability of excess profits should attract new entrants, thereby causing the supply curve to shift rightward, as shown in Figure 3.8 (b), with prices falling as a result. Assuming that each individual entrant is sufficiently small relative to the overall market, the price should fall gradually with each instance of new entry, thereby (eventually) driving excess profits down to zero and causing new entry to cease. Figure 3.9 illustrates this process, with the box at the bottom depicting the **industry's long-run equilibrium**. We have thus arrived at the following important relationship:

> Long-run equilibrium industry price = minimum long-run average cost (LAC)

We conclude by considering an industry's long-run equilibrium in the face of fluctuating demand. The analysis above shows that, in the long run, the price will always end up gravitating toward the level that is equal to the minimum LAC after fluctuations in demand have caused new firms to enter and/or existing firms to exit. Joining up these post-adjustment points leaves us with a horizontal line at which the price p* is equal to the minimum LAC, as shown in Figure 3.10. This is the **industry's long-run supply curve**.

(c) Consumer Surplus

Economists refer to the monetary value of the benefits received by consumers from market transactions as "consumer surplus." We begin with a (not necessarily all that rigorous) intuitive explanation and then proceed with a more formal treatment couched in the consumer behavior framework laid out in Chapter 1.

[i] An intuitive explanation

Sally is considering buying one or more laptops and views the situation as follows.

- She is willing to pay up to $1,200 for the first laptop.
- She is willing to pay up to $800 for the second laptop.
- She is willing to pay up to $200 for the third laptop.

Assuming that the laptops are priced at $500, she will end up buying two laptops based on the following decision-making process.

Figure 3.11 Demand for laptops and consumer surplus

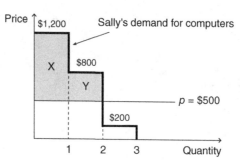

- First: amount she is willing to pay ($1,200) > price ($500)
  → Buy
- Second: amount she is willing to pay ($800) > price ($500)
  → Buy
- Third: amount she is willing to pay ($200) < price ($500)
  → Don't buy

Sally's demand curve is as shown in Figure 3.11. Note that its stepped shape stems from the fact that the amount of laptops takes on values 1, 2, 3, ... and cannot be varied continuously; below we will consider an example where the amount consumed can be varied more continuously, as in the case of gasoline.

How much has Sally "gained" from her purchase of two laptops? Her effective gain on the first laptop is $700, corresponding to the difference between the price she was willing to pay ($1,200) and the price she was required to pay ($500). This is denoted by the area X in Figure 3.11.

X in Figure 3.11 (1,200 – 500 = $700) = gain from purchasing first laptop

Similarly:

Y in Figure 3.11 (800 – 500 = $300) = gain from purchasing second laptop

In other words, Sally's purchase of two laptops made her better off to the tune of X + Y (700 + 300 = $1,000). It is this shaded area X + Y that we refer to as **consumer surplus**.

The same reasoning applies for products such as gasoline, where the amount consumed can be varied continuously. In Figure 3.12 consumer surplus – *or the increase in consumer satisfaction derived from a market transaction* – corresponds to the area bounded by the market price and the consumer's demand curve.

[ii] A more rigorous explanation

In order to make our explanation more precise – and ensure that consumer surplus can indeed be depicted as shown in Figure 3.12 – *we need to impose the requirement that the consumer's utility function takes a particular form.*

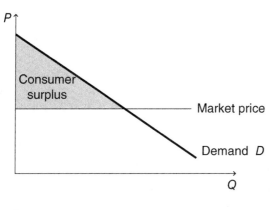

Figure 3.12 Consumer surplus with continuous consumption

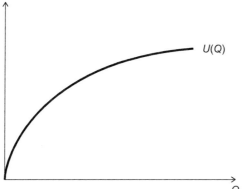

Figure 3.13 Shape of $U(Q)$

Suppose that $V(Q, m)$ denotes the utility derived from purchasing Q liters of Coke and then using one's remaining money m to consume other (non-Coke) goods in optimal fashion. Let us also suppose that this function takes the form

$$V(Q, m) = U(Q) + m.$$

This equation is linear only in m; for this reason, we refer to V as a **quasilinear utility function**. I want to draw your attention to a hidden but very important message of the above formula: in the above inequality, we are adding together the utility $U(Q)$ and the monetary amount m, which implies that *utility $U(Q)$ can be viewed as the monetary value of the benefit derived from consuming Q liters of Coke*. For example, if $U(Q) = 10$, then we can say that our consumer derives $10 worth of benefit (utility) from drinking Q liters of Coke. We also assume that $U(Q)$ – the utility derived from Coke – is concave (bowed upward), as shown in Figure 3.13.[1] This basically means that the marginal utility of Coke (the slope of the graph) declines as the quantity consumed (Q) increases.

When the utility function is quasilinear, the benefit derived by the consumer from the market can be expressed as consumer surplus. Let us now explain what we mean by this.

---

[1] As we learned in Section 2.3 (c), a function with a graph that is bowed upward is known as a concave function.

Figure 3.14 Demand curve under quasilinear utility

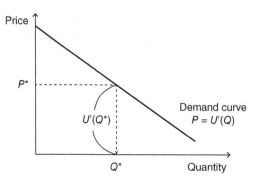

More specifically, provided that the above assumptions are satisfied, we will explain that the optimal level of consumption Q under price P is determined by

$$P = U'(Q).$$

First, consider the case where $U'(Q) = 2$ at the current level of consumption. Then the consumer is \$2 better off if she drinks another unit of Coke. If Coke is priced at \$1 per unit, then the net gain from drinking another unit of Coke will be $U'(Q) - P$, or $2 - 1 = \$1$. The consumer should therefore keep on drinking for as long as $U'(Q) > P$, and, by the same token, she should decrease her consumption if $U'(Q) < P$. This means that the optimal amount of Coke must satisfy $P = U'(Q)$. In other words, for a given price P, the optimal level of demand (consumption) will be that at which $U'(Q) = P$.

For the consumer to be able to purchase the optimal amount of Coke Q that satisfies $U'(Q) = P$, she needs sufficient income (i.e. income more than PQ). So, when economists say that the consumer has quasi-linear utility, not only the utility function has a special form $V(Q,m) = U(Q) + m$, but also it is assumed that the consumer has enough income to purchse the optimal amout given by $P = U'(Q)$. Note that, as long as the consumer has enough income, the optimal consumption level (or demand) is insensitive to the change in income and always equal to the same amount Q that satisfies $P = U'(Q)$. This leads us to the very important observation that there are *no income effects* under quasilinear utility.

The above argument is summarized by Figure 3.14. In other words, *given quasilinear utility, we find that the height of the demand curve denotes the marginal utility $U'(Q)$, or the marginal monetary benefit, of the good in question.*

The demand curve $P = U'(Q)$ is downward-sloping, as shown in Figure 3.14, because marginal utility $U'(Q)$ usually decreases as Q increases.

Quasilinear utility also enables us to view utility as the monetary value of the benefit derived by the consumer. For example, $U(Q) = 10$ *means that the consumer is \$10 better off if she consumes Q units of the good.* Adding up (or integrating) marginal utility for all the amounts up to and including Q gives us the shaded area in Figure 3.15, which corresponds to *the total utility (monetary value) derived from drinking Q liters of Coke,* or $U(Q)$.[2]

Subtracting the total amount paid – $P \times Q$, or the area of the rectangle $PBQ0$ in Figure 3.15 – gives us the net benefit derived from the market transaction, or the area of the triangle APB. This corresponds to consumer surplus.

---

[2] Here our utility function is "normalized" such that $U(0) = 0$, meaning that no utility is derived from zero consumption.

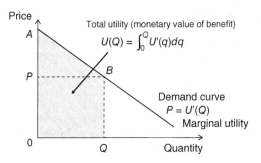

Figure 3.15 Consumer utility under quasilinear utility

The above can be summarized as follows.

When a consumer has a **quasilinear utility function** (and sufficient income):

(i)   the benefit derived by the consumer from the market can be expressed as **consumer surplus**; and

(ii) income effects are zero.

The point of the above discussion is *not* to say that quasilinear utility is realistic and that it is safe to assume that these assumptions are satisfied but, rather, to explain that analysis of surplus is actually possible only when the utility function takes a particular form. So why do we assume this special form[3] in the first place?

- Analysis of surplus (based on the strong assumption of quasilinear utility) provides us with an intuitive means of analyzing market mechanisms.
- Analysis of surplus can be used to identify facts – for example, "Efficiency will be impeded by policies that distort market prices" – that will very often also hold true more generally (that is, *without* imposing the strong assumption of quasilinear utility).

In other words, microeconomics starts out by explaining market mechanisms using a simple (but somewhat "special") framework that enables analysis of surplus, and then uses more sophisticated techniques to show that the same points apply more generally.

These "more sophisticated techniques" come into play from Section 3.3, where we discuss general equilibrium analysis and what are known as the *fundamental theorems of welfare economics*.[4] But let us first use a number of concrete examples to demonstrate the power of the partial equilibrium analysis of surplus.

---

[3] We usually do not know exactly the kind of utility functions that consumers have, and, even if we do, it might be very rare that the utility functions are exactly quasilinear. This leads us to the following very important question: given that consumers have general utility functions that are not quasilinear, when can we assert that the consumer's surplus is a reasonably accurate representation of consumer benefit? A rigorous analysis (presented in Appendix C) reveals that *consumer surplus is an accurate measure of consumer benefit if and only if there are no income effects*. So, when analyzing the market for Coke, for example, if Coke has small income effects, then we can safely use consumer surplus to (approximately) measure consumer benefit.

[4] See Appendix C for a discussion of how to use the demand function to estimate the benefit derived by a consumer under (more realistic) circumstances, where the strong assumption of quasilinear utility does not hold true.

(d)   Putting Partial Equilibrium Analysis to Practical Use

We next show how the concepts of partial equilibrium analysis and consumer surplus can be used to demonstrate that taxes cause markets to lose their efficiency.

[i] Inefficiency of indirect taxes

Figure 3.16 shows the equilibrium in the beer market in the absence of taxes. Under the conditions discussed in Section 3.1 (c), the benefit derived by a consumer of Coke beer can be expressed as consumer surplus. There is also a concept of "producer surplus," which is, roughly speaking, equivalent to profits (or, more precisely, to the profit remaining before subtracting out the producer's sunk fixed costs[5]). Total surplus is equal to the sum of producer surplus and consumer surplus, and represents the total benefit to society that is derived from transactions in the beer market.

If an **indirect tax** (liquor excise) is imposed, then that will make the price paid by the consumer that much higher than the price received by the producer. There are, basically, two ways in which an indirect tax can be applied. If we express the price paid by the consumer as P^D, the price received by the producer as P^S, and the tax rate as t, then a per-unit or **specific tax** is one for which

$$P^D = P^S + t.$$

A liquor excise falls into this category: as of 2022, a ¥70 tax was applicable to each 350 ml can of beer sold in Japan (meaning that $t = 70$ in the above equation). In contrast, a percentage or **ad valorem tax** is calculated as some fixed proportion of sales, such that

$$P^D = P^S(1 + t).$$

Japan's consumption tax is an example, with the government applying a 10 percent tax to sales as of 2022 (meaning that $t = 0.10$ in the above equation). Since the two taxes have similar impacts, we use the example of a per-unit alcohol tax for the following analysis.

The equilibrium in a market where beer is taxed is as shown in Figure 3.17. The price paid by the consumer is P^D, meaning that demand is equal to Q^0. The price received by the producer is P^S, with supply once again equal to Q^0. Figure 3.17 thus shows a situation in which demand

Figure 3.16 Beer market equilibrium without taxation

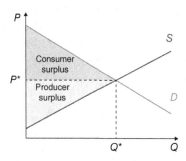

---

[5] Readers may recall that we discussed the relationship between sunk fixed costs, producer surplus, and profits in Section 2.2 (c).

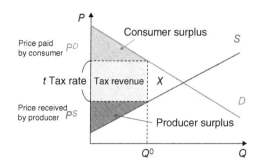

Figure 3.17 Equilibrium and surplus under indirect taxation

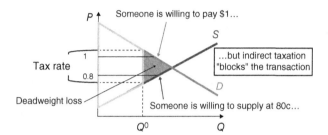

Figure 3.18 Reason for deadweight loss

is equal to supply. Where an indirect tax is applicable, the price P^D paid by the consumer and the price P^S received by the producer are determined so as to equate demand and supply. Total surplus under this framework is equal to the sum of consumer surplus, government tax revenue, and producer surplus. Each of these areas has been identified in Figure 3.17. It can be seen that total surplus is less than in Figure 3.16 – where no indirect tax applied – to the tune of the area of the triangle denoted by X. This reduction in total surplus is known as a **deadweight loss**. We have thus shown how *the existence of an indirect tax makes the market less efficient by causing total surplus to decline.*

What is the source of this inefficiency? As illustrated in Figure 3.18, the deadweight loss arises due to the indirect tax preventing transactions from taking place between a consumer who would be willing to buy at a high price (such as $1) and a producer that would be willing to sell at a lower price (such as 80¢).

[ii] Pareto improvements and lump-sum taxes

Abolishing indirect taxes would boost total surplus for society as a whole, but would leave the government without the revenues needed to fund essential services. So how can taxes be collected in a more efficient fashion?

The answer is not to touch the price of beer while charging *a fixed tax amount* that is not affected by the volume of beer supplied and consumed, or what is known as a **lump-sum tax**.

Abolishing the alcohol tax results in a new equilibrium with price P^* and quantity Q^*, as shown in Figure 3.19. By charging the consumer T_1 and the producer T_2, the government will be able to raise the same amount of revenue as it did using an indirect tax without causing total

Figure 3.19 Equilibrium and surplus under lump-sum taxation

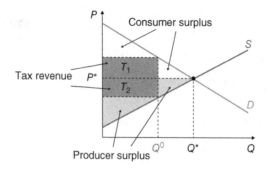

surplus to be reduced. It can also be seen that both the consumer and the producer receive greater surplus than they did in Figure 3.17. In other words, switching from an indirect tax to a lump-sum tax will leave both consumers and producers more satisfied without reducing the amount of revenue received by the government. This sort of "win-win" arrangement – a change that harms no one and benefits at least one economic agent – is known as a **Pareto improvement**.[6]

Comment 3.2 Won't Demand Fall under a Fixed Tax?

Won't charging the consumer T_1 in tax as shown in Figure 3.19 reduce her income and thereby cause demand to fall? This is a perfectly reasonable question: as we discussed above, if beer is a "normal good", then demand for beer should indeed drop away as income falls, meaning that the demand curve will shift downward and to the left. However, as readers will recall from Section 3.1 (c) above, when analyzing surplus we are assuming that the consumer has a quasi-linear utility function, meaning that income effects are non-existent. In other words, *analysis of surplus – premised as it is on quasilinear utility – does not make allowance for shifts in the demand curve due to transfers of income.* That said, our basic conclusion – that switching from an indirect tax to a lump-sum tax constitutes a Pareto improvement – remains the same even if we do allow for demand to be impacted by transfers of income. We explain this point in the context of general equilibrium analysis in Section 3.3 (j).

Let us now summarize our key conclusions derived from analysis of surplus.

– **The market equilibrium maximizes total surplus** (Figure 3.20).
– Indirect taxes are inefficient (entailing a loss of surplus).
– A **lump-sum tax** – whereby the government collects a fixed amount irrespective of the level of economic activity (consumption, production, etc.) – does not entail any such loss of efficiency (surplus).

So what are some concrete examples of lump-sum taxes? Personal and corporate income taxes do *not* fall under this category. For example, personal income tax payments are determined by

---

[6] A more detailed discussion of Pareto improvements can be found in Section 3.3 (f).

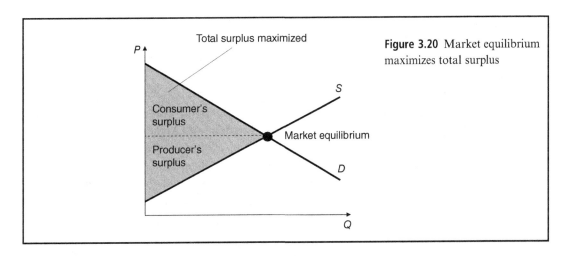

Figure 3.20 Market equilibrium maximizes total surplus

the amount of labor income received, and will therefore vary depending on the level of economic activity (supply and demand in the labor market). Similarly, corporate income tax payments depend on the amount of profits generated by the business in question. A per capita or poll tax, whereby each person is required to pay the same amount, is perhaps the best "real-world" example of something close to a lump-sum tax, although that "real world" did admittedly exist only from ancient times through the Middle Ages. So why are lump-sum taxes so seldom used in practice despite their demonstrable theoretical advantages from a theoretical perspective?

– The amount of tax that can be paid by individuals and businesses will depend on the level of economic activity (including income and profit levels), meaning that a lump-sum tax – levied irrespective of the level of economic activity – may leave some individuals and businesses unable to meet their payment obligations.
– Economic changes (such as a change in policy) may have significant pros and cons for individuals and firms. Using a lump-sum tax to make a Pareto improvement in response to such changes will require different tax amounts to be imposed on different individuals and firms. However, calculating these amounts is far from easy, and there may also be significant political resistance to the idea of imposing higher taxes on some people than on others.

These practical obstacles notwithstanding, understanding that a lump-sum tax can be used to achieve more efficient allocations should prove invaluable when contemplating potential policy actions and their ability to improve upon the status quo. This point should become clearer from the following section.

3.2 What You Need to Know about the Trans-Pacific Partnership: TPP and Liberalization of Rice Imports

The frameworks of partial equilibrium analysis and broader economic theory are extremely useful when thinking about topical issues and assessing policies. In this section we address a particularly contentious issue by using partial equilibrium analysis to perform full-fledged economic analysis of the Trans-Pacific Partnership (TPP). It should become clear from the following discussion how taking a microeconomic perspective helps in identifying the types of data that need to be collected and investigated in order to estimate the impact of "liberalization" at each level of society.

The TPP agreement is aimed at *creating a new free trade zone* through the elimination of tariffs, and it was signed by Brunei, Chile, Singapore, New Zealand, the United States, Australia, Peru, Vietnam, Malaysia, Japan, Canada, and Mexico in 2016. Later, in 2017, the United States dropped out, and the remaining 11 countries signed a revised agreement, called the CPTTP (Comprehensive and Progressive Agreement for Trans-Pacific Partnership), in 2018. The basic idea is that all tariffs should be eliminated for trade between its members, but there is still scope for limited exceptions. Below we take the example of rice tariffs in demonstrating how the use of microeconomic tools (partial equilibrium analysis) can serve to illustrate both *the pros and cons of free trade*.

(i) How do we obtain the rice supply curve?

One important question is the degree to which TPP might impact on the livelihoods of agricultural households. A closely linked question is the degree to which a liberalization-driven decline in the price of rice might reduce domestic rice supply, for which reason we start out by investigating the rice supply curve.

However, practical issues soon arise. The price of rice has never been as low as it will probably be once liberalization kicks in, meaning that we have no real way of knowing just how much supply might disappear. But, rather than just giving up, we can use our knowledge of production theory – or the fact that the supply curve is essentially the same as the marginal cost curve – for the purposes of estimation. The marginal cost curve can then be obtained as the differential of total cost with respect to output... OK, OK, I hear you screaming that this is hardly making things any easier.

But please stick with me. Let's start with Figure 3.21.

It is not all that unreasonable to assume that the cost of producing a kilogram of rice will be constant for each farming household. Below we make an *important* distinction between

(1) c*osts that must be paid to other people*, such as in order to purchase seeds and fertilizer or for help in harvesting; and
(2) *costs associated with using one's own production factors*, such as family labor and family-owned land.

Each farming household has an inverse-L-shaped supply curve determined by these factors, and starting with the lowest-cost household and "summing" the individual supply curves enables us to obtain the nationwide supply curve, as shown in Figure 3.21 (b). Let us next explain why this is so.

The (given) price p in Figure 3.21 (b) is higher than Household A's unit cost of production ((1) + (2) above, including raw material costs and compensation for family labor), meaning that Household A will produce rice. But the price p is meanwhile too low to cover the unit costs

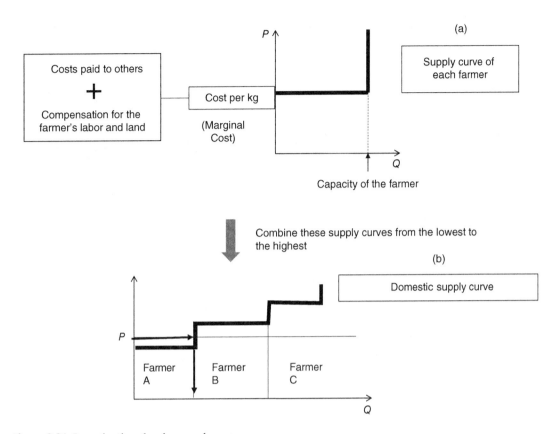

Figure 3.21 Investigating the rice supply curve

for Households B and C, meaning that they will not produce rice. The supply of rice thus ends up being determined by the supply curve shown in Figure 3.21 (b).[7]

We would ideally like to know each farming household's cost of producing a kilogram of rice, but the availability of such data is obviously too much to hope for. However, we do know that rice production costs vary with land area (the size of the farmland), with larger rice paddies able to produce rice more efficiently (at lower cost). The Ministry of Agriculture, Forestry and Fisheries (MAFF) does indeed publish statistics on average production cost by land area, grouping rice-producing households into categories such as "over 15 hectares" (ha) or "10–15 hectares". Figure 3.22 (a) shows a plot of the data for 2010.

Strictly speaking, we should be dealing with an eight-stepped graph given that there are eight categories of households ("over 15 hectares," "10–15 hectares," etc.), but we have smoothed this out into a curve that slopes upward to the right under the assumption that each category will include both large and small farming households, with costs effectively varying in near-continuous fashion as a result. Moreover, although we were unable to find information on each

---

[7] Recall that we used the same approach in Case Study 2.2 when using generation costs for individual plants to derive Tohoku Electric Power's marginal cost curve.

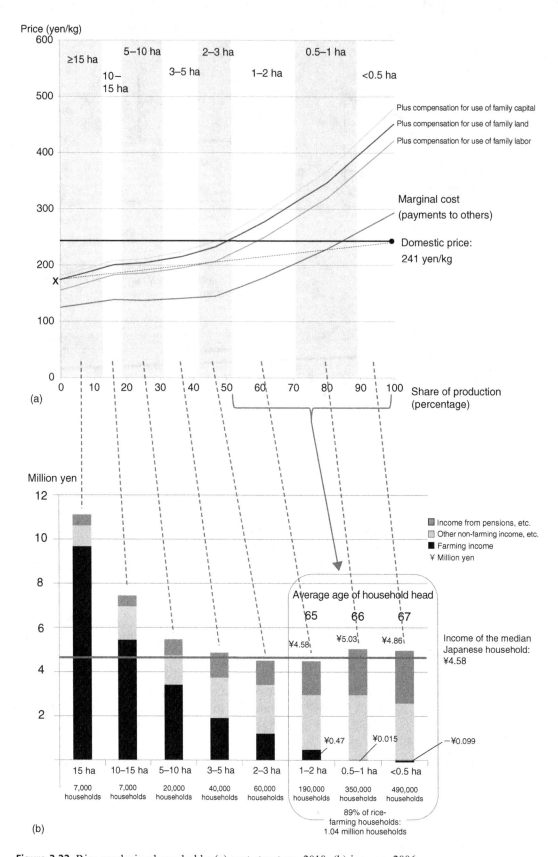

Figure 3.22 Rice-producing households: (a) cost structure, 2010; (b) income, 2006

category's production capacity, the total size of farmlands is published,[8] and Figure 3.22 assumes that the production capacity of each category is proportional to the total size of the farmland in the category.[9]

The next point is important: MAFF statistics use the following market prices for the purpose of estimating costs for household-owned production factors.

Cost of family labor = average wage for small manufacturers.

Cost of family land = rent that could be received if let out to another small rice producer.

Cost of family capital = 4 percent annual interest.

If all people seek compensation for these costs listed above, then the supply curve will be the highest curve shown in Figure 3.22 (a). Conversely, the supply curve will be lower if some people are prepared to produce rice without being fully compensated.

How do rice producers look to compensate themselves for use of their own labor and land in practice? Figure 3.22 (a) offers a slightly surprising insight, with the "domestic rice price"[10] turning out to be quite low by comparison with costs. But households of all sizes nevertheless opted to produce rice. With this in mind, we next set aside our estimation of the supply curve for the time being and use the aforementioned cost structure to investigate the actual income levels of rice-producing households.

(ii) What sort of people produce rice?

Looking at the relationship between the price of rice and costs for smaller rice-producing households with land of 2 ha or less (corresponding to the right half of Figure 3.22 (a)), we find the following.

– In the 1ha – 2ha category the rice price is roughly equal to the cost of family labor (as estimated by MAFF) plus costs paid to other people, meaning that such households basically receive *the "standard" labor income for a small business* but are not compensated for use of their own land or capital.

– In the 0.5 ha – 1 ha category households receive *only meager compensation for their own labor*.

– In the < 0.5 ha category *rice is being produced at a loss*, with the price not even enough to cover costs paid to other people.

Figure 3.22 (*cont.*)

Note: Since there are only recent data on bonuses, which are part of the wage, I did the calculations without including bonuses, even though this is slightly inaccurate.

Sources: (a): Ministry of Agriculture, Forestry and Fisheries, *Report on Results of 2010 World Census of Agriculture and Forestry in Japan* (Tokyo: MAFF, 2011); (b): Ministry of Health, Labour and Welfare, "Comprehensive Survey of Living Conditions" (Tokyo: Ministry of Health, Labour and Welfare, 2006).

[8] As published by MAFF; here we have adjusted the categories for compatibility with our other data sources.

[9] Figure 3.22 (a) may actually be underestimating the capacity of big producers, as larger farms are in reality likely to obtain better yields for a given area.

[10] Here we have used the average wholesale brown rice price for 2006 to 2011 with a view to smoothing out year-to-year fluctuations.

In other words, the statistics show that households are producing rice even when they are not "fairly" compensated for doing so (as assessed in terms of market prices). Moreover, *around a half of Japan's total rice supply comes from the aforementioned households that are struggling to eke out a profit.* This should help put to rest the popular myth that rice-producing households benefit from generous government subsidies and thus live an easy life. But a detailed look at the data reveals that there is more to the story than just that.

The above data might suggest that micro rice producers – those with no more than 2ha to farm – are among Japan's lowest-income households, but is that actually the case? Figure 3.22 (b) addresses this question using (admittedly slightly old) data for 2006.[11] Surprisingly, these *micro rice producers turn out to have comparable incomes to middle-class Japanese households.*[12] As should be clear from the income breakdowns in Figure 3.22 (b), this is because *micro rice producers derive most of their income from pensions and other (non-agricultural) sources.* This non-specialization is possible because automation has enabled households to farm areas of around 1ha while expending very little labor. It also bears noting that the average age of the "proprietor" of a rice-producing household is quite high. In other words, the supply of rice by micro producers relies quite heavily on the retired elderly as a labor source. Finally, it is also surprising to learn that, *although micro rice producers account for around 50 percent of total output, they actually account for the lion's share (89 percent) of all rice-producing households.*

Focusing on the enclosed portion of Figure 3.22 (b), the attributes of an "average" Japanese rice-producing household – i.e. one of the 1.04 million households that account for almost 90 percent of the total – can perhaps be summarized as follows.

– Rice is grown using only around 1 ha of land (100 m by 100 m, or roughly the size of a baseball field).
– Rice production is only a supplementary source of income, with labor supplied mostly on days off and by the retired elderly (with automation helping to make things easier).
– Average total household income is on par with the "middle class," with agricultural income making only a very small contribution (somewhere between ¥(−100,000) and ¥500,000 per year).
– Rice production appears to be motivated by something other than profitability (such as a desire to carry on family traditions to produce rice).
– Micro rice producers typically have elderly proprietors who are also receiving a pension.

(iii) Estimating the rice supply curve

Let us now get back to estimating the rice supply curve. Given that all producers in Figure 3.22 (a) were supplying rice at a price of ¥241 per kilogram, the supply curve should be an upward-sloping

---

[11] Once again I have used MAFF data, this time from a 2007 White Paper. However, I have used 2010 data on household numbers for consistency with Figure 3.22 (a).

[12] Figure 3.22 (b) shows median household income for 2006, or the income earned by the household that falls precisely in the middle when ordered from poorest to richest.

curve passing through the black circle at the right edge of the chart. Moreover, except for the smallest rice producers, for whom income from rice production constitutes only a very small percentage of their total income, we can assume that households will be looking to (1) cover all costs that must be paid to others and (2) receive some amount of compensation for their provision of labor and land. This implies that the supply curve should lie somewhere between the lowest and highest curves shown in Figure 3.22 (a). Because we have no real idea as to the curve's shape, we have assumed a linear supply curve, as denoted by the dotted line.

Point X at the left edge of Figure 3.22 (a) – the lowest point on the supply curve – is important when considering the potential ramifications of liberalization. For example, if $X = ¥190$, then that implies that Japanese rice production would be wiped out altogether if liberalization were to drive the price of rice below ¥190. Given this importance, it is worth going to some effort to justify our estimate. The statistics on which we based Figure 3.22 (a) indicate that the most efficient rice producers (in the ≥ 15 ha category) have an average total cost (including all compensation for owned production factors) of ¥192/kg. However, not all producers within this category will be equally efficient, so we must also ask what costs are faced by the most efficient producers and how much rice they are capable of producing.

Detailed statistics on the distribution of costs are, fortunately, available,[13] and indicate that the most competitive farming households face a unit cost (including all compensation for owned production factors) of ¥132/kg. Moreover, *households facing a unit cost less than or equal to ¥168/kg account for some 5 percent of total rice production.* We have therefore used a conservative estimate of ¥170/kg for the lowest point on the supply curve (X in Figure 3.22 (a)).

(iv) Rice market equilibrium prior to liberalization

Let us now use our estimated supply function to illustrate the pre-liberalization state of the Japanese rice market. Doing so requires us to *estimate the rice demand function.* Prior research indicates that demand for rice has an extremely low price elasticity, in the order of 0.13,[14] meaning that a 1 percent fall in price will cause demand to increase only by around 0.13 percent. For the purposes of our analysis we thus assume that demand for rice exhibits constant price elasticity (of 0.13) and that the curve passes through the actually observed price/quantity combination.

Figure 3.23 shows the pre-liberalization rice market equilibrium and is intended to reflect real-world data to the greatest extent possible. Japanese rice production for 2010 totaled some 8.5 million tonnes.[15] The "Supply subject to production adjustments" curve has been estimated as explained above, using actual cost data for the farming households that supplied this 8.5 million tonnes of rice.

One important point needs to be explained regarding Japanese rice production. The domestic rice price is determined in the free market, but MAFF looks to keep the price artificially high

[13] MAFF data on rice production costs include a frequency distribution for the total cost of producing 60 kg.

[14] Toshiyuki Kako, Masahiko Gemma, and Shoichi Ito, "Implications of the Minimum Access Rice Import on Supply and Demand of Rice in Japan," *Agricultural Economics*, 16(3) (1997), 193–204.

[15] MAFF data for "irrigated rice."

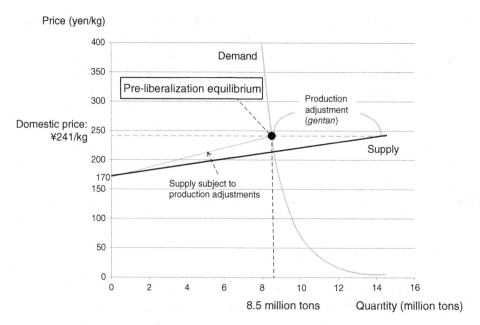

Figure 3.23 The pre-liberalization rice market

via a quota-based program known as *gentan*, or "output reduction." Our best estimate is that these production adjustments serve to reduce output by around 40 percent.[16] Roughly speaking, the program asks all domestic rice producers to use around 40 percent of their land for other crops. Compliance is not strictly mandatory, but is rewarded via subsidies. "Supply subject to production adjustments" can thus be viewed as 60 percent of the "true" supply in the absence of the *gentan* program,[17] which is what we have denoted by "Supply" in Figure 3.23.

(v) By how much will the price of rice fall as a result of liberalization?

Quantifying the impact of liberalization next requires us to investigate the price of rice. Rice imports are currently subject to a tariff of ¥341/kg.[18] This tariff of ¥341/kg is significantly higher than the domestic rice price of around ¥241/kg, and can thus be considered prohibitively high in the sense that *no rice whatsoever would be imported even if the foreign rice price were to be zero.*

[16] Figures on the area of rice paddies subject to *gentan* production adjustments are only available through 2003 (40 percent for that year), at which point MAFF switched to more direct output reductions. The *gentan* system itself was abolished in FY2018.

[17] In other words, we are effectively assuming that each household uses only 60 percent of its true supply capacity to produce rice. Some producers opt not to comply with the program, assessing that subsidies are not worth the (opportunity) cost of reducing output. If high-productivity large producers do not comply with the program, then "supply" in Figure 3.23 may turn out to be overestimating the supply capacity of those producers.

[18] This figure is taken from the Ministry of Finance's "Trade Statistics of Japan," and excludes government imports for special purposes.

So where should the price of rice end up if the aforementioned tariff is abolished under TPP? Answering this is not simple, given that "rice" comes in a range of types and qualities. One useful yardstick might be to consider the sort of rice that is chosen by a Japanese person living in the United States, where tariffs on rice imports are virtually zero. In my own experience the Nishiki and Tamaki brands were particularly popular among the local Japanese community. Nishiki was cheap and thus popular with students, while Tamaki is closer in taste to "made in Japan" rice and would therefore be favored by wealthier expatriates and their families. To the best of my knowledge, none of my Japanese acquaintances ate cheaper short grain prices. Let us now compare the retail prices of these rice products in the United States with comparable domestic rice products sold in supermarkets in Japan.[19]

– Nishiki price/cheap Japanese rice = ¥237/¥400 = 59%.
– Tamaki price/cheap Japanese rice = ¥349/¥400 = 87%.
– Tamaki price/standard Japanese rice = ¥349/¥500 = 70%.

MAFF has used the price of Chinese short grain rice in estimating that TPP-based liberalization would reduce the price to one-quarter of current levels,[20] but this appears to be an overestimate of the price impact. Based on the above price comparison, we assume that *liberalization would cause the price of rice to fall by 25 percent* (as opposed to 75 percent), *from ¥241 to ¥181 per kilogram.*

(vi) How will liberalization impact domestic rice production?

Figure 3.24 shows the post-liberalization rice market equilibrium based on the above assumptions. Free entry of rice from overseas will make it impossible to keep prices artificially high via *gentan* production adjustments. We have thus assumed that liberalization will result in abolition of the *gentan* program, meaning that we can use the "Supply" curve – as opposed to the "Supply subject to production adjustments" curve – from Figure 3.23. The key points regarding the post-liberalization state of the rice market are as follows.

– Post-liberalization consumption is determined by the intersection of the post-liberalization price (¥181/kg) with the demand curve (the "Post-liberalization equilibrium" dot in Figure 3.24).
– Domestic production at the post-liberalization price is determined by the supply curve ("Domestic production" in Figure 3.24).
– The difference between consumption and domestic production corresponds to the quantity of imports ("Imports" in Figure 3.24).

---

[19] At the time of investigation, the website for California-headquartered Japanese grocery store chain Mitsuwa Marketplace listed prices of $16.88/lb for Nishiki and $24.99/lb for Tamaki Gold. I have converted this based on an exchange rate of $1 = ¥95. The retail prices listed here are higher than the domestic rice price (¥241/kg) discussed above because the latter is the wholesale price for unmilled brown rice. Milling rice entails removal of the husk and the bran layers, and thus has a significant impact on the per-kilogram price.

[20] Based on National Policy Unit materials released (in Japanese only) on 27 October 2010.

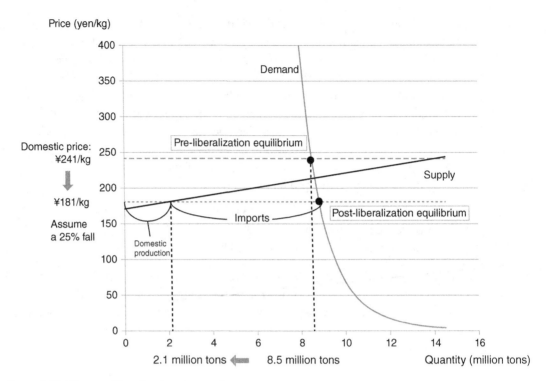

Figure 3.24 The post-liberalization rice market

If our various assumptions are correct and domestic production does drop to 2.1 million tonnes as a result of liberalization, that would translate into a massive 75 percent reduction from current levels. Moreover, the figure of 2.1 million tonnes would be roughly equal to current output by large producers with at least 15 ha in land. The "75%" figure may of course be sensitive to our assumptions, given that even a small change in the shape of the (quite flat) supply curve in Figure 3.24 is liable to have a major impact on the equilibrium production level, but it does seem reasonably safe to conclude that *small producers growing rice as a supplementary income source* – who account for some 90 percent of all Japanese rice-producing households, and were already struggling to make a profit even at the pre-liberalization price – *are likely to find things even harder in a post-liberalization world.*

(vii) Who will benefit from liberalization?

So, who stands to benefit from the liberalization of Japanese rice imports? Figure 3.25 is based on a comparison of the pre-liberalization (Figure 3.23) and post-liberalization (Figure 3.24) markets and looks at consumer surplus (consumer benefits) and producer surplus (rice producer profits).

It can be seen that producer surplus is reduced significantly by liberalization, but that this is more than offset by an increase in consumer surplus. Figure 3.26 shows the increase in the shaded area (total surplus) obtained by moving from the top to the bottom chart in Figure 3.25, with this net increase in total surplus corresponding to the benefit of liberalization to the Japanese economy as a whole.

This benefit consists mostly of *cost savings to consumers as they become free to purchase rice from countries with lower production costs* (denoted by the light gray shading in Figure 3.26), but also includes the profits stemming from increased consumption at lower prices (darker gray shading on the right) and more efficient use of agricultural land due to abolition of the *gentan* system (darker gray shading on the left).

These points can be summarized as follows.

Gains from Free Trade

– Liberalization is negative for domestic rice producers but positive for consumers (Figure 3.25).
– The benefits to consumers exceed the hit to domestic rice producers (Figure 3.26).

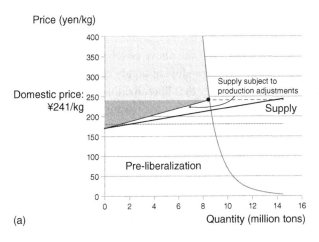

(a)

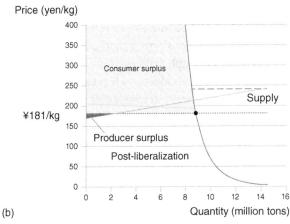

(b)

Figure 3.25 Change in surplus due to the liberalization of rice imports

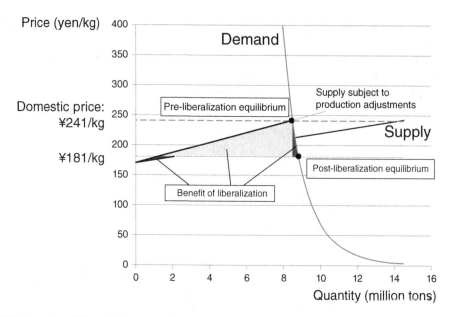

Figure 3.26 Benefit of liberalization to Japan as a whole

It should be clear from Figures 3.25 and 3.26 that **the above conclusion will hold true for all shapes of downward-sloping demand curves and upward-sloping supply curves. In other words, our microeconomic analysis has demonstrated conclusively that liberalization will be a net positive** for the Japanese economy as a whole, with gains invariably exceeding losses. (Those who are worried about the fates of those suffering losses need only wait for two more paragraphs until Subsection (viii).)

Let us next look more closely at who benefits from liberalization. Rice is a staple food for most people living in Japan, meaning that lower prices will tend to benefit most members of the population. But, as illustrated in Figure 3.27, the greatest benefit will be seen by people for whom food accounts for a substantial proportion of total expenditures.

Engel's coefficient measures the percentage of total household expenditures that is accounted for by food. Figure 3.27 groups households into seven equally sized categories by income, ranging from lowest income at the left to highest income at the right. The overall picture is clearly one of higher-income households having lower Engel's coefficients. This observation is known as **Engel's law.** The roughly 30 percent of people with the lowest income in Figure 3.27 (in Groups 1 and 2) spend around 40 percent of their budgets on food and thus stand to benefit disproportionately from liberalization (lower rice prices). *It would thus be wrong to suppose that liberalization is only of benefit to the rich.* There were around 14 million households in Groups 1 and 2 – corresponding roughly to annual income of less than ¥3 million – as of 2012.[21] *The biggest "victims" of liberalization, meanwhile, will be the roughly 1.04 million small rice producers* that collectively account for some 90 percent of all rice-producing households (here it is

[21] Based on figures from the Ministry of Health, Labour and Welfare's "Comprehensive Survey of Living Conditions" for FY2011.

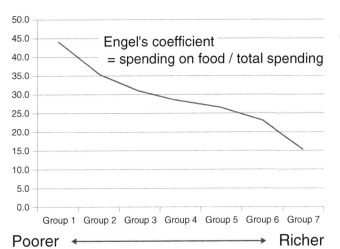

Figure 3.27 Income level versus food expenditures, Tokyo, 2012

perhaps worth reviewing the enclosed portion of Figure 3.22 (b)). Talk of liberalization being a "net positive" is all well and good, but it is clearly also important to understand just who stands to benefit and who is likely to be left worse off.

(viii) Should rice imports be liberalized?

The above focuses solely on the impact of liberalization and is thus an example of what we earlier (in the Introduction) termed **positive analysis**. The next step is to perform **normative analysis**, by making a value judgment as to whether or not liberalizing rice imports would be the "right" option.

In subsection (vii) we learned that the total benefit received by consumers as a result of liberalization exceeds the total damage suffered by rice-farming households. It should thus be possible to devise some sort of arrangement whereby consumers pay **subsidies** to rice-farming households so that *all participants in the economy can end up benefiting from liberalization*.

How can we do that? Well, the solution in fact ends up being quite simple.

A subsidy scheme that enables everyone to benefit from liberalization:

> – will require each consumer to pay an amount equal to (the amount consumed prior to liberalization) multiplied by (the price fall stemming from liberalization); and
> – will use that revenue to pay each rice-producing household an amount equal to (the amount produced prior to liberalization) multiplied by (the price fall stemming from liberalization).

Let us now explain why this would make each and every participant in the economy happier.[22] We begin by noting that the above subsidy scheme is "balanced," in the sense that

---

[22] A key aspect of this arrangement is that it is based on *pre-liberalization* consumption and production amounts. Consumers are thus being asked to pay a lump-sum tax that is not affected by their post-liberalization consumption behavior, while farming households receive a lump-sum subsidy that is not affected by their post-liberalization production behavior. We have already seen in Section 3.1 (d) that lump-sum taxes entail no inefficiency, and the same also turns out to be true for lump-sum subsidies.

the total amount paid by consumers is equal to the total amount received by farming house-holds. This stems from the fact that the total amount being consumed prior to liberalization was equal to the total amount being produced.

Consider things from the perspective of the consumer. Liberalization makes rice cheaper, meaning that money will be left over if pre-liberalization consumption levels are maintained. Note that this leftover amount is exactly equal to the amount each consumer is supposed to pay in the above subsidy scheme, and therefore *sticking with the previous consumption amount is a viable option if one so desires under the scheme.* In reality, consumption behavior is likely to be altered as a consequence of rice becoming cheaper. Such a change in behavior – despite the previous consumption pattern still being attainable – can be viewed as clear evidence of consumers having benefited from liberalization under the above subsidy scheme.

This also holds true for producers, who would be *able to generate the same income as before* by sticking with the pre-liberalization production level and receiving the aforementioned subsidy. However, it should be possible to achieve an even better outcome – i.e. a higher level of satisfaction – by choosing the level of production that is optimal at the post-liberalization price. The above framework thus enables both consumers and producers to benefit from liberalization while leaving no one worse off.

The reality, of course, is that such a judiciously constructed subsidy scheme may indeed prove difficult to fully implement in practice, in which case some people may end up suffering as a consequence of liberalization while others benefit. The question as to whether liberalization should be allowed to proceed then boils down to a value judgment on the part of voters (or other people with a voice in the decision-making process), while *microeconomics does not tell us the kind of value judgment we should make.* However, what microeconomics can do is ensure that any such value judgment is based on an accurate understanding as to (1) *who will benefit or lose out* as a consequence of liberalization (and to what degree) and (2) *how this might be corrected* via some sort of subsidy scheme whereby money is transferred from "winners" to "losers."[23]

Comment 3.3 What's been missing from the debate over TPP?

The above microeconomic analysis differs quite considerably in tone from the debate that one tends to encounter in the media, where arguments tend to be couched as follows.

– TPP is all about imposing Western rules on other nations; the "Westernization" of Japan would go against its national interests.

---

[23] If domestic rice production ends up falling as a consequence of liberalization, then other potential problems might include negative externalities pertaining to flood control and landscape degradation (as discussed in Chapter 4) as well as a decline in Japan's food self-sufficiency ratio. The latter refers to the risk that Japan might end up being unable to feed its people in the event of some natural disaster or military conflict. However, the same sort of problem also arises when it comes to energy, an area in which Japan has already stopped using domestically available coal in favor of imported oil. Japan has sought to mitigate the risk associated with low energy self-sufficiency by maintaining a roughly half-year stockpile of oil, and concerns about low food self-sufficiency could conceivably be addressed in similar fashion.

– South Korea has been quick to liberalize; Japan runs the risk of becoming internationally uncompetitive if it fails to join the free trade bandwagon.

While such views might appear reasonable at first glance, it is important to recognize that they are *rooted in value judgments that pay little attention to the interests of individual citizens*. There is no intrinsic value associated with "avoiding Westernization" or "joining the free trade bandwagon"; indeed, doing so will be beneficial only to the extent that it somehow enriches the lives of individual citizens. Failure to properly understand who stands to benefit and who stands to lose out from any given change is liable to lead to the following sort of fruitless and emotionally charged arguing.

(1) *Sketchy and sweeping judgments* that effectively ignore the interests of individual citizens.
(2) Rigid insistence on one's own correctness while *branding others with labels* such as "anti-reformist" or "market fundamentalist."
(3) A *refusal to change one's opinion* and/or *blinkered thinking that focuses solely on one's own interests*.

A more productive debate needs to ask just who will benefit and who will lose out if Japan "avoids Westernization" or "fails to ride the global tide towards free trade." Microeconomics offers the ideal tools for this purpose.

Comment 3.4 Problems with Japan's policy-making process

The above case study will hopefully have helped to highlight some of the problems inherent to Japan's economic policy-making process. Rice happens to fall under the remit of the Ministry of Agriculture, Forestry and Fisheries, and there is always some government ministry or agency involved when it comes to the formulation and implementation of policy. MAFF is well known for publishing estimates as to just how much damage TPP would do to Japan, but in doing so fails to make any allowance whatsoever for potential benefits to consumers. More generally, it is typical for the relevant government ministry or agency to appoint a "panel of experts" when some new economic policy is being proposed, but the panel members are mostly the representatives of producers, and all concerned will tend to consider things almost entirely from the perspective of the producer. Improving the nationwide livelihood is obviously not possible if the interests of consumers go completely ignored, but Japan's policy-making process is unfortunately notorious for offering consumers only scant representation at best. Rectifying this situation will require greater *economic literacy* on the part of individual citizens and the mass media, along with a willingness to advocate for consumer interests. Thinking about all of these issues in general and abstract terms may leave one skeptical and unconvinced, but the above case study should have helped to demonstrate that economists are in fact all about walking the walk, not just talking the talk.

3.3   General Equilibrium Analysis

Partial equilibrium analysis focusing on a single market has the advantage of being intuitively easy to follow, but unfortunately it fails to shed light on the various spillover effects that can also impact other markets. Our next step is thus to employ "general equilibrium analysis" to look at all markets simultaneously. The behavior of a single market can generally be understood by drawing on one's own social experience and common sense, but interactions between multiple markets may be harder to keep track of without making appropriate use of mathematical economic models. In explaining this "big picture" framework below we – as usual – take care to illustrate its relevance to real-world economic phenomena.

(a)   Viewing the Economy as a Whole: General Equilibrium Models

We begin by using the subscript $n(=1, \ldots, N)$ to denote all the goods that exist in the economy. The list of all prices p_n that is $p = (p_1, \ldots, p_N)$ is known as the **price profile**. The next step is to incorporate the firms and consumers that comprise the economy into our model.

Firms: we use the subscript $j(=1, \ldots, J)$ to denote all the firms that exist in the economy. In the case of the Japanese economy, the number J would be somewhere in the order of 4.2 million.[24] As we saw in Section 2.4, firm j's production activity can be expressed by the following **production plan**:

$$y^j = \left(y^j_1, \ldots, y^j_N\right).$$

If the nth element of the production plan y^j_n is positive, then it represents firm j's output of good n, while a negative element signifies that firm j is using good n as an input. For example, the production plan $y^j = (-5, 0, 0, 1)$ means that firm j is using five units of good 1 to produce one unit of good 4. The set of all production plans that are feasible for firm j is known as that firm's **production possibility** set (Y^j). This can be determined through thorough investigation of what is and isn't possible for the firm in question, thereby allowing for all firms and their myriad production technologies to be incorporated within a single model of the economy.

Example 3.1

The following should help to illustrate the nature of the production possibility set. In a two-good economy where good $1(n = 1)$ is labor and good $2(n = 2)$ is the output (such as wheat), firm j's production plan entailing the use of labor to produce wheat can be written as follows:

$$y^j = \left(\underset{\substack{(-) \\ \text{labor input}}}{y^j_1}, \quad \underset{\substack{(+) \\ \text{wheat output}}}{y^j_2}\right)$$

---

[24] The total figure for large and smaller enterprises outside the primary industry as of FY2009 is taken from Small and Medium Enterprise Agency statistics.

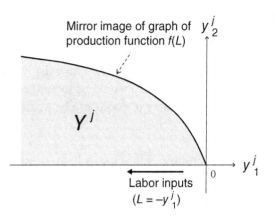

Mirror image of graph of production function $f(L)$

Y^j

Labor inputs
$(L = -y^j_1)$

Figure 3.28 Firm j's production possibility set

For example, if $y^j = (-8, 2)$, then firm j is using eight units of labor to produce two units of wheat. A typical production possibility set for firm j is as shown in Figure 3.28, with the upper boundary of that set corresponding to the production function.

Using the production plan y^j to express production activity, profit can then be expressed very simply as

$$\text{profit} = py^j.$$

Here we should stress that $py^j = p_1 y^j_1 + \cdots + p_N y^j_N$, where $p = (p_1, \ldots, p_{NB})$ and $y^j = \left(y^j_1, \ldots, y^j_N\right)$. For example, in the above case of $y^j = (-8, 2)$, profit is given by

$$y^j = \underset{\text{wages}}{-8p_1} + \underset{\text{sales}}{2p_2}.$$

The profit maximization problem of a perfectly competitive firm can then be expressed as

$$\max_{y^j} py^j$$

$$\text{s.t. } y^j \in Y^j$$

firm j's profit-maximizing behavior

(2)

This optimization problem boils down to requiring firm j to choose the particular feasible production plan that maximizes profit.[25] Each of the millions of firms in an economy can thus be incorporated into our model in this very compact form. The solution to this profit maximization problem (2) is dependent on the price profile p and can thus be written as follows:

[25] "s.t." can be read as either "such that" or "subject to"; "s.t. $y^j \in Y^j$ "thus means "such that y^j is in y^j" or "subject to the constraint that y^j is in y^j."

$$y^j(p) = \text{firm } j\text{'s \textbf{optimal production plan}}$$

Consumers: we use the subscript $i(=1,\ldots,I)$ to denote all the consumers who exist in the economy. Treating each household as a single consumer, the number I would be somewhere in the order of 48 million for Japan.[26] Consumer i's **initial endowment** of goods can be written as

$$w^i = \left(w^i_1, \ldots, w^i_N\right).$$

Corporate profit is ultimately distributed to the public (consumers) in some fashion, which we express as follows:

$$\theta_{ij} = \text{fraction of firm } j\text{'s profit distributed to household } i.$$

Example 3.2

If consumer i owns 10 percent of firm j's stock and is entitled to receive 10 percent of profit as a dividend, then $\theta_{ij} = 0.1$.

$\theta_{1j} + \cdots + \theta_{Ij} = 1$ must hold true for each firm j given that the firm's entire profit must be distributed across consumers $i(=1,\ldots,I)$.

Writing consumer i's **consumption bundle** as $x^i = \left(x^i_1, \ldots, x^i_N\right)$ and recalling that firm j's profit is equal to $py^j(p)$, the **budget constraint** can then be expressed as[27]

$$\underset{\text{spending}}{px^i} \quad = \quad \underset{\text{income from endowment}}{pw^i} \quad + \quad \underset{\text{profit distribution from firms}}{\sum_{j=1}^{J}\theta_{ij}py^j(p)}. \tag{3}$$

Each consumer's optimization problem then boils down to selecting the best consumption bundle (that which maximizes utility) subject to that consumer's budget constraint.

$$\max_{x^i} u^i\left(x^i\right)$$
$$\text{s.t. } px^i = pw^i + \sum_{j=1}^{J}\theta_{ij}py^j(p). \tag{4}$$

consumer i's utility-maximizing behavior

The consumption bundle that solves this problem (4) is dependent on the price profile p and can thus be written as follows:

$$x^i(p) = \text{consumer } i\text{'s \textbf{optimal production bundle}}$$

---

[26] The total number of households in the Ministry of Health, Labour and Welfare's 2012 "Comprehensive Survey of Living Conditions."

[27] Σ means "summing for values of j from 1 to J," meaning that $\sum_{j=1}^{J}\theta_{ij}py^j = \theta_{i1}py^1 + \theta_{i2}py^2 + \ldots + \theta_{iJ}py^J$ (i.e. the sum of profit distribution to consumer i from all firms j).

(b)   Labor supply

Looking at the right-hand side of the budget constraint (3), it may appear as though there is no equivalent of labor income, with the two terms corresponding to "income from endowment" and "profit distribution from firms". However, as we shall now explain, labor income and labor supply are indeed incorporated into the above consumer model. Let us now suppose that one of the goods in the economy, say good 1, is **leisure**, or time spent not working. This point should be a little easier to understand if we consider things from the perspective of consumer i:

- w_1^i = endowment of leisure = 24 hours (each person has 24 hours that they are free to devote to leisure)
- x_1^i = consumption of leisure (that portion of the 24 hours that is actually devoted to leisure)
- $w_1^i - x_1^i$ supply of labor (that portion of the 24 hours that is spent working rather than on leisure)

p_1, or the price of the good corresponding to leisure/labor supply, can then be interpreted as the wage.

Let us now revisit the budget constraint. (3) can be expanded as follows:

$$\boxed{p_1 x_1^i} + \left(p_2 x_2^i + \cdots + p_N x_N^i\right) = p_1 w_1^i + \left(p_2 w_2^i + \cdots + p_N w_N^i\right) + \sum_{j=1}^{J} \theta_{ij} p y^j(p)$$

Moving the first term on the left over to the right hand side of the equation gives us

$$\overset{A}{\left(p_2 x_2^i + \cdots + p_N x_N^i\right)} = p_1 \underset{\substack{\text{24 hours} - \text{non-work hours} \\ \text{wage} \times \text{work hours} \\ \text{labor income}}}{\underbrace{\left(w_1^i - x_1^i\right)}} + \overset{C}{\left(p_2 w_2^i + \cdots + p_N w_N^i\right)} + \overset{D}{\sum_{j=1}^{J} \theta_{ij} p y^j(p)}$$

It should therefore be clear that the budget constraint (3) for the general equilibrium model does indeed incorporate the concept of labor income.

$$\underset{\text{spending}}{A} = \underset{\text{labor income}}{B} + \underset{\text{income from endowment}}{C} + \underset{\text{profit distributions received}}{D}$$

So how is labor supply determined? To keep things simple we assume that there are just two goods – good 1 = leisure and good 2 = consumption good – and that labor income is the sole income source. The consumer's behavior for this simple case, where x_1 = consumption of leisure and p_1 = wage, is determined by the following optimization problem:

$$\max_{x_1, x_2} u(x_1, x_2)$$

$$\text{s.t. } \underset{\text{spending}}{p_2 x_2} = \underset{\text{labor income}}{p_1(24 - x_1)}. \tag{5}$$

Work hours are equal to the endowment of leisure w_1 (= 24 hours) minus consumption of leisure x_1, while labor income is equal to work hours multiplied by the wage p_1. It should be intuitively obvious that leisure x_1 confers positive utility (like other goods), given that it is generally a case of "the more, the better." The budget constraint for the labor supply problem (5) can be rewritten as follows:

$$x_2 = \frac{p_1}{p_2} 24 - \boxed{\frac{p_1}{p_2}} x_1$$
$$\underset{\text{slope}}{}$$

The slope of the straight line (budget line) denoting the budget constraint is thus given by the price ratio p_1/p_2.

Substituting $x_1 = 24$ into this equation gives $x_2 = 0$. *The budget line must therefore pass through the point labelled "24" on the horizontal axis in Figure 3.29.* This means that, if all 24 hours are devoted to leisure ($x_1 = 24$), then the consumer has zero income and is thus unable to buy any of the consumption good ($x_2 = 0$). No work, no consumption. Optimal labor supply is determined, as shown in Figure 3.29, as the point where the budget line is tangential to the consumer's indifference curve.

"Tangential" means that the slope of the indifference curve will be equal to the slope of the budget curve (p_1/p_2) at this optimal point. Recalling what we learned about consumer behavior in Section 1.5 (c), the slope of the indifference curve (marginal rate of substitution) is equal to marginal cost, meaning that labor supply ends up being determined by the following:

$$\underset{\text{MRS (indifference curve slope)}}{\frac{\partial u/\partial x_1}{\partial u/\partial x_2}} = \underset{\text{price ratio (budget line slope)}}{\frac{p_1}{p_2}} \tag{6}$$

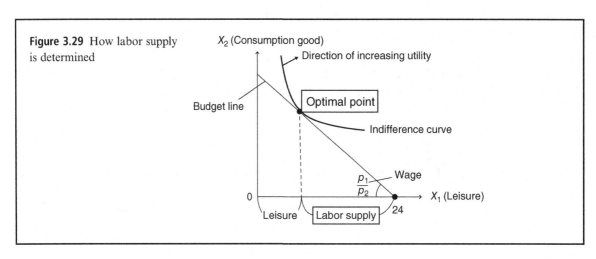

Figure 3.29 How labor supply is determined

$\partial u / \partial x_1$ – the numerator of the fraction on the left-hand side – is the marginal utility of leisure. The numerator on the right-hand side is the wage p_1, meaning that we are basically just saying that the wage is proportional to the marginal utility of leisure. That alone may mean little, but a different interpretation should help. $\partial u / \partial x_1$ is the marginal utility of leisure, meaning that an incremental reduction in leisure will reduce satisfaction (utility) by $\partial u / \partial x_1$. Reducing leisure means increasing time spent working, meaning that $\partial u / \partial x_1$ can also be viewed as *the reduction in satisfaction resulting from an incremental increase in work hours, or the marginal disutility of labor.* The above optimality condition (6) can then be written in word form as follows:

$$\frac{\text{marginal disutility of labor}}{\text{marginal utility of consumption good}} = \frac{\text{wage}}{\text{consumption good price}}$$

optimal labor supply condition

In other words, from the perspective of the person supplying labor, *the wage is proportional to the marginal disutility of labor (marginal utility of leisure).* This makes perfect intuitive sense. If you ask people to work a little more and they complain that they really don't want to (implying a high marginal disutility of labor), then you will need to pay them a high wage in order to get them to work. Conversely, if people say that they would have no problem whatsoever working a little more (implying a low marginal disutility of labor), then a low wage should suffice.

Let us next consider how a change in the wage level may impact labor supply. Changing the wage p_1 in Figure 3.29 will typically cause the optimal point to shift, as shown in Figure 3.30. Increasing the wage from a low level will lead to an increase in labor supply as people see a high incentive to work, but supply will eventually start declining once the wage level rises beyond a certain point. For example, a person who is willing to work a full eight-hour shift if paid $10 an

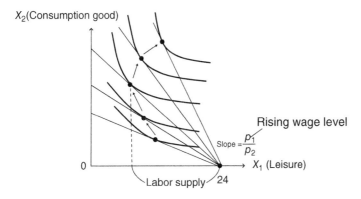

Figure 3.30 How does a change in the wage level impact labor supply?

Figure 3.31 The labor supply curve may often be backward-bending

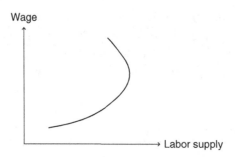

hour might very well be content to work just two hours at an hourly wage of $500. Linking optimal points leads us to the **backward-bending labor supply curve** shown in Figure 3.31, which can probably be considered representative of most workers (consumers).

(c)   General Equilibrium Models (continued)

The economy as a whole can then be completely described as follows:[28]

$$
(u^i, \qquad w^i, \qquad Y^j, \qquad \theta^{ij}) \quad \begin{array}{l} i=1,...,I \\ j=1,...,J \end{array}
$$

utility of each consumer | endowment of each consumer | production possibility set of each firm | profit share

Let us now use the optimal production plan $y^j(p)$, which solves firm j's profit maximization problem, and the optimal consumption bundle $x^i(p)$, which solves consumer i's utility maximization problem, to define the following. Our purpose in doing so is to investigate demand and supply at the economy-wide level.

$$
y(p) = \sum_{j=1}^{J} y^j(p) \quad \text{(aggregate production plan)}
$$

$$
x(p) = \sum_{i=1}^{I} x^i(p) \quad \text{(aggregate consumption bundle)}
$$

Recall once again that $y(p)$, $x(p)$, and w are not single numbers but, rather, vectors comprised of multiple elements (for example, $y(p) = (y_1(p), \ldots, y_N(p))$). The supply/demand equilibrium in the market for good n can then be expressed as

---

[28] As we explained in Section 1.1, individual utility u^i represents individual preferences $\succsim^i$, which may in turn be represented by a range of different utility functions. A more precise description of the economy might therefore be $(\succsim, w^i, Y^j, \theta_{ij})_{j=1,...,J}^{i=1,...,I}$. Note also that the government sector is an important part of the economy but has been omitted here for simplification purposes.

$$x_n(p) = \underset{\text{output}-\text{input}}{y_n(p)} + \underset{\text{original endowment}}{w_n}$$

$$\underset{\text{demand}}{x_n(p)} = \underset{\text{output}-\text{input}}{y_n(p)} + \underset{\text{original endowment}}{w_n}$$

Subtracting the right from the left gives us the **excess demand function** for good n:

$$z_n(p) = x_n(p) - y_n(p) - w_n.$$

If this is positive ($z_n(p) > 0$), then good n is scarce in the sense that demand exceeds supply. Conversely, negative excess demand means that supply of good n exceeds demand. Zero excess demand signifies that the market for good n is in equilibrium, with supply and demand in perfect balance. Let us now simplify our notation by using $z(p)$ to denote the excess demand vector $(z_1(p), \ldots, z_N(p))$.

The following condition in all markets is then satisfied by the equilibrium price profile $p^* = (p_1^*, \ldots, p_N^*)$:

$$z_n(p^*) = 0, \quad n = 1, \ldots, N.$$

The economy's **resource allocation**, which I explained in the Introduction, is thus given by:

$x^1(p^*), \ldots, x^I(p^*)$	Who receives how much of what?
$y^1(p^*), \ldots, y^J(p^*)$	Who makes how much of what, and how?

This **general equilibrium model** is a clear-cut and full-fledged mathematical formulation of what has been variously described as the "market mechanism," "price mechanism" or "capitalist economy" since the days of Adam Smith. Below we use this general equilibrium model to examine market functions in greater detail.

(d) Properties of the Excess Demand Function

What properties must be satisfied by an excess demand function, and what are their significance?

(i) Walras's law

Excess demand for any particular good cannot be completely independent of excess demand for others, although this may not be apparent without some clearly specified model of the economy as a whole. Below we explain what "Walras's law" tells us about interdependences across various markets.

Walras's law is derived from the following consumer budget constraint:

$$px^i(p) = pw^i + \sum_{j=1}^{J} \theta_{ij}py^j(p).$$

Summing across all consumers $i (= 1, \ldots, I)$ gives us the following:

$$p\sum_{i=1}^{I} x^i(p) = p\sum_{i=1}^{I} w^i + \sum_{i=1}^{I}\sum_{J=1}^{J} \theta_{ij}py^j(p).$$

The final term on the right-hand side is the total profit received by consumers, which must be equal to the total profit generated by producers given that no profit is left undistributed.

Actually calculating this should help to make things clearer. Changing the order of summation makes no difference:

$$\sum_{i=1}^{I} \boxed{\sum_{j=1}^{J} \theta_{ij}} = \sum_{j=1}^{J} \boxed{\sum_{i=1}^{I} \theta_{ij}}$$

(1) first sum across all firms j

(2) then sum across all consumers i

(1) first sum across all consumers i

(2) then sum across all firms j

The right-hand side can then be rewritten as follows using the fact that all profit is distributed to consumers ($\sum_{i=1}^{I} \theta_{ij} = 1$):

$$= \sum_{j=1}^{J} \left(\sum_{i=1}^{I} \theta_{ij} \right) py^j(p) = \sum_{j=1}^{J} py^j(p).$$

This is indeed equal to the total profit generated by producers ($py^i(p)$).

Adding together all of the household budget constraints thus gives us

$$p \sum_{i=1}^{I} x^i(p) = p \sum_{i=1}^{I} w^i + p \sum_{j=1}^{J} y^j(p)$$

Using the aggregate consumption bundle x, aggregate endowment w, and aggregate production plan y – as defined above in (c) – we then arrive at the following very simple equation:

$$px(p) = pw + py(p)$$

This can be rewritten as

$$p(x(p) - w - y(p)) = 0$$

Recalling that $z(p) = x(p) - w - y(p)$ is excess demand, we are able to state Walras's law as follows:

For all price profiles p and excess demand functions $z(p), pz(p) = 0$, or:

$$p_1 z_1(p) + \cdots + p_N z_N(p) = 0. \qquad (7)$$

Walras's law thus boils down to a statement that the values of excess demand must sum to zero. This implies the following in the case where all prices are positive (i.e. no good is "free").

- The existence of excess demand in one market means that there must be excess supply in some other market.
- If $N - 1$ out of N markets are in equilibrium, then the remaining market must also be in equilibrium.

Walras's law plays an important role in macroeconomics and trade theory as a basic expression of interdependences across various markets.

Example 3.3

A simple macroeconomic model consists of markets in two goods, namely a consumption good and labor. Looking at the equilibria for any two of these markets is sufficient in order to gain a complete picture. In other words, if, say, the consumption good market is in equilibrium, then Walras's law tells us that the labor market must also be in equilibrium.

(ii) Homogeneity of degree zero

How will firms and consumers react if all prices are multiplied by t? Let us now suppose that the original price profile $p = (p_1, \ldots, p_N)$ is replaced by the new price profile $tp = (tp_1, \ldots, tp_N)$.

We start with the behavior of firms. After all prices have been multiplied by t, firm j will choose the feasible production plan $y^j \in Y^j$ that maximizes its profit tpy^j. This is the optimal production plan $y^j(tp)$ under the new price profile tp. The optimal production plan under the old price profile $p - y^j(p)$ – maximized profit under the old price profile, or py^j. Let us now consider the relationship between these two production plans.

Because tpy^j is simply py^j multiplied by t, it turns out that maximizing tpy^j is the same as maximizing py^j (i.e. maximizing py^j will also maximize tpy^j). This means that the new production plan maximizing tpy^j, or $y^j(tp)$, is the same as the old production plan maximizing py^j, or $y^j(p)$. In other words, the firm's optimal production plan remains unchanged even if all prices are multiplied by t.

Let us now offer a more intuitive explanation. Suppose that the US government wishes to redenominate its currency in terms of cents. This will effectively mean replacing the old price profile p with a new price profile tp, where $t = 100$. This change – which is basically just a relabeling of the currency – should have no impact on the determination of the optimal production level. That is the meaning of optimal production plan $y^j(tp)$ being equal to optimal production plan $y^j(p)$. In other words, *a firm's optimal production plan is not affected even if all prices are multiplied by t*:

For all p and $t > 0$ and for each firm j,

$$y^j(tp) = y^j(p). \tag{8}$$

The function $y^j(p)$ is said to be **homogeneous of degree zero** if (8) holds true.

What about consumer behavior? After all prices are multiplied by t, the budget constraint becomes

$$tpx^i(p) = tpw^i + \sum_{j=1}^{J} \theta_{ij} tpy^j(tp).$$

Using the fact that $y^j(tp) = y^j(p)$ (as we discovered above) and dividing both sides by t, we obtain the following budget constraint:

$$px^i(p) = pw^i + \sum_{j=1}^{J} \theta_{ij} py^j(p).$$

In other words, multiplying all prices by p has no impact on the budget constraint. This in turn implies that *the optimal consumption bundle will also be the same as before*:

For all p and $t > 0$ and for each firm j,

$$x^i(tp) = x^i(p).$$

Combining the above tells us that the excess demand function $z(p) = x(p) - w - y(p)$ is also homogeneous of degree zero.

For all p and $t > 0$, the excess demand function $z(p)$ satisfies the condition

$$z(tp) = z(p).$$
homogeneity of degree zero of the excess demand function

What this tells us is that, if p^* is an equilibrium price profile $(z(p^*) = 0)$, then tp^* – or the vector of prices obtained by multiplying each individual price by t – will also be an equilibrium price profile $(z(tp^*) = 0)$. In other words, *equilibrium turns out to be determined by price ratios (relative prices) as opposed to absolute price levels*.

Some might consider this a divergence from reality (where prices are uniquely determined), but the following should help in understanding why this is not actually the case. In an actual economy, price levels are determined by setting the price of the good known as "currency equal to one." This good is called the **numeraire**.

Example 3.4

The equilibrium in an economy consisting of just apples (good 1) and gold (good 2) will be determined solely by the apple/gold price ratio (relative price) p_1/p_2. For example, if the equilibrium price ratio is $p_1/p_2 = 2/5$ and if one gram of gold is used to make a coin that is then called a "dollar," then the price profile will be given by $p = (2/5, 1)$ (meaning that the price of an apple is $2/5 = 0.4$ dollars). Price levels in this economy are thus determined with gold serving as the numeraire.

This example may have been applicable during the era of the gold standard, but price levels in the US economy of today are effectively determined using a \$1 bill – i.e. a type of good known as "currency" – as the numeraire. It should thus be clear that the situation described above whereby all prices are multiplied by t does *not* correspond to inflation, or a situation in which the price of a \$1 bill remains at \$1 but all other (non-currency) prices are multiplied by t. Inflation is a phenomenon where the value of a special good – known as currency – is reduced in relative terms, whereas multiplication of all prices by t (without exception) corresponds to redenomination or a change in the units in which a currency is denominated (such that what used to be referred to as "\$1" is subsequently referred to as "\$$t$"). Redenomination leaves all relative prices unchanged, including for the currency good. Saying that the excess demand function is homogeneous of degree zero simply means that a redenomination of the currency will have no impact on the real economy, which is of course what one would expect unless people are susceptible to (currency) illusions.

(e)   Existence of an Equilibrium

> ### Comment 3.5
>
> This section (e) covers a more advanced topic, but is designed to be comprehensible without much mathematical background knowledge. I would therefore urge even those readers who consider themselves "allergic" to advanced topics to at least peruse the discussion that follows, which offers some valuable insight into a fundamental problem in economics and the way in which they are analyzed.

Is it really possible for us to find a price profile $p^* = (p_1^*, \ldots, p_N^*)$ that supports simultaneous equilibrium in all markets? This is not as purely technical a question as it might appear at first glance. The desirability of market equilibrium is one of the central tenets of microeconomics, so the whole point is lost if market equilibrium simply does not exist.

Therefore, we must seriously examine if an equilibrium price profile actually exists. It is obviously not immediately apparent whether a solution $p^* = (p_1^*, \ldots, p_N^*)$ does in fact exist for the set of simultaneous equations $z_1(p) = 0 \ldots, z_N(p) = 0$. Even the quadratic equations that we studied in high school did not always have solutions (at least in real numbers), so some might understandably start to lose hope when it comes to a much larger system of potentially more complex equations.

This extremely important problem in the field of theoretical economics was in fact solved back in the 1950s, and, quite remarkably, it turns out that a system of prices consistent with simultaneous equilibrium in all markets does indeed exist under extremely general conditions. Below we sketch out the process of proving this.

We begin by generalizing the conditions for market equilibrium. Above we have equated equilibrium in market n with zero excess demand ($z_n = 0$) or a perfect match between supply and demand, but let us now augment our definition of equilibrium so as to allow for the existence of goods that are "left over" and thus made available free of charge. Here we use the term **free good** to describe a good that is in excess supply ($z_n(p^*) < 0$) and for which $p_n^* = 0$. One example might be when farmers have a bumper crop and offer their surplus produce for free to passing travelers rather than simply letting it rot or otherwise go to waste. The air that we breathe would possibly be a free good if it were traded on competitive markets. In any case, allowing for free goods enables us to define market equilibrium as follows.

Definition: an equilibrium price profile p^* is one for which either $z_n(p^*) = 0$ (demand = supply) or $\{z_n(p^*) < 0$ and $(p_n^* = 0)\}$ (free good) for all goods n.

Now we show that an equilibrium price profile always exists provided that certain very weak conditions are satisfied. More precisely, we require only that the excess demand function is continuous in prices, meaning that it does not jump suddenly in response to an incremental price change (Figure 3.32).

> **Market equilibrium existence theorem**: if excess demand $z(p) = (z_1(p), \ldots, z_N(p))$ is a continuous function of price p, then there exists an equilibrium price profile $p^* = (p_1^*, \ldots, p_N^*)$ consistent with simultaneous equilibrium in all markets.

Figure 3.32 Continuous excess demand and discontinuous excess demand

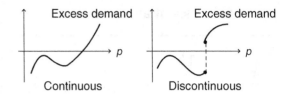

Some preparations are necessary before presenting a proof. As we saw in the previous section, equilibrium is determined not by absolute price levels but by price ratios. Real-world price profiles are "normalized" by setting the price of the currency good to 1, but for the purpose of proving the existence of an equilibrium it is convenient to normalize prices so that they sum to 1 ($p_1 + \cdots + p_N = 1$).

Let us next define S to be the set of price profiles p satisfying

- $p_1 + \cdots + p_N = 1$; and
- $p_n \geq 0$ for all n.

Our task then becomes one of finding the equilibrium price profile from within S. Figure 3.33 illustrates this for a two-good economy ($N = 2$).

Determining whether S contains an equilibrium price profile becomes relatively simple if we use the following theorem from the mathematical field of topology.

> **Fixed-point theorem**: a continuous function $f(p)$ mapping S to S will always have at least one fixed point such that $p^* = f(p^*)$.

A detailed proof is best left to more specialist texts,[29] but below we present an intuitive explanation of what this theorem is saying and why it is correct. What does it mean to say that a function f maps S to S? For each point p in S, $f(p)$ will also be found in S. In the simple two-good case illustrated in Figure 3.33, S is effectively a straight line (with finite length), meaning that we can graph the mapping from S to S as shown in Figure 3.34.

Figure 3.33 Where to look for the equilibrium price (two-good case)

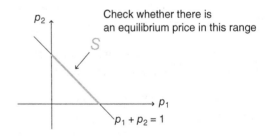

---

[29] This version is actually known as the "Brouwer fixed-point theorem."

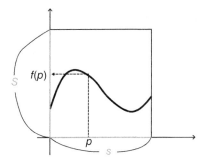

Figure 3.34 Function mapping S to S

Each point p in S is mapped to some point $f(p)$ in S

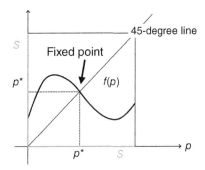

Figure 3.35 Fixed point exists if graph is continuous

If this graph is continuous, then, as shown in Figure 3.35, *it will have to cross the 45-degree line at some point*. The original point p^* and the mapped point $f(p)^*$ are obviously equal because they are on the 45-degree line, and thus give us the fixed point $(p^* = f(p^*))$ that we are looking for. Readers may wish to get out their pencils and demonstrate for themselves that any continuous graph must without exception cross the 45-degree line (meaning that a fixed point must exist). This is the essence of the above fixed-point theorem.

We now have the tools that we need to prove the existence of an equilibrium. The key lies in constructing the function $f(p)$ so that the equilibrium price profile corresponds to a fixed point. The intuition behind our proof is that we adjust the prices p in accordance with supply/demand gaps such that the adjusted price profile is given by $f(p) = (f_1(p), \ldots, f_N(p))$. The fixed point $p^* = f(p^*))$ will be such that there is no longer any scope to adjust prices, meaning that supply/demand gaps have been eliminated and the economy is in equilibrium.

A simple adjustment process would be the following: we adjust the price of good n upward if excess demand is positive ($z_n(p) > 0$, meaning that some people want to buy that good but are unable to) or downward if excess demand is negative ($z_n(p) < 0$, meaning that some of that good is going unsold). The price profile obtained after applying this adjustment process across the board can be written as

$$f_n(p) = p_n + z_n(p).$$

However, the adjusted price $f_n(p)$ could be negative if there is significant excess supply ($z_n(p) < 0$). So, let us focus on raising the prices of those goods for which demand exceeds supply (you may wonder if this works, but it turns out below that this is OK).

Proof of the equilibrium existence theorem: we begin by defining the function $f(p)$ that maps S to S.

To do this we first define the adjusted price p'_n as follows:

$$p'_n = p_n + \max\{z_n(p), 0\}.$$

$\max\{z_n(p), 0\}$ means "whichever is the greater out of $z_n(p)$ and 0" and represents the adjustment whereby we boost the price of good n if it faces excess demand ($z_n(p) > 0$). We also need to normalize our prices so that they sum to one, which is not the case with our adjusted prices p'_n. We therefore opt to normalize these adjusted prices as follows:

$$f_n(p) = \frac{p'_n}{p'_1 + \cdots + p'_N}. \tag{9}$$

We first verify that $f(p) = (f_1(p), \ldots, f_N(p))$ is a continuous function. The $\max\{z_n(p), 0\}$ part does merit special attention, but, as demonstrated in Figure 3.36, this is in fact continuous provided that excess demand $z_n(p)$ is continuous. This means that both the numerator and the denominator in (9) vary in continuous fashion, which in turn makes $f_n(p)$ continuous and ensures that $f(p) = (f_1(p), \ldots, f_N(p))$ is also a continuous function.

The above fixed-point theorem thus tells us that some price structure p^* exists such that $p^* = f(p^*)$. That just leaves us needing to show that p^* is indeed an equilibrium price structure. The denominator of $f_n(p)$ in (9) ($p'_1 + \cdots + p'_N$) is determined by p and can therefore be written as $c(p)$, which means that the following is true at the fixed point:

$$p_n^* = \frac{1}{c(p^*)} \left(p_n^* + \max\{z_n(p^*), 0\} \right)$$

Figure 3.36 Continuity of max $\{z_n(p), 0\}$

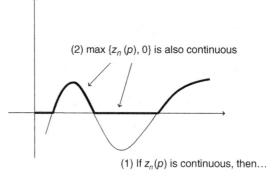

(2) max $\{z_n(p), 0\}$ is also continuous

(1) If $z_n(p)$ is continuous, then…

Multiplying both sides by $c(p^*)z_n(p^*)$ and summing for $n = 1,\ldots,N$ then lets us use Walras's law $\sum_{n=1}^{N}p_n^*z_n(p^*) = 0$ to obtain the following:

$$0 = \sum_{n=1}^{N} z_n(p^*)\max\{z_n(p^*),0\}.$$

Each term being summed on the right-hand side $z_n(p^*)\max\{z_n(p^*),0\}$ is positive if $z_n > 0$ or zero if $z_n \leq 0$. This means that the sum can be equal to zero only if no term is positive – i.e. all terms are zero. This is true if

$$z_n(p^*) \leq 0, n = 1, \ldots, N. \tag{10}$$

Moreover, Walras's law tells us that

$$p_1^*z_1(p^*) + \cdots + p_N^*z_n(p^*) = 0.$$

Given that prices are positive or zero (i.e. non-negative) and (10) holds, each term on the left-hand side must be either zero or negative. The sum of all such terms can only be zero if all terms are zero:

$$p_n^*Zn(p^*) = 0, n = 1, \ldots, N. \tag{11}$$

Comparing (10) $(z_n(p^*) \leq 0)$ and (11) $(p^*_n z_n(p^*) = 0)$, we can say that one of the following is true for each and every good n:

$$z_n(p^*) = 0 \text{ (demand = supply); or}$$
$$z_n(p^*) < p_n^* = 0 \text{ (free good)}$$

We have thus shown that p^* is an equilibrium price profile. (Q.E.D.)

(f)   Analyzing an Exchange Economy: The Edgeworth Box

Above we have introduced a general equilibrium model that describes the economy as a whole and have then shown that an equilibrium does in fact exist for that model. Our next step is to look at whether the resource allocation that is delivered by the market equilibrium turns out to satisfy the needs (preferences) of each individual member of the citizenry.

Jumping straight in by analyzing a general equilibrium model with many firms and many consumers might be a step too far for now, so we begin by solving a smaller model in order to demonstrate the basic market mechanism. More specifically, we assume that the economy consists of just two goods and two consumers. There is no firm producing goods; rather, the two consumers simply trade the goods that they already own in a competitive market. This sort of model without production is known as a **(pure) exchange economy**.

We write the endowment of consumer i (= A, B) as $w^i = \left(w_1^i, w_2^i\right)$. Supposing that A and B together own 100 units of good 1 and 50 units of good 2, the resource allocation in this exchange economy will be represented by some point within the 100 × 50 "box" shown in Figure 3.37.

Corner O_A at the bottom left is the origin from the perspective of A, meaning that positive consumption will entail moving upward and to the right. Similarly, corner O_B at the top right is the origin from the perspective of B, meaning that positive consumption will entail moving downward and to the left. At point x, A is consuming 40 units of good 1 and 20 units of good 2, with B consuming the remainders. Adding in the indifference curves of the two consumers gives us the **Edgeworth box** – named for Anglo-Irish philosopher and political economist Francis Ysidro Edgeworth (1845–1926) – as shown in Figure 3.38.

Let us now use the Edgeworth box to examine how exchange impacts the utility of the two consumers. We start out by assuming that the two consumers' indifference curves intersect at the endowment (initial allocation) point w, as shown in Figure 3.39.

I denotes A's indifference curve, meaning that at any point on that curve A will receive the same utility as at the endowment point. Moving upward and to the right will make A better off than at the endowment point. Similarly, I' denotes B's indifference curve, and moving

Figure 3.37 Resource allocation in an exchange economy

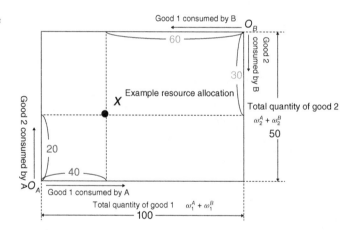

Figure 3.38 Edgeworth box

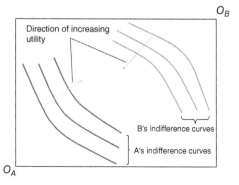

downward and to the left will make B better off than at the endowment point. In other words, an exchange of goods between A and B that moves them into the gray-shaded lens-like area will make both A and B better off. Something that leaves everyone happier in this fashion is known as a "Pareto improvement" – or, more precisely, see Figure 3.39.

> **Definition**: a **Pareto improvement** is a change that harms no one and benefits at least one person.

Will exchange stop at point x in Figure 3.39? If the two consumers' indifference curves intersect at that point, then it should be possible to make both consumers happier through further exchange (Figure 3.40 (a)). This process continues until there are no more gains to be made from exchange, which is when the two consumers' indifference curves touch, as at point x^* (Figure 3.40 (b)).

Figure 3.40 (b) shows the economy's resources allocated with maximum efficiency, meaning that neither consumer can be made happier and there is no waste. This situation is known as "Pareto efficiency."

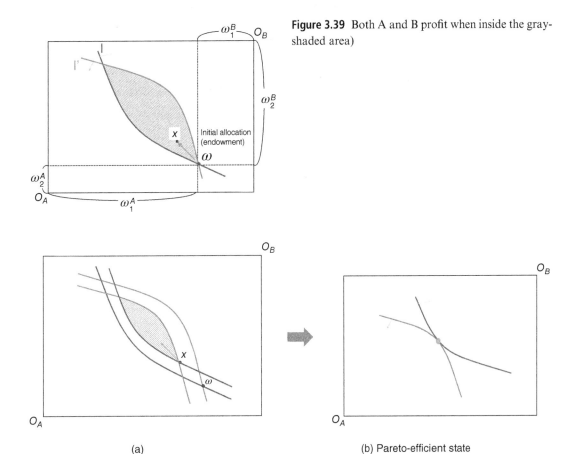

Figure 3.39 Both A and B profit when inside the gray-shaded area)

(a)

(b) Pareto-efficient state

Figure 3.40 Where does exchange stop?

> **Definition**: **Pareto efficiency** (or Pareto optimality) is a situation in which no Pareto improvement is possible, meaning that there is no possible change that will harm no one while benefiting at least one person.

As we shall discuss below, Pareto efficiency is an important criterion for assessing the desirability (or otherwise) of outcomes in a society where multiple people have competing interests. This concept should become clearer through an understanding of Figure 3.41.

Figure 3.41 shows the achievable utility region (or set) for society as a whole. A Pareto improvement is possible at point *x*, meaning that the utility of A and B can be simultaneously improved. Moreover, at point *y* it is possible to boost A's utility without making B any worse off, which is also a Pareto improvement (moving in the direction indicated by the arrow). Pareto-efficient points – those at which a Pareto improvement is not possible – thus correspond to the portion of the boundary of the achievable utility region that is *downward-sloping to the right*.

There are *many Pareto-efficient allocations* in an exchange economy represented by an Edgeworth box. As shown in Figure 3.42, all points at which the two consumers' indifference curves touch (rather than intersect) are Pareto-efficient. The set of these Pareto-efficient allocations within the Edgeworth box is sometimes known as the **contract curve**.

It should be evident from Figure 3.42 that Pareto efficiency is not necessarily a perfect yardstick for "desirability." For example, point O_B is Pareto-efficient. A is consuming all of good 1 and all of good 2 at this point, and, if we try to make B better off, we need to transfer goods from A to B, which would leave A worse off. In other words, while point O_B is clearly "unfair" in the sense that A gets everything and B gets nothing, it is nevertheless Pareto-efficient

Figure 3.41 What is Pareto efficiency?

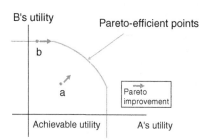

Figure 3.42 Many Pareto-efficient allocations

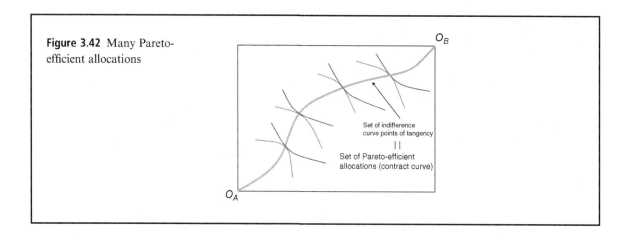

in as much as there is no way to make everyone happier. We should therefore stress that *Pareto efficiency is not necessarily the same thing as "desirability."* Alternatively, just because no "Pareto improvement" can be made it doesn't necessarily mean that the outcome is socially desirable.

But consider the flipside. Most would probably agree that *a "desirable" outcome* – as measured in terms of the happiness of each individual citizen – *needs to be Pareto-efficient*. By definition, if an outcome is not Pareto-efficient, then it is possible to make at least one person better off and no one worse off. That Pareto improvement should be considered desirable as long as what is desirable is based on the happiness of individual citizens. Put simply, an allocation that is not Pareto-efficient is not desirable, meaning that a desirable allocation must be Pareto-efficient.

Let us now summarize the above.

- There are generally many Pareto-efficient allocations, not just one.
- Some Pareto-efficient allocations may be extremely "unfair."
- That said, if "desirability" is to be assessed in terms of the happiness of each individual citizen, then *a desirable outcome must be Pareto-efficient.*

The relationship between Pareto efficiency and social desirability

---

Let us next consider the conditions for achieving Pareto efficiency in an exchange economy. As we saw from the Edgeworth box, the indifference curves of consumers A and B must touch (rather than intersect) at a Pareto-efficient point. Recalling that the slope of the indifference curve is the marginal rate of substitution, we are then able to express *the condition for Pareto efficiency in an exchange economy* as follows:

$$\underset{\text{A's marginal rate of substitution}}{\text{MRS}^A_{12}} = \underset{\text{B's marginal rate of substitution}}{\text{MRS}^B_{12}}$$

In other words, *the marginal rates of substitution of different consumers must all be equal* in order for goods to be allocated without waste and in accordance with the various needs of individual consumers (i.e. in a Pareto-efficient fashion). This is true not only for a two-good, two-consumer model but also more generally. The reason is simple: if there are any two consumers and two goods for which the equality of the marginal rate of substitution fails, then an exchange such as that shown in Figure 3.39 would serve to improve the satisfaction of both consumers, and therefore the existing allocation must be (Pareto-)inefficient.

What happens if a market is introduced to an exchange economy represented by an Edgeworth box? So as to avoid any misunderstanding, I should once again stress that an Edgeworth box is not intended to be (and, indeed, is not) a realistic market model, but is merely an easy-to-handle and easy-to-understand tool for demonstrating basic market mechanisms. What holds true for such a small and simple model may of course break down once we start working with a more realistic general model, but, as we show below, the efficiency of a market equilibrium is in fact a fundamental property of the market mechanism that holds true even for more general cases.

We begin by considering the behavior of consumer A in the face of given market prices. Writing A's consumption plan as $x^A = (x_1^A, x_2^A)$, A's budget constraint is then given by

$$p_1 x_1^A + p_2 x_2^A = p_1 w_1^A + p_1 w_2^A.$$

The left-hand side corresponds to spending, while the right-hand side represents income from A's endowment. It is always possible to simply consume one's endowment, meaning that $x^A = w^A$ satisfies the budget constraint. *A's budget line must therefore pass through A's endowment point.* As should be evident from rewriting the budget constraint as follows, *the slope of the budget line is the price ratio p_1/p_2:*

$$x_2^A = -\underbrace{\left|\frac{p_1}{p_2}\right|}_{\text{slope}} x_1^A + \frac{p_1 w_1^A + p_2 w_2^A}{p_2}.$$

Figure 3.43 (a) uses this to show A's optimal consumption under given market prices. Similarly, consumer B's optimal consumption is shown in Figure 3.43 (b).

Combining the two charts in Figure 3.43, we find that supply and demand are not in balance (Figure 3.44). This is because A's desired consumption point x^A and B's desired consumption point x^B do not match up within the box. This point warrants further explanation. Focusing on good 1, whereas A is supplying ten units of that good, B is only demanding two units. The market for good 1 is thus in a state of excess supply, meaning that the price of good 1 should fall.[30] If the price does indeed adjust "properly" in this fashion, then the slope of the budget line (price ratio) will change such that the optimal consumption point ends up corresponding to the market equilibrium shown in Figure 3.45.

Note that Figure 3.45 is an example of general equilibrium having been achieved in as much as the markets for both goods (all the goods in this economy) are in simultaneous equilibrium (with demand equal to supply).

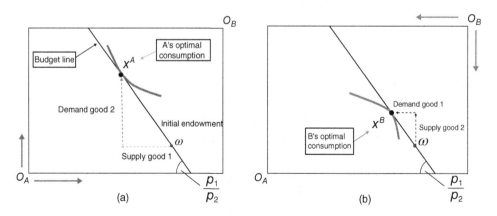

Figure 3.43 Consumer behavior when faced with fixed market prices

[30] As we learned in Section 3.3 (d), Walras's law tells us that, if one market is in a state of excess supply, then some other market must be in a state of excess demand. In this two-good case, the market for good 2 must be in a state of excess demand. Interested readers should use the above charts to verify this for themselves.

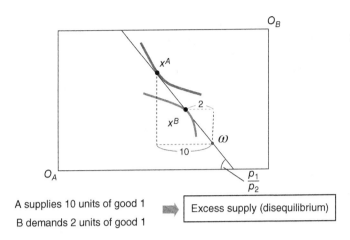

Figure 3.44 An out-of-equilibrium market

A supplies 10 units of good 1

B demands 2 units of good 1

➡ Excess supply (disequilibrium)

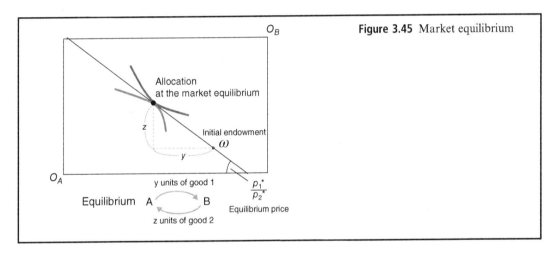

Figure 3.45 Market equilibrium

This sort of market equilibrium is Pareto-efficient, with the two consumers' indifference curves touching rather than intersecting. Let us know consider why market equilibrium delivers Pareto-efficient outcomes. As we saw in Section 1.5 (d), the marginal rate of substitution for a consumer pursuing optimal consumption (utility maximization) under given market prices will be equal to the price ratio. All consumers will of course face the same market prices, meaning that all will have equal marginal rates of substitution and thus satisfy the condition for Pareto efficiency in an exchange economy.

$$\text{A's marginal rate of substitution} = \frac{p_1^*}{p_2^*} = \text{B's marginal rate of substitution}$$

Utility maximization by individuals

The fact that the market equilibrium is Pareto-efficient holds true not only for a two-good, two-consumer exchange economy but also for a general case of many consumers and many firms.

Microeconomics has, of course, revealed many truths over the years, but this is one of the most important and is known as the first fundamental theorem of welfare economics.

First fundamental theorem of welfare economics: the perfectly competitive market equilibrium is Pareto-efficient.

We will explain the precise conditions under which this holds and present a general proof in Section 3.3 (g). But Figure 3.45 should hopefully have demonstrated why this theorem holds true in a simple economy.

We have already shown that the market will achieve one out of the many possible Pareto-efficient allocations. For example, if endowments (initial allocations) are skewed as shown in Figure 3.46, then the market equilibrium will end up favoring the richer individual (in this case A).

How can we go about achieving the fairer (and still efficient) allocation denoted by x? This question is addressed by the following theorem.

Second fundamental theorem of welfare economics: any Pareto-efficient allocation can be achieved as a perfectly competitive market equilibrium under some income redistribution policy using lump-sum taxes and lump-sum subsidies.

We will explain the precise conditions under which this holds and present a general proof in Sections 3.3 (g) and (i), along with Appendix D. But let us first understand why it holds true in a two-good, two-consumer exchange economy.

One way of achieving point x in Figure 3.46 – which is fairer than the market equilibrium shown – is to transfer some of good 1 from A to B prior to opening the market (Figure 3.47).

Figure 3.46 Market allocation favors the wealthier consumer (A)

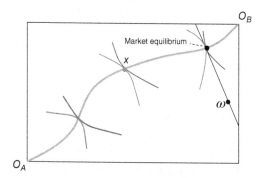

Figure 3.47 Second fundamental theorem of welfare economics

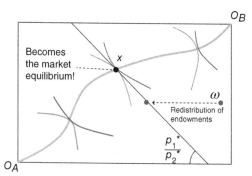

As we have seen above, while value judgments can of course be made from a wide range of perspectives, any outcome that is considered "desirable" in terms of the happiness of individual citizens must be Pareto-efficient. The second fundamental theorem of welfare economics effectively states that *any such desirable outcome can be achieved through a combination of income redistribution policy and the market mechanism.*

Let us now summarize the discussion to date. Markets function in the following fashion in order to achieve an allocation of resources that is "good" or "desirable" for the people.

– Market equilibrium achieves a waste-free (Pareto-efficient) allocation of resources (in accordance with the first fundamental theorem of welfare economics).
– However, given that there are multiple possible Pareto-efficient allocations, the equilibrium allocation may end up being "efficient but unfair."
– Government intervention is then needed to achieve a fairer (but still efficient) allocation of resources.
– This intervention need not be particularly dramatic or obstructionist; rather, the government can simply let the market function as usual after first redistributing income via a combination of lump-sum taxes and lump-sum subsidies (as promised by the second fundamental theorem of welfare economics).

The two fundamental theorems of welfare economics should thus be considered among the most important tenets of microeconomics when it comes to explaining the basic function of market mechanisms. Below we explain these two theorems in more general form.

(g) Demonstrating the Efficiency of Market Mechanisms: The First Fundamental Theorem of Welfare Economics

In this section we offer a more precise explanation of the conditions under which the first fundamental theorem of welfare economics ("the competitive market equilibrium is efficient") holds true even under a more general case in which the economy is populated by large numbers of consumers and firms. Some people might view the "competitive markets are efficient" claim as nothing more than groundless ideology, but we will now use a rigorous theoretical framework to demonstrate that it is in fact true, and clarify that it is true under a very general condition.

First, some preparation. The following notational promise will make our proof much easier to follow.

Notation (vector inequality): if $b = (b_1, \ldots, b_N)$ and $c = (c_1, \ldots, c_N)$, then

$$b \geq c$$

means that each element of b is at least as large as the corresponding element of c – i.e. $b_n \geq c_n$ for all $n = 1, \ldots, N$.

We also need to define "resource allocation" and "Pareto efficiency". A **resource allocation** can be represented as follows:

$$a = \left(\underset{\substack{\text{consumption} \\ \text{bundles}}}{x^1, \ldots, x^I,} \quad \underset{\substack{\text{production} \\ \text{plan}}}{y^1, \ldots, y^J} \right)$$

A resource allocation is **feasible** provided that

$$\underbrace{\sum_{i=1}^{I} x^i}_{\text{consumption}} \leq \underbrace{\sum_{i=1}^{I} w^i}_{\text{endowment}} + \underbrace{\sum_{j=1}^{J} y^i}_{\text{output−inputs}}$$

(i.e. the consumption bundle is achievable under the production plans)

and

$$y^j \in Y^j$$
(each firm's production plan is achievable)

for all firms $j = 1, \ldots, J$.

Shifting from the feasible resource allocation $a = \left(x^1, \ldots, x^I, y^1, \ldots, y^J \right)$ to another feasible resource allocation $\overline{a} = \left(\overline{x}^1, \ldots, \overline{x}^I, \overline{y}^1, \ldots, \overline{y}^J \right)$ constitutes a **Pareto improvement** ("$\overline{a}$ Pareto-improves a") if it gives at least one consumer higher utility without reducing the utility of anyone else – i.e. if

$u^i\left(\overline{x}^i\right) \geq u^i(x^i)$ holds true for all consumers $i = 1, \ldots, I$ and the strong inequality $(>)$ holds true for at least one consumer.

Saying that allocation a is **Pareto-efficient** means that

(1) a is feasible; and
(2) no other feasible allocation $\overline{a}$ exists that would constitute a Pareto improvement over a.

Many might wonder why we have gone to all this notational and definitional trouble, but this sort of clarity and precision turns out to be vital when rigorously demonstrating market efficiency.

We are now in a position to prove the following.

> **First fundamental theorem of welfare economics**: the perfectly competitive market equilibrium always achieves a Pareto-efficient allocation of resources under the following condition. **Condition**: there is one good for each consumer for which consumption can be varied continuously (as in the case of water or sugar) and for which an increase in consumption will increase utility.

Note that the condition that must be satisfied in order for the market to achieve an efficient outcome is extremely weak. This might come as a surprise to readers who have grown accustomed to stricter assumptions, such as requiring the utility function and production function to be differential, requiring indifference curves to be convex toward the origin, or requiring consumption to be continuously variable (rather than taking on discrete values 0, 1, 2, ...) *for all goods*. To reiterate, we are requiring only that there be *one good* for each consumer for which consumption can be varied continuously (as in the case of water or sugar) and for which an increase in consumption will translate into greater utility.[31]

---

[31] This is known as the **local non-satiation** assumption.

Proof: Here we take a perfectly competitive market equilibrium consisting of price profile $p = (p_1, \ldots, p_N)$ and resource allocation $a = (x^1, \ldots, x^I, y^1, \ldots, y^J)$, and then show that a contradiction arises if we assume this allocation to be Pareto-inefficient. If the allocation is indeed Pareto-inefficient, then it should be possible to find some other feasible allocation $\bar{a} = (\bar{x}^1, \ldots, \bar{x}^I, \bar{y}^1, \ldots, \bar{y}^J)$ such that

$u^i(\bar{x}^i \geq u^i(x^i))$ for all $i = 1, \ldots I$ and the strong inequality ($>$) holds for at least one consumer.

The following (1) and (2) will then hold under this assumption.

(1) $p\bar{x}^i > px^i$ must be true for any consumer i for whom $u^i(\bar{x}^i) > u^i(x^i)$.

This part is simple.

Reason (this part is very easy to prove): If $p\bar{x}^i \leq px^i$, then consumer i should have been able to buy $\bar{x}^i$ instead of x^i under price profile p and achieve higher utility by doing so. This contradicts the fact that x^i was an element of the optimal consumption plan under p.

---

(2) $p\bar{x}^i <$ weak inequality $>\geq px^i$ must be true for any consumer i for whom $u^i(\bar{x}^i) = u^i(x^i)$.

This is the only part of the proof that requires some careful thinking. So read the following carefully!

Reason: If $p\bar{x}^i < px^i$, then, instead of buying x^i under price profile p, consumer i could instead:

- buy $\bar{x}^i$ in order to achieve the same level of utility; and then
- use the leftover money $p(x^i - \bar{x}^i) > 0$ to buy the (assumed-to-exist) good, such as sugar, for which any amount can be purchased to increase utility, thereby achieving greater total utility while spending the same amount as was originally spent on x^i. Once again, this contradicts the fact that x^i was an element of the optimal consumption plan under p.

This leads us to the following:

$$\sum_{i=1}^{I} p\bar{x}^i > \sum_{i=1}^{I} px^i$$

(from (1) and (2)).

$$= \sum_{i=1}^{I} pw^i + \sum_{j=1}^{J} py^j$$

(from the market equilibrium condition).[32]

---

[32] This equality holds if supply equals demand for each good n ($\sum_i x_n^i = \sum_i w_n^i + \sum_j y_n^j$). It also holds true if we generalize the market equilibrium as we did in Section 3.3 (f) so as to allow for the existence of free goods (goods that are priced at zero due to excess supply). This is because $p_n = 0$ for a free good, meaning that $\sum_i p_n x_n^i = \sum_i p_n w_n^i + \sum_i p_n y_n^i$. Moreover, if the budget constraint holds true as an equality (spending = income) rather than an inequality (spending $\leq$ income), then the same equality can be proved using the sum of the budget constraints (this is the same as for Walras's law).

$$\geq \sum_{i=1}^{I} pw^i + \sum_{j=1}^{J} p\bar{y}^j$$

($py^j \geq p\bar{y}^j$, since y^j maximizes profit under p).

Comparing the start and the end, we obtain:

$$0 > p\left(\sum_{i=1}^{I} w^i + \sum_{j=1}^{J} \bar{y}^j - \sum_{i=1}^{I} \bar{x}^i\right).$$

This contradicts both the fact that allocation $\bar{a}$ is achievable ($\sum_{i=1}^{I} w^i + \sum_{j=1}^{J} \bar{y}^j + \sum_{i=1}^{I} \bar{x}^i \geq 0$) and the fact that $p \geq 0$ (**Q.E.D.**).

Comment 3.6 What's the Point of Studying Proofs?

Some might consider the above discussion to be overly abstract, pointless, and a waste of time because, if the first fundamental theorem of welfare economics is known to be true, then we can just use it without understanding why it is true. So why bother?

It is perhaps no exaggeration to say that many arguments about important social issues are based on simple preconception with no logical basis. Some might therefore worry that a statement to the effect that "the market mechanism achieves an efficient allocation of resources" is also nothing more than pure ideological conjecture. However, it is indeed possible to rigorously prove that this statement does in fact hold true under an extremely weak condition. One of the most startling and important twentieth-century advances in the social sciences was the demonstration that, even though social phenomena are much more complicated and chaotic than those in physics and chemistry, there are in fact certain things that can be proved. Moreover, those who simply take the claims of (purportedly) authoritative people and books at face value without asking *why* such claims are true may end up believing pure ideological conjecture as something unquestionably true.

I have presented the above proof of the first fundamental theorem of welfare economics to offer you a fuller understanding as to the reasons why markets achieve efficient outcomes and the conditions that must be satisfied in order for that to happen.

Comment 3.7 A Common Misunderstanding

The word "efficiency" may often be misconstrued as a propensity for "cutting costs while ignoring consumer interests." For example, one often hears arguments to the effect that "leaving things up to the market will result in *economic efficiency being prioritized above all else*, such that consumers will end up being forced to eat easy-to-grow but chemical-laden vegetables." However, *the concept of Pareto efficiency is in fact based on waste-free allocation of resources in accordance with consumer preferences.* If people really are willing to pay a higher price for organically grown vegetables, then they will end up being supplied via competitive market. The first fundamental theorem of welfare economics actually tells us that "markets achieve **consumer sovereignty**," not that "markets cause economic efficiency to be prioritized over human happiness."

(h)   Background to "Globalization": Market Equilibrium and the Core

"Globalization" (or "globalism") remains a hot topic in the context of market economies. Historically, numerous disparate regional economies in each country ended up being brought together by the market mechanism, and more recently we have started to see markets "make the world smaller" by linking and integrating economies that may be quite geographically remote from one another.

The true essence of "globalization" lies in allowing markets to transcend national borders and geographical distance. However, the more you think about it, the more this seems at least a little puzzling. Why should "markets" keep on growing without limits while limits ("natural" or otherwise) continue to be placed on the growth of other social organizations, such as firms? We do not see all of a nation's firms merged together into a single huge conglomerate; indeed, split-offs and spin-offs are often seen when a firm becomes in some sense "too big." So why don't we see a similar push for "independence" when it comes to the seemingly inexorable globalization of markets?

One commonly heard claim – both in the traditional mass media and on the Internet – is that globalization is being promoted at the political behest of society's "winners." According to this view, globalization benefits only a select few wealthy individuals and wealthy nations (such as the United States) while leaving the vast majority of the population worse off, and is occurring only as a consequence of these "winners" wielding significant political and economic power.

However, it is unlikely that the political power of a small minority would be capable of completely withstanding opposition from the remainder of the population over an extended period of time. As such, if the above explanation is correct, it should be a relatively simple matter to find examples of action having been successfully taken to curb market growth at some point in history. Such efforts to "strike independence" should have been widely applauded by the general public, and, indeed, their benefits should have been so obvious as to encourage other nations and regions to go down a similar road. However, the reality is that such examples are very rare. Some occasional attempts have indeed been made to "break away" from the global market, such as Japan's isolationist foreign policy under the Tokugawa shogunate, which essentially banned foreign trade for nearly 300 years, and the formation of economic "blocs" prior to World War II, which severely restricted trade across the blocs and exacerbated the global economic crisis.

But none of these initiatives stood the test of time, and nor have we heard widespread longing for the "good old days," when the rest of the world was shut out. One notable exception is Brexit, whereby the United Kingdom left the European Union's free trade zone in 2020. However, we are yet to see if Brexit actually signifies the end of globalization, and whether breaking away from the global market is going to be the norm rather than an exception. The following analysis helps you think about this issue, and throws light on the continuing process by revealing who benefits from globalization.

Microeconomics helps to explain the continued progress of globalization in a manner consistent with these observed facts. Consider what would happen if some of the consumers $i = 1, \ldots, I$ participating in a market were to "break away" from the rest (based, say, on their country or region of residence). Let S be the set of such consumers (for example, if the first 100 out of 10,000 consumers opt to break away, then $S = \{1, \ldots, 100\}$). Similarly, of the $j = 1, \ldots, J$ firms participating in the market, let T denote the set of firms located in the "breakaway" region and suppose that these firms are owned by the members of set S.[33]

Let p denote the pre-breakaway price profile and $(x^1, \ldots, x^I, y^1, \ldots, y^J)$ the allocation of resources. Suppose next that the members of set S shift to the new "independent" allocation denoted by $(\bar{x}^i, \bar{y}^j)_{i \in S, j \in T}$. The following will then apply.

> **Proposition**: splitting off some part of a perfectly competitive market cannot constitute a Pareto improvement for the residents of that part.

In the context of this proposition, a "Pareto improvement" would leave all the breakaway residents happier than before (or, more precisely, would make at least one person happier without making anyone unhappier). In other words, the above proposition is effectively saying that a breakaway will force all residents to settle for a share of a smaller overall pie (which obviously leaves no way of making everyone happier).

Conditions will of course need to be satisfied in order for this proposition to hold true. Those conditions are the same as for the first fundamental theorem of welfare economics, namely that we require only that, for each consumer, there exists some good for which a slight increase in consumption will result in higher utility.

Proof of proposition: suppose that the breakaway consumers do in fact achieve a Pareto improvement – i.e. $u^i(\bar{x}^i) \geq u^i(x^i)$ holds for all consumers $i \in S$, and the strong inequality ($>$) holds for at least one such consumer. Using the same argument as in our proof of the first fundamental theorem of welfare economics, we find that

$$0 > p \left(\sum_{i \in S} w^i + \sum_{j \in T} \bar{y}^j - \sum_{i \in S} \bar{x}^i \right).$$

This contradicts both the fact that the post-breakaway allocation $(\bar{x}^i, \bar{y}^j)_{i \in S, j \in T}$ is achievable and the fact that $p \geq 0$ (**Q.E.D.**).

If group S breaks away and shifting to an allocation achievable by S in isolation constitutes a Pareto improvement for the members of S, then S is said to **block** the pre-breakaway allocation. In other words, S blocks the original allocation if breaking away enables all members of S to

---

[33] If the firms in set T were owned by someone else (consumers outside S), then the breakaway might enable these ownership rights to be "stolen" to the benefit of consumers inside S. However, our focus here is on whether a breakaway might enable consumers to benefit in some other – less legally problematic – way.

become happier. Defining the **core** as the set of resource allocations that cannot be blocked by any group, we arrive at the following theorem as a rewording of the above proposition.

> **Theorem**: *The resource allocation achieved by a perfectly competitive equilibrium belongs to the core.*

The condition that must be satisfied in order for this to hold true is the same as for the first fundamental theorem of welfare economics, namely that, "for each consumer, there exists some good for which a slight increase in consumption will result in higher utility." *The proof also turns out to be almost exactly the same as that for the first fundamental theorem of welfare economics* presented above.

I personally am (almost) convinced that globalization – or the continued growth of markets to transcend national borders and geographical barriers – occurs not so much as a consequence of "winners" wielding their political power but, rather, because the market equilibrium belongs to the core. Well, do you agree or disagree?

Comment 3.8 The Core Is, Essentially, Equal to Competitive Market Equilibrium in Large Economies

Generally speaking, there will be many core allocations, not just one. You can easily demonstrate this by using a simple Edgeworth box. However, it can be shown that the core shrinks as the number of people in the economy becomes larger, and ends up converging to the perfectly competitive equilibrium allocation in the limit, where the economy is infinitely populated. This is known as the **Debreu–Scarf core limit theorem**. In other words, once the number of people is sufficiently large, the market mechanism becomes the only means of determining a resource allocation that will resist any temptation to break away (i.e. to block the process of globalization). The relationship between globalization and market forces thus turns out to be surprisingly profound.

(i) The Second Fundamental Theorem of Welfare Economics and Conditions for Efficiency

The next two sections are aimed at gaining a more thorough understanding of the second fundamental theorem of welfare economics, which states that any Pareto-efficient allocation can be achieved by a perfectly competitive market subject to some appropriate redistribution of income (via lump-sum taxes and subsidies). Our basic roadmap is as follows.

(1) We first explain the *main conditions* in order for the second fundamental theorem of welfare economics to hold true.

(2) The second fundamental theorem of welfare economics also provides us with *general conditions that must be satisfied by an efficient allocation*. These can then be used to gain

an understanding as to the circumstances under which inefficiencies (resource allocation distortions or imbalances) might be expected to arise.

(3) Employing a *general framework* that does not rely on the strong assumptions needed for our surplus-based partial equilibrium analysis, we then show how *competition policy* can be used to eliminate such efficiencies.

First recall Section 3.3 (f), in which we used an Edgeworth box to confirm that the second fundamental theorem of welfare economics holds true. We have reproduced this analysis in Figure 3.48 (a). Taking x as an arbitrary Pareto-efficient point, we note that the indifference curves of A and B (I_A and I_B) touch each other (rather than intersect) at that point. Provided that each indifference curve is *convex* toward the origin, as shown in Figure 3.48 (a), we can then draw *a straight line l that "separates" the two curves*. Shifting the endowment (initial allocation) to some point along this line will enable the efficient point x to be achieved as a market equilibrium. The straight line l represents the budget line for both A and B, with point x turning out to be optimal for both parties.

But what if A's indifference curve is not convex toward the origin, as shown in Figure 3.48 (b)? It will no longer be possible to achieve the Pareto-efficient point x as a perfectly competitive market equilibrium. Let us now consider why not. In order for B's consumption at point x to be a market equilibrium, B's budget line must be tangential to B's indifference curve I_B at point x. This in turn implies that l must be B's budget line. Note once again that, in an Edgeworth box framework, the same line – passing through the endowment point w and with slope equal to the price ratio – represents the budget line for both A and B. As such, A's budget line should also be given by l. However, A's optimal consumption subject to the budget line l will actually correspond not to x but to some other point, as shown in Figure 3.48 (b). It is thus impossible to achieve a market equilibrium in which both A and B consume at point x.

It should be clear from the above that a number of somewhat stronger conditions (by comparison with the first fundamental theorem of welfare economics) must be satisfied in order for the second fundamental theorem of welfare economics to hold true. One of those

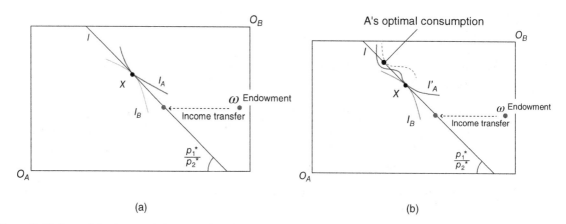

(a)   (b)

Figure 3.48 Second fundamental theorem of welfare economics does not hold unless indifferences curves are convex to the origin

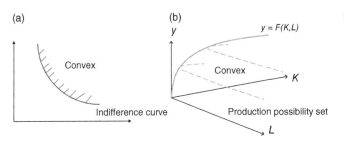

Figure 3.49 Convexity assumptions

is that the area above each consumer's indifference curve (upper contour set) needs to be a convex set (Figure 3.49 (a)). Another, as it turns out, is that each firm's production possibility set needs to be convex (Figure 3.49 (b)).

In the preceding chapters we have seen that these conditions hold up in a variety of real-world examples. Moreover, as explained in Appendix D.6, these conditions can be relaxed quite considerably for the case of a large economy populated by sufficiently large numbers of consumers and firms.

These convexity assumptions are the main conditions that must be satisfied in order for the second fundamental theorem of welfare economics to hold true. There are some additional conditions of a slightly technical nature for the second welfare theorem to hold, and the interested reader can find them in Appendix D.5.

Let us now summarize the above.

Second fundamental theorem of welfare economics: If

– the upper contour set of each consumer's indifference curve is convex,
– each firm's production possibility set is convex, and
– some additional conditions are satisfied,[34]

then *it will be possible to achieve any Pareto-efficient resource allocation as a perfectly competitive market equilibrium* by using lump-sum taxes and lump-sum subsidies to redistribute income in an appropriate manner.

The proof is, admittedly, a little long and involved, but Appendix D explains it in a way that should be easy for undergraduates to follow (and thereby improve their understanding of market mechanisms and the role of prices).

The second fundamental theorem of welfare economics should serve as the guiding principle for government economic policy. Opinion is course likely to be divided as to just what is "best" for society as a whole, but any "desirable" outcome must be Pareto-efficient if we are using the happiness of individual citizens as our basis of judgment. In order to achieve that outcome, policy-makers need only redistribute income via (non-distortionary) lump-sum taxes and lump-sum subsidies and then simply leave the market to do its work. This general-purpose guideline for economic policy – as embodied in the second fundamental theorem of welfare economics – is *one of the most important lessons of microeconomics.*

---

[34] Conditions 1, 2, 3, 4a, 4b, and 4c are in Appendix D.5.

Another (perhaps less obvious) contribution of the second fundamental theorem of welfare economics lies in clarifying the *general conditions that must be satisfied by an efficient allocation of resources*. These conditions boil down to all consumers and all producers facing identical prices. The key message is thus that price-distorting institutional practices and regulations must be avoided to the greatest extent possible from an efficiency perspective.

Let us now explain this all in greater detail. The second fundamental theorem of welfare economics tells us that an efficient allocation of resources can be achieved as a perfectly competitive market equilibrium (via some appropriate redistribution of income). This in turn implies that each consumer's marginal rate of substitution and each firm's marginal productivity must satisfy the following conditions at the efficient allocation.

Proposition relating to efficiency conditions (a corollary of the second fundamental theorem of welfare economics):

There exist $p_1, \ldots, p_K$ satisfying the following conditions for any Pareto-efficient allocation of resources.

(1) For any consumer i and any two goods a and b:

$$MRS^i_{ab} = \frac{p_a}{p_b}$$

marginal rate of substitution $\uparrow$

(2) For any firm j using good h to produce good k:

$$p_k \frac{\partial F^j}{\partial x_h} = p_h$$

$\uparrow$

marginal productivity

---

(1) corresponds to the consumer's utility maximization condition for a competitive equilibrium, while (2) corresponds to the firm's profit maximization condition (since F^j denotes firm j's production function). It is important to note that here we are talking about *any* Pareto-efficient allocation, not only the allocation that is actually achieved by the market. For example, even if some almighty economic planner were to bypass the market altogether and use a supercomputer to allocate people and resources as efficiently as possible, the outcome – if truly efficient – would be such that some $p_1, \ldots, p_K$ must satisfy the above. These are the prices that would arise if the efficient allocation under consideration were achieved by competitive markets and income redistribution, and such "theoretical prices" are known as "**shadow prices**." The second fundamental theorem of welfare economics thus also plays an important role in *demonstrating the true nature of prices, with any efficient allocation able to be characterized by a set of clearly defined theoretical prices*.

The above proposition enables us to derive a number of conditions pertaining to efficiency. Exploring these in some detail should prove invaluable in understanding the true relationship between efficiency and prices. A certain amount of patience and perseverance will indeed be necessary, but for now you will just have to trust me that the journey is worth it! (More on this later.)

The first condition follows immediately from part (1) of the above proposition.

Efficiency condition A: For any two goods, all consumers (who consume those goods) must have identical marginal rates of substitution.

We have already shown this in our Section 3.3 (f) discussion of Edgeworth boxes, but it is worth taking some additional time to explain both the significance of this condition and why it needs to be satisfied in order to achieve an efficient outcome.

Significance of condition A: Recall that the marginal rate of substitution of good a for good b $\left(MRS_{ab}^i\right)$ represents the amount of b that consumer i would need to receive in order to maintain the same level of satisfaction while (slightly) reducing consumption of a. For example, suppose that a = organic orange juice and b = regular orange juice. If $MRS_{ab}^i = 1.5$, then, if for some reason she is forced to reduce her consumption of organic orange juice by some amount, consumer i would need to drink an additional 1.5 times that amount of the inferior-tasting regular orange juice in order to maintain the same level of satisfaction. Very roughly speaking, *organic orange juice has 1.5 times the value of the regular orange juice* to consumer i when tweaking consumption amounts. This marginal rate of substitution – the degree to which organic orange juice is considered more valuable than regular orange juice – will generally differ from one consumer to the next, but needs to be identical for all consumers at an efficient equilibrium. In other words, if organic orange juice and regular orange juice are being allocated efficiently, then *all those who consume both organic orange juice and regular orange juice will need to agree that the former is worth, say, 1.5 times as much as the latter*. If this efficient allocation is achieved via the market, then the price of organic orange juice should be 1.5 times the price of regular orange juice. Prices can thus be viewed as a reflection of consumer attitudes toward individual goods (and their relative merits) in aggregate form.

Need for condition A: if this condition is not satisfied and marginal rates of substitution differ across individuals, then a good that is considered precious by one consumer might be dismissed as less valuable by another, in which case an exchange of the good between those two individuals would serve to improve the satisfaction of both (as we showed in Figure 3.39 as part of our Section 3.3 (f) Edgeworth box discussion). It should thus be clear that condition A needs to be satisfied in order for an allocation to be efficient.

The next condition follows immediately from part (2) of the above proposition.

Efficiency condition B: The marginal productivity of a given production factor must be the same for all firms producing the same good.

For example, if an allocation is efficient, then the marginal productivity of labor with regard to steel must be the same for all steelworks. If this were not the case, then it should be possible to produce more steel using the same amount of labor by simply shifting workers from a less efficient (lower-productivity) plant to a more efficient (higher-productivity) plant. If an efficient allocation is being achieved, then the marginal productivity of labor should be the same for all steelworks, and this amount must be embodied appropriately in both the wages received by steelworkers and the price of steel (part (2) of our proposition states that marginal productivity $\frac{\partial F^j}{\partial x_h}$ is equal to the ratio of the steelworker's wage to the price of steel, or p_h/p_k).

Condition B pertains to the efficient allocation of production factors among *firms that are producing the same good*. Condition C – which also follows from part (2) of our proposition –

addresses how production factors should be efficiently allocated among firms producing different goods.

Efficiency condition C: the marginal rate of technical substitution across given production factors must be the same for all firms.

In other words, the following (which we can obtain from part (2) of our proposition) must be true for all firms j:

$$\frac{\partial F^j/\partial x_h}{\partial F^j/\partial x_{h'}} = \frac{p_h}{p_{h'}}$$

As we learned in Section 2.3 (b), the left-hand side of this equation is the marginal rate of (technical) substitution for production factors good h and good h'. For example, if good h is labor and good h' is fuel and if firm j's marginal rate of substitution $\frac{\partial F^j/\partial x_h}{\partial F^j/\partial x_{h'}}$ is three, then that would imply that the same amount of steel can be produced by reducing labor inputs by one unit while increasing fuel inputs by three units. Condition C states that all firms using labor and fuel (including those that produce goods other than steel) must have identical marginal rates of substitution for labor and fuel in order for an allocation to be efficient.[35] In a competitive market this common marginal rate of substitution will be equal to the production factor price ratio $\frac{p_h}{p_{h'}}$.

Let us conclude with a condition that spans the efficiency of both production and consumption (in the sense that firms are producing just the sorts of goods that consumers want). Consider two firms α and β. Both use the same production factor h (e.g. labor), but α produces juice ($k =$ good a) whereas β produces milk ($k =$ good b). Using part (2) of our proposition, we obtain

$$\frac{p_a \frac{\partial F^\alpha}{\partial x_h}}{p_b \frac{\partial F^\beta}{\partial x_h}} = \frac{p_h}{p_h} = 1.$$

This can be rewritten as

$$\frac{p_a}{p_b} = \frac{\left(\frac{\partial F^\beta}{\partial x_h}\right)}{\left(\frac{\partial F^\alpha}{\partial x_h}\right)}. \tag{12}$$

How can we interpret the right-hand side of this equation? Suppose that a small amount of labor (ΔL) is shifted from the juice-producing firm α to the milk-producing firm β, thereby slightly reducing output of juice (by Δy_a) and slightly increasing output of milk (by Δy_b). This transfer of labor has effectively enabled us to **transform juice into milk** (which is admittedly less impressive than "water into wine"). How much additional milk can be produced? This is given by

$$\frac{\text{increase in milk}}{\text{decrease in juice}} = \frac{\Delta y_b}{\Delta y_a} = \frac{\left(\frac{\partial F^\beta}{\partial x_h}\right)}{\left(\frac{\partial F^\alpha}{\partial x_h}\right)}$$

---

[35] The rationale is virtually the same as for condition A. If the marginal rate of substitution of labor for fuel were three for a steelworks and five for an oil company, then it should be possible to simultaneously boost output of steel and oil by having the steelworks provide labor to the oil company in exchange for additional fuel.

In other words, the right-hand side of (12) is the **marginal rate of transformation (MRT$_{ab}$)** of good a for good b, or the additional amount of good b (milk) that can be produced by slightly reducing production of good a (juice).

This is an important aspect of the perfectly competitive market equilibrium that we have yet to discuss, so let us summarize as follows.

For a perfectly competitive equilibrium, **the price ratio is equal to the marginal rate of transformation**:

$$\frac{p_a}{p_b} = MRT_{ab} = \frac{\left(\frac{\partial F^\beta}{\partial x_h}\right)}{\left(\frac{\partial F^\alpha}{\partial x_h}\right)}. \tag{13}$$

Let us once again explain how we calculate the marginal rate of transformation. Taking any single production factor (such as labor, or good h) that is used to produce both juice (good a) and milk (good b), we can write the marginal rate of transformation of juice for milk as

$$MRT_{ab} = \frac{\text{marginal productivity of labor in the production of } (b) \text{ milk } \left(\frac{\partial F^\beta}{\partial x_h}\right)}{\text{marginal productivity of labor in the production of } (a) \text{ juice } \left(\frac{\partial F^\alpha}{\partial x_h}\right)}.$$

How to calculate the marginal rate of transformation

Transferring a small amount of labor from the juice-producing firm α to the milk-producing firm β effectively enables us to convert juice into milk based on the "exchange rate" given by the right-hand side of the equation.

Combining (13) – the efficiency condition pertaining to the marginal rate of transformation – with the efficiency condition pertaining to each consumer's marginal rate of substitution from part (1) of our proposition gives us the following condition:

$$MRT_{ab} = \frac{\left(\frac{\partial F^\beta}{\partial x_h}\right)}{\left(\frac{\partial F^\alpha}{\partial x_h}\right)} = MRS_{ab}^i. \tag{14}$$

How can we interpret this? The left-hand side is the marginal rate of transformation of juice (good a) for milk (good b). The first equality $MRT_{ab} = \frac{\left(\frac{\partial F^\beta}{\partial x_h}\right)}{\left(\frac{\partial F^\alpha}{\partial x_h}\right)}$ is thus saying that, for any production factor h and any two firms α and β making use of that factor, marginal rates of transformation will need to be equal. In other words, if an allocation of resources is efficient, marginal rates of transformation will need to be equal irrespective of the path by which juice is transformed into milk.[36] As such, if production is efficiently handled, then there will be just a

---

[36] More generally, juice might be transformed into milk less directly by transferring some production factor from the juice-producing firm to firm 1, some other production factor from firm 1 to firm 2, ..., and yet another production factor from firm 10 to the milk-producing firm.

single marginal rate of transformation of juice for milk for society as a whole. This corresponds to MRT_{ab} on the left-hand side of (14).

Ignoring the middle part of (14) gives us the following:

For all consumers i,

$$MRT_{ab} = MRS^i_{ab}$$

marginal rate of transformation   marginal rate of substitution

(15)

In other words, the social marginal rate of transformation must be equal to each consumer's marginal rate of substitution. Suppose that this condition does not hold and that the marginal rate of transformation of juice for milk is five, whereas there is some consumer for whom the marginal rate of substitution of juice for milk is two. Reducing that consumer's consumption of juice by one unit makes it possible to increase production of milk by five units. The consumer's marginal rate of substitution is two, meaning that satisfaction would be left unchanged by reducing consumption of juice by one unit while increasing consumption of milk by two units. But milk production has been increased by more than two units, meaning that the consumer can be made even better off than before without impacting any other part of the economy. Such an adjustment should not be possible if starting from an efficient equilibrium, which is why the above condition (14) needs to be satisfied.

The above can be summarized as follows.

Efficiency condition D: the marginal rate of transformation for any two goods must be the same irrespective of the path of transformation, and must also be equal to each consumer's marginal rate of substitution.

This is basically just condition (14) in word form. Moreover, both the marginal rate of transformation and the marginal rate of substitution turn out to be equal to the ratio of prices for the two goods.

We have thus used the second fundamental theorem of welfare economics to derive four conditions (A) to (D) that must be satisfied in order to achieve an efficient allocation of resources.

Comment 3.9 Price Is a Simple Tool for Expressing "Efficiency"

Readers will no doubt agree that the above was quite a mouthful to get through. (I must confess I myself also feel so.) I once again hear many of you screaming *"I hate these complicated efficiency conditions, so why bother?"* If that is what you think, you are on the right track, because **these conditions being annoyingly complicated is exactly the point I wanted to make**. Let me explain what I mean.

Recall that each of the quite bothersome (some might even say annoying) efficiency conditions (A) to (D) was derived from the simpler "Proposition relating to efficiency conditions" (p. 190). This proposition is simpler because it uses the parameters $p_1, \ldots, p_K$ to express conditions (A) to (D) in an extremely compact form. These parameters are the market equilibrium prices, or the theoretical prices associated with an efficient equilibrium. Finding an efficient allocation requires all the painstaking trouble of checking whether each of the very complicated conditions (A), (B), (C), and (D) is satisfied, but the market mechanism makes that task very much easier by setting prices at the appropriate levels and letting consumers and firms achieve the simpler efficiency conditions in terms of prices. This is indeed the secret of success of the market mechanism!

(j)   The Second Fundamental Theorem of Welfare Economics and Economic Policy

As we discussed earlier, the importance of the second fundamental theorem of welfare economics lies in providing a general-purpose guideline for use in formulating economic policy (for example, when contemplating some form of deregulation- or competitin-promoting measure). This importance cannot be overstated. In this section I attempt to convince you of this by effectively providing *a manual for using the second fundamental theorem of welfare economics to formulate economic policy*.

We start by recalling Section 3.1 (d), in which we assessed competition policy using a partial equilibrium framework of the sort typically found in introductory textbooks. That analysis of a liquor excise (indirect tax) is reproduced in Figure 3.50.

As shown in Figure 3.50 (a), the imposition of a liquor tax results in a deadweight loss (of surplus) corresponding to the area of the white triangle X at the market equilibrium. Abolishing this tax shifts the consumption amount and the price to the point where supply and demand intersect, as shown in Figure 3.50 (b), thereby eliminating the deadweight loss. If the government instead imposes lump-sum taxes of T_1 on the consumer and T_2 on the producer, as shown in Figure 3.50 (b), it can collect the same amount of revenue while leaving both consumers and producers better off (i.e. with a greater surplus) than under the indirect taxation regime.

This explanation based on partial equilibrium analysis has the benefit of being intuitively easy to understand, but unfortunately lacks generality in the following respects.

(1) Partial equilibrium analysis explains the inefficiency of an indirect liquor tax in terms of a decline in total surplus (deadweight loss). This approach depends on the assumption that a

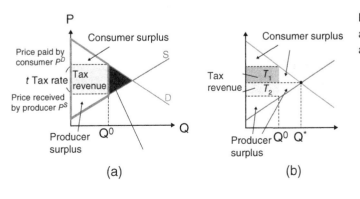

Figure 3.50 Partial equilibrium analysis of an alcohol tax

consumer's satisfaction can be expressed in monetary terms as "consumer surplus" (or the area of the upper triangle in Figure 3.50 (a)), but in reality that assumption will hold true only provided that the consumer's preferences satisfy quite "special" properties.[37] So can we find some way of *showing that an indirect liquor tax is inefficient without imposing the strong assumption that consumer satisfaction can be measured in terms of consumer surplus?*

(2) Partial equilibrium analysis enables us to focus on a single market in demonstrating the desirability of switching from an indirect liquor tax to lump-sum taxation, meaning that we look solely at the government's tax revenue, the profits of liquor producers, and consumer surplus in the liquor market. However, in reality the abolition of a liquor tax would be expected to have a range of spillover ramifications for other markets. For example, if liquor becomes cheaper, then more people might decide to drink wine rather than, say, sparkling water at restaurants, in which case sparkling water producers might suffer losses. An increase in liquor production should also be a good thing for suppliers of raw materials (to produce liquor). Is there some way to *conclude that abolishing an indirect liquor tax is indeed desirable even after allowing for these various spillover ramifications?*

Such issues are *best addressed via general equilibrium theory, or, more specifically, by using the second fundamental theorem of welfare economics.* General equilibrium theory employs sophisticated analytical techniques not simply as a means of pursuing theory for theory's sake but, rather, for the purpose of solving real-world problems in an intellectually satisfying fashion (i.e. without imposing unrealistic simplifying assumptions).

Let us now explain why an indirect liquor tax is inefficient without imposing the (strong) assumption that consumer satisfaction can be expressed in terms of consumer surplus (point (1) above). The price paid by the consumer under indirect taxation is higher than the price received by the producer (by an amount equal to the liquor tax). This violates the efficiency condition (discussed in subsection (i) above) requiring that all economic agents face the same price profile when optimizing their consumption and production. We are therefore able to conclude that imposition of an indirect liquor tax leads to an inefficient outcome.

Deepening our understanding will once again require us to get our hands a little "dirty," but let us now offer a more precise explanation of why an indirect liquor tax creates inefficiency. Condition D from the previous section – which pertains to the relationship between the marginal rate of transformation and the marginal rate of substitution – turns out not to be satisfied. For example, if a = sparkling water and b = wine and the prices faced by producers are p_a and p_b, then, as explained in (12) above, the following holds true for a competitive equilibrium:

$$\frac{p_a}{p_b} = \frac{\text{marginal productivity of labor with regard to wine}}{\text{marginal productivity of labor with regard to sparkling water}} = MTR_{ab},$$

---

[37] As we explained in Section 3.1 (c), the utility function must be quasilinear in order for the above assumption to be satisfied.

where p_b is the wine price faced by producers (with no tax included). The consumer, meanwhile, faces the higher tax-inclusive price, which can be written as $(1 + t)p_b$, where $t > 0$ is the tax rate. As we discussed in Chapter 1, at the optimal consumption point consumer i's marginal rate of substitution MRS_{ab}^i will be equal to the price ratio faced by the consumer:

$$\frac{p_a}{(1 + t)p_b} = MRS_{ab}^i.$$

The higher the tax rate t, the lower this ratio. Summarizing the above:

$$\underset{\substack{\text{marginal rate of} \\ \text{transformation}}}{MRT_{ab} = \frac{p_a}{p_b}} > \underset{\substack{\text{marginal rate of} \\ \text{substitution}}}{\frac{p_a}{(1 + t)p_b} = MRS_{ab}^i}$$

In other words, efficiency condition D is not satisfied, because the marginal rate of transformation does not equal the marginal rate of substitution.

Suppose that a restaurant sells sparkling water for \$5 a glass ($= p_a$) and wine for \$6 a glass ($= (1 + t)p_b$). The consumer's marginal rate of substitution will be 5/6, or approximately 0.83. In other words, the consumer will be left equally satisfied if her consumption of sparkling water is reduced by 100 ml while her consumption of wine is increased by around 83 ml. Conversely, if she receives more than 83 ml, then her satisfaction will improve. If the tax rate is set at 20 percent ($t = 0.2$), then the price faced by the wine producer will be $p_b = 6/(1 + t) = \$5$, or the same as the price of sparkling water. The marginal rate of transformation will thus be equal to 1 ($\frac{p_b}{p_a} = \frac{5}{5} = 1$). In other words, shifting (a small amount of) labor from the sparkling water factory to the wine factory will enable sparkling water to be transformed into wine at a 1:1 ratio. The fact that the marginal rate of transformation (1) is higher than the consumer's marginal rate of substitution (0.83) means that such a transformation will leave the consumer better off (more satisfied). The possibility of such improvement means that the allocation under the liquor tax is inefficient.

Some might be tempted to dismiss the above as an unreliable conclusion based on excessive reliance on complicated and unrealistic mathematical models. But is that really the case? Societies in which many goods are taxed are known for being uncomfortably expensive to live in. For example, drinking just a single glass of whisky in Sweden will set you back a small fortune. Similarly, imported meat can be astonishingly expensive in Japan owing to the imposition of high tariffs (for example, a 25.8 percent tariff applied to imported beef as of 2022). Such uncomfortably high prices must ultimately be blamed on the government's use of taxation to (however unintentionally) block a range of transactions that would "naturally" cause prices to fall to more comfortable levels. The above model-based discussion is, basically, just intended to offer a general framework for discussing what our life experience already tells us.

So what have we learned? A deep understanding of the circumstances under which market inefficiencies arise requires us to check each of the individual efficiency conditions (A) to (D), which in turn requires at least some degree of patience. However, our compact "Proposition relating to efficiency conditions" (p.190) offers a simpler means of checking for market inefficiency in terms of (theoretical) prices. This proposition states that, in order for an efficient allocation to be achieved, all economic agents must (in effect) be facing *the same price structure* and behaving in *perfectly competitive* fashion. This helps us identify the circumstances under which market inefficiencies arise.

General causes of inefficiency

(1) **Price distortions**: inefficiencies will arise if all consumers and all producers do not face identical prices.
    Examples: commodity taxes such as a liquor excise, tariffs, student discounts, shareholder discounts, etc.

(2) **Restrictions on competition**: even if all consumers and producers face identical prices, inefficiencies will arise if they do not behave in perfectly competitive fashion.
    Examples: monopolies, oligopolies, restrictions on competition such as a guaranteed minimum wage.

Firms have pricing power under a monopoly or oligopoly, meaning that *they do not maximize profits subject to given market prices* (as in the case of perfect competition), and that inefficiencies arise as a result. We will discuss this point in greater detail soon. An inefficient market outcome is generally referred to as a **distortion of resource allocation**. The second fundamental theorem of welfare economics serves to clarify the causes of resource allocation distortions, and as such represents one of the most important reasons for studying and understanding microeconomics.

Let us now consider the sorts of policy responses that need to be considered if markets are operating inefficiently for one (or more) of the above reasons. Recall first that a situation is considered "Pareto-inefficient" if it is possible to boost at least one person's satisfaction without reducing the satisfaction of anyone else – i.e. if a "Pareto improvement" is possible. There are almost as many different ways of making value judgments as there are people in the world, with some people placing greater weight on addressing inequality and protecting the vulnerable while others may believe that the victors in a fair competition deserve to be richly rewarded. No matter which value judgment is to be employed, the desirable outcome must be Pareto efficient if "desirability" is measured in terms of the happiness of individual citizens, which most would surely agree is a very reasonable metric. And, as we have seen from the second fundamental theorem of welfare economics, achieving a desired Pareto-efficient outcome ultimately just boils down to eliminating price distortions and restrictions on competition – thereby allowing for perfect competition – while also ensuring that income is appropriately redistributed via some combination of lump-sum transfers (taxes and subsidies).

Returning to our liquor excise example, we found that abolishing an indirect tax in order to make the liquor market perfectly competitive will also have spillover ramifications for various other markets. However, the second fundamental theorem of welfare economics guarantees that, even after these spillovers are taken into consideration, the entire citizenry will be made better off by abolishing indirect taxation and instead implementing appropriate income redistribution. The following general guidelines for policy-makers – which stem in their entirety from the second fundamental theorem of welfare economics – constitute one of the most important takeaways when you learn economics.

General guidelines for "desirable" economic policy

(1) Irrespective of the specific basis on which value judgments are made, *it is always desirable for inefficiencies to be eliminated*.

(2) Inefficiencies will arise unless all consumers and all producers face *identical prices*. And, even if all consumers and all producers do face identical prices, inefficiencies will still arise unless consumers and producers behave in *perfectly competitive* fashion.

(3) The entire citizenry can be made better off – or, more precisely, at least some people can be made better off without leaving anyone worse off – by *creating a perfectly competitive environment* (including through the elimination of price distortions and restrictions on competition) and *redistributing income through some appropriate combination of lump-sum transfers* (taxes and subsidies).

Comment 3.10 How Should Income Be Distributed?

The second fundamental theorem of welfare economics guarantees that an appropriate redistribution of income can indeed be found, as required by point (3). But how might this be achieved in practice? For example, if a liquor excise is to be abolished, how much tax should be collected (and from whom) and how much should be paid out in subsidies (and to whom) in order to make everyone better off via the perfectly competitive market mechanism? Massive amounts of information may need to be collected in order to answer this question, and setting different levels of tax and subsidies at the individual level could prove extremely costly from an administrative perspective. Perfect implementation of (3) may therefore prove difficult if not impossible in the real world. Given this practical limitation, what is the point of the above guidelines?

The value of these guidelines is twofold. First, an understanding that price distortions and restrictions on competition are negative for overall happiness should prove invaluable when assessing the social "desirability" of any given policy action. Making everyone better off by eliminating price distortions and restrictions on competition may of course be easier said than done, owing to the difficulty of determining precisely how income should be redistributed, but understanding the theoretical possibilities should nevertheless help to ensure that the policy debate takes place in as rational and productive a fashion as possible.

Second, and perhaps more important from the perspective of actual implementation, policies that eliminate price distortions and restrictions on competition will tend to benefit many (or perhaps even most) people over the longer term *even if not accompanied by income redistribution* as outlined in (3). Income redistribution at the individual level may ultimately be impossible to achieve in practice, but *the longer-term national interests can nevertheless be served* – possibly quite effectively – *by looking to eliminate price distortions and encourage free competition at every available opportunity*. This idea – known as the **compensation principle** – will be discussed in detail in the final chapter of this book.

(k)   The Big Picture: Decentralized Decision-Making, Information, and Incentives

So much for the technicalities; let us now try to get the big picture. Don't say, *"OK, just skip this part, because the professor won't make any exam questions out of this section."* Believe me; **this is the most important part of the entire book!**

Here I examine "what exactly the market mechanism is," "how it works," and "why it works well in certain senses," which are the central questions in economics. Ever since the days of Adam Smith, the case for "market forces" has run along something like the following lines. The many producers and many consumers that participate in markets possess information only about themselves and act only with their own interests in mind. In other words, consumers and producers strive to maximize their own satisfaction (utility) or profits without knowing anything about other consumers' preferences and other producers' technologies. But, notwithstanding this completely **decentralized decision-making**, competitive markets are still capable of achieving an efficient resource allocation that balances supply and demand. Smith himself referred to this ability of markets to translate individual self-interest into the best interests of society as an **"invisible hand."** According to this philosophy, the market mechanism essentially serves two important purposes.

First, *market prices offer an efficient and succinct means of conveying relevant information for the various agents* (consumers and producers) *that comprise society*. This characteristic of the market mechanism is known as **information efficiency**. For example, suppose that an increase in demand serves to drive up prices of notebooks. Notebook producers will then ramp up their output without any knowledge as to just who wants more notebooks or why (and, indeed, without any need for such knowledge). In other words, the price of a notebook offers an extremely clear and succinct signal as to the level of social demand for notebooks and whether notebook suppliers should be producing more or fewer.

Second, *markets end up producing socially desirable (and efficient) outcomes despite each individual economic agent acting solely in its own interests*. This characteristic of the market mechanism is known as **incentive compatibility**. A very good place to read more about these two characteristics of the market mechanism – information efficiency and incentive compatibility – is the 1945 paper titled "The Use of Knowledge in Society" by Austrian-British economist and philosopher Friedrich August von Hayek (1899–1992).[38]

The significance of these characteristics should be easier to understand if we compare a (socialist) planned economy with a market economy. Whereas prices in a market economy serve to convey necessary information in a timely and concise manner, those responsible for a planned economy will need to collect massive amounts of information about individual production technologies and consumer needs and then use this information to perform a series of massively complicated calculations. A planned economy thus leaves much to be desired from

---

[38] Friedrich A. Hayek, "The Use of Knowledge in Society," *American Economic Review*, 35(4) (1945), 519–530.

an information efficiency perspective. Incentive compatibility has also proved problematic. For example, there is a danger that consumers and producers in a planned economy might not provide the authorities with honest information about their needs and technologies. People who want to wear jeans are liable to exaggerate the importance of doing so, while producers wanting to do as little as possible may be tempted to overstate their own production costs. People might also end up refusing to comply with the official production quotas and consumer allocations. Socialist economies have invariably found themselves hampered by the existence both of producer sabotage and of "black markets," which is, ultimately, a reflection of planned economies failing to provide appropriate incentives for people to behave in (socially) desirable fashion.

The philosophy outlined above might be termed the **liberal economic school of thought**, and it falls under the category of "ideology." Microeconomic model-based analysis is aimed at formalizing *a portion* of this ideology and demonstrating its validity. For example, the "competitive equilibrium existence theorem" in microeconomics guarantees that it is possible to achieve supply/demand balance in all markets simultaneously, while the "fundamental theorems of welfare economics" promise that this supply/demand balance will be efficient.

However, there is something of a gap between the liberal economic school of thought and the perfectly competitive market model used in microeconomics. The latter shows that it is possible to achieve simultaneous equilibrium in all markets, but offers no clear guidance as to how those equilibrium prices can be achieved. Moreover, while the liberal economic school of thought contends that the market mechanism is the best possible means of allocating resources, it would perhaps be a step too far to argue that the perfectly competitive market model has conclusively demonstrated this. We say this because, although the perfectly competitive market model does serve to clarify how the market mechanism works, it does nothing to explain how various other conceivable resource allocation methods work, and, as such, is ultimately incapable of saying which particular method might be "best."[39]

It also needs to be recognized that there is an unavoidable gap between microeconomic model-based analysis and actual reality. The perfectly competitive market model that we have studied above does not incorporate either "time" or "uncertainty." Nor does it specify the process by which exchange and distribution are mediated by "currency" (a critical component of a real-world market economy), and nor does it make allowance for the limits of human computational power. But that is not to say that research has ground to a complete halt. Indeed, a perusal of the more advanced literature in fields such as microeconomics, macroeconomics, and finance will uncover a range of efforts to successfully incorporate time and uncertainty into economic models, and issues such as the role of currency as a mediunm of exchange, the limits of computational power and behavioral biases (systematic departure of human decision making from perfect rationality) also continue to be studied by cutting-edge researchers I want you to understand that the models you study in this book is just a fruitful first step to capture the function of the market mechanism, and more exciting research is to be

---

[39] Our discussion of game theory and the economics of information from Chapter 6 onward should help to clarify what progress has been made in this regard.

Figure 3.51 The relationship between reality, ideas, and models

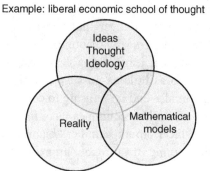

Example: liberal economic school of thought

Reality

Ideas Thought Ideology

Mathematical models

Example: collapse of socialism   Example: general equilibrium model

done to fully incorporate what we observe in reality and what has been informally captured by "ideas, thoghts and ideology".

As explained above and illustrated in Figure 3.51, there are, clearly, areas in which the liberal economic school of thought (ideology) and the perfectly competitive market model overlap as well as areas in which they differ. Failure to appropriately distinguish between "ideology," "reality," and "mathematical models" is unfortunately all too common, and a proper understanding of overlaps and boundaries will prove invaluable when contemplating real-world socio-economic phenomena. Modern economic theory has played a crucial role in this regard by using clearly specified models and rigorous logic to identify those aspects of "ideology" that hold (reasonably) true in reality as well as those that are best taken with a grain of salt (or dismissed altogether).

4   Market Failures

The above discussion has focused on the ways in which the market mechanism gets things right, or, more specifically, on the ability of perfectly competitive markets to allocate various resources (efficiently) in accordance with the needs of the people when all goes well. However, it is important to acknowledge that the market mechanism may also occasionally get things wrong. In this chapter we focus on so-called **market failures**, or typical cases in which the market mechanism fails to achieve an efficient allocation of resources – for whatever reason – and how they might be best addressed. Our discussion focuses on the following two themes in particular.

- **Externalities**, or problems such as environmental pollution that markets are unable to resolve if simply left to their own accord.
- **Public goods**, or things such as parks that need to be provided by the government because these things are difficult to supply via the market mechanism.

4.1   Externalities

In this section we learn about issues such as air pollution, noise from factories and highways, and access to sunlight, which prove incapable of being resolved via natural market forces. Let us begin with the definition of such "externalities."

The consumers and firms that comprise an economy will naturally impact on one another in various ways. Figure 4.1 looks at the two basic channels via which the production or consumption of a given economic agent (firm or consumer) may end up impacting on the utility or profits of another economic agent.

The first channel reflects the indirect impact through a change in market prices, such as when a firm lays off so many workers that wages are driven lower (thereby causing other workers to lose out) or when the construction of a new subway station serves to drive up surrounding land prices (thereby benefiting landowners). This indirect impact of a change in market prices is known as a **pecuniary externality**. The second – more direct – channel is that via which so-called **technical externalities** arise, with typical examples including environmental pollution, cigarette smoke, and noise. These examples would all be referred to as **negative externalities**, given that

Figure 4.1 Externalities

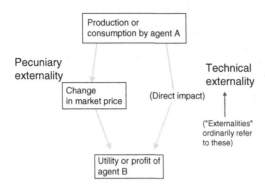

they entail consumers and/or firms suffering direct harm as a consequence of the actions of others, but there are also examples of **positive** (technical) **externalities**, such as when an orchard's yield may be boosted by the arrival of a beekeeper due to an increase in pollination.

Pecuniary externalities arising indirectly via changes in market prices do not actually result in market failure, but, as we shall see below, markets do indeed fail to achieve the "desired" or "efficient" outcome in cases where technical externalities are present (whether negative or positive). As such, economists will generally be referring to technical externalities – those that cause market failures – when they simply say "externality."

(a)   Market Equilibrium with Externalities

A good example of a negative technical externality is a steelworks that dumps sludge into a nearby river, thereby making it harder for downstream fishermen to earn a good living. Suppose that, for each ton of steel produced, the associated dumping of sludge (environment pollution) inflicts $500 in damage on downstream fishermen. How will the socially desirable level of steel output compare with the actual equilibrium level resulting from the market mechanism?

Let us begin by recalling that the steel plant's marginal cost MC(Q) represents the additional cost incurred when increasing steel output by a tiny amount from Q. This cost must be paid by the steel plant itself, and as such is sometimes referred to as the **private marginal cost**. However, there is also a social cost associated with the damages suffered by fishermen as a consequence of steel production. In this example, these damages amount to $500 per ton of steel produced, meaning that the marginal cost of steel production for the society as a whole is MC + 500, which is called the **social marginal cost**. Here the "500" part of the social marginal cost corresponds to the additional loss suffered by others (fishermen) due to a tiny (or marginal) increase in steel output, and is referred to as the **marginal loss**. The definition of social marginal cost thus boils down to the following when a negative externality is present:

> **Social marginal cost** = private marginal cost + **marginal loss**
> **marginal loss**   ↑
> the additional loss suffered by
> others due to a marginal increase
> in output

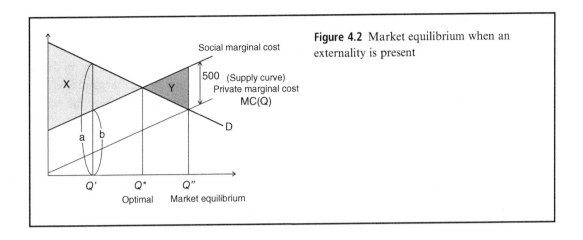

Figure 4.2 Market equilibrium when an externality is present

Figure 4.2 uses this concept in determining the socially optimal level of steel production. Suppose that output is given by Q'. The height of the demand curve denotes the amount that consumers are willing to pay for steel, meaning that consumers are willing to pay $\$a$ in order for steel production to be increased by a tiny amount from Q'. Increasing production by a tiny amount from Q' will meanwhile impose the cost $\$b$ (= social marginal cost) on society. The benefit for increasing production (a) is in this case greater than the cost (b), meaning that it is socially desirable for output to be increased. The net upshot is that output should be increased up to the point Q^*, where the demand curve equals (intersects with) the social marginal cost. This is the socially optimal steel output level, and it delivers society as a whole the surplus denoted by area X in Figure 4.2.

But how much steel will end up being produced if the market is simply left to its own devices? As we learned in Section 2.2 (c) (1), in the benchmark case the supply curve will be equal to the (private) marginal cost. A competitive market will thus see the (excessively high) output level Q'' determined by the intersection between the private marginal cost (supply) curve and the demand curve. For each unit of steel that is produced beyond the socially optimal amount Q^*, a loss will be incurred that is equal to the social marginal cost minus the height of the demand curve. The sum of these losses at the above-optimal output level Q'' is thus given by the area Y in Figure 4.2, which represents the amount by which surplus for society as a whole falls short of the level at the optimal production amount Q^*. The above is thus an example of how the market mechanism fails to achieve an efficient allocation of resources in the face of a negative externality (pollution).

What is the cause of this market failure? Put simply, market failure happens because *the firm does not regard the part of the social cost associated with the harm caused by sludge to fisherman as something it must pay out of its own pocket*. The level of steel production thus ends up being higher than desirable from a social perspective. A possible solution quickly springs to mind: if the **externality** can somehow be **internalized** – in other words, if we can somehow make sure that the firm factors social costs into its production decisions – then it should be possible to steer the economy toward the socially optimal output level. As we show in the following section, this desired outcome can be achieved via judicious application of a tax and/or subsidy.

(b)   Pigovian Taxes

Let us now internalize the costs associated with pollution (sludge emissions) by taxing steel producers by an amount equal to the marginal loss imposed on fishermen, or, in this example, by $500 per ton of steel output. A tax that is set at a level equal to the marginal loss is known as a **Pigovian (or Pigouvian) tax**.[1] A general definition of a Pigovian tax where the production of some good entails negative externalities is as follows:

> **Pigovian tax rate** = marginal loss
> = additional loss incurred by others due to a marginal increase in production.

How will the producer behave under a Pigovian tax regime? Suppose that

$$\underset{\text{Marginal cost}}{\text{MC}} + \underset{\text{Pigovian tax rate}}{500} < \underset{\text{steel price}}{P}.$$

The cost of increasing output by a tiny amount (MC + 500) will be less than the revenue earned by increasing output by a tiny amount (P), making it worthwhile to do so. Conversely, the producer will want to reduce output of MC + 500 > P. The optimal production amount will thus be determined by

$$\underset{\text{Marginal cost}}{\text{MC}} + \underset{\text{Pigovian tax rate}}{500} = \underset{\text{output price}}{P}.$$

As can be seen from Figure 4.3, the supply curve under a Pigovian tax is given by MC + the tax rate. But the Pigovian tax rate is equal to the marginal loss, meaning that

Supply curve under a Pigovian tax → MC + marginal loss = **social marginal cost**.

The market equilibrium under a Pigovian tax is thus determined by the intersection between the demand curve and the social marginal cost (supply curve) and achieves the socially optimal production level (as should once again be clear from Figure 4.2).

(c)   Pigovian Subsidies

Above we have shown how taxing steel production is an effective means of reining in pollution (a negative externality) by preventing above-optimal output levels. It turns out that it is also possible to achieve the socially desirable output level by *subsidizing producers that refrain from overproduction*.

As we saw in Figure 4.2, in the absence of some sort of government intervention, equilibrium output Q'' turns out to be higher than the socially optimal level Q^*. But what about if the government offers steel producers a subsidy of $500 for each ton by which they reduce production from Q''? Recall that $500 represents the marginal loss to fishermen associated with a ton of steel production. This is referred to as a **Pigovian subsidy**.

[1] Named for English economist Arthur Cecil Pigou (1877–1959).

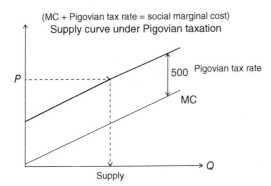

(MC + Pigovian tax rate = social marginal cost)
Supply curve under Pigovian taxation

Figure 4.3 Supply curve under Pigovian taxation

> **Pigovian subsidy**: a subsidy equal to the marginal loss is paid to producers for each unit by which they reduce output from an excessive (above-optimal) level.

If the cost of producing steel is C(Q), then the steel producer will choose its output level so as to maximize profits as follows:

$$\text{Profit}: PQ - C(Q) + 500(Q'' - Q)$$

Pigovian subsidy

(subsidy received for

reducing output

excessive level Q'').

In this expression $500Q''$ is a constant term (i.e. is not affected by the level of output), meaning that it suffices for the producer to maximize the remaining part:

$$PQ - C(Q) - 500Q. \qquad (1)$$

This turns out to be the same as the profit under a Pigovian tax. In other words, surprising though it might seem, the producer ends up maximizing (1) irrespective of whether it faces a Pigovian tax or a Pigovian subsidy, meaning that the optimal output level from the producer's perspective is ultimately the same. We have thus shown that a Pigovian tax and a Pigovian subsidy are both capable of *achieving the socially optimal output level.*

(d)   Taxes or Subsidies?

This leads us to an obvious question: if either a tax or a subsidy is capable of limiting pollution to the socially optimal level, then which should we use? Above we have shown that either policy instrument will serve to maximize the overall social "pie" (total surplus), but it does need to be recognized that the way in which this pie is divided up will differ depending on whether producers are taxed or subsidized. Figure 4.4 should help to make this all clear.

Figure 4.4 (a) shows the breakdown of total surplus under a Pigovian tax. Area C is equal to output (Q^*) × 500, which is in turn equal to the total revenue raised by the Pigovian tax given that the tax rate is 500. The damage inflicted upon fishermen per unit of output is also

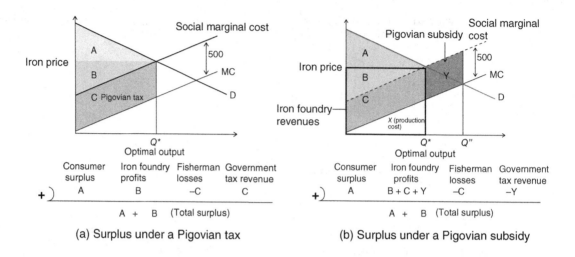

Figure 4.4 Pigovian policy and allocation of surplus

equal to 500, meaning that area C can, alternatively, be viewed as the total damage done to fishermen.

Figure 4.4 (b) considers the case of a Pigovian subsidy. Assuming that steel production does not entail any fixed costs, the cost of producing Q^* will be given by the area of the white triangle X, which is effectively the sum of marginal costs. The producer's revenue will be equal to the steel price multiplied by Q^*, which corresponds to the rectangle area (B + C + X). Subtracting out the cost X leaves profit (excluding subsidies), or B + C. The total subsidy received by the producer for reducing output from Q'' to Q^* – at a rate of 50 per unit of output – is, meanwhile, given by area Y.

Total surplus A + B ends up being the same under either a Pigovian tax or a Pigovian subsidy, but the breakdown of this surplus clearly differs, as illustrated in Figure 4.4. What if the government were to compensate fishermen for their losses C? In Figure 4.4 (a), this could be done without any net impact on the government's coffers by simply paying fishermen an amount equal to the tax revenues raised from steel producers. Such an approach would likely be agreeable to many from a fairness perspective.

If the government instead decides to compensate fishermen under a Pigovian subsidy regime, then it will face a deficit of $Y + C$, while steel producers will earn a very sizable profit of $B + C + Y$. This might seem unfair, in as much as steel producers would effectively be profiting from their status as polluters, but could nevertheless make sense under certain circumstances. For example, consider a case in which people suddenly start fishing downstream from a steelworks that has been operating for many years. The steel producer might have reasonable grounds for asserting a right to keep producing at previous levels, in which case a policy of having the government subsidize the producer for reducing its output might not actually seem all that unreasonable.

In other words, *whereas a Pigovian tax might seem fairer if one focuses on the right of fishermen not to suffer from pollution, a Pigovian subsidy might seem fairer if one instead focuses on the right of steelmakers to pollute the river.*

Case Study 4.1 London Congestion Charging as an Example of a Pigovian Tax

If you think that Pigovian tax is only a theoretical possibility, now is probably a good time for a real-world example in the form of the London congestion charge.[2] London has long suffered from a negative externality in the form of traffic jams, whereby the larger the number of cars that are on the road, the lower the speed at which traffic will be able to move. Indeed, the average speed is said to have been on a rough par with the horse-drawn carriages of the nineteenth century at one point. The London congestion charge was launched as a form of Pigovian tax in 2003 by then mayor of London, Ken Livingstone, and it remains in operation to this day. The congestion charge was originally set at £11.50 per day for cars entering the charging zone – as marked by signs such as the one shown in Figure 4.5 (a) – between 7:00 a. m. and 10:00 p.m. on weekdays.

Drivers were asked to pay this charge either in advance or by 10:00 p.m. on the date of travel, typically via the Internet, at a convenience store, or by using an automated payment machine. The system is enforced via a camera-based surveillance system (Figure 4.5 (b)), which allows for the registration numbers of cars in the charging zone to be automatically checked against a database of congestion charge payments. Non-payment was originally punished by a £130 fine. As of 2011 the

(a)   (b)

A congestion charging sign is displayed on October 24, 2021, in London
Credit: Hollie Adams / Getty Images

Congestion Zone cameras, April 2008
Credit: Daniel Berehulak / Getty Images

Figure 4.5 London congestion charging
Source: Photographs: Aflo Co., Ltd.

---

[2] Basic information can be found at the Transport for London website: https://tfl.gov.uk/modes/driving/congestion-charge.

Case Study 4.1 (cont.)

relatively complex scheme cost some £90 million to administer, but this amounted to less than half the approximately £227 million in revenue from charges and fines.

So, just how effective has the scheme been in reducing congestion?

As can be seen from Figure 4.6 (a), the number of (private) cars on the road in central London declined significantly following the scheme's introduction. Congestion – as measured by the time

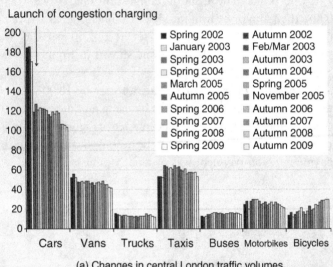

(a) Changes in central London traffic volumes

(Vertical axis shows traffic volumes at congestion charging
times in thousands of vehicles)

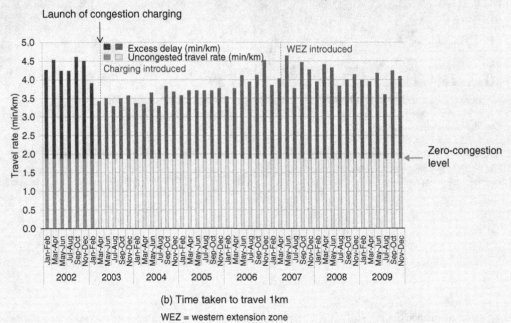

(b) Time taken to travel 1km

WEZ = western extension zone

Figure 4.6 Impact of London congestion charging

taken to travel 1km – was alleviated to some degree initially, but has since gradually deteriorated once again (Figure 4.6 (b)).[3] However, given that the congestion charge has proved successful in keeping traffic volumes down (Figure 4.6 (a)), it seems likely that the situation would have been even worse if not for the scheme's introduction. A strong case can therefore be made that the London congestion charge has indeed proved reasonably successful in alleviating traffic jams on central London roads.

(e)   Some Important Remarks

Two points about externalities and Pigovian taxes and subsidies warrant further comment.

[i] Problems with Pigovian taxes and subsidies

Using Pigovian taxes and subsidies to achieve an optimal outcome requires knowledge of the marginal loss, which in many cases may be difficult if not impossible to measure with any real confidence. Taking the above example, only the fishermen themselves can truly know just how severely they are impacted by pollution from an upstream steelworks. The government can of course ask them, but there is no guarantee that the fishermen will not exaggerate the severity of their losses. *Calculating the optimal Pigovian tax or subsidy rate* (based on the marginal loss) *will thus require some means of extracting the private information* known only to the fishermen. Modern economic theory has already made some progress in showing what degree of "efficiency" is achievable under such circumstances and how various "mechanisms" (institutional arrangements) might best be designed for that purpose.[4]

In practice, policy-makers will tend to set the Pigovian tax rate based on either a rough estimate of the marginal loss or a rough idea as to the degree to which production (and, in the above example, pollution) should be reduced. The aforementioned London congestion charge scheme was also designed in this necessarily "approximate" fashion. In such instances the tax rate cannot realistically be expected to achieve a truly "optimal" allocation of resources, but the outcome should nevertheless be considerably better than if no Pigovian taxes or subsidies were used whatsoever and externalities were simply left unchecked. (This is one reason why the phrase "Never let the perfect be the enemy of good" is quite popular among economists.)

[ii] Why do externalities prevent the market from making efficient allocations?

As we have explained above, the reason why pollution (and other externalities) prevent efficient allocations from being achieved is that polluters do not count the marginal loss (inflicted on others) as part of their own costs. Let us now use economic theory to explain why externalities cause market failures from a slightly different perspective. In Section 3.3 the first fundamental theorem of welfare economics told us that an efficient allocation of resources is achievable

---

[3] Transport for London attributes this deterioration to the impact of various roadworks as well as the adoption of new more pedestrian-friendly traffic rules.

[4] We conclude Section 4.1 (f) with a brief discussion of some recent research in the fields of information economics and mechanism design.

provided that all goods are traded in perfectly competitive markets. Why does the existence of an externality prevent this from holding true? The answer is that the steelworks is producing not only steel, but also a "good" – pollution (sludge) – that confers negative utility on the recipient. Achieving an efficient allocation of resources will thus require both steel and sludge to be traded in competitive markets, but the unfortunate reality is that no such market for sludge (usually) exists. This is the reason why markets fail to effectively limit pollution. Put simply, *inefficient allocations of resources (market failures) arise* – at least in standard cases – *due to a lack of markets in which externalities* (such as pollution) *can be freely traded.*

Case Study 4.2 Global Warming and Emission Rights Trading

Markets to trade externalities such as pollution were long considered little more than a theoretical construct, but a number of nations have responded to worsening climate change by launching markets in which greenhouse gases (such as CO_2) can effectively be traded. Rather than having greenhouse gas emitters and climate change sufferers trade directly in the emissions themselves, the government instead determines the total amount of emissions that is "desirable" (or at least acceptable) and then issues producers with rights to emit up to that level. Producers are then free to trade those rights among themselves, which should, ideally, result in an efficient allocation. "Carbon emission allowances" are in fact already very actively traded on the London Intercontinental Exchange (ICE).

(f)   Negotiating Externalities Away: The Coase Theorem

Some argue that, even if the government does not intervene by introducing Pigovian taxes or subsidies and even if there is no market in which pollution can be traded, it should still be possible to achieve an efficient outcome if the parties affected by pollution or other externalities negotiate rationally. This view is popular among members of the so-called Chicago School of economists, who (generally speaking) believe that competitive markets should be left to do their own thing with only a bare minimum of government intervention (if any). The possibility of solving the problem with externalities via rational negotiation was notably formalized by prominent economist and author Ronald Coase in what is today known as the **Coase theorem**.

Coase theorem: *even in the presence of externalities,*

(1) *it is possible to achieve an efficient level of externalities through negotiations between the parties involved* provided that negotiation costs are sufficiently low; and

(2) furthermore, provided that consumer satisfaction can be measured in terms of consumer surplus, *the same level of externalities is achieved irrespective of how* (externality-related) *property rights are initially allocated.*

Each of these claims requires some further explanation. Claim (1) is grounded in the following way of thinking. Consider the example of a negative externality whereby the construction of a skyscraper blocks out the sunlight of local residents. Suppose also that the planned building is going to be "too tall" and thus result in an inefficient outcome. Recalling the definition of (Pareto) efficiency, when starting from an inefficient allocation it should be possible to find some way of making everyone better off.[5] In this case, it should be possible to make everyone happier by having the developer reduce the height of the building and then arranging appropriate compensation. This follows directly from the definition of inefficiency: it is possible to make everyone happier if the initial state is inefficient. If the developer and the local residents are rational, they must realize that there is a way to make all of them happier. The Coase theorem then goes on to argue that, provided that the cost of negotiating an agreement to shift to a better-for-everyone allocation is sufficiently low, then the agreement should be made and the inefficiency associated with the negative externality should be eliminated. This is what the first part of the Coase theorem – claim (1) – is asserting.

Comment 4.1

The above may seem eminently reasonable, but, as we discuss at the end of this section, subsequent economic research has demonstrated that a number of important auxiliary conditions must be satisfied in order for the first part of the Coase theorem to hold true.

What about the second claim? Returning to our skyscraper/sunlight example, the following two cases are possible with regard to externality-related rights: either local residents can stake claim to a *right to receive unfettered sunlight,* or the property developer can insist that he has the *right to build as tall a building as he wishes.* Intuitively, one would expect the building to end up being lower under the former case and taller under the latter, but the second part of the Coase theorem, surprisingly, tells us that *the height of the building will be exactly the same in either case.*

Why? If consumer satisfaction can be represented by consumer surplus, then the combined satisfaction of all parties – or total surplus – will be equal to the sum of consumer surplus and profits. Negotiating an efficient outcome will thus entail:

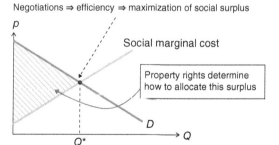

Negotiations ⇒ efficiency ⇒ maximization of social surplus

Figure 4.7 Second part of the Coase theorem

Level of production (and therefore the level of externalities) does not depend on the allocation of property rights

(It maximizes total surplus)

---

[5] Or, more precisely, it should be possible to make at least someone better off without making anyone worse off.

– choosing the level of externalities (the height of the skyscraper) to maximize total surplus (the size of the overall pie); and then
– apportioning maximized surplus based on the rights of the parties concerned.

In other words, *irrespective of how rights are initially allocated, the level of externality – in this example the height of the building – should end up being set at the level that maximizes total surplus* (Figure 4.7).

A slightly technical note: what are the ramifications of assuming that "consumer satisfaction can be represented by consumer surplus"? As we explained in Section 3.1 (c) in the context of partial equilibrium analysis, the consumer's utility function will need to be "quasilinear" in order for this assumption to hold true. When the consumer does have a utility function of that particular form, consumer surplus will not be impacted in any way by the level of income (i.e. there will be no "income effects"). In other words, *the second part of the Coase theorem requires a "no income effects" condition*, which in the above example boils down to an assumption that neither the rights of the property developer (or those who will live in the skyscraper) nor the harm suffered by local residents due to deprivation of sunlight will be affected in any way by income levels.

Let us conclude this section with some points pertaining to the first half of the Coase theorem, or the claim that an efficient outcome can be negotiated provided that negotiation costs are sufficiently low. We should begin by stressing that *this claim is not actually expressed as a "theorem" that can be rigorously proved*. We say this because "negotiation costs" have not been clearly defined. If negotiation costs are defined in such a way that they will be low when the outcome of negotiation is efficient and high when inefficient, then the claim will hold true automatically and thus be essentially meaningless.[6] The first part of the Coase theorem should thus be regarded *not* as a "theorem" that has been proved to be true but as a sort of loosely formulated conjecture that leads us to ask important questions about the nature of negotiation costs and factors that might make them higher or lower. The field of economics has, of course, advanced to some degree since the above claim was first made by Coase, with developments in areas such as information economics and game theory – discussed in the second part of this book – helping to shed light on the aforementioned questions.

Second, recall how we went about explaining the first part of the Coase theorem. The argument can be generalized as follows.

A naive laissez-faire philosophy: by definition, an "inefficient" outcome implies that there is some change that improves the satisfaction of all parties. If all parties are rational, then they will want to shift to this better outcome rather than contenting themselves with the (inefficient) status quo. Outcomes should therefore be efficient provided only that rational individuals are permitted to act freely.

---

[6] This would be a good example of a tautology. If negotiation costs are defined in this way, then nothing else will be necessary in order for the claim to hold true, and the claim will be capable of "explaining" even things that cannot occur in practice. *A tautologous theorem is thus one that explains both everything and nothing at the same time.*

This claim appeared to be phrased in a way that makes it impossible to dispute from a purely logical perspective. It seems that the conclusion automatically follows from the definitions of inefficiency and rationality. For that reason, the "laissez-faire" philosophy was once highly influential among economists, particularly those of a more conservative bent, but subsequent advances in economic theory – particularly in the field of game theory – have actually revealed it to be "incorrect" in its simplest form. Those who are eager to learn more about this issue – where the above claim falls down, and what the right claim should be – should look forward to Section 6.4 in the second part of this book.

Comment 4.2 Situations where the First Part of the Coase Theorem Is Known to Fail

For the time being let us just present a preview of how advances in game theory and information economics have helped to make things clearer. Suppose that a pollution-emitting firm and polluted individuals are looking to negotiate the installation of some pollution-reducing device. If the cost of the device is c and its installation will reduce pollution-related harm by b, then it will be efficient to install the device provided that the benefit exceeds the cost, or if $c < b$. However, generally speaking, the cost c may be known only to the firm while the benefit b may be known only to those suffering from pollution.

Negotiations might therefore be liable to break down as a consequence of the firm overstating the cost c of installing the pollution-reducing device and/or pollution sufferers looking to hide the true benefit b. It turns out that, if both sides expect the cost c and benefit b to be continuously distributed between some minimum value (such as zero) and some maximum value (such as $1 million), then *an efficient outcome will never be achieved even if all parties are completely rational and there is zero cost associated with negotiating and drawing up contracts*. In other words, there is a very real danger that, no matter how cleverly formulated the rules of negotiation, the tendencies of the firm to overstate costs and of pollution sufferers to hide benefits will end up preventing the pollution-reducing device from being installed even in cases where $c < b$ (meaning that the true benefits outweigh the true cost).

This major result from the fields of game theory and information economics is known as the **Myerson–Satterthwaite theorem** and is one of the reasons why University of Chicago professor Roger Myerson was awarded the Nobel Memorial Prize in Economic Sciences in 2007. The theorem itself goes beyond the scope of this book,[7] but Part II will at least introduce some of the basic theoretical tools – fundamentals of game theory and information economics – that can be used to perform analysis such as the above.

---

[7] Paul Milgrom, *Putting Auction Theory to Work* (New York: Cambridge University Press, 2004), chap. 3, provides a good exposition.

4.2   Public Goods

In this section we discuss public goods as the second case in which markets fail to achieve efficient allocations of resources. We use the phrase "public good" in our everyday language to refer to something that provides benefits to the general public. However, in economics "**public good**" is a technical term referring to a very specific class of goods that satisfy the following two properties (1) and (2).

> Properties of a public good (1) **non-rivalry of consumption**: consumption of the good by one person does not reduce the amount available to be consumed by others.

An ordinary good does not satisfy this property. For example, if I eat an apple, then that obviously means that there is one less apple available for others to eat. An ordinary good such as an apple may therefore be referred to as a **private good**. However, satellite TV does satisfy the above property. Just because I watch a given broadcast, that has no impact whatsoever on the ability of other people to watch the same broadcast. In addition to this "non-rivalry of consumption" property, a public good will also need to satisfy the following.

> Properties of a public good (2) **non-excludability of consumption**: it is difficult or even impossible to prevent certain individuals from consuming the good.

Requiring some sort of decoder in order to watch a satellite broadcast is a means of excluding those who do not pay the relevant subscription fee. So, satellite TV does not satisfy this property (2) even though it satisfies (1). However, when it comes to matters of national defense, it will seldom be practical for the military to refuse to defend the homes of certain individuals. National defense can thus be viewed as satisfying the "non-excludability of consumption" property.

Because a public good satisfies the above two properties, for mathematical modeling purposes it can be treated as a good for which *the supply of some amount Q allows everyone to consume that amount Q*. It turns out that there are not actually all that many real-world examples of pure public goods. The best examples perhaps include national defense, diplomacy, a natural landscape that has been spared environmental degradation, or a beautiful streetscape (scenery). Other goods such as parks may share certain attributes of public goods, so the analysis in this section applies to some extent.

As I mentioned earlier, we should note that the general public may use the term "public good" in a slightly different way from economists. For example, aged care services and education may often be described as "public goods" by virtue of their quite significant benefits to the public. However, both are actually examples of private goods in as much as they satisfy neither (1) nor (2) above. Economists focus on goods satisfying (1) and (2) because *those properties make it difficult to design a market in which such goods can be traded*. Properties (1) and (2) mean that, even if someone were to pay money to produce a public good, everyone would be able to consume that good in the same quantity (including those who did not pay for it), which would of course make it difficult – or, in practice, impossible – to solicit contributions via any sort of free market mechanism. I mean, would you pay for something if you would be able to use it for free anyway?[8] In such cases the government will, basically, need to step in to supply the public good owing to the inability of the market to do so. However, aged care services and education are what economists term "private goods" (their public benefits notwithstanding), which means it is possible to supply them via markets on a "pay for what you consume" basis.

(a)   Optimal Supply of a Public Good: Partial Equilibrium Analysis

So, how should public goods be supplied? Let us begin with a partial equilibrium analysis focusing solely on the public good itself. In doing so, let us first introduce the concept of the "marginal value" assigned to the public good by each consumer.

> The **marginal value of a public good** $V_i(Q)$ is *the amount that consumer i would be prepared to pay in order to* (marginally) *increase consumption of that good by one unit* from Q.

Figure 4.8 is a graph of marginal value. Our public good here is a park, and the graph shows that, if the park currently has an area of $100 \, m^2$, then consumer i would be prepared to pay $500 in order to expand the park by $1 \, m^2$. The bigger the park gets, the less that consumer i will be willing to pay in order to make it even bigger. As such, the graph of marginal value will generally be downward-sloping to the right.

The marginal value of a public good to society as a whole ("**social marginal value of a public good**") can be derived from the marginal values of individual consumers, as shown in Figure 4.9. In order to expand a $100 \, m^2$ park by a further $1 \, m^2$, consumer 1 is willing to pay $800 while consumer 2 is prepared to pay $500. Society as a whole – in this simple two-consumer world – is thus willing to pay a total of $1,300 in order to expand the park. *The social marginal value of a public good is thus equal to the sum of the marginal values of individuals*, meaning that in graphical terms we can obtain the social marginal value curve as the *vertical* summation of the individual marginal value curves.[9]

Figure 4.8 Marginal value of a public good

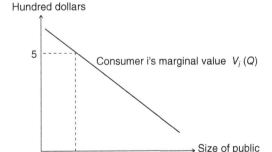

Hundred dollars

5

Consumer i's marginal value $V_i(Q)$

Size of public good Q (park)

$100 \, m^2$

---

[8] As we shall discuss in (b) below, this is referred to as "the free rider problem."

[9] This is in contrast to the situation with private goods, where we obtain the market demand curve as the *horizontal* summation of individual demand curves.

Figure 4.9 Social marginal value of a public good

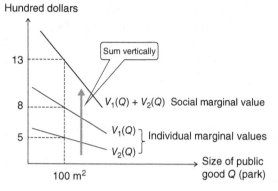

Figure 4.10 Optimal supply of a public good

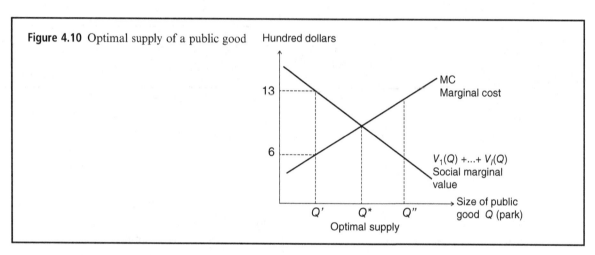

The optimal supply of a public good can be determined as shown in Figure 4.10, using the social marginal value and the marginal cost (MC) of supplying the public good.

At point Q' the marginal cost is lower than the social marginal value. Since it would cost only $600 to expand the park by $1\,m^2$ (the marginal cost) and the people as a whole are actually prepared to pay $1,300 (the social marginal value), it makes sense to go ahead and expand the park. Conversely, at point Q'' the social marginal value is less than the marginal cost, meaning that society would be better off if the park were shrunk. Optimal supply will thus correspond to the point at which the social marginal value is equal to the marginal cost:

Optimal supply condition for a public good (partial equilibrium analysis)

$$\underset{\text{sum of individual marginal values}}{V_1(Q^*) + \cdots + V_1(Q^*)} = \underset{\text{marginal cost}}{MC(Q^*).}$$

(b)   Lindahl Equilibrium

Above we have shown how to determine the optimal supply of a public good. But how much should be collected from whom in order to fund that supply, and how much should be paid to the producer of the public good? In considering one possible answer to this question, let us stick with the example of a park and assume that it is produced by a private company, a property developer.

Step 0 (gathering relevant information): the government needs to find out the marginal value assigned to the park by each individual and then calculates the (optimal) supply Q^* – and the corresponding social marginal value $V(Q^*)$ – for which the social marginal value $V(Q) = V_1(Q) + \ldots + V_1(Q)$ is equal to the marginal cost MC(Q).

Step 1: the government asks the property developer to supply the park at price $V(Q^*)$.

The supply curve for the (perfectly competitive) developer will be given by the marginal cost MC, meaning that the park will be supplied at the optimal level Q^* (Figure 4.11).

The amount paid by the government to the developer is equal to the area of the shaded rectangle in Figure 4.11, or $V(Q^*) \times Q^*$. How should this cost be covered? The following step allows for just the right amount to be collected from consumers.

Step 2: each consumer i pays $V_i(Q^*) \times Q^*$ – an amount proportional to their own marginal value – to the producer.

The total amount paid to the producer will thus be precisely equal to the area of the gray shaded rectangle in Figure 4.11:

$$(V_1(Q^*) + \cdots + V_1(Q^*))Q^* = V(Q^*)Q^*.$$

This three-step process was devised by Swedish economist Erik Lindahl (1891–1960) and leads to what is now known as a **Lindahl equilibrium**.

Lindahl equilibrium: suppose that the marginal value of a public good to consumer i is given by $V_i(Q)$.

Step 0: the government gathers information about individual marginal values and calculates the (optimal) supply Q^* and $V(Q^*)$ such that

$$V(Q^*) = V_1(Q^*) + \ldots + V_1(Q^*) = MC(Q^*).$$

Step 1: the government orders Q^* of the public good from the perfectly competitive producer at price $V(Q^*)$, which is equal to the marginal social value of the public good.

Step 2: each consumer i pays $V_i(Q^*) \times Q^*$ – an amount proportional to their own marginal value – to the producer.

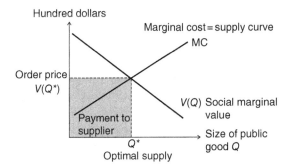

Figure 4.11 Ordering a public good

Case Study 4.3 Streetlights as a Public Good

The next example should illustrate how concepts such as "public good" and "Lindahl equilibrium" can be usefully applied to real-world situations. Three residents of an apartment block – conveniently named A, B, and C – are considering having streetlights installed on the narrow path to the entry. There is space for up to three streetlights, and each resident's enthusiasm for the project differs, as summarized in Table 4.1.

Table 4.1 Maximum amount each resident is willing to pay for each streetlight

	First streetlight	Second streetlight	Third streetlight
A	$900	$600	$300
B	$500	$400	$300
C	$1,000	$600	$400

For example, reading along A's row, we see that A is prepared to pay up to $900 to have the first streetlight installed, $600 for the second, and $300 for the third.

Each streetlight costs $1,500 to install. So how do we go about determining the following?

- How many streetlights should be installed?
- How much should A, B, and C be asked to pay?

Microeconomics offers a satisfyingly neat solution.

Is streetlighting a public good? It certainly satisfies the first necessary property – non-rivalry of consumption – given that the benefit of streetlighting to A does not detract from the benefit to B in any way. It also satisfies the second necessary property – non-excludability of consumption – given that there is no practical way of preventing C from benefiting from whatever streetlights end up being installed. Streetlights can thus be considered quite a pure example of a public good.

Next consider the meaning of Table 4.1. For example, the "$600" figure for "Second streetlight" for A means that A is prepared to pay up to $600 to have a second streetlight installed. This corresponds to A's **marginal value** (for a second streetlight) and can be written as $V_A(2)$. In other words, the "A" row of the table gives A's marginal values as follows:

$$V_A(1) = 900 \quad V_A(2) = 600 \quad V_A(3) = 300 \quad \text{(measured in \$100)}$$

The **social marginal value** is calculated by summing the individual marginal values of A, B, and C. For example, the social marginal value of a first streetlight is equal to the "vertical" sum of the entries in the "First streetlight" column, or $900 + 500 + 1,000 = 2,400$ (in $100). The social marginal values of a second and a third streetlight can also be calculated by vertically summing the corresponding rows, leading us to the graph shown in Figure 4.12.

It is possible to supply any number of streetlights at $1,500 each, meaning that the marginal cost can be viewed as $1,500. Figure 4.12 shows that the social marginal value of a first streetlight ($2,400) exceeds this marginal cost ($1,500). It therefore makes perfect sense for a first streetlight to be installed for the following reasons.

Case Study 4.3 (cont.)

Table 4.2 Amount per streetlight to be paid by each resident

	Amount paid per streetlight
A	$600
B	$400
C	$600

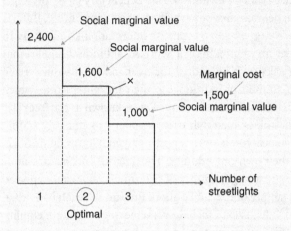

Figure 4.12 Social marginal value

– The three residents are together willing to pay $2,400 to have a first streetlight installed.
– The cost of doing so is just $1,500.

The same argument applies to a second streetlight, given that the social marginal value ($1,600) exceeds the marginal cost (constant at $1,500). However, the social marginal value of a third streetlight is less than the marginal cost, meaning that installation would not be worth it.

The optimal supply of streetlights (the public good) thus turns out to be two, and is determined by the point at which the social marginal value and the marginal cost intersect.

Let us now use the **Lindahl equilibrium** approach to consider how much each of A, B, and C should be asked to pay. Two streetlights are to be installed, so we charge each individual an amount *per streetlight* equal to their marginal value for a second streetlight. The relevant column from Table 4.1 has been extracted in Table 4.2. Note that, because two streetlights are being installed, each resident's total payment will be twice that shown.

Some money – corresponding to the segment X in Figure 4.12 – will be left over given that the entries in Table 4.2 sum to $1,600 whereas the cost of procuring each streetlight is $1,500, but we can refund this money to A, B, and C via some sort of appropriate method.[10]

---

[10] This issue stems from the fact that it is not possible to supply a fraction of a streetlight. Where supply can be varied continuously – such as for the area of a park – the amount required and the amount paid will match up perfectly at the intersection of the social marginal benefit curve and the marginal cost curve, meaning that no money will be left over.

Case Study 4.3 (cont.)

Following the Lindahl equilibrium approach thus results in streetlights (a public good) being supplied in the optimal quantity, with costs collected in accordance with a **"beneficiary pays"** principle in the sense that an individual with a higher marginal value will be asked to pay more.

Let us conclude with some **very important caveats** regarding the use of a Lindahl equilibrium approach to supply a public good. As we learned from Case Study 4.3, a "beneficiary pays" principle applies in the sense that an individual with a higher marginal value will be asked to pay more. But it is important to recognize that each individual's marginal value is **private information** known only to that individual. Suppose that the government announces that it will use a Lindahl equilibrium approach to supply a public good, and then asks each individual for their marginal values. Each individual will end up being asked to pay an amount proportional to their marginal value, which gives them an obvious incentive to understate their willingness to pay. This is known as the **free rider problem**. In our above example of streetlights we assumed that each resident was honestly stating their marginal values, but in reality one might expect residents to report somewhat lower figures – i.e. hide the true benefit – in the hope of reducing their own expenditures. The free rider problem is liable to be particularly serious in cases where there are a large number of consumers, and each reported marginal value has only a minimal impact on supply of the public good. Put simply, each individual consumer may claim that their own marginal value is extremely low. Achieving a Lindahl equilibrium may thus prove difficult in cases where this sort of asymmetry of information applies.

Is there some way of achieving the optimal supply level for a public good by encouraging (or forcing) each individual to be honest in reporting their marginal value? This falls under the domain of "mechanism design," and it is currently a hot topic within the field of information economics and game theory.

(c)   Optimal Supply of a Public Good: General Equilibrium Analysis

Let us now move on to a general equilibrium framework and consider a public good as just one of the many goods that exist in an economy. For the purpose of the previous section we assumed that the satisfaction derived by a consumer from a public good could be expressed in monetary terms as "marginal value," but in this section we demonstrate the sort of analysis that can be performed without imposing such a strong assumption.[11] Once again using a park as our example of a public good, we consider a society that has a total of 10,000 m^2 in land and is looking to divide it between a park (public good) and residential lots (private goods). The possible combinations of land use can thus be expressed as shown in Figure 4.13.

Point A corresponds to all of the land being used for a park, while point B corresponds to all of the land being used for housing. If we are willing to consider the possibility that some land might be used for neither purpose (and, basically, just go to waste), then any allocation within the shaded

---

[11] The above partial equilibrium analysis assumed "quasilinear utility," a concept that we first explained in the context of consumer surplus. This boils down to a strong "no income effects" condition, or an assumption that the desirability of a public good will not be influenced in any way by income levels.

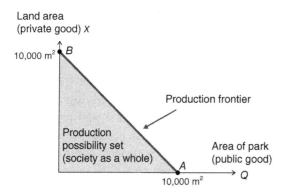

Figure 4.13 Production possibility set for society as a whole

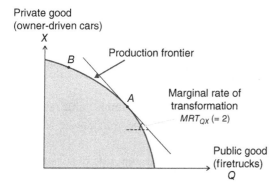

Figure 4.14 Marginal rate of transformation

triangle will be achievable. For our simple two-good economy in which only residential lots and a park (public good) are produced, this area denotes the **production possibility set** for society as a whole. The upper boundary of this set is known as the **production frontier** and corresponds to allocations where all land is used to produce one of the two goods with none going to waste.

The slope of this production frontier plays an important role in determining the optimal supply of a public good, and is known as the **marginal rate of transformation** of the public good with respect to the private good. In the above example, reducing the area of the public good (park) by 1 m^2 will allow for supply of the private good (residential lots) to be increased by 1m^2, meaning that the marginal rate of transformation is always equal to one. However, as illustrated in Figure 4.14, the marginal rate of transformation will not necessarily be constant in more general cases.

The shaded area in Figure 4.14 is the set of combinations of owner-driven cars (private good) and firetrucks (public good) that can be produced by the economy as a whole, with its boundary corresponding to the production frontier. At point A the slope of the tangent line to the production frontier – that is, the marginal rate of transformation – is equal to two, meaning that it will be necessary to reduce production of cars by (roughly) two units in order to produce an additional firetruck. In other words, the marginal rate of transformation can be defined more generally as follows.

The **marginal rate of transformation** of a public good with respect to a private good (MRT$_{QX}$)

= the slope of the (tangent line to the) production frontier;

$\cong$ **the amount of the private good that must** be **sacrificed in order** to **increase the private good by one unit**.

Comment 4.3

Unlike in our example of land use, the marginal rate of transformation is unlikely to be constant when it comes to the production of cars. Many firetrucks are being produced at point A in Figure 4.14, suggesting that the production facilities for firetrucks are operating near full capacity, meaning that producing an additional firetruck is a demanding task and requires a large amount of inputs. As such, producing an additional firetruck will necessitate quite a large reduction in production of owner-driven cars in order to free up sufficient inputs such as labor and raw materials (meaning that the marginal rate of transformation will be relatively high). In contrast, relatively few firetrucks are being produced at point B, suggesting that fewer resources will need to be diverted away from the production of private vehicles in order to produce an additional firetruck (meaning that the marginal rate of transformation will be relatively low). Therefore, the production frontier is likely to be "bowed upward" as in Figure 4.14 (i.e., the production pssibility set is likely to be convex).

Returning to our park example, let us now consider how consumers value residential lots (the private good) and parkland (the private good). This can be understood in terms of each individual's indifference curves, as illustrated in Figure 4.15.

At point A the slope of the indifference curve – or the marginal rate of substitution – is equal to 0.4. This effectively means that consumer i is willing to provide (almost) 0.4 units of the private good in order to increase the public good by one unit. In other words:

Consumer i's **marginal rate of substitution** for the public good with respect to the private good $\left(\text{MRS}^i_{QX}\right)$

$\cong$ **the amount of the private good that consumer i is willing to provide in order to increase the private good by one unit**.

Figure 4.15 Marginal rate of transformation and value of a public good

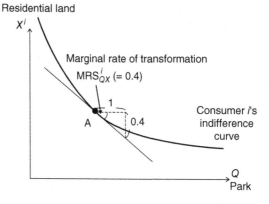

It should then be a relatively simple matter to determine the optimal supply of a public good by comparing the amount of the private good needed to increase the public good (marginal rate of transformation) with the amount of the private good that consumers are prepared to provide in order to increase the public good (marginal rate of substitution). Suppose that there are two consumers ($I = 1,2$) in our park example, and that consumer 1's marginal rate of substitution $\left(\text{MRS}^1_{QX}\right)$ is equal to 0.4 while consumer 2's $\left(\text{MRS}^2_{QX}\right)$ is equal to 0.8. This means that the two consumers – in this case, the entire public – are willing to provide $1.2\,\text{m}^2$ of residential land to be used as the park. This is greater than the marginal rate of transformation (MRT_{QX}) – or the $1\,\text{m}^2$ of land that is needed to produce an additional $1\,\text{m}^2$ of parkland – and means that it makes sense to expand the park. In other words:

$$
\underset{\underset{\begin{array}{c}\text{residential land that the}\\\text{public is willing to provide}\\\text{to expand the park by } 1\,\text{m}^2\end{array}}{\underbrace{\phantom{\text{MRS}^1_{QX} \;+\; \text{MRS}^2_{QX}}}}}{\overset{0.4\qquad\quad 0.8}{\text{MRS}^1_{QX} \;+\; \text{MRS}^2_{QX}}} \;>\; \underset{\underset{\begin{array}{c}\text{residential land necessary to}\\\text{expand the park by } 1\,\text{m}^2\end{array}}{\underbrace{\phantom{\text{MRT}_{QX}}}}}{\overset{1}{\text{MRT}_{QX}}}
$$

Conversely, if $\text{MRS}^1_{QX} + \text{MRS}^2_{QX} < \text{MRT}_{QX}$, then society as a whole would be better off if the park were to be shrunk. Optimal supply will thus require $\text{MRS}^1_{QX} + \text{MRS}^2_{QX} = \text{MRT}_{QX}$. The general condition for an economy with I consumers can be stated as follows.

Optimal supply condition for a public good (general equilibrium analysis)

For a public good Q and private good X,

sum of individual marginal rates of substitution   marginal rate of transformation

$$
\underset{\underset{\begin{array}{c}\text{amount of the private good that}\\\text{consumers are willing to provide to}\\\text{marginally increase the public good}\end{array}}{\underbrace{\phantom{\text{MRS}^1_{QX} + \cdots + \text{MRS}^I_{QX}}}}}{\text{MRS}^1_{QX} + \cdots + \text{MRS}^I_{QX}} = \underset{\underset{\begin{array}{c}\text{amount by which the private}\\\text{good must be reduced to marginally}\\\text{increase the public good}\end{array}}{\underbrace{\phantom{\text{MRT}_{QX}}}}}{\text{MRT}_{QX}}
$$

This is known as the "**Samuelson condition** (or Samuelson rule) for optimal provision of public goods" and is named after US economist Paul Samuelson (1915–2009).

Let us conclude: if we combine what we have learned about externalities and public goods with what we learned in Chapter 3 about the efficiency of a market equilibrium, we obtain the following general principle – or, you might say, an "iron law" – to guide how all economic policies should be designed and applied. This is one of the most important things you should learn in microeconomics!

General principles for economic policy: markets are flawed in the following three respects.

(1) Income is distributed unfairly, with wealth concentrated among those who own relatively scarce resources.
(2) Externalities such as pollution cannot be adequately controlled.
(3) Public goods are not supplied in the optimal amounts.

Government intervention in markets should be limited to measures aimed at addressing these three flaws, with everything else best left to the competitive market mechanism.

---

5   Monopolies

Our discussion to this point has focused entirely on perfectly competitive markets, or scenarios in which the economy is populated by large numbers of producers and consumers who individually have no ability to influence market prices. However, in reality, we may sometimes encounter cases of **imperfect competition**, whereby the number of producers is so small that individual producers do indeed wield some sort of **pricing power**. In this chapter we consider a polar case: that of a **monopoly** in which there is just a single producer. Terms such as "monopolistic" are often used in daily conversation to describe large and powerful corporations, but for the purposes of economic theory *a "monopoly" is literally a market with just one producer*. An imperfectly competitive market populated by a small number of firms is known as an **oligopoly**. A special case where there are two firms is called duopoly. Analysis of oligopolies requires new tools from the field of game theory and has thus been left for Part II of this book.

5.1   Behavior of a Monopolistic Firm

Unlike in a perfectly competitive world, where producers must take market prices as "given," a monopolistic firm will be mindful of its ability to impact the market price by altering its level of output.

    The monopolistic firm wields **pricing power** in the sense that a change in the output level Q causes the market price P to change in accordance with the demand curve D as shown in Figure 5.1 (a). Choosing output level Q results in revenue of $Q \times P$, as denoted by the thick rectangle in Figure 5.1 (b). Note that the area of this rectangle (the producer's revenue) will change as the output level Q is adjusted and the market price responds as shown in Figure 5.1 (a). If we make the simplifying assumption that the producer faces no fixed costs, then the cost of producing Q units of output will be given by the white trapezoid in Figure 5.1 (b).[1] The

---

[1] Here we are adding up (or, more accurately, integrating) marginal costs (MC) for output levels from zero to Q.

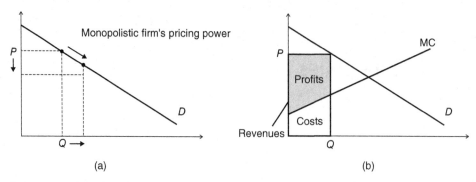

Figure 5.1 Monopolistic firm's profit maximization problem

remaining gray area thus corresponds to revenues minus costs, or the profit earned by the producer. The goal of a monopolistic firm will be to maximize this gray area.

In considering the optimal production level from the perspective of the monopolistic firm, let us first look at the relationship between output and revenue. The demand curve can be written as $P = P(Q)$, and the monopolistic firm will act in full recognition that an increase in output will drive the price lower. Revenue can then be written as $R(Q) = \text{price} \times \text{quantity} = P(Q)Q$. By how much will the monopolistic firm's revenue grow if output is increased by just a tiny (infinitesimal) amount? In other words, what is the derivative $R'(Q)$ of revenue $R(Q)$? This is known as **marginal revenue** and can be written as $\text{MR}(Q)$. Let us now explain the importance of marginal revenue when considering the profit maximization problem faced by a monopolistic firm.

Suppose that marginal revenue is greater than marginal cost – i.e. $\text{MR}(Q) > \text{MC}(Q)$. The revenue generated from a tiny increase in output ($\text{MR}(Q)$) will be greater than the cost of doing so ($\text{MC}(Q)$), meaning that increasing production will lead to higher profits. Conversely, profits will be boosted by reducing production if $\text{MR}(Q) < \text{MC}(Q)$. At the optimal output level it should no longer be possible to increase profits by adjusting production in either direction, meaning that marginal revenue and marginal cost should be equal. To summarize:

Optimal production (profit maximization) condition for a monopolistic firm

$$\underset{\text{marginal revenue}}{\text{MR}} = \underset{\text{marginal cost}}{\text{MC}}$$

The above explanation is perhaps a little abstract, so let us illustrate for the case of a downward-sloping demand curve given by $P = a - bQ$. For a given quantity of output Q, revenue $R(Q)$ is given by

$$\underset{\text{revenue}}{R(Q)} = \underset{\text{price} \times \text{quantity}}{P \times Q} = (a - bQ)Q = aQ - bQ^2.$$

Marginal revenue MR is equal to the derivative of $R(Q)$ with respect to Q, or

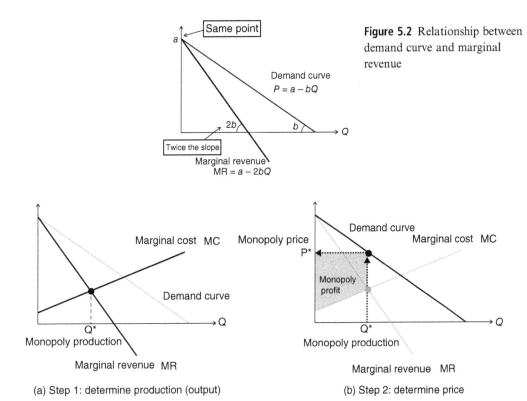

Figure 5.2 Relationship between demand curve and marginal revenue

Figure 5.3 Monopolistic firm's output and price

$$\underset{\text{marginal revenue}}{\mathrm{MR}(Q)} = \underset{\text{derivative of the revenue function}}{R'(Q) = a - 2bQ.}$$

Figure 5.2 compares this with the demand curve $P = a - bQ$.
What have we found?

> If the demand curve is a downward-sloping straight line, then the graph of **marginal revenue** *will intersect the vertical (price) axis at the same point as the demand curve, but will have twice the slope of the demand curve.*

Incorporating the marginal cost graph then enables us to determine the monopolistic firm's optimal output level and the corresponding market price, as shown in Figure 5.3.

Step 1 (Figure 5.3 (a)): the (optimal) output level in a monopoly will be determined by the intersection of marginal revenue and marginal cost.

Step 2 (Figure 5.3 (b)): the **monopoly price** will be determined by the above output level and the demand curve (with the gray area corresponding to monopoly profits).

Let us try to understand once again why Q^* is the optimal output level. If output were lower than Q^*, then – as should be clear from Figure 5.3 – marginal revenue would be greater than marginal cost. In other words, the revenue earned from increasing production by a tiny amount (marginal revenue) would be greater than the cost of doing so (marginal cost), meaning that greater profits would be earned by increasing production. Conversely, if output were higher than $Q*$, then marginal cost would be greater than marginal revenue, meaning that it would be more profitable to cut back production. The monopolistic firm thus ends up maximizing its profit by producing at level $Q*$.

5.2   What Is Wrong with Monopolies?

So, what sort of problems can we encounter when we face a monopoly rather than a perfectly competitive world? Figure 5.4 considers this question in some detail.

Recall that, under perfect competition, the output and price levels are determined by the intersection of the demand curve and supply curve, with total surplus given by the large triangle enclosed by those two curves. But what about when there is just a single (monopolistic) producer?

(1) Output is lower and the price is higher.
(2) The producer generates more profits,[2] while consumer surplus is lower (**inequality** of distribution).
(3) The damage suffered by consumers (reduction in consumer surplus) is invariably greater than the increase in producer profits, meaning that total surplus is lower (**inefficiency** of distribution).

Opinions expressed in media and blogs along the lines of "monopolies are bad" often focus on *inequality* of distribution, or the tendency of monopolistic producers to earn lucrative profits at the expense of the public (consumers). However, as I explain in the following comment, economists tend to be more concerned about *inefficiency* of distribution, or the way in which a monopoly will "shrink the pie" for society as a whole.

Figure 5.4 Surplus under a monopoly

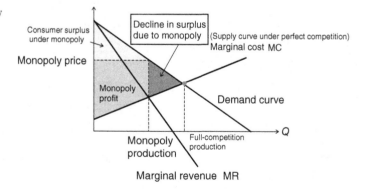

---

[2] One way to understand why this happens is to note that the monopolist could choose the perfectly competitive output level. If it does not, that implies that it can earn larger profits by choosing the monopoly output level.

Comment 5.1

Why do economists spend so much time worrying about *inefficiency* of allocation rather than the inequality of distribution caused by monopolies? One reason is that shrinkage of the overall social pie may not be immediately apparent without appropriate economic analysis, whereas *inequality* of distribution – monopolistic producers earning massive profits while the general public struggles under the burden of high prices – tends to be much more obvious even to the untrained eye.

If you focus on the equality of distribution without paying attention to efficiency, you may often end up representing and protecting the interests of a small fraction of people in the society at the expense of the general public. History is of course replete with examples of certain parts of society receiving special protection from the powers that be. For example, the government agency responsible for supervising a given industry is liable to focus almost exclusively on the interests of those particular constituents. In cases where an industry is not populated entirely by well-performing blue-chip firms, policy-makers often look to boost the profits of the industry by restricting competition and fostering monopoly-like conditions, with such action justified quite vaguely in terms of "protecting the weak," "preventing over-competition," or "developing a healthy industry." So who loses out? Consumers, of course, but also potential competitors to the industry that are excluded by the protection policy. *Restrictions on competition may deliver quite noticeable profits to a privileged few protected firms, but the losses suffered by consumers tend to be much more broadly shared and are thus liable to go unnoticed because the loss of each individual consumer tends to be small.* Huge losses may be suffered by consumers in the aggregate (with total surplus declining as a result), but individual losses are usually much more modest. The net upshot may be a very unfortunate erosion of the overall social pie – reduction in total surplus – if restrictions on competition are broadly applied and general prices end up reaching uncomfortably high levels as a result.

The role of economists – and, indeed, those studying microeconomics – is to deploy the power of economic analysis in explaining how *policies should be tailored to the needs of the masses rather than just the interests of a (more conspicuous) privileged few.* Such analysis is all the more important in *cases where policy ramifications may not be intuitively obvious.*

Case Study 5.1 Soaring Oil Prices and Price Pass-Through (revisited)

Let us now revisit our discussion of price pass-through from early in Chapter 1. When faced with a surge in oil prices and soaring raw material prices, which firms will be best positioned to pass the burden through to consumers by hiking their product prices? As we saw above, many would argue that powerful large firms find it relatively easy to pass through costs, whereas smaller firms facing fierce competition are more likely to struggle. Those contending that smaller firms have no option but to pass through costs owing to their lack of power will generally be in the minority. *Each argument may appear reasonable at first glance if we rely solely on common sense, but they cannot*

Case Study 5.1 (cont.)

both be correct. Economic analysis thus has an important role to play in arriving at a "legitimate" or "logically justifiable" conclusion.

So let us now weigh in to the debate. Recall the newspaper article about a gas station from Case Study 0.1. It seems reasonable to use the wholesale price at which gasoline is purchased from the parent company as the gas station's marginal cost. In other words, if the wholesale price is $2/gallon, then the marginal cost MC = $2. If a surge in oil prices causes the wholesale price to rise by 10¢ (per gallon), then the marginal cost curve will shift upward, as shown in Figure 5.5.

How will this 10¢ cost increase be passed through to customers? Consider first a world of perfect competition in which there are many small gas stations. The marginal cost curve is the supply curve under perfect competition, meaning that *the entire cost increase will be passed through to consumers*, as shown in Figure 5.6.

What about if all gas stations are owned by a single large firm, or each gas station is the monopolist in the local area? This monopoly situation is shown in Figure 5.7.

Figure 5.5 Rise in marginal cost for a gas station

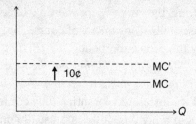

Figure 5.6 Price pass-through under perfect competition

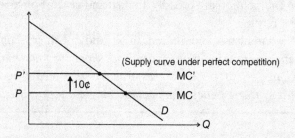

Figure 5.7 Price pass-through under monopoly

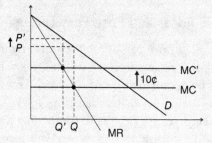

As we learned in Section 5.1, output under a monopoly will be determined by the intersection of marginal cost MC and marginal revenue MR. It can be seen from Figure 5.7 that the price of gas rises by considerably less than the full 10¢ increase in costs. Using the monopoly optimality condition (marginal revenue = marginal cost), we can show that the monopoly price is $P = a/2 + MC/2$.[3] In other words, *only half the increase in marginal cost MC will be passed through to the monopoly price.*

This would suggest that the above (popular and seemingly quite reasonable) argument to the effect that "powerful large firms find it relatively easy to pass through costs, whereas smaller firms facing fierce competition are more likely to struggle" is in fact mistaken, and that the newspaper article was actually correct in contending that "smaller firms have no option but to pass through costs owing to their lack of power." This example should, hopefully, help to demonstrate the importance of using the tools of economic analysis to identify areas where "common sense" may lead to flawed conclusions.

5.3   Natural Monopolies and Price Regulation

Did you know that fees such as gas and electricity tariffs are set by the government (as opposed to being left up to market forces)? In this section we explain why.

Industries with massive fixed costs are more likely to be "monopolistic." Electric power companies are a good example, since there are obviously massive fixed costs associated with building, say, hydro power plants or nuclear reactors. Markets where fixed costs are so massive as to make new entry difficult (prohibitively expensive) are known as **natural monopolies**. "Public utilities" such as electric power and gas companies tend to fall into this category.

Two competing objectives need to be balanced when managing (regulating) a natural monopoly. On the one hand, from the perspective of technological efficiency, a monopoly is probably to be preferred over a situation in which many firms pay huge fixed costs. For example, a single dam should be sufficient in order to generate hydro power in a given region, meaning that it would be inefficient if each of ten different companies were to construct its own dam. On the other hand, the more firms, the better, when it comes to competition-based efficiency. It is obviously not possible to achieve both objectives simultaneously, meaning that policy-makers will generally opt to *allow a monopoly but impose price regulation.*

---

[3] In Section 5.1 we showed that, for a demand curve $P = a - bQ$, marginal revenue will be given by $MR = a - 2bQ$. Applying the monopoly optimality condition (marginal revenue = marginal cost) gives us the monopoly output level of $Q = (a - MC)/2b$. Substituting into the demand curve equation $P = a - bQ$ and rearranging gives us $P = a/2 + MC/2$.

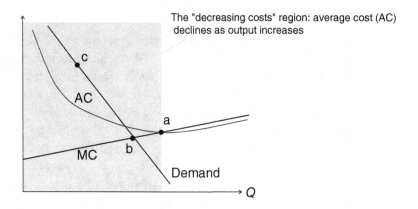

Figure 5.8 Market under a typical natural monopoly

But how should prices be appropriately regulated? Suppose that a firm in a "natural monopoly" industry faces fixed costs F and variable costs VC. The average cost AC is equal to the total cost $F +$ VC divided by output Q, or

$$AC = \frac{F}{Q} + \frac{VC}{Q}.$$

In this equation, $\frac{F}{Q}$, is the fixed cost per unit of output, and it will decline as output Q rises. In other words, each additional unit becomes cheaper to produce (in terms of fixed costs) for higher levels of production. This effect will be extremely large when fixed costs F are massive, meaning that there is likely to be *a very wide range of output levels for which boosting production will reduce overall average costs*.

Figure 5.8 illustrates this point for a "typical" natural monopoly. There are four points that warrant particular attention. First, recall from Chapter 2 that the average cost curve AC is U-shaped, meaning that, to the left of the minimum (point a in Figure 5.8), the curve will be downward-sloping (to the right). In other words,

(i) the "**Decreasing costs**" region – for which the (average) cost falls as output is increased – is given by the *gray area* to the left of the minimum average cost (point a in Figure 5.8).

Second, recall also from Chapter 2 that an upward-sloping marginal cost curve MC passes through the minimum point (a) of a U-shaped average cost curve AC:

(ii) *AC will always be higher than MC within the (gray) "Decreasing costs" region.*

This can be checked using Figure 5.8.

Third, the "Decreasing costs" region will tend to be very wide when fixed costs are huge, meaning that

(iii) the point at which demand and marginal cost (MC) intersect (b in Figure 5.8) will very often lie within the "Decreasing costs" region.

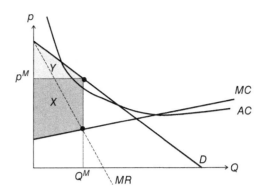

Figure 5.9 Leaving a natural monopoly unregulated

Finally, note also that

(iv) there are points (such as c in Figure 5.8) where demand exceeds the average cost AC.

Why do such points exist in a natural monopoly? Such industries are typically producing essential items such as gas and electricity, demand for which is unlikely to decline appreciably even when prices are hiked. In other words, the demand curve is likely to be reasonably close to vertical, meaning that there will be points (c) at which demand exceeds average cost AC.

Figure 5.9 looks at what could be expected to happen in such a market if it were left as an unregulated monopoly.

Total surplus will end up being equal to just $X + Y$, as output and price are set at the low and high monopoly levels respectively. As we learned in Section 2.2, the producer's profit will be equal to producer surplus X minus fixed costs F.[4] Whether or not this profit $(X - F)$ is positive will depend on the relationship between the monopoly price p^M and the average cost curve AC. Figure 5.9 shows p^M to be above AC (by virtue of (iv) above), meaning that it is sufficiently high for profits to be left over after average costs are recovered.

How could prices be regulated in order to maximize total surplus? This is achieved by setting the price at the point where the marginal cost curve intersects with the demand curve, which is known as a **marginal cost pricing rule**.

Total surplus will be maximized under marginal cost pricing (area Z in Figure 5.10). Marginal cost pricing might thus seem like an "optimal" policy, but, unfortunately, it is impractical in the following respects. As we saw in Figure 5.9, the marginal cost MC is always lower than the average cost AC within the "Decreasing costs" region (property (ii) above). As such, when the optimal output level – determined by the intersection of the demand and marginal cost curves – lies within the "Decreasing costs" region (as is quite likely by virtue of property (iii) above), setting the price equal to MC will result in it being lower than AC, meaning that *the producer will end up incurring losses*. Furthermore, it will likely be

[4] Consider the fixed costs to be "sunk."

Figure 5.10 Marginal cost pricing rule

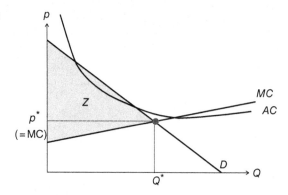

Figure 5.11 Average cost pricing rule

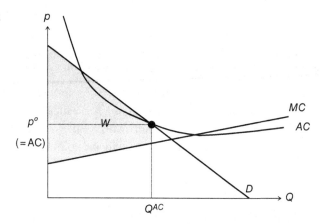

very *difficult for the regulatory authorities to accurately measure (estimate) marginal costs.* It is primarily for these two reasons that marginal cost pricing is seldom used in practice.

Real-world regulators typically apply an **average cost pricing rule** by way of a compromise, setting the price at the point where the demand and average cost curves intersect, as illustrated in Figure 5.11.[5] Note that average cost is fairly easy to measure (just divide the total cost by total quantity), in contrast to the marginal cost.

Total surplus W will be smaller than under marginal cost pricing, but considerably greater than under an unregulated monopoly. Moreover, setting the price equal to average cost means that the producer will not end up incurring any losses. However, nor will the producer earn any profits. As such, *regulators will typically treat "normal profits" as a cost when calculating average costs*, thereby providing the producer with some incentive to operate. "Normal profits" are often calculated based on average profit margins for other (comparable) industries.

[5] The demand curve and the average cost curve actually intersect at two points in Figure 5.11, but regulators will choose the point where output is higher with a view to making surplus as large as possible.

Case Study 5.2 Regulated Price for Tohoku Electric Power

Let us now return to the example of Tohoku Electric Power presented in Section 2.2 (d). Figure 5.12 shows the utility's estimated marginal cost and estimated average cost including normal profits. As is the case for power companies operating elsewhere in Japan, Tohoku Electric Power's supply price is determined by average cost pricing, or by the point at which the demand curve intersects with the average cost curve (with normal profits included in the calculation of average cost; note that the demand curve in Figure 5.12 is a hypothetical one that passes through the (average production, average tariff) point, just as the (unknown) "real" demand curve does. The average tariff of ¥13.1 (per kWh) thus ends up being equal to the average cost plus some measure of "normal profit" per unit of power generated.[6]

So what are the pros and cons of average cost pricing? On the plus side of the ledger, the producer does not incur losses. Moreover, as I argued before, the average cost is equal to actual costs divided by the actual output level, which makes it easier to measure than the marginal cost. On the minus side, total surplus does not end up being maximized, and *the producer is not provided with an incentive to minimize costs.* Indeed, average cost pricing guarantees that the firm will always be paid enough to cover its actual costs – however wasteful – while also earning a "normal" profit. There are numerous examples in history of such inefficiencies eventually becoming too great to ignore. And the overall direction of policy is changing, with technological progress serving to lower fixed costs in, say, the electric power and telecommunications industries, to the point where *many policy-makers now find it preferable to encourage new entry and promote free competition rather than persisting with a natural monopoly and an average cost pricing regime.*

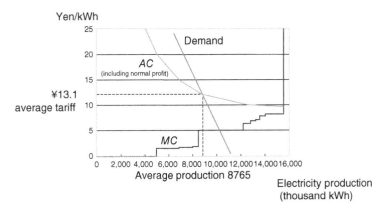

Figure 5.12 Tohoku Electric Power's average cost price
Note: AC and MC are estimates.

---

[6] The average cost graph in Chapter 2 (Figure 2.30) did not include normal profits, meaning that the average cost at the average production level ended up being that much lower (¥12.3).

Part II

Game Theory and Economics of Information: New Frontiers in Economic Theory

In Part II I explain the basic principles of game theory and economics of information, which are relatively new areas of economic theory compared to Part I. The development of game theory and economics of information was motivated by the need to analyze general economic and social problems beyond the realm of perfectly competitive markets. Prior to the invention of these new fields, the theory and tools available to economists were only applicable to the study of perfectly competitive markets, and as such our tools were narrowly limited.

Introduction: Why Do We Need Game Theory?

Let me explain what exactly "game theory" is and why we need it. A central, yet simple, principle in the theory of competitive markets (which we studied in Part I) is that each agent makes choices that are most beneficial to him- or herself. For example, firms want to earn as much profit as possible, and consumers want to buy the goods they want at the lowest possible cost. Of course, in reality, decision-making is more complex and nuanced. However, as far as economic problems are concerned, the main driving force is rational behavior (i.e. choosing the most preferable option out of those available), and, as we saw in Part I, how the market mechanism works can clearly be analyzed by means of its main driving force: rational behavior.

Let's review the theory of perfect competition. In a perfectly competitive market, there are many consumers and many firms. Therefore, the behavior of a single consumer or firm will not change the market price. Consequently, consumers and firms maximize their utility or profits, taking the market price as given. *Thus, we can model the behavior of consumers and firms as mathematical maximization problems ("utility maximization" and "profit maximization" problems).* We might ask: even outside perfectly competitive markets, *in more general economic and social problems, can we understand human behavior using the simple but important principle of rational behavior*, which states that each person will choose the option that is more beneficial to him- or herself? Can we frame all economic and social problems as mathematical maximization problems? Surprisingly, the answer is "Not really." In order to understand why, let's consider an example.

Suppose that Toyota and Honda are developing new cars. What kind of car should Toyota design? On the one hand, if Honda releases a new hybrid car, it might be good for Toyota to release a hybrid car as well. On the other hand, if Honda releases a new minivan, it might be better for Toyota to release a small car. The difficulty for Toyota managers is that, until Honda actually unveils its new car, they won't know what kind of car they should have developed. This stands in contrast to the case in which firms can observe market prices before making production decisions. In essence, when deciding what type of car to develop, Toyota must predict what kind of car Honda will decide to develop. This type of situation is called a "strategic situation."

A **strategic situation** is a situation in which

- one's optimal decision *depends on the decision another person makes,*
- and, therefore, one needs to *predict what decisions other people will make.*

Apart from the problems of perfectly competitive markets and problems in which a single isolated person makes a decision (such as a monopoly problem), it's safe to say that *almost all social and economic problems are strategic situations.*

Now, let's consider how to predict others' decisions. Once Toyota makes a prediction about the type of car Honda will release, we can analyze Toyota's behavior using a maximization problem and the principle that Toyota, given its prediction about Honda's behavior, will try to maximize its own profit (see Figure II.1).

So far, so good: Toyota's behavior can successfully be modeled by a maximization problem, *given* Toyota's expectation about what Honda will do. However, you should notice that Honda's decision is not mechanically determined, like the weather or a roll of dice. Honda is in the same situation as Toyota. *Like Toyota, Honda will make a prediction about the type of car Toyota will release, and choose the type of car it releases based on that prediction.* Therefore, in order to better predict Honda's decision, Toyota should consider the prediction Honda will make about the type of car Toyota will release. This is shown in Figure II.2.

Figure II.1 A simple way to predict others' decisions.

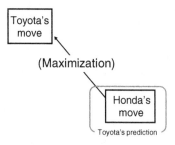

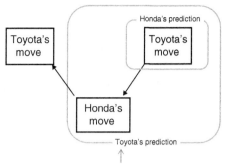

Figure II.2 Predicting others' decisions by anticipating others' predictions

What Toyota thinks about "What Honda thinks about Toyota's move"

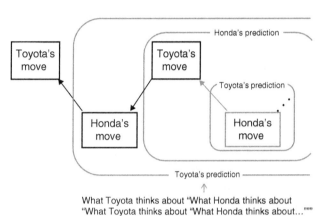

Figure II.3 Predicting others' decisions by anticipating others' predictions about predictions about...

What Toyota thinks about "What Honda thinks about "What Toyota thinks about "What Honda thinks about...""""

That is, when making a prediction about Honda's decision, Toyota needs to consider

what Honda believes Toyota's decision will be.

But this is not the end of the story, and you should go one step further. Now you must realize that

what Honda believes Toyota's decision will be depends on what Honda believes about what Toyota believes about what Honda's decisions will be.

This line of reasoning never stops, and goes on indefinitely: when making a prediction about Honda's decision, Toyota needs to consider

what Honda believes about what Toyota believes about what Honda believes ... (this goes on forever) (see Figure II.3).

This chain of beliefs about beliefs continues infinitely, and therefore rationality alone fails to pin down what Toyota does. *In other words, outside the world of perfectly competitive markets, the principle of rational behavior is not enough to allow us to analyze more general social and economic problems. We need to have a theory that considers how to predict others' beliefs, and hence their decisions.* It was John von Neumann (1903–1957), a math genius who studied theoretical physics and computer science, and Oskar Morgenstern (1902–1977), an economist, who first observed this fact and developed game theory, a new academic field that systematically deals with these issues. Note that problems such as the example with Toyota and Honda can arise only in a "society" in which multiple strategic people interact and predict one another's decisions. For a long time, economics borrowed tools from the mathematical theories of optimization or probability. However, with game theory, economists developed a mathematical theory unique to the social sciences and pioneered a new field of research in mathematical science.

Even within economics, there are many subfields that use game theory. While *game theory is necessary for analyzing almost all problems other than in perfectly competitive markets and monopolies*, there are a few areas of applications where game theory is especially useful:

- analysis of imperfect competition – i.e. oligopolies (industrial organization);
- analysis of activity within firms (economics of organization, contract theory);
- analysis of government and the public sector (political economy);
  - how do politicians and bureaucrats make decisions?
- analysis of asymmetric information;
  - how can one make decisions using only the information known to oneself?
- analysis of institutional design.
  - how can we design desirable institutions (rules of the game) to achieve good outcomes?

Apart from economics, game theory is also useful in management science, political science, sociology, biology, computer science, and other fields. The applications of game theory have spread widely beyond just economics. In what follows, I explain game theory by paying special attention to the main ideas hidden behind the formulas and mathematical models.

6   Simultaneous-Move Games and Nash Equilibrium

First, let's begin with the simplest situation, which we call the case of "*simultaneous moves*," in which everyone makes his or her decision at the same time. In order to analyze such a situation, we will express the situation using a model, which we call a "game."

6.1   What Is a "Game"?

In order to express a situation in which multiple people have to make decisions based on predictions about the other peoples' decisions, we need to clearly describe ① the participants, ② the possible actions each person can take, and ③ the players' payoffs given the decisions of each player. A model that describes each of these three components is called a game.

> A **game** is a model consisting of the following three components:
>
> ① **players**, denoted $i = 1, 2, \ldots, N$;
> ② the **strategy** a_i of player i
>   (we denote by A_i the set of all strategies that player i can take); and
> ③ the **payoff** function $g_i(a_1, \ldots, a_N)$ of player i.

Virtually all economic and social problems can be formulated as a game. For example, in our earlier example with Toyota and Honda, we can describe the situation in the following way.

- The players are $i =$ Honda, Toyota.
- The players' strategies are the possible types of cars to release – that is, each player i chooses a strategy from

$$A_i = \{\text{hybrid, minivan, compact sedan, } \ldots\}.$$

(for instance, player i might choose $a_i = $ minivan).

- The players' payoffs are their total profits; each company's profit is determined by the types of cars that Toyota and Honda choose.

In the next section, I'll introduce some more concrete examples.

6.2   Nash Equilibrium

Now, what happens in the games that we described in Section 6.1? Using the mathematical model of games that we just introduced, we can formulate various social and economic problems, such as the competition between Toyota and Honda, the political battle between Democrats and Republicans, trade agreements between the United States and China, and more. Using our past experience and common sense, we can make *a prediction about the outcome in each particular instance*. This is called an "ad hoc" prediction. For instance, by using our common sense, we might guess that Toyota will produce a hybrid, or that the United States and China will make such and such agreement. However, our goal as economists is not to make such ad hoc predictions but to determine whether there are any *general* principles that govern human behavior in various social and economic settings.

In modern game theory, we suppose that Nash equilibria (named after US genius mathematician John Nash Jr. (1928–2015), which I'll define below, are the outcomes of games that model general social and economic problems.

In order to more clearly explain what a Nash equilibrium is, we'll make use of the following notation. First, let us call a combination of players' strategy $a = (a_1, \ldots, a_N)$ as a strategy profile. Given a strategy profile $a^* = \left(a_1^*, \ldots, a_N^*\right)$, we write *the strategy profile in which only player i changes her strategy, from* a_i^* *to* a_i, *as*

$$\left(a_{-1}^*, a_i\right).^1$$

Using this notation, a Nash equilibrium is defined as follows.

Definition

If a strategy profile a^* satisfies the property that for every player i and every strategy a_i,

$$g_i(a^*) \geq g_i\left(a_{-i}^*, a_i\right),$$

then we say that a^* is a **Nash equilibrium**.

This is a simple definition, but it may be hard to grasp its meaning at first glance, so let me explain it carefully. Let's take a closer look at the condition $g_i(a^*) \geq g_i\left(a_{-i}^*, a_i\right)$.

- The left-hand side of the inequality is player i's payoff when each player uses the strategy specified in a^*.

---

[1] That is, $\left(a_{-i}^*, a_i\right) = (a_1^*, \ldots, a_{i-1}^*, a_i, a_{i+1}^*, \ldots a_N^*)$.

- The right-hand side of the inequality is player i's payoff when player i uses a different strategy a_i, but all other players use the strategy specified in a^*.

The inequality holds if player i cannot achieve a strictly higher payoff by unilaterally changing her strategy. Thus, we can restate our definition of a Nash equilibrium in the following way.

> A Nash equilibrium is a strategy profile for which **no player can gain from unilaterally changing his or her strategy**.

Put differently, we have this.

> A Nash equilibrium is a strategy profile for which each player's strategy is a best response to the other players' strategies (players are taking **mutual best replies**).

In modern game theory, we suppose that *people behave according to a Nash equilibrium in simultaneous-move games*. It is far from obvious if that is actually a reasonable thing to assume, so let me offer a detailed explanation. First, using several examples, I would like you to understand the kind of behavior that corresponds to a Nash equilibrium. In each example, I'll present a simple game and its Nash equilibria along with a real-life situation that mirrors the model. Once you have a clearer idea of the kind of behavior that a Nash equilibrium represents, in Section 6.3 we'll discuss a crucial question: why can we suppose that people behave according to a Nash equilibrium?

(a) Equilibrium in Four Games and Real-Life Situations

Here, I will explain the following four games:

- prisoner's dilemma;
- technology choice;
- location game;
- road traffic.

With each game, I'll use a real-life example to motivate the problem. First, let's take a look at the famous game called "prisoner's dilemma."

Example 6.1 Prisoner's Dilemma

Two suspects, 1 and 2, are held in solitary cells and are separately interrogated by the police. The police know that 1 and 2 were involved in a crime and are seeking detailed confessions from the prisoners. Each prisoner has two possible strategies: remain silent; or admit to the crime and tell the police the full story. When the situation involves a small number of players and strategies, as in this example, we can express the game (i.e., the players, the players' strategies, and the players' payoff functions) through a **payoff table** or matrix, as shown in Table 6.1.

Example 6.1 (cont.)

Table 6.1 The Payoff Table for Prisoner's Dilemma

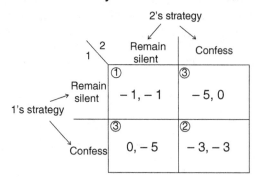

The first and second numbers in each cell of the matrix in Table 6.1 represent 1's payoff and 2's payoff respectively. The number gives the length of the player's prison sentence. Since the usual convention is that higher payoffs are better, we put negative signs in front of the prison sentences. I labeled the cells of the table ① to ③. For each cell, let me explain the players' payoffs.

① "−1, −1": if both prisoners are silent, then each is sentenced to one year in prison. (Therefore, the payoffs for both players are −1.)

② "−3, −3": if both prisoners confess, then the details of the vicious crime are revealed and each is sentenced to three years in prison.

It's easy to see that, *from the prisoners' perspectives, it would be better for both to keep silent than for both to confess.*

③ The rest: if one prisoner confesses and the other prisoner is silent, then the prisoner who confessed will receive leniency for his cooperation and walk free, while the one who kept silent is punished more severely for a lack of remorse and is sentenced to five years in prison.

In this situation, what would the prisoners choose to do? If we carefully examine the payoff table, we can see that *the Nash equilibrium of this game is for both prisoners to confess.* Why is this a Nash equilibrium? Let's look at Table 6.2.

Table 6.2 Checking the Nash-equilibrium condition

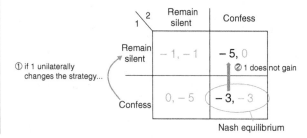

The Nash equilibrium is circled. Starting from this outcome, what happens if only player 1 changes his strategy? As you can see from the table, 1's payoff changes from –3 to –5, which leaves him worse off. The same holds for player 2. Thus, *when both prisoners confess, neither player can gain from unilaterally changing his strategy.* Therefore, by definition, this is a Nash equilibrium of the game. Put differently,

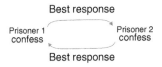

and we call this outcome a Nash equilibrium.

By examining the payoff table more closely, we can see that, *no matter what decision his partner makes, it is always better for a prisoner to confess than to remain silent.* Table 6.3 demonstrates why this is so.

As you can see in Table 6.3, no matter what player 2 chooses to do, player 1 earns a higher payoff by confessing than he does by remaining silent. A strategy, such as confessing in prisoner's dilemma, that is always optimal regardless of what the other players do is called a **dominant strategy**.[2]

Since it is better to confess no matter what the other prisoner chooses to do, any outcome in which a prisoner chooses to remain silent is not a Nash equilibrium. In particular, despite the fact that both prisoners prefer their payoffs when they both remain silent to their payoffs when they both confess, the outcome in which both prisoners remain silent is not a Nash equilibrium. The reason is that, if a prisoner knows his partner is going to remain silent, he can choose to confess, in which case he serves no time in prison, as opposed to one year in prison. In other words, the prisoner can gain by unilaterally changing his action.

Thus, *although both prisoners would benefit if they both remained silent, self-interested prisoners are bound to confess, and so the prisoners are trapped in a situation that they do not like.* This surprising feature is why this game is called the prisoner's "dilemma" (see Table 6.4).

Table 6.3 No matter what the other prisoner does, it's best to confess

1 \ 2	Remain silent	Confess
Remain silent	– 1, –	– 5, 0
Confess	0, – 5	– 3, – 3

---

[2] As you will see in various examples, a dominant strategy does not always exist. In fact, in most games players will not have a dominant strategy.

Example 6.1 (cont.)

Table 6.4 The reason this game is called "prisoner's dilemma"

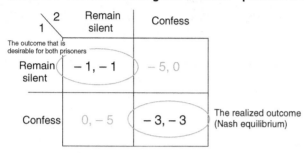

Comment 6.1 What Are the Payoffs in a Game?

In the above game, the players' payoffs were the negative values of the lengths of their prison sentences (for example, for a three-year prison sentence the payoff is –3). How can we assign players' payoffs in an arbitrary game? The answer is as follows.

> *If there is no uncertainty*, we can determine a player's payoffs by *assigning larger numbers to outcomes that player finds more desirable*. (The actual numbers used can be arbitrary, as long as, for each player, more desirable outcomes are assigned higher outcomes than less desirable outcomes.)

When we say "If there is no uncertainty," we are referring to situations in which there are no factors that are probabilistically determined (i.e. by stock market outcomes, a roll of dice, etc.) and no player behaves randomly (i.e. using "mixed strategies, which we'll discuss later).

This method of assigning players' payoffs is based on the same principle we discussed when we learned about consumers' utility functions (Chapter 1, Section 1.1). As long as we assign higher payoffs to more desirable outcomes, we can use any numbers we like because, regardless of what specific numbers are assigned, the Nash-equilibrium outcome is the same.

By contrast, if there is uncertainty, we need to be more careful in selecting numbers for the players' payoffs. This is because payoffs will reflect a player's attitude toward risk, as well as a player's preferences over deterministic outcomes. I will explain this in greater detail in Section 6.6.

Case Study 6.1 Leniency Program

Are there situations like the prisoner's dilemma in the real world? In fact, a successful new policy that has been implemented in the United States, Japan, and other countries creates the situation described in the prisoner's dilemma to uncover illegal activity.

In many developed countries, antitrust laws outlaw practices (such as collusion between firms or formation of cartels) that are meant to raise prices by limiting competition. The Japan Fair Trade Commission is the governing body in charge of Japanese antitrust regulation. Firms that are caught violating antitrust laws are punished with a fine.[3] A new "leniency program" *reduces the fine a firm receives if, prior to being investigated by the Fair Trade Commission, the firm confesses that it was involved in illegal collusion or was a member of a cartel.* More specifically, in Japan, the first firm that confesses faces no fine, the second firm that confesses has its fine reduced by 50 percent, and the third firm that confesses has its fine reduced by 30 percent.

Suppose that firm 1 and firm 2 have colluded with each other. There is a possibility that the collusion is uncovered even if neither firm confesses. Let p be the probability of this occurring. What is the payoff table if the fine for collusion is x dollars? We'll see that the payoff table for firm 1 is as follows.

Table 6.5 Firm 1's payoffs under the leniency program

1 \ 2	Remain silent	Report
Remain silent	① $-px$	③ $-x$
Report	② 0	④ $-\frac{1}{4}x$

Let's walk through how we determined that this is firm 1's payoff table (Table 6.5).

① Even if both firms are silent, the collusion is uncovered with probability p. Therefore, the expected loss for firm 1 is $-px$.

② If firm 1 is the only firm to confess to being involved in the collusion, then it faces no fine.

③ If firm 1 remains silent but firm 2 confesses, then firm 1 faces the full fine, $-x$.

④ What happens if both firms confess? The order of the confessions is determined, in Japan, by when the fax arrives at the Fair Trade Commission. Assuming that each firm's fax arrives first with equal probability, and there are no ties in the time of arrival, there is a 1/2 chance that firm 1 was the first to confess and receives no fine. However, there is also a 1/2 chance that firm 1 was the second to confess, and therefore pays 50 percent of the fine. Thus, the expected loss for firm 1 is $1/2 \times (50\% \text{ of } -x) = -(1/4)x$.

---

[3] In particularly serious cases, individuals can be criminally prosecuted.

Case Study 6.1 (cont.)

Table 6.6 The effect of the leniency program

Fiscal year	The number of detected cases of cartels/bid collusions	The number of companies self-reporting	The number of leniency applications*	The number of companies that received a reduced fine*
2005	17	26	0	0
2006	9	79	6	16
2007	20	74	16	37
2008	10	85	8	21
2009	22	85	21	50
2010	10	131	7	10
2011	17	143	9	27

Note: * Only those that the company agreed to publicize.

Looking at Table 6.5, we see that, as long as p (the probability of collusion being detected even if both firms are silent) is positive, it is always best for the firm to confess, regardless of what the other firm chooses to do. However, if $p < 1/4$, each firm is better off if neither firm confesses than if both firms confess. This is exactly the same situation that we saw in the prisoner's dilemma.[4]

Let's take a look at the actual effect of the leniency program in Japan. In Table 6.6[5] the second and third columns show the total numbers, while the fourth and fifth columns show just the numbers for cases where the involved firms agreed to allow the case to be publicly reported. Even if we restrict our attention to the cases that were publicized, we can see that a very high fraction of cases were self-reported by colluding firms (see the first and third column of the table). In addition, the number of firms that admit to collusion increases each year, and there were 143 self-reported cases in the 2011 fiscal year.[6] This suggests that the leniency program has successfully encouraged self-reporting of illegal activity, by creating a situation similar to the prisoner's dilemma.

[4] In reality, if a firm betrays its partner and confesses to collusion, it may face retaliation in the future. Therefore, if we also consider future payoffs, it might be that firms choose not to confess out of fear of retaliation. The fact that not all firms report collusion seems to suggest that the decision to report collusion is indeed influenced by the possibility of future retaliation.

[5] This figure is based on data the author received from the Japan Fair Trade Commission.

[6] Why is it that the number of firms that admit to collusion (the third column) is much greater than the number of firms that have their fines reduced (the last column)? There are several reasons: (1) a firm's fine may not be reduced, even if it confesses, because it was not one of the earliest firms to confess; (2) there may be companies that had their fines reduced but did not agree to disclose this fact; (3) there may be instances in which firms confess and the government does not officially detect the behavior. We don't know exactly how many cases these potential explanations can account for, but, from what I understand from speaking to some authorities, each explanation accounts for a non-trivial number of cases.

Let's look at another example of a game that can be expressed with a payoff table.

Example 6.2 Technology Choice

Two students working together on a project are buying laptop computers and need to decide whether to buy Apple or Windows devices. Suppose that, for their joint work, it's more convenient if they both buy the same type of computer. Moreover, suppose that the Apple computer is better suited for their work. The payoff table in Table 6.7 describes this situation.

Table 6.7 Technology choice game

1 \ 2	Apple	Windows
Apple	3, 3	0, 0
Windows	0, 0	2, 2

In this game, the outcome in which both students buy Apple computers and the outcome in which both students buy Windows computers are both Nash equilibria.[7] If a student knows that his partner is going to buy an Apple, he will be worse off if he buys a Windows computer instead of an Apple. Likewise, if a student knows that his partner is going to buy a Windows computer, he will be worse off if he buys an Apple computer instead of a Windows. In this sense, it's best for each player to take the same action as the other player. In other words, they have a mutual interest in taking the same action. Such situations are said to have **network externalities** and are abundant in real life. It's common that there are multiple equilibria in this type of situation. Let me introduce a real-world example of such a situation.

Case Study 6.2 Industry "De Facto" Standard for New Technology

When new technologies are invented, it's common for several different "industry standards" to be proposed. For example, when video cassettes were invented as a way to store videos, the two formats "Beta" and "VHS" competed vigorously for market share. In more recent years, we've seen competition between "Blu-ray" and "HD DVD" in the optical disk arena. In these cases, customers prefer to buy the type of product that is more common, because a wider range of compatible software and better customer support are available. Thus, for the Blu-ray versus HD DVD example, *there are multiple equilibria in which everyone chooses the same product: everyone choosing Blu-ray* and *everyone choosing HD DVD* could both be Nash equilibria, since, if everyone is already using Blu-ray, there would be no reason for an individual to switch to HD

---

[7] This game is sometimes called a "**coordination game**."

Case Study 6.2 (cont.)

Figure 6.1 Evolution of market shares of Blu-ray and HD DVD

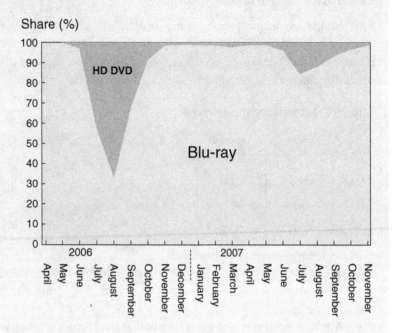

DVD, and vice versa. However, between these two possible equilibria, it's difficult to predict in advance which will actually occur. One possibility that might occur is that, *by chance, one format gets an early head start in market share, which means that it attracts even more future customers and eventually becomes the industry standard while the other format becomes irrelevant.* Looking back, we can see that for our two examples, VHS and Blu-ray beat out Beta and HD DVD respectively, and became the standard video formats.

Figure 6.1 shows the evolution of the market share of HD DVD starting around 2006 in Japan. HD DVD debuted in June 2006 and began capturing a growing share of the market. However, when the new format Blu-ray was introduced by another company in November, Blu-ray became the dominant technology, and the share of HD DVD has never recovered fully. In this way, the market converged to the equilibrium in which Blu-ray alone is used.

An important conclusion from our study of the technology choice game is the following.

> It is possible for a game to have multiple Nash equilibria. Moreover, it may be that one equilibrium is better for everyone than another equilibrium.

In the game described by Table 6.7, we can see that the equilibrium in which both students purchase Apple computers is better for both players than the equilibrium in which both students buy Windows computers. In this example, since there are only two players, the students can talk and agree to choose the better equilibrium (Apple). By contrast, in the case of the choice of technology standards for society as a whole, it's not possible for everyone to discuss and agree on what action to take. Therefore, *it could be that everyone coalesces around the technology that just happens to get a larger market share near the beginning, and it may not be that the better technology is the one that becomes standard.* VHS and Windows became the industry standards for video cassettes and personal computers respectively, but there are people who believe that Beta and Apple were the superior technologies. In much the same way, English is used as the language of international communication; however, some argue that the invented language "Esperanto," which was specifically designed to be efficient and easy to learn, would be a better choice. These examples motivate the following important lesson of game theory.

Once society as a whole gets stuck in the worse equilibrium, it is not easy to get out of it through individual efforts.

So far, we've seen two examples of games that can be expressed by simple payoff tables, but I don't want you to conclude that game theory is all about payoff tables. In fact, game theory can be used to describe and analyze situations far beyond just the simple cases that can be expressed as payoff tables. Next, let's consider a situation that cannot be described with a simple payoff table and try to find its Nash equilibrium.

Example 6.3 Location Game

Suppose there are two students, A and B, who will each sell hot dogs from a food stall at their school festival. They can set up their food stalls on a street on the school campus, which we'll represent as a straight line, as in Figure 6.2.

The two students, A and B, simultaneously decide where on the street to locate their food stalls. Customers are equally distributed along the street and will choose to go to the closer stall. If the two food stalls are located at exactly the same place, then we'll assume that each stall gets one-half of the customers. Each player wants to pick the location of her stall to maximize the number of customers who buy her food.

This is a simultaneous-move game in which the players' possible strategies are the possible locations of their food stalls and the players' payoffs are the number of customers who go to their stall. What is the Nash equilibrium of this game? In order to determine the Nash equilibrium, let's check if the locations of the stalls shown in Figure 6.2 constitute a Nash equilibrium (see Figure 6.3).

Figure 6.2 Location game

Example 6.3 (cont.)

Since the customers on the street will go to the closer food stall, the customers are divided at *the point halfway between the two stalls*: the left portion goes to A's stall and the right portion goes to B's stall (see the upper part of the figure). However, this outcome is *not* a Nash equilibrium. Note that, if one student unilaterally decides to move closer to the other student's stall, she can steal some of her competitor's customers, while keeping all her original customers (see the lower part of the figure).

Therefore, if the two students set up their stalls at different locations, a student can increase her payoff (her number of customers) by moving her stall closer to her opponent's stall. Consequently, such an arrangement cannot be a Nash equilibrium. How about the outcome shown in the upper part of Figure 6.4? If the two students set up their stalls at the exact same location, is that a Nash equilibrium?

Unfortunately, this outcome is not a Nash equilibrium either. In this arrangement, each student gets one-half of the customers. However, if student A moves her stall slightly to the left, then she can attract more than half (in fact, almost two-thirds) of the customers (see the lower part of Figure 6.4).

Figure 6.3 This outcome is not a Nash equilibrium (#1)

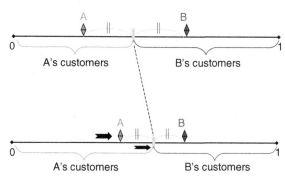

A would have more customers if she were to move closer to B

Figure 6.4 This outcome is not a Nash equilibrium (#2)

In the above state, A and B each have 1/2 of all customers.

But, if A moves slightly to the left, then she can take almost 2/3 of the customers.

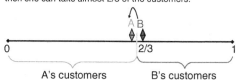

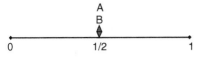

Figure 6.5 The Nash equilibrium of the location game

Given these observations, we can deduce that the Nash equilibrium of this game is the outcome in which the two food stalls are both placed at the exact midpoint of the ginkgo-lined street (see Figure 6.5).

In this outcome, A and B each get half the customers, and, if a player unilaterally decides to move her stall to either side of the midpoint, she will lose customers to her competitor. Thus, the Nash-equilibrium condition that no player can profit by unilaterally changing his strategy holds. For the customers, it would probably be more convenient if the food stalls were more spread out along the street, but such an arrangement would not occur if A and B are allowed to choose where they set up their stalls.

This result was discovered by Harold Hotelling (1895–1973), a pioneer of theoretical economics, and is sometimes called **Hotelling's location game**. Next, let's look at a real-life example that can be modeled by this game.

Case Study 6.3 The Platforms of Two Major Political Parties

We can reframe the location model to model competition between political parties for voters. Suppose that the line segment from 0 to 1 in the location game represents the political platforms declared by the parties. A point close to 0 represents a liberal platform and a point close to 1 represents a conservative platform. The two parties simultaneously choose where on this spectrum to set their platform. The preferences of the voters are distributed equally on this line and each person votes for the party with the platform that is closest to his own position. Suppose that each party's payoff is equal to the number of votes it receives. If we reinterpret the model in this way, the location game becomes a model of electoral competition, and its Nash equilibrium is the outcome in which both parties declare the exact same platform at the point 1/2. In other words, *both parties would declare platforms exactly at the middle of the voters' preferences*. This is a prediction of game theory, and in political science it is called the "**median voter theorem**." In fact, in the runoff of the 2007 French presidential election, the left-wing candidate Ségolène Royal and the right-wing candidate Nicolas Sarkozy tried to soften their left- and right-wing policies to appeal to centrist voters.[8]

---

[8] *Asahi* newspaper, April 24, 2007.

Let's look at one last example.

Example 6.4 Road Traffic Game

Suppose that there are 150 cars that want to go from city A to city B. They can choose one of the three routes of different lengths shown in Figure 6.6.

In general, the shorter routes take less time to travel, but heavy traffic increases the travel time. Therefore, the length of a car's journey from city A to city B depends both on the length of the route it selects and the amount of traffic on that route. The exact relationship between the amount of traffic and the length of the trip is complicated (I'll soon show you a real-life example in Case Study 6.4), so, for simplicity, we'll say that the transit time on a route is given by a simple linear formula:

$$\text{(the length of the route (km))} + \text{(the number of cars on that route}/10). \tag{1}$$

In this case, *what is the amount of traffic and the transit time on each route?* In order to solve this problem, which is of clear practical importance, we can use the notion of Nash equilibrium.

Assuming that each person wants to arrive at city B as quickly as possible, we can solve for the following Nash equilibrium.

- 50 cars travel on route 1, and the transit time is $25 + (50/10) = 30$ minutes.
- 100 cars travel on route 2, and the transit time is $20 + (100/10) = 30$ minutes.
- No cars travel on route 3.

Beginning from this outcome, no person could achieve a shorter transit time by choosing a different route. Suppose a driver who had chosen route 1 was debating whether or not to switch to route 2 or route 3. If he switches to route 2, his transit time will be 30.1 minutes, and, if he switches to route 3, his transit time will be 35.1 minutes, both of which are longer than his transit time of 30 minutes on route 1. By the same reasoning, we can see that a driver who had chosen route 2 also will have no incentive to unilaterally choose a different route. Therefore, this outcome satisfies the Nash-equilibrium condition that no player can gain by unilaterally adopting a different strategy.

Figure 6.6 Road traffic game

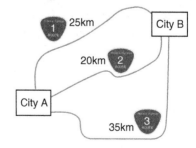

Case Study 6.4 Predicting the Amount of Road Traffic

In this case study we'll look at the problem of predicting road traffic around Hamamatsu City in Japan, using the same logic as in the road traffic game we just studied.[9] In order to predict the amount of road traffic, one first needs to know how many cars travel from location to location. This is possible using statistics from sources such as the road traffic census. Next, one needs to determine the relationship between the amount of traffic and transit time. In the toy model we studied in Example 6.4, this relationship was assumed to be described by the simple linear formula (1), but what about in real life? The actual relationship between traffic and transit time, estimated from real data, is shown in Figure 6.7.

Using this information, we can use the same logic we used in the road traffic game to compute the amount of traffic in a Nash-equilibrium outcome. The calculations involved are very complex, but fortunately, there is a nice computer program to solve for the equilibrium. The results are shown in Figure 6.8. Bolder lines indicate heavier traffic.

Now, how accurate is this prediction? This is answered in Figure 6.9. According to the data, the Nash-equilibrium prediction explains 85 percent of the variation in the real-world data. The predictive power of our model is reasonably good.

In the United States and Europe, it is common to predict and analyze traffic using Nash equilibria of road traffic games. In fact, there are some commercial software programs designed specifically for this task.

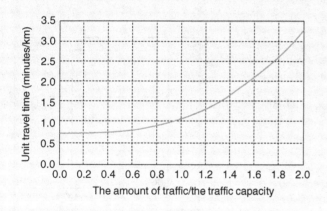

Figure 6.7 The calculated relationship between the amount of traffic and transit time

---

[9] Committee of Infrastructure Planning and Management (ed.), *Theory and Applications of Demand Prediction for Road Traffic*, part I: *Towards the Application of the Equilibrium User Distribution* (Tokyo: Japan Society of Civil Engineers, 2003). Figures 6.7 to 6.9 are excerpts from this book (pp. 72, 101, and 103 respectively).

Case Study 6.4 (cont.)

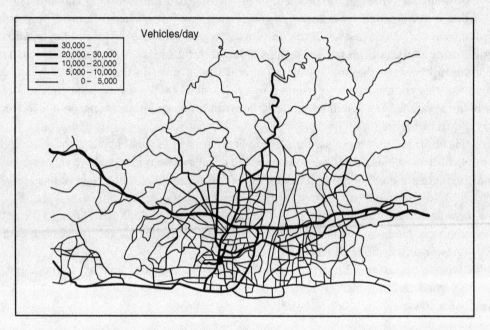

Figure 6.8 The predicted amount of traffic in a Nash equilibrium

Figure 6.9 Comparison of the Nash equilibrium and reality
Note: Each dot expresses one road section.

Predicted amount of traffic according to the Nash equilibrium

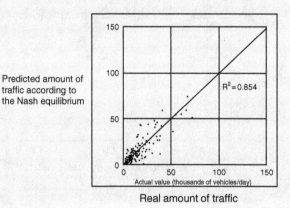

Real amount of traffic

The four examples we've studied should make clear that, even though Nash equilibrium is a very simple concept, we can use it to explain a wide variety of socio-economic phenomena, including detection of cartels, industry standards for technology, electoral competition, the amount of road traffic, etc. Since you now have a more concrete grasp of what Nash equilibria are, let's use the real-world examples we've just seen to consider why (or in what situations) people behave according to a Nash equilibrium.

6.3 The Reason Why a Nash Equilibrium Arises

The following are the three main reasons why people behave according to a Nash equilibrium.

> ① As a result of **rational inference**, people arrive at a Nash equilibrium.
> ② Through a process of **trial and error**, people arrive at a Nash equilibrium.
> ③ As a result of **pre-play communication**, people arrive at a Nash equilibrium.

Which one applies will depend on the context of the situation. Of course, it's also possible that none of these reasons applies, and that people do not behave according to a Nash equilibrium. Let me now elaborate on these three reasons.

① Rational Inference Leads to a Nash Equilibrium

If people with strong reasoning abilities analyze the game thoroughly prior to playing the game, in some situations a Nash equilibrium is realized. One example is the prisoner's dilemma game we saw earlier. In this game, regardless of what one's opponent does, it's better to confess than to remain silent. Therefore, players who choose their strategy rationally (i.e. in order to maximize their own payoffs) would choose to confess, and the Nash equilibrium realizes. However, there are examples in which rational inference alone will not necessarily lead to a Nash-equilibrium outcome. Consider the following example.

Example 6.5 The Battle of the Sexes

A boyfriend and girlfriend are planning a date; they can either watch a football match or shop at the mall. On the one hand, if they choose different activities and show up at different places, they miss out on a date and receive a payoff of zero. On the other hand, if they both choose the same activity, they'll have their date and receive higher payoffs. However, the boyfriend would be happier if they go to the football match, while the girlfriend would be happier if they went shopping at the mall. This game is summarized in the payoff table shown in Table 6.8.

Table 6.8 The battle of the sexes

Man \ Woman	Football	Shopping
Football	(3, 2)	0, 0
Shopping	0, 0	(2, 3)

Example 6.5 (cont.)

In this game, there are two Nash equilibria, which are circled in Table 6.8. Both of the outcomes in which both the boyfriend and girlfriend choose the same activity are Nash equilibria. However, *when each one is separately considering where to go, they cannot possibly reach a conclusion, since they don't know in advance what the other will choose.*

As you can see from this example, in order for a Nash-equilibrium outcome to occur, it's not enough for players to rationally analyze the game. We need an additional condition: correctly predicting the other players' moves.

> Rationality + **Correct prediction of the other player's moves**   ⇒   Nash equilibrium

Except for situations such as the prisoner's dilemma, in which there is a single action that is best for each player, regardless of what the other players do, it is important for a Nash equilibrium that players correctly predict the opponents' moves. I am going to list two additional reasons why a Nash equilibrium may emerge (②,③), and these will tell you where the "correct predictions about other players' moves" might come from.

② Trial and Error Lead to a Nash Equilibrium

People do not always behave fully rationally, and it's possible that they make wrong predictions about the other players' moves. However, *if they accumulate experience in identical or similar situations through trial and error*, they might learn how to predict the other players' moves and also identify what their best action is. Here are two real-world examples that will illustrate this process.

The first example is the road traffic game from earlier (Example 6.4, Case Study 6.4). Drivers may not be totally rational, but, with the experience they accumulate from making that drive repeatedly, they might learn to avoid congested roads and take less-traveled roads. Through this process of trial and error, they learn how congested various roads are (i.e. correct predictions about the other players' moves) and they come to choose the most convenient road based on this knowledge (i.e. behave rationally). Presumably by such a process of trial and error, the drivers in Case Study 6.4 reached a situation that is close to a Nash equilibrium, where no driver could benefit by independently switching routes. Next, I'll provide another example in which trial and error may give rise to a Nash equilibrium.

Case Study 6.5 Standing to the Left on Escalators

On escalators in the railway stations in Tokyo, people who are not in a hurry stand on the left side and leave the right side open so that people in a hurry can pass. If someone who was not in a hurry decided to stand on the right side, he would probably get some nasty comments from people who were in a hurry and trying to pass on the right. In this sense, we can view this outcome as a Nash equilibrium, where no one wants to change his or her behavior unilaterally.

This outcome is not the unique Nash equilibrium. In fact, the opposite convention of standing on the right side and leaving the left side for people to pass, which is also a Nash equilibrium, is common in the United Kingdom, the United States, and Osaka, the second largest city in Japan. How did these conventions (Nash equilibria) arise? Search on the Internet, and you'll find various plausible or amusing stories to explain why people stand on one particular side in a particular country. Many of these stories appear to be urban legends. To find out the truth, at least for the Japanese case, my research assistant, Toshiaki Kouno, extensively studied the newspaper archives at the University of Tokyo, and found that it was in 1992 that a newspaper article first mentioned opening the right on escalators in Japan.[10]

In the time before this convention emerged, people presumably stood on different sides of the escalator and gained experience about what to do through trial and error. There is nothing inherently special about leaving the right side open; the convention could just as easily have been to leave the left side open. It just so happened that people settled on this arrangement. The newspaper article says, "For the last year or so, standing on the left side has become noticeable during the morning and evening rush hours ... It seems to be a **spontaneous order** developed among the busy Tokyo commuters."

From the above examples, you can see that there are indeed cases in which a Nash equilibrium emerges as a result of repeated trial and error. However, we can't definitively say that "a Nash equilibrium *always* emerges" as a result of trial and error. It's possible that the adjustment process of trial and error takes a very long time, or that peoples' behavior never actually converges over time. Then, in what kind of situations might we believe that a Nash equilibrium emerges? One important answer is the following.

A **stable pattern of behavior that is established in society** is likely to be a Nash equilibrium.

The reason for this is simple: if a behavior that is not a Nash equilibrium were established in society, then (by the definition of Nash equilibrium) there would be someone who could gain by unilaterally changing his or her behavior. Such a person would notice this fact sooner or later and then would change his or her behavior. Therefore, a mode of behavior that is not a Nash equilibrium cannot persist for a long time. In other words (by looking at the contraposition), we conclude that, if a certain mode of behavior persists in a society, it must be a Nash equilibrium.

Established modes of behavior that are repeatedly observed are sometimes called "**stylized facts**." *A major objective of social science is to explain the origins of and reasons for such stylized facts.* Nash equilibrium is a very useful concept for this purpose. Game theory does not boldly claim that people *always* act according to a Nash equilibrium. Instead, the message of game

---

[10] *Asahi* newspaper, February 22, 1992.

theory is much more restrained, but nonetheless useful: Nash equilibrium captures stable modes of behavior (or stylized facts) that persist in a society. I'd like you to recall the earlier examples of road traffic around Hamamatsu City and opening the right on escalators to appreciate this assertion.

③ Pre-Play Communication Leads to a Nash Equilibrium

There are cases in which a Nash equilibrium may be achieved not as a result of repeated trial and error but as a result of conscious discussion by the parties involved before playing a game. Let me explain this point using a few examples.

Let's return to the battle of the sexes that we saw beforehand (Example 6.5). If the boyfriend and girlfriend separately ponder whether to go to the soccer game or to the mall, they won't arrive at a clear answer. So, what do they do? In reality, of course, they talk to each other to decide where they should go. If they talk before playing the battle of the sexes and agree to go shopping at the mall, then there will be no confusion when it comes time for them to leave their houses at meet up for their date.

That is, pre-play communication makes it possible to implement the Nash equilibrium in which they both go shopping at the mall. There are two important points I would like you to understand from this example. The first is that, in the following explanation,

> Rationality + **Correct prediction of the other players' moves**   ⇒   Nash equilibrium

which I gave previously, *"correct prediction of the other players' moves" can be achieved as a result of pre-play communication.*

The other point is that *the players will follow through on the plan they agree on.* Since the outcome in which the boyfriend and girlfriend both go to the mall is a Nash equilibrium, if either person breaks the agreement and chooses to go to the soccer game instead, then that person is worse off. This ensures that people actually honor the non-binding commitments they made. In order to understand this more clearly, let's look back at the prisoner's dilemma.

We saw that it's good for the prisoners if they both remain silent. What if, before being interrogated, they both agreed to remain silent? Unfortunately, this is not a Nash equilibrium, and therefore neither prisoner has an incentive to keep his promise. Even if one prisoner expects his partner to remain silent, it's in his interest to betray his partner and confess.

In order to ensure the prisoners to follow through on their promise to remain silent, which is not a Nash equilibrium, it's necessary for there to be negative consequences for any player who reneges on the agreement. For instance, if whoever breaks the agreement will be killed by a mob boss, it's almost certain that neither will confess. By contrast, in the battle of the sexes, it's possible to achieve the outcome in which both players go to the mall just by making a verbal agreement without the threat of punishment, since this is a Nash-equilibrium outcome.

Now, you should be able to see that we can characterize Nash equilibria in the following way.

> A Nash equilibrium is an **outcome that can be achieved by verbal agreement**, without using any additional penalty or reward.

We call an arrangement that individuals will honor even without penalty or reward a **self-enforcing agreement**. In summary, a Nash equilibrium can be seen as a self-enforcing agreement. This is a very important interpretation of Nash equilibrium.

6.4 The Relationship Between an Individual's Self-Interest and Socially Desirable Outcomes

A major contribution of game theory and the concept of Nash equilibrium is that it gives us a general framework for thinking about the relationship between socially desirable outcomes and the decisions that self-interested individuals make.

Recall that, in our analysis in Part I, we saw that in competitive markets, with individuals and firms that act in their own interest, the "size of the pie" is maximized. In other words, despite the fact that each individual and firm cares only about their own outcomes, through the market forces that Adam Smith dubbed the "invisible hand" competitive markets maximize social gains – that is, competitive markets maximize the total gains that are divided among the members of society. In this sense, competitive markets are (Pareto-)efficient; there is no alternative arrangement that could make *everyone* better off.[11]

Other than in competitive markets, how do self-interested individuals' decisions relate to socially desirable outcomes? Is it still the case that, in more general social and economic problems, the decisions of self-interested individuals will maximize social welfare? There is a line of social thought, called *laissez-faire*, that believes the answer is "Yes." In Chapter 4, Section 4.1, part (f), I introduced Coase's theorem, which states that the problem of "externalities" such as pollution can be solved by rational discussion among the affected parties. I presented the following line of thought.

Naïve Laissez-Faire

In an inefficient state, there is (by the very definition of inefficiency) another state that is better for everyone involved. If the parties are rational, they will notice this and will work together to move from the inefficient state to the efficient one. Therefore, *when individuals are rational, social outcomes must always be efficient, so there is no need for intervention.*

---

[11] More precisely, there is no alternative arrangement that could make anyone better off without leaving at least one person worse off.

At first glance, doesn't this seem to be a logically flawless argument? In fact, until the late 1970s this philosophy had very strong support, (mainly) among conservative economists.

However, if this reasoning were correct, then, in the prisoner's dilemma, rational prisoners would remain silent and arrive at the socially optimal outcome. In fact, our analysis of the prisoner's dilemma showed that this outcome is never reached, even when the (rational) prisoners are allowed to talk to each other. By carefully analyzing individual incentives, game-theoretic analysis has revealed that laissez-faire reasoning is flawed.

What is wrong with laissez-faire reasoning? There is nothing wrong with the claim that rational people will recognize that they are in an inefficient state and that there is an alternative state that is better for everyone. The issue lies in the claim that, if rational people recognize that they are in an inefficient state, they will work together to move to an efficient state.

In order to actually move from an inefficient state to an efficient state, *it's not enough for the people involved to simply agree to do so. The reason is that, once people enter into the agreement, they might find it is in their best interest to violate the agreement. Consequently, to "work together to move to an efficient state," they must install some sort of mechanism to ensure that people actually honor the agreement.* For instance, we saw in the prisoner's dilemma that, even if both prisoners agree to remain silent, each prisoner has an incentive to disregard the agreement and confess. Therefore, in order to ensure that both prisoners actually remain silent, they should install a certain mechanism to remove the incentive to break the agreement. For instance, if the prisoners know they will be killed if they break the agreement, they will honor the agreement to remain silent. You might think that implementing such a mechanism is a simple and easy task, but in most cases it is actually easier said than done.

Let's summarize what we've discussed so far. *In competitive markets, the self-interested behavior of individuals ensures a socially desirable (efficient) outcome. However, in more general social and economic problems, this is not necessarily the case.* In my opinion, this revelation, which is now widely accepted by almost all economists, is one of the most important contributions of game theory to the social sciences. In general, the behavior of self-interested individuals results in a Nash-equilibrium outcome. But, since each individual is concerned only with his or her own well-being, it is likely the case that

• cooperative actions that benefit others but are individually costly are not taken,
• and actions that benefit the player at the expense of others are taken.

Therefore, it's often the case that Nash equilibria, unlike competitive market outcomes, are inefficient. In order to avoid inefficient Nash equilibria, *it's necessary to design rules or institutions that provide incentives for people to take socially optimal actions.* Game theory reveals this principle in a very elegant manner and brought an end to economists' single-minded focus on promoting free competition through markets. Economists now pay more attention to designing rules and institutions that provide appropriate individual incentives.

6.5   Application to Oligopoly (I): Quantity Competition and Price Competition

Using game theory, let's analyze an **oligopoly (imperfect competition)** in which a small number of firms try to interact with the other firms. In this section, we consider a simple case in which the firms simultaneously choose their strategies. This case is further divided into the case in which firms compete by deciding the quantities they supply (output) and the case in which firms compete by deciding the price they sell the good at. We will see that these two cases result in very different outcomes. First, let's consider the case of quantity competition.

(a)   Quantity Competition (Cournot Model)[12]

Suppose there are two firms, $i = 1, 2$, that have common constant marginal cost c (i.e. the cost of producing one unit of output is c) in a market in which the (downward-sloping) demand curve is defined by $P = a - bQ$. An oligopoly in which there are two firms is sometimes called a **duopoly**. Assume that the firms simultaneously decide their outputs, q_1 and q_2. What happens if each firm chooses its output based on a prediction of what its competitor will choose? In order to answer this question, let's use game theory and solve for a Nash equilibrium.

First, by examining the relationship between firm 1's profit and the combined output of both firms, we conclude that

$$\pi_1 = \underbrace{(a - b(q_1 + q_2)) - c)q_1}_{\text{Price } P}. \tag{2}$$

This is a quadratic equation with respect to firm 1's own output q_1, so the graph of firm 1's profit function has a shape that is bowed upward (i.e. it is a parabola), as in Figure 6.10. Let's consider in detail what happens at the Nash equilibrium (q_1^*, q_2^*). Figure 6.10 depicts firm 1's profit when firm 2 produces the Nash-equilibrium output q_2^*. When firm 1 varies its output q_1, its profit π_1 changes as depicted in Figure 6.10. The quantity at which this graph

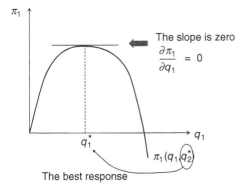

Figure 6.10 The graph of firm 1's profit function

The slope is zero
$$\frac{\partial \pi_1}{\partial q_1} = 0$$

$\pi_1(q_1, q_2^*)$

The best response

---

[12] Antoine Augustin Cournot (1801–1877), a French economist, developed this model.

peaks (i.e. the profit-maximizing quantity) is firm 1's **best response** q_1^* when firm 2 chooses q_2^* (since both firms are choosing optimally at the Nash equilibrium $\left(q_1^*, q_2^*\right)$, the best response to q_2^* must be q_1^*).

Let's try to use equations to express the idea that a best response is a point at which the graph of the profit functions peaks. We know that, at the peak of the graph, the slope of the tangent line is zero. We also know that the slope of the tangent line is given by the derivative of π_1 with respect to q_1, $\partial \pi_1 / \partial q_1$ Therefore, *the equation that determines firm 1's best response* is simply

$$\frac{\partial \pi_1}{\partial q_1} = 0.$$

Using the expression for π_1 given by Equation (2) and differentiating with respect to q_1, we obtain

$$\frac{\partial \pi_1}{\partial q_1} = a - 2bq_1 - bq_2 - c = 0. \tag{3}$$

This is sometimes called **the first-order condition** for optimality. An analogous argument holds for firm 2, so the *Nash-equilibrium condition* that both firms are best responding to each other can be expressed by the system of equations of each firm's first-order conditions for optimality:

$$\begin{cases} \mathbf{0} = \dfrac{\partial \pi_1}{\partial q_1} = a - 2bq_1 - bq_2 - c \\[4mm] \mathbf{0} = \dfrac{\partial \pi_2}{\partial q_2} = a - 2bq_2 - bq_1 - c \end{cases}$$

Nash-equilibrium condition (1)

If we solve this system of equations,[13] we obtain the Nash-equilibrium outputs for the two firms. Since these equations are symmetric for firms 1 and 2, let us guess that the solution must also be symmetric: $q_1^* = q_1^* = q^*$. Substituting this into (3), we obtain $0 = a - 3bq^* - c$, and solving for q^* we find that

$$q_1^* = q_2^* = \frac{a - c}{3b} \tag{4}$$

is a Nash equilibrium, which is called the **Cournot–Nash equilibrium**.

Analysis Using a Graphical Representation

In order to deepen our understanding, let's look at the Nash equilibrium from a graphical perspective. Since the first-order condition for Optimality (3) determines firm 1's optimal

---

[13] We can state this more rigorously in the following way: if the graph in which each player's payoff π_1 is on the vertical axis and that player's strategy a_1 is on the horizontal axis (for any fixed strategy of the opponent) and is bowed upward (i.e. π_1 is a concave function of a_1), then a Nash equilibrium is obtained by solving the system of equations of the first-order conditions of the players.

output q_1 given firm 2's output q_2, if we solve the equation (3) for q_1, then we obtain firm 1's best response as a function of firm 2's output:

$$q_1 = \frac{a-c}{2b} - \frac{1}{2}q_2 = R_1(q_2).$$

We call this firm 1's **best response function**. Since firm 2's best response function has exactly the same shape, it is given by $R_2(q_1) = \frac{a-c}{2b} - \frac{1}{2}q_1$. The Nash equilibrium (q_1^*, q_2^*) is the state in which the two firms are optimally responding to each other, so we can express this by

$$\begin{cases} q_1^* = R_1(q_2^*) \\ q_2^* = R_2(q_1^*) \end{cases}.$$

Nash-equilibrium condition (2)

This is depicted in Figure 6.11.

Since firm 2's best response is $R_2(q_1) = \frac{a-c}{2b} - \frac{1}{2}q_1$, its graph (sometimes called the reaction function) is a downward-sloping straight line with slope equal to $1/2$, as shown in the figure. Firm 1's reaction function is analogous. *The intersection of these reaction functions (i.e. the point at which each player is best responding to the other) is the Nash equilibrium.*

Using Figure 6.11, let's check whether the Nash equilibrium maximizes the combined profits of the firms. Denoting the total output by $Q = q_1 + q_2$, we can write the sum of the profits of the two firms as

$$\begin{aligned} \pi_1 + \pi_2 &= (P(Q) - c)q_1 + (P(Q) - c)q_1 \\ &= (P(Q) - c)Q. \end{aligned}$$

This is exactly equal to the profit of a single monopolistic firm with the same constant marginal cost c that produces output Q. Therefore, in order to maximize the combined profits, $\pi_1 + \pi_2$, of the two firms, we can set total output $Q = q_1 + q_2$ equal to the optimal output of a single monopolistic firm.

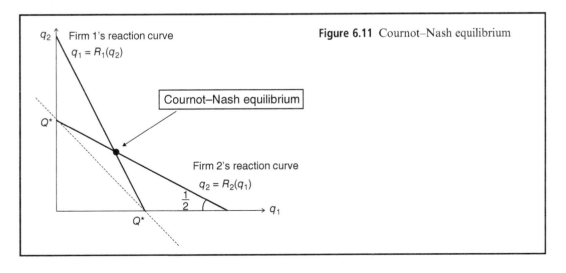

Figure 6.11 Cournot–Nash equilibrium

Now, here is a fun question for you. Somewhere in Figure 6.11, the optimal output of a single monopolistic firm is depicted; can you spot where? The answer is Q^* in the figure. The reason Q^* gives the optimal output of a single monopolistic firm is that Q^* is the optimal output of a duopolistic firm *when the other firm produces no output*, which is exactly the same situation as the monopoly case.

Keeping this in mind, you should notice that, on the dashed line in Figure 6.11, the sum of the outputs of the two firms is equal to the optimal output of the monopolistic firm (i.e. $q_1 + q_2 = Q^*$). In other words, along this dashed line, the combined profits of the two firms are maximized. Since the Nash equilibrium is to the top right of this line, the combined profits of the two firms are not maximized at the Nash equilibrium. *That is, if oligopolistic firms compete in quantity, the outputs are too large relative to the point that maximizes the combined profits.*

Next, let's compare outputs under perfect competition and under the Nash equilibrium. Under perfect competition, the price is equal to the marginal cost of production, so $P = c$. If we denote the total output under perfect competition by Q^0, since $P = a - bQ^0 = c$, we have that the total output under perfect competition is equal to

$$Q^0 = \frac{a - c}{b}.$$

By contrast, according to Equation (4), the total output of the two firms under the Cournot–Nash equilibrium is

$$\frac{2}{3}\left(\frac{a - c}{b}\right),$$

which is less than the total output under perfect competition. Thus, if oligopolistic firms compete in quantity, the combined output is less than it is under perfect competition, and, as a result, the price is too high relative to the market price under perfect competition.

Summarizing the above, using game-theoretic analysis we have shown the following.

Output under monopoly	<	total output under oligopoly (quantity competition)	< total output under perfect competition

(b)   Price Competition (Bertrand Model)[14]

Let's consider the same situation as above: there are two firms, $i = 1, 2$, that have common and constant marginal cost c in a market with demand curve $P = a - bQ$, but, this time, suppose that the two firms simultaneously decide prices p_1 and p_2 as opposed to quantities q_1 and q_2.

[14] Joseph Louis François Bertrand (1822–1900), a French mathematician, developed this model in response to Cournot's model.

First, let me explain the concept of "**product differentiation**," which is important for the analysis of price competition. Starbucks coffee and Dunkin' Donuts coffee have different tastes, though both are coffee.[15] In such a case, the two products are distinguishable. When there is product differentiation such as this, people don't necessarily just buy the cheaper product; they might be willing to pay slightly more, because they happen to prefer the more expensive option. It's clear that many people are willing to pay for Starbucks coffee, even though it costs more than Dunkin' Donuts coffee. By contrast, for a product such as gasoline, most people can't tell the difference between various companies' products and simply choose the least expensive option. In this case, we say there is no differentiation.

In the Bertrand model, we usually consider the case with *no product differentiation* and assume that the firm with the lower price gets all the demand. If two firms set the same price, we assume that each firm gets half the demand.

Let's get straight to the conclusion.

Nash Equilibrium of the Bertrand Model (Price Competition)

$p_1^* = p_2^* = c$, firms earn zero profits

We saw before that, in perfectly competitive markets, the market price coincides with the marginal cost of production. Since c is the marginal cost in the market we are considering, *the Nash equilibrium of the Bertrand model (price competition) with no product differentiation is the same as the perfectly competitive equilibrium.*

Let's verify that this is indeed a Nash-equilibrium outcome. It suffices to show that the Nash-equilibrium condition that

"no player can gain by unilaterally changing his or her strategy (price)"   (*)

holds. Suppose the opposing firm sets the price equal to the marginal cost of production, c. What happens if the firm unilaterally changes its price?

[1] When the Firm Unilaterally Raises Its Price

If the firm unilaterally raises its price, it will have no customers, since all customers will buy from the opponent at a lower price. Therefore, the firm earns zero profits. Since the firm also earns zero profits in the equilibrium state (price is equal to cost), we can clearly see that the firm does not benefit from unilaterally increasing its price.

[2] When the Firm Unilaterally Lowers Its Price

If the firm unilaterally lowers its price, it attracts all the customers. However, since the firm is selling at a price that is lower than the cost, c, it actually earns negative profits. This is worse

---

[15] In my opinion.

than earning zero profits, as it did in the equilibrium state. As a result, the firm does not benefit from unilaterally decreasing its price.

Thus, we've shown that the outcome $p_1^* = p_2^* = c$ satisfies the Nash-equilibrium condition (*).

In order to understand price competition more deeply, let's consider the scenario in which the two firms collude and raise the price above the cost, c, and earn positive profits – that is, $p_1^0 = p_2^0 > c$. In this case, if one firm deviates from the agreement and sets a price just below the other firm's price, it steals all of its competitor's customers. Since the price is barely less than before, it practically doubles its profits by absorbing its competitor's profits. Consequently, although the state $p_1^0 = p_2^0 > c$ in which both firms earn positive profits is desirable from the perspective of the firms, the condition (*) is not satisfied, so it is not a Nash equilibrium. Therefore, it's unlikely that such an outcome could actually occur, unless there is a way to punish the firm that deviates from the agreement.[16]

If we check the various other cases, we'll see that there are no other Nash equilibria apart from "$p_1^* = p_2^* = c$, zero profits." (I leave this as a practice problem for the reader.)

Comment 6.2 Which Is the Correct Model of an Oligopoly?

The only difference between the Cournot model and the Bertrand model is what the firms' strategies are: in the Cournot model, the firms compete by choosing quantities; in the Bertrand model, the firms compete by choosing prices. Yet these two models make dramatically different predictions. The outcome of the Cournot model (quantity competition) is an intermediate case between a perfectly competitive market and a monopoly, while the outcome of the Bertrand model (price competition) is the same as the outcome in a perfectly competitive market. Which model should we take more seriously?

In fact, there is no single "right" model, and there are some cases in the real world that closely resemble quantity competition, and others that closely resemble price competition. For instance, nearby gas stations compete by displaying their prices, such as "$3.23/gallon," on a billboard in front of the station. This situation could be modeled using the Bertrand model of price competition. By contrast, local fish markets closely resemble the Cournot model of quantity competition. Every morning, fishermen (who we can think of as the firms) go out in their boats, catch fish (i.e. they choose their quantity), and bring them to the local fish market. The fish are then sold in auctions at the market. The auction prices of the fish depend negatively on the quantity of fish available for sale, as with a demand curve. This situation is well modeled using the Cournot model of quantity competition.

What about the sale of more "common" types of goods, such as household electrical appliances such as TVs or refrigerators? These are more complicated cases. Ultimately, producers have little control over the price their goods are sold at, since they wholesale their products to retailers. The

---

[16] In Chapter 7, Section 7.5, I'll explain in greater detail a method to sustain high prices in price competitions by preventing firms from deviating.

market prices of these goods are determined when the retailers resell to consumers. Therefore, this situation could reasonably be described by a model of quantity competition between producers, in which the firms deliver a certain quantity of the product, for which later a competitive price is set in the market.

6.6   Uncertainty and Expected Utility

Let's change topics slightly and discuss the basics of dealing with uncertainty in economics and game theory. So far we have ignored uncertainty, but in the real world there are many situations that involve some kind of uncertainty. Now that we are in the latter half of this book, we'll finally deal with these issues. First, let me list several situations in which uncertainty is an issue.

- **Fluctuations of the environment**: it might be necessary to consider aspects of the (natural or social) environment, such as weather, stock prices, or exchange rates, that fluctuate randomly and can affect the decisions of firms and consumers.
- **The opponents' moves cannot be precisely predicted**: we need to consider the various actions the opponents potentially take and how likely each of the possible actions is.
- **Asymmetry of information**: we need to consider the various pieces of information the opponents might have, and how likely it is that the opponent has any given piece of information.

To study such situations, we need to understand how humans behave under uncertainty. I'm going to introduce the "expected utility model," a simple and tractable model that formulates how people make decisions under uncertainty. This model can describe

- cautious people who dislike risks;
- risk-loving people, such as gamblers; and
- people in between, who don't care whether there are risks or not,

in a simple and easily understood manner. This model is the basis for economics of uncertainty, so, although the discussion will be a bit abstract and will require your patience, it is a useful analytic tool that will seem logical once you understand it! Bear with me for a while.

Instead of diving straight into the model, let's first work through a simple example that will illustrate the various ways that people may behave under uncertainty.

Example 6.6

Suppose there is a lottery that gives $3,000 or $1,000 with equal probability. In your opinion, what is the value of this lottery? Equivalently, how much would you pay to play this lottery? One possible answer that often appears in mathematics and statistics textbooks is that the value of this lottery is equal to the expected value of the prize money.

If we denote the prize money of this lottery by $\tilde{x}$, we can say that $\tilde{x}$ takes value 3,000 with probability 1/2 and takes value 1,000 with probability 1/2. Therefore, the expected value of this

Example 6.6 (cont.)

lottery, which we denote by E[$\tilde{x}$], is just the average of the possible outcomes weighted by their respective probabilities. That is,

$$E[\tilde{x}] = \frac{1}{2} \times 3,000 + \frac{1}{2} \times 1,000 = 2,000.$$

What does it mean that the expected value of this lottery is $2,000? It means that, if you play this lottery many times, *on average you will win $2,000*.

Since "expected values" play a key role in our discussion of decision-making under uncertainty, let's briefly review what an expected value is. A variable $\tilde{x}$ that takes a random value, such as the prize money of this lottery, is called a random variable. (We attach the notation $\sim$ to express that it is a random variable.) The expected value of a random variable expresses the value this random variable takes on average. We define it as follows.

Suppose that $\tilde{x}$ is a **random variable** that takes one of the values $x_1, \ldots, x_K$. We denote by p_k the probability of $\tilde{x}$ taking value x_k. In this case,

$$p_1 x_1 + \ldots + p_K x_K$$

is called the **expected value** of $\tilde{x}$, and is denoted by E[$\tilde{x}$].

Do people always make decisions based on expected values? Example 6.7 will help us answer this question.

Example 6.7 St. Petersburg Paradox[17]

Suppose I offer you the following gamble. I will toss a coin until tails appears. Once a tails appears, I pay you $2^{(\text{the number of coin tosses})}$.

Let me give you a few examples to clarify how the prize money is determined.

- Tails (tossing ends here)   →   I pay you $2^1 = \$2$.
- Heads, Tails   →   I pay you $2^2 = \$4$.
- Heads, Heads, Tails   →   I pay you $2^3 = \$8$.

How much would you pay me to play this game? Try flipping a coin yourself to check how much prize money you would win. My guess is that most people would pay $5 or $10 to play, perhaps $100 at most.

Let's calculate the expected value of the prize money. Let us denote the probability of heads and tails by Pr(Heads) and Pr(Tails), and assume that they are equal to 1/2. Then, the expected value is

---

[17] This is called the St. Petersburg paradox because it first appeared in a 1738 paper by the mathematician Daniel Bernoulli that was published in an academic journal in the Russian city of St. Petersburg.

$$\left(\tfrac{1}{2}\right) \cdot 2 \quad + \quad \left(\tfrac{1}{2}\right)^2 \cdot 2^2 \quad + \quad \left(\tfrac{1}{2}\right)^3 2^3 \quad + \cdots = 1 + 1 + 1 + \ldots = \infty \,(\text{infinity}).$$

$Pr(\text{Heads})$	$Pr(\text{Heads})\,Pr(\text{Tails})$	$Pr(\text{Heads})Pr(\text{Heads})Pr(\text{Tails})$

That is, the expected value of the prize money in this gamble is – oh, dear – infinity!

If someone made decisions based only on expected values, he or she would be willing to pay me $1 million, or even $100 million, to take this gamble! Of course, hardly anyone would actually do such a thing. It's safe to say that people have other considerations besides just expected values.

Based on the two examples above, let's think about how to build a model that can capture how people make decisions under uncertainty. Returning to the lottery in Example 6.6, which pays $3,000 or $1,000 with equal probability, would people rather take that gamble, or receive its expected value $2,000 with certainty? We can broadly classify attitudes toward risk in the following manner.

- A cautious person who dislikes risks and would rather receive the expected value of the prize money than play the lottery is said to be **risk-averse**.
- Someone who likes gambles and would rather play the lottery than receive the expected value of the prize money is said to be **risk-loving**.
- Someone who cares only about the expected value of the prize money and is indifferent between playing the lottery and receiving the expected value of the prize money is said to be **risk-neutral**.

Is there *a model that can express these various attitudes toward risk*? Yes; the expected utility model, described below, can do just this!

The Expected Utility Model

$x =$ the realized outcome (i.e. the prize money, income, etc.).
$u(x) =$ the "utility" that the outcome provides the decision-maker.

When the outcome is uncertain, the decision maker **maximizes the expected utility** $E[u(\tilde{x})]$.

The expected utility is just the expected value of the utility. Expressing the uncertain outcome by a random variable $\tilde{x} = x_1, \ldots, x_K$ and denoting the probability of the kth outcome x_k by p_k, we have that the expected utility is given by

$$E[u(\tilde{x})] = p_1 u(x_1) + \ldots + p_K u(x_K).$$

Example 6.8

The expected utility from the lottery in Example 6.6 that pays \$3,000 and \$1,000 with equal probability is given by

$$E[u(\tilde{x})] = \frac{1}{2}u(1,000) + \frac{1}{2}u(3,000).$$

In the expected utility model, the curvature of a person's utility function tells us whether he or she is risk-loving, risk-neutral, or risk-averse (see Figure 6.12). Let me explain why this is so.

First, let me explain the case of the risk-averse person whose utility function is shown at the top of Figure 6.12. We can use the graph of this person's utility function to determine whether she prefers to play the lottery in Example 6.6 or take the expected value of the lottery with certainty. Before we go further, I want to make sure you understand how the expected utility of a lottery is calculated. Take a look at Figure 6.13.

If this person plays the lottery, she receives utility $u(1,000)$ with probability $1/2$ and utility $u(3,000)$ with probability $1/2$, so the expected utility of the lottery is just the average of these two

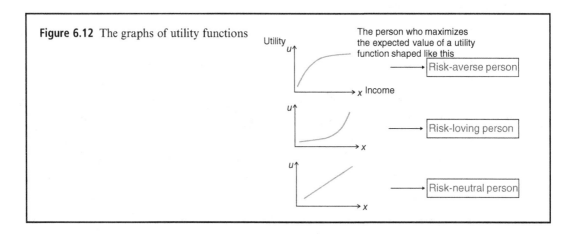

Figure 6.12 The graphs of utility functions

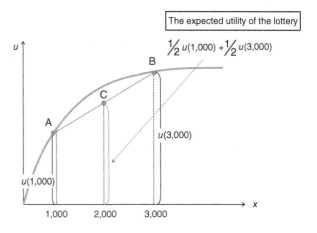

Figure 6.13 Utility function of the risk-averse person

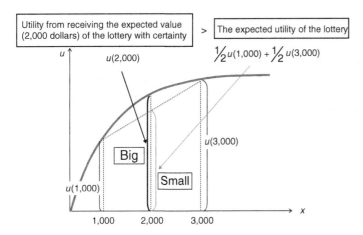

Figure 6.14 The risk-averse person

numbers. Graphically, this is given by the height of the midpoint C of the line segment between points A and B in Figure 6.13.

By contrast, the utility from receiving the expected value of the lottery, $2,000, with certainty is $u(2,000)$. Graphically, this is given by the height of the graph of the utility function at $x = 2,000$ in Figure 6.13. In Figure 6.14, I explain both steps.

From this example, you should see that, if the graph of a person's utility function is bowed upward, then this person is risk-averse and would prefer to receive the expected value of the lottery with certainty rather than play the lottery.

Think back to Chapter 2, Section 2.3, part (c), in which we learned about production functions. You might remember from that discussion that functions that are bowed upward (i.e. the area below the graph is a convex set) are said to be concave functions. The utility function u that we discussed above is clearly a concave function. However, it also satisfies an additional property: *there is no part of the graph that is a straight line*. In other words, it is curved everywhere. Concave functions that satisfy this additional property are said to be **strictly concave** functions. Using this terminology, we can summarize our analysis in a succinct way: *a person whose utility function is a strictly concave function is risk-averse.*

Comment 6.3 An Explanation Using a Formula

Recall that in Chapter 2, Section 2.3, part (c), we saw that a function $u(x)$ is said to be a concave function if, for any t satisfying $0 < t < 1$ and any two points a, b with $a \neq b$,

$$u(ta + (1 - t)b) \geq tu(a) + (1 - t)u(b)$$

holds. In particular, *when this condition is satisfied with a strict inequality ($>$), u is said to be a strictly concave function*. Figure 6.14 is nothing but a graphical depiction of this inequality for $t = 1/2, a = 1,000$, and $b = 3,000$.

How can we interpret the above condition being satisfied with a strict inequality? Suppose that there is a lottery that pays a dollars with probability t and pays b dollars with probability $1 - t$. The left-hand side of the above expression gives the utility from receiving the expected value of the lottery, $ta + (1 - t)b$ dollars, with certainty. The right-hand side is the expected utility from playing the lottery and is smaller than the left-hand side. In this way, from the mathematical formula that defines a strictly concave function, we can see that a person whose utility function is strictly concave will always prefer to receive the expected value of a lottery with certainty rather than play the lottery. That is, such a person is risk-averse.

Next, I'll explain the risk-loving case shown in the middle of Figure 6.12. A function whose graph is bowed downward and has no straight portions is said to be a strictly convex function. To analyze this case, let us change the graph of the utility function in Figure 6.14 in such a way that it is bowed downward (meaning that the person has **strictly convex** utility function). Then, you will see that the labels "Big" and "Small" should be switched. Such a person would prefer playing the lottery to receiving the expected value of the lottery with certainty and is risk-loving.

Last, consider the case in which the graph of the utility function is a straight line, as in the bottom part of Figure 6.12. To analyse this case, modify the graph of the utility function in Figure 6.14 with a straight line. Then you will see that the parts labeled "Big" and "Small" should be the same size. Therefore, a person having such a utility function is indifferent between playing the lottery and receiving the expected value of the lottery with certainty, and so is risk-neutral. If the graph of a utility function is a straight line, then we can express the utility function using a linear equation of the form $u(x) = kx + c$. In particular, if we consider the utility function $u(x) = x$, it's easy to see that maximizing the expected utility, $E[u(x)]$, is the same as maximizing the expected value of the lottery, $E[x]$. A person having this utility function is clearly risk-neutral.

We can summarize our findings, shown graphically in Figure 6.12, as follows.

In the expected utility model:

- the utility function is a **strictly concave** function ⇔ **risk-averse** person;
- the utility function is a **strictly convex** function ⇔ **risk-loving** person;
- the utility function is a **linear** function ⇔ **risk-neutral** person.

Below, I'll make two detailed remarks.

Comment 6.4 "Utility" to Represent a Consumer's Preferences versus the "Utility" in the Expected Utility Model

In Chapter 1 we saw how utility functions capture a consumer's preferences, and now we have learned how utility functions express a person's attitudes toward risk. However, the meaning of "utility" in the former and the latter cases is not the same. When we talk about a utility function to represent a consumer's preferences, *any function that assigns larger numbers to more desirable items is a valid utility function*. The exact numbers could be arbitrary. In contrast, when we talk about utility functions in the expected utility model, not only should we assign larger numbers (levels of utility) to more desirable outcomes but also *we must carefully choose those numbers to capture a person's attitudes toward risk*. As you can see in Figure 6.12, which depicts various utility functions in the context of the expected utility model, each utility function assigns larger utility values to higher dollar payoffs. However, the exact shapes of those utility functions have different implications for the person's attitude toward risk. For instance, if each additional dollar of payoff gives the person less and less utility, as in the top case of Figure 6.12, the person is risk-averse.

In this way, using utility functions to describe a person's preferences in the presence of uncertainty (i.e. in the expected utility model) requires more thought than using utility functions to describe a person's preferences in the absence of uncertainty. We sometimes refer to utility functions that describe a person's attitude toward risk or uncertainty as **von Neumann–Morgenstern utility functions** (after the names of the people who invented them).

Comment 6.5 What Are the "Payoffs" Used in Game Theory?

One of the things that may puzzle you when you first study game theory is what exactly the players' "payoffs" are. If the situation the game describes involves monetary payoffs, the numbers in the payoff table could be dollar amounts. But what about the case of the battle of the sexes (Table 6.8)? What does it mean to have a payoff of three or two or zero in this context?

In many textbooks on game theory, there is either no answer to this question or the answer is that the numbers are von Neumann–Morgenstern utilities. However, let me give a more practical and appropriate interpretation. First, we should separate cases in which people make decisions in the presence of uncertainty from cases in which people make decisions in the absence of uncertainty. Some scenarios in which people must make decisions in the presence of uncertainty are:

- the environment surrounding players fluctuates randomly (rolling dice, being affected by stock prices or exchange rates, etc.); or

- players take random actions (the case of "mixed-strategy" equilibria, which I'll explain in Section 6.7).

In these cases, since it's necessary to consider the players' attitudes toward risk, we have to set payoffs equal to von Neumann–Morgenstern utilities.

Example 6.9

If the amount of money a player receives is subject to random events such as fluctuations in stock prices or exchange rates, the player's payoff should not be modeled as a set dollar amount x but the von Neumann–Morgenstern utility $u(x)$ that the player receives from the dollar amount x.

(In this way, we can build in a player's attitudes toward risk.)

By contrast, in the absence of uncertainty, the players' payoffs can be arbitrary as long as more desirable outcomes are assigned larger numbers. The reason is that, in the absence of uncertainty, the Nash-equilibrium outcome is not changed by assignment of numbers.[18] Most applications of game theory use Nash equilibria in the absence of uncertainty. When we consider such applications, determining the players' payoffs is easy: just assign larger numbers to more desirable outcomes.

To summarize.

> *The players' payoffs in game theory* must assign larger numbers to more desirable outcomes, but
>
> - *in the absence of uncertainty*, the exact numbers can be arbitrary;
> - *in the presence of uncertainty*, the numbers must be assigned in a way that captures the players' attitudes toward risk (i.e. payoffs = von Neumann–Morgenstern utilities).

6.7   Mixed-Strategy Equilibria and the Existence of Nash Equilibria

Now back to game theory. In the various examples that we've seen so far, there has always existed a state in which all players are best responding to one another – i.e. a Nash equilibrium. Does every game have a Nash equilibrium? Let's take a look at the following example.

---

[18] A Nash equilibrium is a state in which *no player can gain* from unilaterally changing her behavior. If we assign higher payoffs to more desirable outcomes, then, whatever numbers we use, in Nash equilibrium a player *cannot improve her payoff* by unilaterally changing her strategy. That is, the Nash-equilibrium outcome does not change depending on the numbers we use.

Example 6.10 Rock, Paper, Scissors

Rock, paper, scissors is a hand game in which players simultaneously choose one of three actions: rock, paper, or scissors. It can be expressed as a payoff table, as in Table 6.9. If a player wins, her payoff is 1; if a player loses, her payoff is -1; and, if there is a tie, her payoff is 0.

In rock, paper, scissors, rock beats scissors, scissors beat paper, and paper beats rock, so it appears that *there is no state in which all players are optimally responding to each other's actions – i.e. there is no Nash equilibrium.* In fact, you can check that no entry of the payoff table in Table 6.9 is a Nash equilibrium. What, then, do most people do in reality? Well, they would like their actions to be unpredictable, and so they randomly choose one of the actions. Moreover, a player wouldn't like to choose one action much more frequently than the others; most players seem to choose each action with roughly equal probability.

Let's think carefully about what is happening here. Imagine that you are player 1 and you know that player 2 will play rock, paper, or scissors, each with 1/3 probability. Take a look at Table 6.10. If you know that your opponent will randomly play rock, paper, or scissors with equal probability, it's easy to see that your expected payoff if you play rock is 0. Likewise, if you play paper or scissors, your expected payoff is still 0.

Thus, your expected payoff is the same regardless of what action you take. In conclusion, if you are trying to *maximize your expected payoff* and your opponent randomly selects rock, paper, or scissors, each with 1/3 probability,

- any action you take is optimal;
- in particular, it is one of the optimal actions for you to randomly select rock, paper, or scissors, each with 1/3 probability;
- therefore, when all players randomly select rock, paper, or scissors, each with 1/3 probability, all players are *optimally responding to one another.*

Table 6.9 The payoff table for rock, paper, scissors

1 \ 2	Rock	Scissors	Paper
Rock	0, 0	1, −1	−1, 1
Scissors	−1, 1	0, 0	1, −1
Paper	1, −1	−1, 1	0, 0

Table 6.10 Calculating the expected payoff

1 \ 2	Rock $\frac{1}{3}$	Scissors $\frac{1}{3}$	Paper $\frac{1}{3}$
Rock	0, 0	1, −1	−1, 1

Player 1's expected payoff

$$\frac{1}{3} \times 0 + \frac{1}{3} \times 1 + \frac{1}{3} \times (-1) = 0$$

In this sense, we can think of this outcome as a version of a Nash equilibrium. When a player behaves randomly, we say that this player is using a **mixed strategy**. By contrast, if a player's strategy does not involve randomizing what action she takes (for instance, deciding to play rock with certainty), we say that the player is using a **pure strategy**.[19] A state in which players use mixed strategies such that they are optimally responding to one another is called a mixed-strategy equilibrium. A **mixed-strategy equilibrium** is just a Nash equilibrium in which players maximize their expected payoffs by using mixed strategies.

Rock, paper, scissors is not the only example of a scenario in which people behave randomly. When investigating tax compliance, the United States' Internal Revenue Service (IRS) randomly selects people to audit. If they followed a known deterministic rule (last names beginning with "A" get audited this year, last names beginning with "B" get audited next year, etc.), then people would pay taxes only in years they know they will be audited. In effect, the IRS could not enforce tax policy. If the IRS randomly selects who is audited, people are more likely to pay taxes since there is a possibility of getting caught cheating. This can be viewed as a mixed-strategy equilibrium. Mixed strategies are also used in sports. Tennis players might randomly decide whether to hit their serves to their opponent's forehand or backhand. Similarly, soccer players taking penalty kicks may randomly decide whether to kick the ball to the left or right. Let's look more carefully at the example of penalty kicks in soccer.

Case Study 6.6 Penalty Kicks in Soccer

In soccer games, there are situations called "penalty kicks" in which a player and goalkeeper face off. We can think of the player taking the penalty kick as having two strategies: kicking the ball to the left and kicking the ball to the right. (It is rare to kick the ball down the middle.) Since professional players can kick the ball very hard, the goalkeeper does not have time to look at the direction of the ball after it is kicked and move in that direction. Instead, the goalkeeper has to take a guess as to which direction the kicker will shoot and move in that direction at approximately the same time that the ball is kicked (see Figure 6.15).

Let's analyze this situation using game theory. We can think of the kicker's payoff as the probability that his shot scores. Since the goalkeeper wants to make this probability as small as possible, we can think of the goalkeeper's payoff as the negative of the probability that the kicker

---

[19] More precisely, a mixed strategy is a probability distribution over pure strategies, which gives the probability with which the player adopts each pure strategy.

Source: Markus Gilliar - GES Sportfoto / Contributor/Getty Images

Figure 6.15 Penalty kick

scores. Games such as this, in which the two players' payoffs are negatives of each other, are called **two-player zero-sum games**.

To determine these payoffs, we can use statistics from real soccer matches. For example, we can calculate from data the frequency with which a shot scores if the goalkeeper correctly guesses left. When you have a large data set, this is a good estimate of the payoff (i.e. the probability that a shot scores) when the kicker kicks to the left and the goalkeeper jumps to the left.

In fact, there is a researcher who did this by watching *a large number* of European matches between 1995 and 2000, and calculated such statistics based on 1,417 penalty kicks.[20] The payoff table based on his calculations is shown in Table 6.11.

Based on this data, let's solve for the mixed-strategy equilibrium using an analogous procedure to the one we used when we studied the game of rock, paper, scissors. If we let p denote the probability that the goalkeeper jumps to the left, the expected payoff of the kicker can be calculated as shown in Table 6.12.

[20] Ignacio Palacios-Huerta, "Professionals Play Minimax," *Review of Economic Studies*, 70(2) (2003), 395–415.

Case Study 6.6 (cont.)

In order for it to be optimal for the kicker to randomly kick to the left or right, the expected payoff from kicking to the left ① must be equal to the expected payoff from kicking to the right ②. (If not, then it would be better for the kicker to kick to the side with the higher expected payoff with certainty.) If we solve the equation ① = ②, we will find the value of p. In the same way, if we analyze the goalkeeper's expected payoffs from jumping to the left and right, we can calculate the probability that the kicker shoots to the left and right. Table 6.13 compares the mixed-strategy equilibrium that we solved for with real data from professional soccer players.

You can see that the mixed-strategy equilibrium that we solved for is in fact very similar to the behavior of professional soccer players in this data set.

Table 6.11 The payoff table for penalty kicks

Kicker \ Goalkeeper	Left	Right
Left (from the goalkeeper's perspective)	58. 30	94. 97
Right	92. 92	69. 92

The Estimated Payoff Of The Kicker
(the probability that the shot scores (%))

Table 6.12 The kicker's expected payoff

	p	1 − p	
Kicker \ Goalkeeper	Left	Right	
Left	58. 30	94. 97	→ $58.30p + 94.97(1 - p)$ ①
Right	92. 92	69. 92	→ $92.92p + 69.92(1 - p)$ ②

Table 6.13 The mixed-strategy equilibrium

	Goalkeeper		Kicker	
	Left	Right	Left	Right
Equilibrium	41.99	58.01	38.54	61.46
Actual frequency	42.31	57.69	39.98	60.02

In all the examples that we've seen so far, there exists a Nash equilibrium. Even when no Nash equilibrium seems to exist, as with rock, paper, scissors, we found that there was a mixed-strategy equilibrium. This is not a coincidence. John Nash Jr., who laid the foundation for modern game theory, proved the following theorem.

Theorem (Existence of a Nash Equilibrium)

For any game with a finite number of players, each of whom has a finite number of pure strategies, there exists a Nash equilibrium (possibly a mixed-strategy equilibrium).

Nash proved this theorem using results from a field of mathematics called topology. The proof is almost identical to the proof of the existence of a perfectly competitive equilibrium that we saw in Chapter 3, Section 3.3, subsection (e). In fact, Nash's theorem pre-dates the theorem on the existence of a competitive market equilibrium, which was later proved drawing inspiration from Nash's proof.

This theorem ensures that, in any social or economic problem, there exists a state in which the players are optimally responding to one another (i.e. a Nash equilibrium). This means that *any social or economic problem can be analyzed using the notion of Nash equilibrium and the tools of game theory*. It is a powerful result that illustrates the vast scope of possible applications of game theory.[21]

---

[21] The proof is found, for example, in Andreu Mas-Colell, Michael D. Whinston, and Jerry R. Green, *Microeconomic Theory* (New York: Oxford University Press, 1995), chap. 8, app. A.

7 Dynamic Games and Credible Strategies

In this chapter we will study a general method for analyzing social and economic problems that take place over time, which we call dynamic games. I'll start by explaining a simple example that will illustrate various key concepts that we will use to solve dynamic games.

7.1 Bank Bailout

Suppose there's a major financial institution that may go bankrupt and the government must decide whether or not to rescue it. We can model this situation as a two-stage game, as seen in Figure 7.1.

This game lasts for two periods: first the bank chooses a move, then the government chooses a move. To better understand how this game works, let's look at the payoffs associated with each outcome.

- If the bank chooses diligent management, it receives a so-so payoff of 1, while the government (and thus, the citizens) receives a large payoff of 10.
- On the other hand, if the bank chooses risky management, such as lending to risky borrowers, there is a danger of bankruptcy. At this point, it is the government's turn to move.
- If the government chooses to rescue the bank, the bank receives a more substantial payoff of 2, while the government (and citizens) receive a payoff of 1, which is much lower than their payoff if the bank had worked diligently.
- If the government chooses to give up on the bank, then the bank goes under and receives a payoff of –1, while the government (and citizens) are hit with a financial crisis and also receive a payoff of –1.

Now, what will happen in this game? First, let's consider the action the bank takes. In order to decide whether to manage itself diligently or not, the bank must know what will happen in the future if it chooses not to manage diligently. That is, *in order to determine the action of the bank in the first stage of the game, it is necessary to first analyze what will happen in the second stage of the game*. If we *consider the second stage*, we can see that, if the bank does not manage diligently, the government will choose to rescue the bank, since it prefers a payoff of

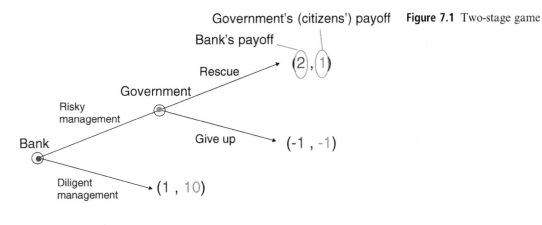

Government's (citizens') payoff   **Figure 7.1** Two-stage game

Figure 7.1 Two-stage game

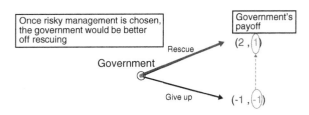

Figure 7.2 What happens in the second stage?

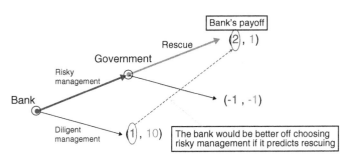

Figure 7.3 What happens in the first stage if the bank predicts what would happen in the second stage?

1 to a payoff of –1 (see Figure 7.2). Knowing this, the bank will decide against diligent management and make more risky management decisions (see Figure 7.3).

Using this game as an example, we can summarize the basics of solving dynamic games in the following manner.

The actions that players should take at the early stages of the game depend on what is going to happen at later stages of the game.

Therefore, in order to determine players' actions, we need to **solve the game** starting at the end and working **backward**.

That is, in order to solve a dynamic game, we should:

- determine how each player behaves at the final stage;
- knowing how each player behaves at the final stage, determine how each payer behaves at the second-to-last stage.
- . . .
- . . .

Note that the outcome of the game that we solved for by moving backward through the game is a Nash equilibrium. If the bank does not manage diligently it is optimal for the government to rescue the bank, and if the government will rescue the bank it is optimal for the bank to not manage diligently. In other words, this is an outcome in which both players are responding optimally to the other's action, so it is a Nash equilibrium. One might say that *this Nash equilibrium that we obtained by solving the game backward is reasonable or realistic in the sense that it correctly predicts the players' moves.*

However, if we analyze this game as a payoff matrix, we can see that *there is another Nash equilibrium* (see Table 7.1).

Let's confirm that this second Nash equilibrium (equilibrium ②) is indeed a Nash equilibrium. Recall that a Nash equilibrium is a state in which no player can gain by unilaterally

Table 7.1 Two Nash equilibria

Bank \ Government	If the bank chooses risky management Rescue	If the bank chooses risky management Give up
Risky management	2 , 1	-1 , -1
Diligent management	1 , 10	1 , 10

The realistic equilibrium obtained by solving the game backwards (equilibrium ①)

The other Nash equilibrium (equilibrium ②)

Table 7.2 Checking the Nash equilibrium condition for the bank

Bank \ Government	If the bank chooses risky management Rescue	If the bank chooses risky management Give up
Risky management	2 , 1	-1 , -1
Diligent management	1 , 10	1 , 10

The bank would not gain by unilaterally changing its strategy

Table 7.3 Checking the Nash equilibrium condition for the government

Bank \ Government	If the bank chooses risky management Rescue	If the bank chooses risky management Give up
Risky management	2 , 1	-1 , -1
Diligent management	1 , (10)	1 , (10)

The government, too, would not gain by unilaterally changing its strategy

changing his or her action. First, let's check if the bank can gain by changing its action. Take a look at Table 7.2. It's easy to see that, when the government chooses not to rescue the bank, it's better for the bank to work diligently.

Now let's check if the government can gain by changing its action. This part is a bit tricky, so take a closer look at Table 7.3. As the table shows, when the bank is already working diligently there is no benefit to the government if it changes its strategy. Therefore, equilibrium ② is indeed a Nash equilibrium. However, note that in the second stage of the original dynamic game, the government's choice not to rescue is not optimal, since it could earn a payoff of 1 instead of −1 if it changed its action and decided to rescue the bank. So how can this be a Nash equilibrium? In a Nash equilibrium, aren't all players optimally responding to one another?

The answer to this apparent contradiction is as follows. If the bank manages diligently, then *in the dynamic game the government does not have the opportunity to choose an action, so whether it plans to rescue or not is irrelevant to the final payoffs.* In this sense, although it may appear suboptimal for the government to choose not to rescue, *it cannot be excluded as a Nash equilibrium since this outcome satisfies the condition that no player earn a higher payoff by unilaterally changing his or her strategy.*

In some sense, the government's strategy in this Nash equilibrium ② is *just a bluff.* The government says that it will not rescue the bank, but, if the bank called the government's bluff and did not manage diligently, the government would change course and rescue it. In equilibrium ②, the bank actually believes the government intends to not rescue the bank. It seems as if a smart player would be able to figure out when another player is just bluffing, so, although this game has two Nash equilibria, ① and ②, the more realistic equilibrium is ①.

Let's summarize our discussion so far. This example illustrates key ideas and principles we use when solving dynamic games.

> [1] Dynamic games can be expressed using a "game tree," as in Figure 7.1. We call this the **extensive form** of a game.

- I will explain the method for expressing dynamic games using game trees in greater detail in Section 7.2.

[2] A **strategy** in dynamic games is a **complete contingent action plan** that specifies what to do after all possible contingencies (i.e. observable history of past events and actions).

- The strategy of the government in the example above is a contingent action plan that specifies what to do if the bank does not choose diligent management.

[3] A dynamic game can be analyzed using Nash equilibria by regarding it as a simultaneous-move game in which all players simultaneously choose an action plan at the start of the game.

- We did this in the prior example using the payoff table presented in Table 7.1.

[4] However, *among the Nash equilibria of a dynamic game, there may be "unrealistic" ones in which non-credible threats (bluffs) are used.*

- The aforementioned equilibrium ② is such an equilibrium.

[5] *In order to* exclude equilibria involving non-credible threats and *solve for a "realistic" equilibrium, we can solve the game backward.*

- Figure 7.4 shows how to solve a game backward. First, we solve the part of the game in the square, and then solve the entire game.

  The part in the square is called a **subgame**, and the result we obtain by solving the game backwards in this manner is called a **subgame-perfect equilibrium**. Of the five points [1] to [5], the most important point is [5]. The other points are important details that are needed to firmly understand the final point. A basic principle in game theory is that *Nash equilibria are used to*

Figure 7.4 Solving the game backward and the notion of subgame-perfect equilibrium

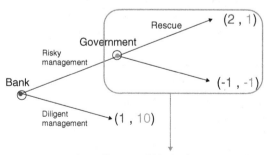

A small game within the larger game (a "subgame")

solve simultaneous-move games and subgame-perfect equilibria are used to solve dynamic games. In Section 7.2 I'll give a detailed explanation of subgame-perfect equilibria.

7.2   Subgame-Perfect Equilibrium

In this section I will answer the following questions.

- How can we express a dynamic game using a game tree?
- What is a strategy in a dynamic game?
- What is a subgame-perfect equilibrium?

Understanding the answers to these questions will require some patience on your part, but please bear with me, as you'll learn the essentials of game theory.

(a)   Extensive Form and Strategies in Dynamic Games

As you saw before, we can use game trees to describe dynamic games. When we express games in this manner, we say that we have written the game's **extensive-form representation**. It is necessary to understand the extensive form of dynamic games in order to discuss subgame-perfect equilibria. Let's begin by taking a look at Example 7.1.

Example 7.1 A Dynamic Version of the Battle of the Sexes

Recall the battle of the sexes game, in which a man and a woman simultaneously decide whether to go to a football match (F) or to go to the shopping mall (S). Suppose we modify the game a little bit and say that the man first decides where to go, after which the woman observes his choice and decides where to go. This new game can be expressed in the manner shown in Figure 7.5.

Using this game as an example, let me explain the key points of describing the extensive form of a dynamic game. An extensive-form representation uses a directed graph called a "game tree" to describe how things happen over time, and a game tree consists of nodes[1] and branches.

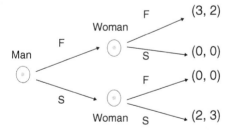

Figure 7.5 A dynamic version of the battle of the sexes

---

[1] We sometimes call these "decision nodes." More precisely, the end points of the tree, where the payoffs are indicated in Figure 7.5, are also regarded as nodes, and they are called "terminal nodes".

A node represents a stage of the game at which a player moves, and *the branches coming out of a node represent the various actions the player can take at that stage of the game.* Look at the two nodes labeled "Woman" in Figure 7.5. The top node represents the state in which the man has chosen to go to the football match (F) and the bottom node represents the state in which the man has chosen to go to the shopping mall (S). Since we assume that the woman can observe the choice that the man makes, the woman can distinguish between the two situations represented by these nodes. To express this in an extensive-form representation, we circle these two nodes with distinct circles, and call each circle the woman's **information set** at that stage of the game. If the woman cannot observe the man's action, the woman cannot distinguish between the two situations represented by the nodes. In this case, both nodes lie in the same information set and the two nodes are enclosed in a single circle, as in Figure 7.6.

Figure 7.6 The case in which the woman cannot observe the man's action

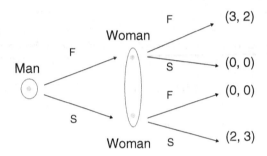

To recap: a player's **information set** is *a collection of nodes at which she moves and expresses the fact that, (i) the player knows if an information set is reached or not, but (ii) within that information set, the player cannot observe which specific node she is at.*

Let me now make a technical but *important remark.* When we construct an extensive form, we adhere to the convention that only one player moves at each node. For example, when we write the extensive form of a dynamic game in which two players move simultaneously, we specify that

- one of the two players moves first; and
- the other player moves afterward, without observing the action taken by the first player.

For example, the game in which the man and the woman choose their destinations simultaneously has the extensive-form representation shown in Figure 7.6, in which formally the man moves first.

Now that we understand how to represent a dynamic game in extensive form, we can define strategies in dynamic games.

Definition I

A **strategy in a dynamic game** designates, at every information set, an action to take.

This is a precise mathematical definition, but it may be a little difficult to digest in the abstract, so let's try to understand this definition using the prior example. Please look at Figure 7.7.

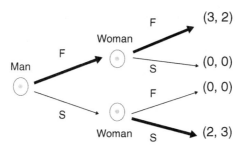

Figure 7.7 Strategies in a dynamic game (the bold arrows)

The bold arrows in the figure express the strategies of the man and the woman. The woman has two information sets, given by the circles at the top and bottom of the figure. Thus, the woman's strategy designates an action that must be taken at each information set: at the top information set she chooses F and at the bottom information set she chooses S. It may help to describe this strategy in the woman's words: "If the man chooses F then I also choose F, and if the man chooses S then I also choose S."

Definition II

A **strategy in a dynamic game** is a **contingent action plan** that specifies what to do after all possible contingencies (i.e. observable past events and actions).

In order to reinforce your understanding of strategies in dynamic games, let's rephrase definitions I and II in yet another way. Consider the case in which player i takes action $x_i(t)$ at time t in a dynamic game.

Definition III

A **strategy of player i in a dynamic game** is a **mapping** $s_i(.)$ that maps each possible **history** of past events and actions that player i observes to an **action that she takes at the current stage**. That is,

$$x_i(t) = s_i \text{ (everything player } i \text{ has observed in the past).}$$

Definition III is the most useful definition of a strategy when we create models that use mathematical formulas. To see this, let's look at Figure 7.7. Let the woman be player 2 and let the time at which the woman moves be t. Since "everything the woman has observed in the past" is just the man's action, the woman's strategy is a mapping

$$x_2(t) = s_2 \text{ (the man's action)}$$

where $x_2(t)$ is either F or S. In particular, the strategy s_2 shown in Figure 7.7 is

$$F = s_2(F)$$

$$S = s_2(S).$$

Comment 7.1 A Strategy Is Not the Same as the Actions the Player Actually Takes

Here I make a technical but *important remark*. In Figure 7.7, *the actions that are actually taken* by each player are: the man goes to the football match (F); and the woman goes to the football match (F). So, you may think that the man's strategy is "Go to the football match" and the woman's strategy is also "Go to the football match." *This is a typical mistake that beginners make.* In fact, the woman's strategy is not "Go to the football match." This is just the action the woman takes given that the man has chosen the football match. Her strategy, in contrast, is *the contingent action plan* described by the following.

- "If the man goes to the football match (F), then I will go to the football match (F)."
- "If the man goes to the shopping mall (S), then I will go to the shopping mall (S)."

Why do we need such a complicated definition? Isn't it simpler if we just define a strategy to be the actions the player actually takes? To think about this more clearly, let's suppose that a strategy consists only of the actions that are actually taken. Please take a look at Figure 7.8.

Figure 7.8 If the woman's strategy is not defined properly. . .

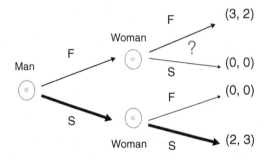

Here, both the man and the woman take action S. However, when we define strategies to be only the actions that are actually taken, we do not know how the woman would react if the man chose F instead of S. This corresponds to the "?" in Figure 7.8. Therefore, since we don't know how the woman would react if the man were to choose F, *we can't see whether the man should choose F or S.* In other words, *if we do not define a strategy to be a contingent action plan that designates what action to take given the preceding actions and events, we will not be able to ask the central question in game theory: how should players optimally react to each other?*

(b)   What Is a Subgame-Perfect Equilibrium?

Now that we understand how to express dynamic games and have defined strategies in dynamic games, let me finally explain what a subgame-perfect equilibrium is. A "subgame" is, roughly speaking, a small game contained within a larger dynamic game. A more precise definition is given below.

Definition of a subgame in words

At some point in a dynamic game, if

- *all players who will move from that point on*
- *observe everything that has happened in the past,*

then *the remainder of the game from that point on* is called a **subgame**.

In order to understand what this is saying, let's return to our previous example. First, let's consider the case in which the woman acts *without observing* the man's choice (see Figure 7.9).

Since we are considering a two-stage game in which the man moves first and the woman moves second, you might be tempted to say that the second stage in which the woman moves is itself a subgame. That is not the case. The reason is because *the player who moves there (the woman) does not observe the past actions of the other players (the man).*

Why is it necessary that the players who will move from that point on have observed the past actions of the other players? The answer to this question is quite important, so I'll explain it carefully.

A subgame is a part of a dynamic game that can be analyzed as a "game" if we remove it from the original game. In particular, each player's payoff in the subgame must be clearly defined. In dynamic games, *past actions can affect the payoffs players eventually obtain.* Therefore, *to make sure that the players involved in the subgame know how their own actions will affect their payoffs, we must require that they observe what has happened in the past.* In fact,

The player who is moving from now on (the woman) *does not* observe what has happened in the past (whether the man has taken F or S)

Figure 7.9 This is not a subgame

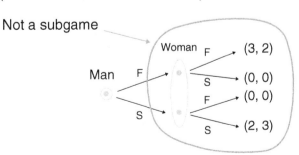

Not a subgame

Figure 7.10 An example of subgames

The player who is moving from now on (the woman) observes what has happened in the past (whether the man has taken F or S)

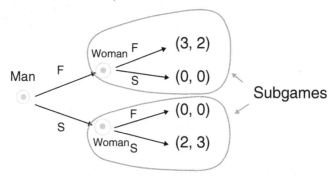

in Figure 7.9, the woman's payoffs from playing F or S depend on the choice the man made in the first stage. Consequently, we can't treat the entire second stage of the game as a subgame, since the woman doesn't know how her actions affect her payoffs.

Next, let's consider the case where we actually obtain subgames. As you might expect from the preceding discussion, if the woman *observes the choice* the man makes in the first stage, then there are two subgames in the second stage, as shown in Figure 7.10.

I want you to pay special attention to the fact that, although you might be tempted to say that the second stage (where the woman moves) is one subgame, there are actually two distinct subgames within the second stage of the game. The first is the subgame after the man chooses F (the top subgame in Figure 7.10) and the second is the subgame after the man chooses S (the bottom subgame in Figure 7.10). While they are both games within the second stage in which the woman chooses F or S, they differ in the past actions of the man and hence in the players' payoffs. This leads to the following important caveat when you define subgames.

Definition of a subgame (continued)

Subgames that begin after different histories are regarded as *distinct subgames*.

So far we have defined subgames in an informal manner using words, but there is always some ambiguity and imprecision in definitions that rely on words alone. So let's define subgames in an unambiguous way by using game trees (i.e. extensive forms).

Definition of a subgame using game trees (extensive forms)

Any part of a game tree that satisfies the following conditions is a subgame:

(i)   it begins at a single node;
(ii) it contains all nodes and branches that follow that single node;
(iii) its information sets do not contain any node outside of the part of the game to be defined as a subgame (i.e. an information set of a subgame should not "go outside" of the subgame).

If we return to Figure 7.10 again, we can verify that both circled portions of the game tree satisfy all three conditions.

Remark: since the entire game itself satisfies conditions (i) to (iii), it is also a subgame. However, some textbooks define subgames to exclude the entire game.

Comment 7.2 User's Guide to Find Subgames

In order to find a subgame, *you could use the definition in words* that we saw first, because the verbal definition is fairly easy to check. However, if you are not confident, *try to draw the game tree and check whether the part of it that you suspect is a subgame actually satisfies mathematical conditions (i) to (iii) above.* I myself do this all the time! (Also try to find subgames in many different examples. That's the best way to develop your ability to identify subgames.)

Now that we've laid the groundwork, let's define subgame-perfect equilibrium.

Definition

A **subgame-perfect equilibrium** is a strategy profile that induces a Nash equilibrium in every subgame.

Put differently, *a subgame-perfect equilibrium is a realistic equilibrium that excludes non-credible threats (bluffs)*, as explained in Section 7.1. The subgame-perfect equilibrium discussed in Section 7.1 is indicated by the bold arrows in Figure 7.11.

Since only the government moves in the subgame shown in Figure 7.11, the Nash equilibrium of the subgame is just the state in which the government takes an optimal action. Keeping in mind that the numbers in the figure are "(the bank's payoff, the government's payoff)," take a moment to verify that the government is taking an optimal action. Thus, the subgame-perfect equilibrium is the one in which the government's bluff to not rescue the bank in the case of bankruptcy is not credible, and the bank correctly forecasts that the government will indeed choose to rescue in the case of bankruptcy.

So far we've seen a lot of definitions. Now let's try to deepen our understanding by solving an example.

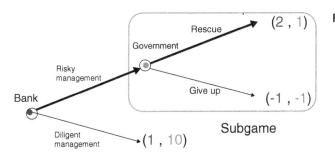

Figure 7.11 Subgame-perfect equilibrium

Example 7.2: Solve for the Subgame-Perfect Equilibrium of the Dynamic Version of the Battle of the Sexes (Figure 7.5) that We Saw at the Beginning of This Section

Recall that the man first chooses whether to go to the football match (F) or the shopping mall (S), after which the woman, having observed the man's choice, chooses her own destination. In order to solve for the subgame-perfect equilibrium, it suffices to take the following two steps.

Step 1: find the subgames in the entire game, and then solve for the Nash equilibrium of each subgame (see Figure 7.12).

The portions encircled in ⌒ are subgames, and the bold arrows represent the Nash equilibria (in this case, the optimal actions of the woman).

Step 2: based on the equilibria of the subgames, solve for the equilibrium of the whole game. According to Figure 7.12, since the woman will always take the same action as the man took, the man will choose to go to the football match (F) (see Figure 7.13).

Therefore, the subgame-perfect equilibrium is given by the bold arrows in Figure 7.13.

Summarizing our discussion, we obtain the following.

Figure 7.12 First, solve for the Nash equilibria of the subgames

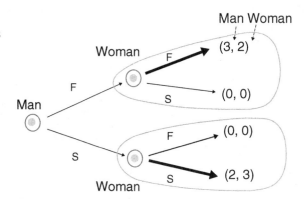

Figure 7.13 Next, solve for the equilibrium of the whole game

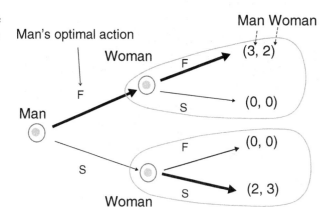

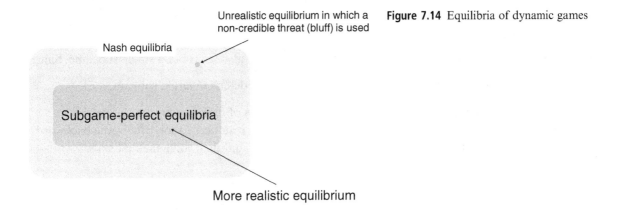

Figure 7.14 Equilibria of dynamic games

- In order to solve a dynamic game, it is helpful to solve the game *backward.*
- "Solving the game backward" means that *we first solve for the equilibria of the subgames and then solve the whole game.*
- In this way, we can solve for *the "realistic" equilibrium that excludes bluffs* (that is, the subgame-perfect equilibrium).

Figure 7.14 depicts the relationship between the different equilibrium concepts we've seen.

7.3 Application to Oligopoly (II): The Stackelberg Model

Now, suppose that in the market with the downward-sloping demand curve given by $P = a - bQ$, there are two firms $i = 1, 2$ that have identical and constant marginal costs $MC_1 = MC_2 = c$. This is the same market we studied when we introduced oligopolies in Chapter 6, Section 6.5. So far we've analyzed the case in which the firms simultaneously choose their quantities (Cournot model) and the case in which the firms simultaneously choose their prices (Bertrand model). Now let's consider the case in which the two firms take actions at different times. Specifically, consider a two-stage quantity competition in which

- first, firm 1 chooses its quantity q_1;
- then, observing firm 1's choice, firm 2 chooses its quantity q_2.

This is called the **Stackelberg model**. The firm that moves first is called the **leader** and the firm that moves second is called the **follower**.

Since this is a dynamic game, in order to find an outcome in which each firm correctly predicts its opponents move (without believing bluffs) we need to find a **subgame-perfect equilibrium**.

First, let's find the subgames. Recalling the definition of subgame that used words, since in the second stage

- *the player who moves from this point on (firm 2) observes what has happened in the past (firm 1's quantity),*

a subgame begins at the second stage. However, the second stage is not a single subgame. Since

- subgames that begin after different histories are regarded as separate subgames,

there are as many subgames as there are possible values of firm 1's quantity q_1.[2]

In order to solve for the subgame-perfect equilibrium, it suffices to solve the game backward. That is, we first solve the subgames in the second stage and then solve the first stage.

Step 1: Solve the subgames after firm 1's quantity q_1 is given.

$$\Rightarrow \text{ firm 2's move (best response) } q_2 = R_2(q_1) \text{ is determined.}$$

Step 2: Foreseeing step 1, firm 1 chooses the optimal quantity q_1. Denoting firm 1's profit by $\pi_1(q_1, q_2)$, firm 1 solves the following problem:

$$\max_{q_1} \pi_1(q_1 \underbrace{R_2(q_1)}_{\uparrow}).$$

correctly forecasting firm 2's move

Let's now do the calculation.

Step 1: firm 2's profit is given by

$$\pi_2 = \underbrace{(a - b(q_1 + q_2)}_{\text{price } P} - c)q_2.$$

Since this is a quadratic equation in q_2, it has a shape that is "bowed upward" (i.e. a parabolic shape). Therefore, the profit maximization point is at the unique peak of the graph. Recall that the slope of the tangent line to the graph is equal to zero at the peak. We can express this "zero-slope" condition (called the "first-order condition for the optimum") using differentiation, which gives us the following equation:

$$0 = \frac{\partial \pi_2}{\partial q_2} = a - bq_1 - 2bq_2 - c.$$

Solving this equation for q_2, we find that firm 2's **best response** to firm 1's choice is

$$q_2 = R_2(q_1) = \frac{a - c}{2b} - \frac{1}{2}q_1. \tag{1}$$

From this equation, it's easy to see that the higher firm 1's quantity q_1 is, the lower firm 2's optimal quantity q_2 is in the second stage.

Step 2: forecasting firm 2's response that we solved for in step 1, firm 1 calculates its profit to be

$$\pi_1(q_1, R_2(q_1)) = (a - b(q_1 + R_2(q_1)) - c)q_1$$
$$= \left(\frac{a - c}{2} - \frac{b}{2}q_1\right)q_1.$$

---

[2] Since firm 1's quantity is a continuous variable, this game has infinitely many subgames.

For the same reason as in step 1, the profit maximization point is given by the first-order condition

$$0 = \frac{d\pi_1}{dq_1} = \frac{a-c}{2} - bq_1.$$

Solving this equation for q_1 and plugging that value back into our equation for firm 2's optimal quantity, we find that the subgame-perfect equilibrium[3] quantities are

$$q_1^* = \frac{a-c}{2b}$$
$$q_2^* = R_1\left(q_1^*\right) = \frac{a-c}{4b}.$$

This is called the Stackelberg solution.

To better understand what is going on, let's go over the analysis we've done using some figures. To this end, it's handy to consider firm 1's **iso-profit curve**. Iso-profit curves are, essentially, a firm's indifference curves: they are collections of points that each give the same profit. Figure 7.15 shows what iso-profit curves look like.

For every point on the top iso-profit curve in Figure 7.15, the firm's profit is 100 ($\pi_1 = 100$). Here are some important properties of iso-profit curves.

① *Lower iso-profit curves correspond to higher profits.*
Reason: compare points A and B in Figure 7.15. Since B is directly below A,[4] if we move from A to B, firm 1's quantity is unchanged while firm 2's quantity decreases. Since total quantity decreases, the price increases according to the downward-sloping demand curve $P = a - bQ$. Since firm 1's quantity remains the same while the price increases, firm 1's profit $(= Pq_1 - cq_1)$ increases.

---

[3] Detailed remark: since a subgame-perfect equilibrium is defined as a profile of the strategies of all players, these quantities are the equilibrium *outcome*, but not actually the equilibrium itself. The subgame-perfect equilibrium is

$$q_1^* = \frac{a-c}{2b} \text{ (firm 1's strategy)}$$
$$q_2 = R_2(q_1) = \frac{a-c}{2b} - \frac{1}{2}q_1 \text{ (firm 2's strategy)}.$$

Note that firm 2's strategy is a *contingent action plan* that determines how to respond given firm 1's production decision.

[4] You may wonder what happens if we compare point A to some point that is not directly below it. By definition, the firm's profit is constant along an iso-profit curve. Therefore, in order to compare the profits corresponding to different iso-profit curves, it suffices to choose two points, one from each curve, and compare the profits at these two points.

Figure 7.15 Iso-profit curves

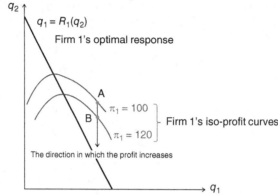

Figure 7.16 The vertex of an iso-profit curve lies on the best response curve

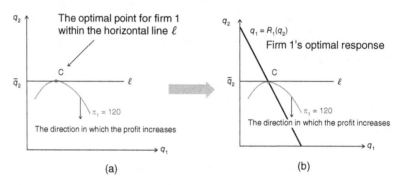

② The vertex of an iso-profit curve lies on the best response curve.

Reason: Figure 7.16 illustrates this fact.

First, I want you to study Figure 7.16 (a). You should see that, when we say that point C is the vertex of firm 1's iso-profit curve, this means that C is the optimal point for firm 1 along the line ℓ. Just as the point at which the budget line and the indifference curve are tangent to one another gives a consumer's optimal point along the budget line, the point at which the line ℓ and the iso-profit curve are tangent to one another gives firm 1's optimal point along ℓ.

Now I'll explain why the optimal point C lies on the best response curve, as in Figure 7.16 (b). Note that line ℓ is the collection of points corresponding to different quantities q_1 for firm 1 while holding firm 2's quantity constant at $\bar{q}_2$. Along this line, firm 1's optimal point is just the point at which it is responding optimally to firm 2's quantity $\bar{q}_2$. That is, firm 1's optimal point lies on the best response curve $q_1 = R_1(q_2)$.

Now we are ready to examine how we can depict the Stackelberg solution graphically. Once firm 1 determines its quantity, firm 2 responds optimally to firm 1's choice. That is, *when firm 1 is making its production decision, it can effectively choose a final outcome from among any of the points along firm 2's best response curve* (see Figure 7.17).

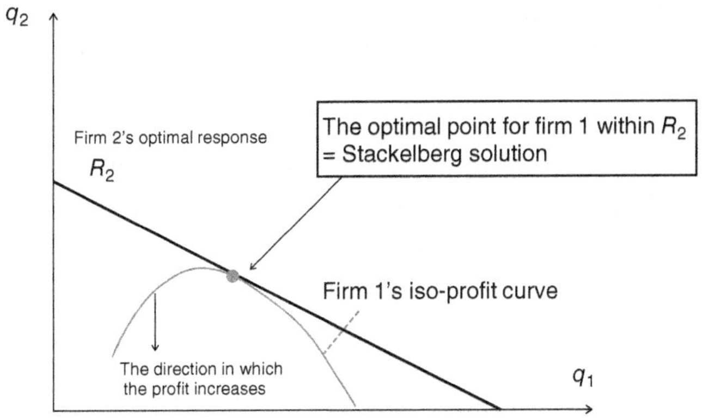

Figure 7.17 The Stackelberg solution

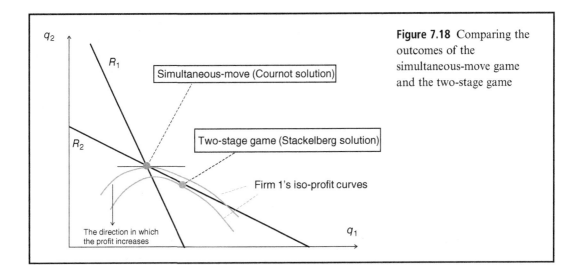

Figure 7.18 Comparing the outcomes of the simultaneous-move game and the two-stage game

The optimal point for firm 1 along firm 2's best response curve R_2 is given by the point at which R_2 and firm 1's iso-profit curve are tangent to one another. This is exactly the Stackelberg solution.

Next, let's compare this outcome with the solution to the Cournot model, in which the firms simultaneously choose their quantities. Please look at Figure 7.18.

Since the Cournot solution is the state in which the two firms are producing optimal quantities given the other firm's production decision, the Cournot solution is given by the intersection of the two best response curves R_1 and R_2. The Stackelberg solution is, as stated above, the point at which R_2 and firm 1's iso-profit curve are tangent. If we examine Figure 7.18, we can make the following observations.

- The leader's (firm 1's) quantity is larger in the two-stage game's outcome than it is in the simultaneous-move game's outcome.
- The leader's (firm 1's) profit is larger in the two-stage game's outcome than it is in the simultaneous-move game's outcome.

Let's pause for a moment to consider what this means. In the simultaneous-move game (the Cournot model), firm 1 is free to choose any quantity when firm 2 makes its choice. In the two-stage game (the Stackelberg model), firm 1's choice is fixed when firm 2 makes its choice. The fact that firm 1 earns a higher profit in the two-stage game suggests that strategically restricting one's own action can be beneficial. When we restrict our options to a single choice, we call this **committing** to a certain action. How in the world could it be beneficial to have fewer choices rather than more? We will consider this puzzle in the next section.

7.4   Commitment

When a *single* individual is making a decision, the wider the range of options, the better. Moreover, when the individual makes decisions over time, *making an optimal decision at every point in time* provides the overall *optimal outcome*. This may seem completely obvious, and perhaps you're wondering why I even bothered to mention it. However, this seemingly obvious conclusion can actually fail in social or economic problems where multiple decision makers interact. This may seem a bit surprising, but in strategic situations involving multiple people it is possible that *people may be better off if they "tie their hands" so that are unable to take the "optimal action."* Since this is a very general and important insight that game theory has provided, I will explain it in great detail in this section.

First, let's begin by looking at a concrete example.

Case Study 7.1 Financial Crises and Bank Bailouts

In recent years Japan and other Western countries have experienced major financial crises that left many financial institutions at the brink of bankruptcy. In order to stabilize the financial system and the economy, many national governments rescued these financial institutions with "bailout" packages. For example, in Japan, over ¥7 trillion (approximately $64 billion) of public funds was spent in just a one-month period in March 1999 in order to bail out banks that were imperiled by the serious financial crisis.

When should the government intervene to rescue a bank that is at risk of going under? Let's consider the following seemingly flawless opinion:

"When a financial institution goes bankrupt, it harms the economy at large (this is true). Therefore, the government's optimal strategy is to carefully weigh the negative effects of the bankruptcy and the cost of rescuing the bank and to rescue the bank if the former exceeds the latter."

What do you think? Doesn't this make a lot of sense? It may be hard for you to imagine that there could be anything wrong with this argument. Many people in the media and on the Internet have echoed similar opinions. However, people who have studied game theory could immediately tell you that this line of thinking contains a *big oversight* and is not necessarily right.

Why not? Let's return to the stylized example of the bank bailout that we saw earlier (Figure 7.1) and reconsider it carefully (see Figure 7.19).

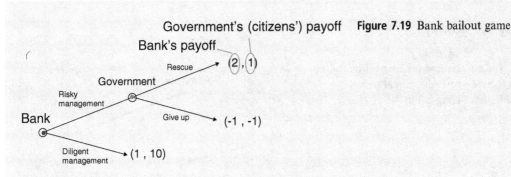

Figure 7.19 Bank bailout game

This game captures the essence of the bank bailout problem, and it goes as follows. First, the bank decides whether to

- lend money to reliable borrowers ("diligent management") or
- lend money to risky borrowers ("risky management").

If the bank lends money to risky borrowers who are unable to repay their loans and the bank is at risk of bankruptcy, the government is called upon to move. The government decides whether to rescue the bank or let it go under.

In order to understand how this game plays out, we can "solve it backward," as we saw in Section 7.1. I'll repeat how we solved it previously. First, we consider what happens when the bank has chosen risky management and is about to go bankrupt. We know that, at this stage, *it is optimal for the government to intervene and rescue the bank*, as shown in Figure 7.20. That is, when the bank is at the brink of bankruptcy, the government weighs the costs of rescuing the bank and the costs of letting the bank fail, and decides it is better to bail out the bank.

However, if the bank knows that the government will rescue it in the event that it is going bankrupt, then it is optimal for the bank to choose risky management in the first stage, as shown in Figure 7.21.

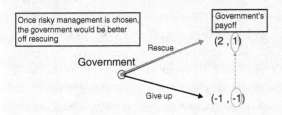

Figure 7.20 What happens after the bank has chosen risky management

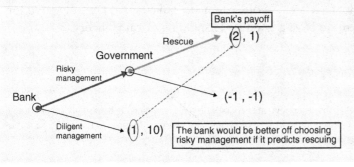

Figure 7.21 The bank's choice with correct anticipation of what is going to happen

Case Study 7.1 (cont.)

Figure 7.22 The government is better off by committing to an ex-post suboptimal action (never to bail out a failing bank)

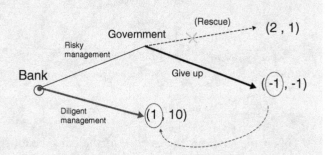

Note that, *if the government takes the optimal action during stage 2, its payoff* (and therefore the citizens' payoff) *is very low* (= 1) *because the bank will choose risky management.*

Now, what happens *if we pass a law that prevents the government from rescuing any banks?* Please look at Figure 7.22.

In this case, if the bank chooses risky management, the government cannot intervene and so the bank goes under, leaving it with a worse payoff than when it chooses diligent management. Therefore, the bank will choose diligent management, and the government and its citizens receive the much higher payoff of 10. In other words, the government would be better off by limiting its range of possible actions in the second stage and committing to a choice that, in the actual event of a bank going under, is suboptimal.[5]

This demonstrates that, when determining whether or not to rescue a financial institution at risk of bankruptcy, it is essential for the government to weigh both

- the value today from avoiding the financial crisis by rescuing the bank; and
- the cost of future bankruptcies that may occur if banks choose risky management, expecting the government to rescue them.

The seemingly flawless opinion we have seen refers only to the former and overlooks the important latter point. In 1999, in the financial crisis mentioned at the beginning of this case study, the former was huge, so I personally believe it exceeded the latter. However, if the government were to choose to rescue every time, there would be no way to keep banks from choosing risky management all the time. It's necessary to draw the line somewhere and rescue sometimes but not always. The main job of policy-makers is to decide where that line ought to be and to create a mechanism through which that line is respected in the future. As we have seen, in order to make policies that are truly good for the citizens in the long run, it's necessary to have a good understanding of game theory.

---

[5] The apparent contradiction that the policy that is optimal at every point in time (rescuing the banks that are about to go bankrupt) is different from the policy that is optimal at the initial time point (committing not to rescue the banks) is called the **time inconsistency of optimal policy**.

To summarize what we've learned from the case study.

- In cases in which only a *single person* is making a decision, it is *better to have a wider range* of possible choices.
- However, in cases in which there are *multiple decision-makers* (people, firms, governments, etc.) who act based on predictions of others' actions, *it can be beneficial to restrict the range of choices to exclude the optimal action* (we call this **committing** to an action).

How can a player possibly benefit from excluding his or her own optimal action? The answer is simple: by doing so, *a player can sometimes induce her opponent to take an action that is better for her*. In Case Study 7.1, by passing the new law, the government can "commit" to not rescuing the bank in the event of a possible bankruptcy. This changes the bank's optimal action from risky management to diligent management, which is better for the government.

At this point, let me clarify what it means to "commit."

To **commit** to an action means to irreversibly restrict one's own choices to make that the *only action available to choose.*

In other words, in game theory, *committing to an action is not just a promise to take that action*. Rather, "making a commitment" means taking some concrete steps or installing some mechanisms to limit one's choices so that there is no option but to take that action. In essence, a player ties her own hands when she commits to an action; there is no possibility of going back on her commitment. To understand this important point, let's look at several examples.

Upon arriving in Mexico in 1521, the Spanish explorer Hernán Cortés *burned all but one of his army's ships*. By removing his own troops' escape option, Cortés committed to establishing a Spanish colony at all costs, since the only way he and his soldiers could survive was by defeating the indigenous people and building a settlement. This move may have intimidated the natives and forced them to reconsider how costly it would be to mount a resistance to the Spanish forces. The point is that it would not have been effective for Cortés to merely announce that the Spanish forces would never retreat, since the native people would have called his bluff and assumed that he would give up if his forces were put in serious danger. By burning his own ships and eliminating his option to escape, Cortés committed to fighting and convinced his adversaries that they would incur serious losses if they fought the Spanish. This may have given Cortés an edge in the conflict that ensued. Let me provide another example which is relevant to the issues of today.

Case Study 7.2 Euro Crisis

From 1999 to 2002 most major countries in Europe (the United Kingdom being the main exception) adopted the euro as their national currency, forming the Eurozone. However, shortly after its inception the Eurozone faced a serious crisis. The crisis was rooted in the fact that, while the European Central Bank (ECB) is in charge of the Eurozone's monetary policy, each member state's government is in charge of its own fiscal policy.

Why was this a problem? A national government or incumbent politicians might be tempted to increase government's spending in order to please the voters and win the next election. The government can finance this by issuing government bonds. However, if the government keeps on doing this, eventually it may not be able to pay off its liabilities. This is exactly what happened to Greece and Italy. Since it would have been a total disaster if these governments had defaulted, the European Central Bank had to step in to buy out the risky government bonds. However, since the ECB manages the currency for the entire Eurozone, which is comprised of many countries, this action amounted to the other member states paying for the overspending of Greece and Italy.[6]

We can reframe this scenario in the language of game theory.

> [1] If *one country is about to default*, then it is *optimal for the rest of Europe to rescue* that country by sharing its debt.
> [2] If each country can foresee this, each has an incentive to overspend at the expense of other countries. This situation is similar to the *prisoner's dilemma*. That is, even if all countries are better off not spending too much, each country is tempted to choose unilaterally to take on too much debt.

This is one of the major reasons behind the euro crisis, and this is obvious to anyone who has a solid understanding of game theory.

Now, what can be done to prevent another crisis? Game theory suggests *committing* to not rescue countries that go bankrupt and instead punishing countries if they do go bankrupt. If it ever comes to actually implementing these actions (i.e. if a country goes bankrupt), people may have second thoughts, since it may be optimal at that point in time to rescue the country. Therefore, it's necessary to create a mechanism upfront so that countries cannot later reverse their decision and choose to rescue. In fact, this is exactly what the Eurozone did.

---

[6] The supply of money (euros) increases by the amount of government debt that the ECB buys. This results in inflation. The inflation devalues the Eurozone citizens' assets, which means that all Eurozone citizens bear the burden of Greece and Italy's national debt. This is sometimes called an "inflation tax." One of the major issues with the euro is that it can lead to people across the Eurozone (or people outside the Eurozone who hold euro-denominated assets) paying for Greek borrowing.

The Eurozone designed a policy that requires member countries to pay a deposit corresponding to 0.2 percent of gross domestic product. If a country fails to reduce its debts, it *automatically triggers* (unless vetoed by a majority vote) a response that stops interest payments on the deposit and, in some cases, permanently confiscates the initial deposit.[7] This is a commitment policy that is consistent with the game-theoretic analysis of the euro crisis.

Since the whole point of making a commitment is to change the opponent's action, once one has committed to an action and has an effective mechanism (commitment device) in place, it is important to *demonstrate the commitment device to the opponent.* In the masterpiece black comedy *Dr. Strangelove*,[8] which is about nuclear war, a disaster unfolds because somebody fails to communicate that he has committed to an action. In a period of high tensions with the United States, the Soviet Union creates a mechanism that automatically detonates a huge number of hydrogen bombs buried on a remote island in the Arctic, making the world uninhabitable, in the event that there is a nuclear attack on the Soviet Union. Of course, were the Soviet Union actually to be attacked by the United States, it would clearly be foolish and suboptimal to take such an action. The idea was that the Soviets could prevent an attack from happening by guaranteeing or committing to a worldwide catastrophe in the event that they were attacked. This seemed like a good plan, but, once the bombs are armed and it comes time to publicize the mechanism, an American commander goes crazy and orders a nuclear attack on the Soviet Union. The Soviet hydrogen bombs then explode and wipe out humanity.

There are many real-world examples in which people can benefit from committing to certain actions. Allow me to describe some of them.

[1]   Counterterrorism

When a hijacking of an airplane occurs, the government may be tempted to negotiate with the terrorists for the safe return of the passengers. However, if the government were to try and meet the terrorists' demands in order to save the passengers, it could cause more hijackings in the future, since the terrorists will believe that they can profit from committing more attacks. In the long run, it may be better for the citizens if the government commits to "never negotiate with terrorists" and uses an armed response, even if the passengers are ultimately harmed. Many Western countries seem to follow similar policies.

---

[7] Source: *Yomiuri Shimbun*, December 6, 2011, morning edition, page 1.

[8] The film is presented with a chilling sense of reality, but it's also loaded with tons of subtle jokes. The names of the characters are all puns, and the three main characters are played by the same actor. If you weren't paying close attention, the satire might go unnoticed, and you would end up wondering why this movie has become a bit of a cult classic that is praised as hysterically funny. This 1964 film directed by Stanley Kubrick is one of my personal favorites.

How can the government effectively commit to an armed response? One possibility is that it can pass a law that requires an armed response to hijackings. A more realistic *method of commitment, which is often used in reality, is to install hawkish political leaders who will deal harshly with terrorists.* This type of leader might make the controversial decision to sacrifice some citizens in the short run to prevent more attacks in the long run. That may sound crazy, but this type of leader can be effective because potential terrorists may think twice about carrying out attacks.

The people who led the response to the euro crisis were leaders such as Angela Merkel of Germany and Nicolas Sarkozy of France, who were both in favor of harsh austerity measures. It may seem a bit odd that *there are many politicians and corporate managers who have strong personalities and are often described as "quite a character,"* but game theory tells you that there could be a good reason for this: it may be beneficial to have a strong personality if it makes it possible to *commit to* difficult but *beneficial actions.* Don't you think this captures some aspect of reality?

[2]   Lowest Price Guarantees

If you go to a big electronics store, you'll probably see signs that say "Price match guarantee." At first glance, this may seem like a good thing for the consumer, but it's actually an ingenious mechanism to raise prices. Let me explain how. In general, it is not optimal for Best Buy to match any discount that another store makes, since that could lead to selling items at a loss. However, by committing to this action, Best Buy makes it impossible for its competitors to steal its customers by offering a lower price than Best Buy. Therefore, if every store has a price match guarantee, then no store can take customers from a competitor by lowering its price. In the end, prices remain high, because no store can gain from offering a discount.

[3]   Artists Destroying Printing Matrices

If we look at the prints of famous artists, there are numbers such as "22/100" around the bottom of the piece. This means that the work was the 22nd print of 100. The number that matters more is the 100; since few prints were made, the artwork is scarce and therefore has a higher value. Artists may want to limit the number of prints they make to a small number, say 100, in order to raise the value of each one and therefore earn a higher income. However, once the original 100 prints sell at a high price, the artist may be tempted to produce more and sell those as well. This would diminish the value of the original 100 prints and could upset the buyers. What's necessary is that the artist *commit to not printing any more.* By doing so, the collectors who purchase the first 100 prints can rely on their art to retain its value and will be willing to pay a higher price. One common way for artists to make this commitment is by destroying the matrix (the plate from which prints are produced) after making 100 prints. This may seem suboptimal once the 100 prints have sold, but, by doing so before the first 100 prints have sold, the artist can ensure that they sell at a high price.

The moral of the story so far is the following. A sad fact of our lives is that our society is full of *stupid bureaucratic red tape, crazy politicians, and aggressive corporate managers*, but game theory reveals that at least some of these things may actually *possess a certain rationality*. Inflexible institutions or rules and crazy leaders could be a device to ensure the optimal outcome by committing to an ex-post suboptimal action.

7.5 Long-Term Relationships and Cooperation

Let me introduce one more very important and general insight from the study of dynamic games: if people interact for a long time, they can develop trust and build a cooperative relationship.

One important takeaway from game theory is that, when people do what's best for themselves, it can have undesirable consequences for society as a whole. For example, in the prisoner's dilemma, despite the fact that it brings about a good outcome if both prisoners cooperate and remain silent, if they just do what's individually best they will choose to betray their partner and confess. In the language of game theory, it is often the case that a Nash equilibrium (the outcome of each person pursuing his or her own self-interest) is (Pareto-) inefficient.

I gave a detailed explanation of this principle in Chapter 6, Section 6.4, but let's review it one more time. Even if cooperation is socially desirable, oftentimes

* there is a cost to cooperation,

and, therefore,

* each individual is tempted to shirk and tries to save the cost of cooperation by free-riding on others' efforts to cooperate.

In such a case,

* if the players *interact only a single time*, they will drag each other down (by shirking) and end up with a bad outcome that nobody likes. (This is the Nash equilibrium of a one-shot game.)

However, if the players know that this group will interact (or play the same game) repeatedly, both now and in the future, then they may think twice about shirking, since it could trigger a punishment by other players at a later time. Alternatively, the players might believe that, by cooperating today, they can ensure that their opponents will also choose to cooperate in the future. Based on those considerations, we expect that, in a long-term relationship, it's possible to achieve cooperation, even among purely self-interested individuals. That is,

* *even selfish individuals can cooperate if they are thrust into a long-term relationship with others.*

The subfield of game theory that formulated this insight is called the **theory of repeated games**. Let me provide an overview of repeated games along with an example. First, let's consider the following case.

Case Study 7.3 Cooperation between Gas Stations

If you look around, you'll sometimes spot two gas stations very close to each other. In extreme cases, there may be two gas stations right next to each other (see Figure 7.23)!

Credit: Nippon Hyoron Sha, Co., Ltd.

Figure 7.23 Two gas stations right next to each other

Each gas station will post a price such as "$3.00 per gallon" on a signboard every morning, so this is a case of

- price competition,

in which each gas station's strategy is the price it posts. Since each company's gas is virtually identical, this is a situation in which

- there is no product differentiation,

and consumers will simply choose whichever station has a lower price. Moreover, the cost of supplying the gasoline is almost the same as the wholesale price of purchasing the gasoline, which does not differ much between the two companies. This means that

- all players' marginal costs are constant and identical (and equal to the wholesale price).

If we think about the gas stations in this way, we can see that *this looks like a near-perfect example of the Bertrand model*, which I explained when we learned about simultaneous-move games (look back at Chapter 6, Section 6.5 (b)). We saw that the unique Nash equilibrium of the Bertrand model is that *the two firms set their prices equal to the wholesale price and earn zero profits*. However, in apparent contradiction of this prediction, we see examples of gas stations right next to each other that continue to operate (presumably because they earn positive profits). What on earth is going on? Let's consider this conundrum in the following way.

The key to this puzzle is the fact that the two gas stations don't just engage in a price competition today but also tomorrow, the day after tomorrow, and so on. Therefore, instead of treating each day's price competition as a separate game, it's more reasonable to analyze the situation by treating each day as a part of one big dynamic game. Since this dynamic game is one in which the players (gas stations) repeatedly play the same game (price competition) over and over into the future, we call this a **repeated game**. We call the game (price competition) that is played in each period $t = 0, 1, 2, \ldots$ of the dynamic game the **stage game**. To summarize, *a repeated game is a game in which*

- *the same players repeatedly play the same stage game over an infinite time horizon $t = 0, 1, 2, \ldots$*

As the starting point for analyzing what happens in the repeated game that the gas stations are playing, let's review why they cannot generate positive profits in the price competition game that lasts for a single period. Please look at Figure 7.24.

The marginal costs for the two gas stations (firms 1 and 2) are identical and constant at value c (which is equal to the wholesale price of gasoline). In the left panel of the figure, the gas stations agree to raise their prices above the marginal cost c ($p_1 = p_2 > c$). Both firms generate high profits, and, overall, this is a desirable arrangement. However, each firm is *tempted to unilaterally deviate from this arrangement and betray the other station*. For example, if firm 1 were to lower its price to a level just below firm 2's price, since there is no product differentiation firm 1 can steal all of firm 2's customers and earn a much higher profit (see the right panel of the figure). In fact, if firm 1's price cut is tiny, then the price is almost unchanged, but it doubles its customer base since, originally, each firm got half the customers.

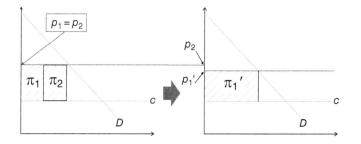

Figure 7.24 If firms cooperate to raise prices, one firm can gain by betraying the other

If firm 1 lowers its price a little, **its profit almost doubles**

This means that *firm 1's profit approximately doubles*. For this reason, in a single price competition game, it is not possible to sustain the state in which both firms set prices above marginal cost and generate positive profits. That is, this state cannot be a Nash equilibrium.

Now, let's think about what happens in the repeated game in which the gas stations repeatedly play the price competition game over time. Let $p_1 = p_2 = p^* > c$ be the price that maximizes the sum of the profits of the two gas stations. Here's one way to sustain a high price over the long run (i.e. in a repeated game).

- In the first period, both firms set their prices at p^*.
- In future periods, if both firms have set their prices at p^*, then both firms set their prices at p^* in the next period too.
- If in some period a firm sets its price at some value besides p^*, the firm sets its price at c in every future period.

If the gas stations follow this strategy, the following occurs.

- In equilibrium, the gas stations cooperate in every period and set their prices at p^*.
- However, once someone deviates from the cooperative action, the gas stations fall into cutthroat price competition for good (i.e. they permanently play the Nash equilibrium of the one-shot price competition game, $p_1 = p_2 = c$ with zero profits).

The repeated game strategy in which one

① *plays the cooperative action in every period in equilibrium, and*
② *plays the Nash equilibrium strategy of the one-shot game (stage game) in every period once the cooperation is broken,*

is called a **trigger strategy**. This name comes from the fact that any deviation from the cooperative strategy triggers an irreversible response that ends cooperation permanently. In other words, a trigger strategy is a strategy that aims to achieve cooperation by using the less favorable Nash equilibrium of the one-shot game as a threat or punishment.

Next, let's check that the trigger strategy constitutes a subgame-perfect equilibrium. It suffices to show that

---

after any history of past prices, the two gas stations are *taking mutual best responses*.[9]
(*)

---

[9] Recall the (verbal) definition of a subgame in Section 7.2 (b), which says that, when all players who move from now on observe all past events, the remaining part of the dynamic game is a subgame. In our gas station repeated game, players observe all past events (prices), and therefore what is going to be played after each period is a subgame. Hence, if the gas stations' strategies induce a Nash equilibrium in each subgame (i.e. after any history of prices, the two gas stations each respond optimally to the other's actions), then it is a subgame-perfect equilibrium.

Table 7.4 What happens when a firm betrays first

	t	$t+1$	$t+2$	$\ldots$
The payoff when the firm plays as in equilibrium	π^*	π^*	π^*	$\ldots$
The maximum payoff when the firm deviates in period t	$2\pi^*$	0	0	$\ldots$

First, let's consider the situation in which one firm has already betrayed. Under the trigger strategy, *in every subsequent period the opponent will always set the prices at c, which is the Nash equilibrium strategy of the stage game*. Therefore, one's best response is to also choose the Nash equilibrium action (setting the price equal to c) in each period. Hence, once one firm has already deviated, the equilibrium condition (*) holds. Note that the best profit one can earn is zero (because the firms set prices equal to c) if someone has already deviated.

Next, let's consider the situation in which neither firm has betrayed yet. Let $\pi^* > 0$ be the profit that each firm earns in each period in equilibrium. The top row of Table 7.4 shows a firm's profit period by period when the local firm plays as in equilibrium.

If the firm follows the equilibrium strategy and sets its price at p^*, it receives a payoff of π^* each period. On the other hand, if the firm deviates in the tth period by slightly undercutting the price, as I explained at the beginning, it can roughly double its profit in that period. However, after that period, the maximum profit one can earn is zero in each period, as I explained above (the second row of Table 7.4).

Now, let's consider which of these two strategies is more profitable. Our intuition tells us that it is more valuable to a firm to earn \$1 today than it is to earn \$1 a year from now. In other words, *firms discount their future profits*. So, let's suppose that each firm discounts the next period's payoff by a factor of $0 < \delta < 1$. The lower-case Greek letter delta, δ, captures the idea that the firm equally values \$1 tomorrow and δ dollars today, and we call it the **discount factor**. We can think of a firm whose *discount factor is large* (i.e. close to one) as being patient. By contrast, we can think of a firm whose *discount factor is small* (i.e. close to zero) as being myopic.

If we take a firm's discounting into account, it's reasonable to suppose that each player i's payoff in a repeated game is the sum of each period's payoff, $\pi_i(t)$, discounted appropriately by the discount factor δ. Hence, the repeated game payoff of firm i is

$$\pi_i(0) + \pi_i(1)\delta + \pi_i(2)\delta^2 + \pi_i(3)\delta^3 + \cdots.$$

A firm's immediate gains from unilaterally betraying its opponent in some period are given by this:

$$(\textit{The upper bound of}) \textit{ immediate gains from betraying} = 2\pi^* - \pi^* = \pi^*.$$

On the other hand, once a firm betrays the opponent, it loses its profit of π^* in every subsequent period. Therefore, using the above expression, we have that a firm's losses from unilaterally betraying its opponent are given by this:

$$\textit{Future losses from betraying} = \pi^*\delta + \pi^*\delta + \pi^*\delta^3 + \cdots.$$

Let this sum of future losses from betraying be equal to X. Note that we can rewrite X as

$$X = \pi^*\delta + \delta\underbrace{\left(\pi^*\delta + \pi^*\delta^2 + \cdots\right)}_{\text{equal to } X},$$

so we have that $X = \pi^*\delta + \delta X$. Solving for X, we obtain this:

$$\textit{Future losses from betraying } (X) = \frac{\delta}{1-\delta}\pi^*.$$

Therefore, if

$$\underset{\substack{\text{immediate gains} \\ \text{from betraying}}}{\pi^*} \quad \leq \quad \underset{\substack{\text{future losses} \\ \text{from betraying}}}{\frac{\delta}{1-\delta}\pi^*}$$

then it is not worth it for the firm to unilaterally choose to betray its opponent. We can rewrite this condition as $1 - \delta \leq \delta$, which implies that, *if the discount factor δ is greater than or equal to $\frac{1}{2}$, then the firm is left worse off if it unilaterally betrays.*

To summarize, if the discount factor δ satisfies $\delta \geq 1/2$, then the trigger strategy satisfies the equilibrium condition that "after any history of prices, the two gas stations are taking mutual best responses in the remaining part of the repeated game." Thus,

> if the discount factor δ is no less than $1/2$, then the two gas stations can sustain the high price p^* that maximizes their profits by using the trigger strategy.

In the example of the gas stations, one period is equal to one day, so the discount factor δ is probably very close to one. That is, it seems unlikely that the gas stations would accept substantially less than \$1 today rather than wait to get \$1 tomorrow. Therefore, it seems reasonable to assume that the condition $\delta \geq 1/2$, under which the trigger strategy constitutes an equilibrium, is satisfied. We don't know whether the actual gas stations in Figure 7.24 follow the trigger strategy, but doesn't it seem plausible that the gas stations would think in the following manner?

"We might earn more money today if we undercut our competitor's prices, but this might cause our competitor to retaliate and undercut us, which would cost us money in the future. In that case, let's keep our price high and avoid starting a price war."

Repeated games are a useful modeling tool for capturing this sort of thinking in real firms. Nearby gas stations are not the only real-world firms that cooperate like this. More generally, in markets with only a small number of firms, it's common to see firms **collude** and raise their prices. We call such a group of a firms a **cartel**. In a cartel, there is always a *temptation for a firm* *to betray the group* by deviating from the agreed-upon plan in order to increase its own profits. In order to ensure the cartel functions successfully, it's necessary to guard against such a betrayal by instituting a rule that punishes any firm that deviates from the group's plan of action. The study of repeated games elucidates the structure of cartels and shows that such a punishment can be a very effective preventative measure due to the firms' long-run relationship.

Comment 7.3

I have now explained all the basics of game theory. In what follows, I will explain what kinds of things happen when firms and consumers have **private information** that only they know. We call such a situation a case of **asymmetric information**. The subfield of economics that studies these situations is called "information economics." Information economics is an important new area that was discovered after the study of perfectly competitive markets was more or less completed. In general, information economics deals with two types of problems, which differ in the nature of people's private information (information that is unknown to others).

- Problems of moral hazard are cases in which players *cannot observe their opponents' actions*.
- Problems of adverse selection are cases in which players *do not have the same information their opponents have*.

For example, in today's market economy, in which ownership and management are separate, a company's shareholders cannot monitor whether the company's management is working diligently. This is a problem of "moral hazard," since the management's actions are hidden from the shareholders. On the other hand, a firm that borrows money knows its own profitability and risk of going bankrupt, but the lending bank does not. This is a problem of "adverse selection," since the bank does not truly know the firm's profitability or risk of going bankrupt. I hope these examples illustrate that problems of asymmetric information are important and pervasive in our society. In Chapter 8, we will study the basics of these two types of asymmetric information.

8   Insurance and Moral Hazard

Shareholders of a company cannot directly monitor what the company's manager is doing in her/his office. So, what can the shareholders do to ensure that the manager works hard for the sake of the company? This is a problem of moral hazard (a problem in which certain people's actions – the manager's effort – are "hidden" from others). To solve this type of problem, one needs to consider the following two issues. One is **risk-sharing** between the shareholders and the manager, and the other is motivating the manager with **incentives**. First, let's study how risk-sharing works.

8.1   Efficient Risk-Sharing and the Role of Insurance

We have seen the importance of allocating the various goods in the economy (for instance, foods such as chicken and beef) in a way that satisfies the needs of the consumers. Allocations that give beef to people who prefer chicken and give chicken to people who prefer beef are inefficient. By altering such an allocation, we can increase the satisfaction and well-being of all consumers. This leads to the idea of an efficient allocation of goods that we learned in the first half of the book.

In the same way that it's necessary to allocate commodities such as chicken and beef according to the needs of the consumers, *it is also necessary to efficiently allocate the risks that are inherent to life in a way that is suitable to each individual's preferences and attitudes toward risk*. This is the theory of **efficient risk-sharing**, which we will now learn. The basic idea is simple: we avoid imposing risk on people who especially hate risk and try to shift the burden onto people who don't mind taking risks. Let me explain using the expected utility model that we learned in Chapter 6, Section 6.6

In our society, there all types of people, from those who particularly dislike taking risks, to those who are indifferent to taking risks, to those who actually enjoy taking risks. The expected utility model we learned in Section 6.6 captures these attitudes toward risk in a simple and easy-to-understand manner.

First, let's recall what an "expected value" is. Suppose that there is a random variable $\tilde{x}$ that takes one of the values $x_1, \ldots, x_k$. We let p_k denote the probability that $\tilde{x}$ takes value x_k. Then the expression

$$p_1 x_1 + \cdots + p_K x_K$$

is called the expected value of $\tilde{x}$ and is denoted by $E[\tilde{x}]$. The expected value represents the value the random variable $\tilde{x}$ takes on average. In the expected utility model, the random variable $\tilde{x}$ might represent an individual's income, and the individual tries to maximize expected utility,

$$E[u(\tilde{x})] = p_1 u(x_1) + \cdots + p_K u(x_K),$$

which is just the expected value of the utility $u(x)$ that he or she receives from earning income x.

Now, let's consider the situation in which an earthquake occurs with probability p. Let x_1 denote the individual's income in the event of an earthquake and let x_2 denote the individual's income in the absence of an earthquake. Each individual tries to maximize her expected utility:

$$pu(x_1) + (1-p)u(x_2).$$

For an individual whose utility is equal to the income she receives (that is, $u(x) = x$),

$$\text{expected utility} = \text{expected value of income.}$$

In other words, *all that matters to this individual is the expected value of her income; she doesn't care whether there is a lot of variability and risk or whether there is no variability or risk.* Such an individual (with $u(x) = x$) is said to be risk-neutral.

On the other hand, we know that an individual whose utility function has a graph that is bowed upward, like the one in Figure 8.1,[1] would prefer to receive the expected value of her income with certainty than to receive various amounts with certain probabilities. Formally, we can express this by

$$\underbrace{pu(x_1) + (1-p)u(x_2)}_{\text{the expected utility from the "risky" income}} < \underbrace{u(px_1 + (1-p)x_2)}_{\text{the expected value of income}}.$$

This type of individual is said to be risk-averse.

Say that we have a risk-averse individual named Amanda and a risk-neutral individual named Brian. How should Amanda and Brian share the risk of a fluctuating income due to the possibility of an earthquake? Figure 8.2 illustrates a solution if there is a risk that Amanda's income varies in the event of an earthquake.

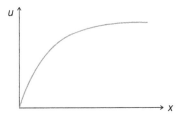

Figure 8.1 The utility function of a risk-averse individual

---

[1] This means that the individual is someone whose utility function is a strictly concave function. Look back at Chapter 6, Section 6.6.

Figure 8.2 Efficient risk-sharing

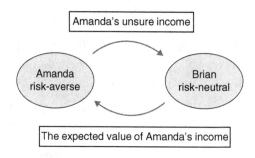

Suppose that an earthquake occurs with probability 1/2. If an earthquake hits, Amanda's income is $0, and, if there is no earthquake, Amanda's income is $100,000. If

- Brian, who is risk-neutral, takes Amanda's risky income ($0 or $100,000), and
- in exchange, pays Amanda $50,000,[2] the expected value of her income,

then we can increase Amanda's satisfaction without lowering Brian's. In other words, we can execute a "Pareto improvement." Here's why.

- Since Brian is risk-neutral, he cares only about the expected value of his income. That is, the satisfaction he gains from receiving $0 with probability 1/2 and receiving $100,000 with probability 1/2 is equal to the satisfaction he gives up by paying $50,000. Therefore, this arrangement with Amanda does not affect Brian's satisfaction.
- Since Amanda is risk-averse, she is better off receiving $50,000 with certainty as opposed to receiving $0 with probability 1/2 and receiving $100,000 with probability 1/2.

After performing the exchange shown in Figure 8.2, Brian, who is risk-neutral, has taken on all the risk, and Amanda, who is risk-averse, faces no risk at all. Under this arrangement, it is not possible to increase someone's satisfaction without lowering the other's satisfaction. Put differently, the outcome of the exchange in Figure 8.2 achieves Pareto-efficient risk-sharing. Let me summarize what we've seen above.

Pareto-Efficient Risk-Sharing

In situations with one risk-averse person and one risk-neutral person, *it is Pareto-efficient if all of the income risk is taken by the risk-neutral person* in a way that gives the risk-averse person an income with certainty.

This is the key to understanding the *role of insurance* in our society. In the real world, consumers are exposed to various risks, such as fires, car accidents, or illnesses and hospitalizations, and many would like to eliminate the risk of negative outcomes associated with these

---

[2] The expected value of Amanda's income can be calculated as $(1/2) \times 0 + (1/2) \times 100{,}000 = 50{,}000$.

events. This means that consumers are risk-averse. On the other hand, insurance companies are owned by many shareholders, who receive a portion of the companies' revenues. In this sense, insurance companies are able to share risks widely.[3] Therefore, we can think of insurance companies as being almost risk-neutral. The insurance companies that sell car insurance, home insurance, or health insurance can be considered as the mechanisms through which we can achieve Pareto-efficient risk-sharing (the risk-neutral individuals bear risks).

8.2 Moral Hazard: The Challenge We Face and What We Can Do

Using the idea of efficient risk-sharing, let's revisit the problem of moral hazard that arises between shareholders and managers. To recap: the manager is hired by the company share-holders to work on their behalf, but the shareholders cannot directly observe whether the manager is working diligently or slacking off. *Situations in which there are "hidden" actions are called **moral hazard** problems.*

Even if the manager's effort cannot be directly observed, if we know that

- the company is *guaranteed* to earn high revenues if the manager works diligently, and
- the company is *guaranteed* to earn low revenues if the manager is lazy,

then the shareholders would be able to figure out the manager's actions just by looking at the company's revenue. In this case, there is no asymmetric information. Solving the moral hazard problem is easy: they agree to pay the manager a lot when the company's revenue is high but pay the manager very little when the company's revenue is low. (The manager will then work diligently in order to earn a higher income.) However, in reality, the shareholders cannot perfectly determine the manager's actions just by looking at the company's revenue. To illustrate this point, let's suppose that the company's revenue is either high ($500 million) or low ($100 million).[4] The following situation would be more realistic.

- Even if the manager is lazy, there is still a possibility of earning the high revenue. Conversely, even if the manager works hard, it's possible that the company will have low revenue due to bad luck.
- However, the probability of earning the high revenue increases if the manager works diligently.

Figure 8.3 gives one such example. In scenarios such as this, even if the company earns the low revenue, it's not necessarily the case that the manager was lazy. It's possible that the manager worked hard but was unlucky. When the company's revenue is subject to these random fluctuations, what can be done to induce the manager to work diligently? Together,

---

[3] Even if an insurance company's revenue fluctuates by $1 million, if there are 5,000 shareholders each shareholder's income fluctuates by only $200, which isn't that big a deal. We might also think that people who bother to become shareholders of insurance companies are risk-neutral people.

[4] For example, we can imagine a scenario in which the company's revenue is high if a project the manager implements is successful and is low if it fails.

Table 8.1 Examples of moral hazard

Principal	Agent	Hidden *action*	Observable *outcome*
Landowner	Farmhand	Effort	Harvest
Boss	Salesperson	Effort	Sales
Defendant	Lawyer	Effort	Verdict
Fire insurance company	Customer	Take proper precautions	Fire
Car insurance company	Driver	Drive safely	Accident

Figure 8.3 The manager's effort and the company's revenue

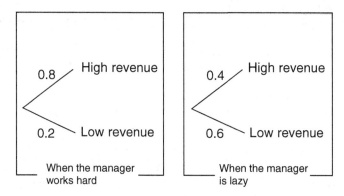

let's determine the most efficient way to do this. We'll find that the idea of efficient risk-sharing plays a key role.

Allow me to summarize the discussion so far. There are many real-world problems that share the following features.

① One person (a **principal**) hires another person (an **agent**) to perform a task, but
② the agent's action cannot be directly observed (there is a moral hazard problem).
③ However, there is an observable outcome that is affected by the agent's action, and
④ the observable outcome does not correspond one to one with the agent's action, but fluctuates randomly due to external random shocks.

In the example above, the principal is the group of shareholders, the agent is the manager, and the observable outcome is the company's revenue. Other prominent "moral hazard" situations that fit points ① to ④ are listed in Table 8.1.

Let me explain some of these examples.

- The landowner (principal) asks the farmhand (agent) to harvest wheat, but cannot always monitor the farmhand's effort (moral hazard). However, the amount of wheat that is harvested can be precisely measured (it is an observable outcome). Good harvests and bad harvests reflect the farmhand's effort, but may also be due to random factors such as the weather. Therefore, if the harvest is poor, it may not be due to a lack of effort by the farmhand. In this kind of situation, what can be done to make the farmhand work hard?
- The probability of a fire occurring depends partly on how cautious people are in their homes. Knowing this, the insurance company (principal) would like its customers (agents) to be careful and take precautions. The problem is that the insurance company does not know whether its customers are careful or reckless (moral hazard). In this kind of situation, what can the insurance company do to make the customers take the proper precautions and avoid reckless behaviors?

Comment 8.1 About the Terminology of "Moral Hazard"

The above example of fire insurance is actually the source of the phrase "moral hazard." "Moral hazard" is a phrase that has long been used in the insurance industry. Economists later adopted it to refer to the problems that can arise from unobservable actions. In the United Kingdom, where the insurance industry developed in the nineteenth century, there were many instances of people who had purchased fire insurance becoming careless since they knew their homes were insured. This led to increases in the number of accidental fires. The phrase "moral hazard" became widely used to refer to risks that arise from people's selfish actions (such as residential fires due to carelessness), as opposed to "physical hazards" that are due to acts of nature (such as hurricanes or earthquakes).[5] Subsequently, economists started using the phrase "moral hazard" to describe any situation in which *it may be difficult to incentivize people to take appropriate actions when their actions are not observable*. During the development of information economics, this terminology was adopted within academia. Nowadays, the phrase "moral hazard" even appears in newspapers and is understood to refer to these types of problems. However, the phrase "moral hazard" tends to give people the false impression that the source of the problem is a lack of ethics, and that the solution might be to persuade people not to be greedy. Economically speaking, moral hazard problems arise when there is asymmetric information because certain actions are not observable. The proper countermeasure is, therefore, not to preach to people to be good citizens, but to design a mechanism that provides the appropriate incentives for people to take the desired actions.

"**Agency theory**"[6] deals with problems like those shown in Table 8.1. This type of problem is common in the real world. In short, answering the question "How can we solve a moral hazard

---

[5] Allard E. Dembe and Leslie I. Boden, "Moral Hazard: A Question of Morality?," *New Solutions*, 10(3) (2000), 257–279.

[6] This is also sometimes called **principal–agent theory**.

Figure 8.4 The problem of moral hazard

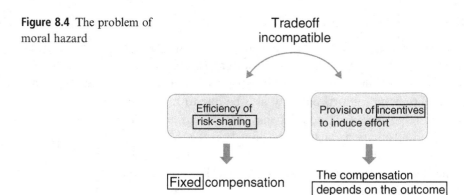

problem?" amounts to answering "What is the best way to induce the agent to take the proper action?" In this section, I will explain the basic ideas of agency theory. For the sake of my explanation, let's assume

- the principal (the group of shareholders) is risk-neutral;[7] and
- the agent (the manager) is risk-averse.

Before solving this problem using a model, let's consider the essence of the moral hazard problem using plain English. Shareholders give a portion of the company's randomly fluctuating revenue to the manager as payment. As we saw in the previous section, from a risk-sharing perspective, it's better if all the risks associated with fluctuating revenue are taken by the risk-neutral shareholders and if the risk-averse manager is paid a constant amount regardless of the company's revenue. However, if the manager's compensation does not depend on the company's revenue, then she has no incentive to work hard. This tradeoff is at the heart of most moral hazard problems. Please take a look at Figure 8.4.

In light of this observation, let's now use a mathematical model to design appropriate incentives when *we have a tradeoff between efficient risk-sharing and incentivizing the desired action*. When choosing how to compensate the manager (agent) in a way that maximizes their profit, the shareholders (principals) need to consider the following two conditions.

① The compensation paid to the manager must be high enough that she does not look for work at a different company.
② The compensation paid to the manager must depend on the company's revenue in such a manner that it prompts her to work diligently.[8]

---

[7] As I explained in the part on insurance in Section 8.1, if there are many shareholders, the risk for each shareholder is small. This enables the shareholders as a group to take on large risks. In other words, when there are many shareholders, the shareholders as a group are nearly risk-neutral.

[8] If the cost of inducing the manager to work diligently is too high, then it may be optimal for the shareholders to have the manager not work at all. In this case, the optimal compensation is simple: the shareholders should pay a fixed amount regardless of the company's performance. This would achieve Pareto-efficient risk-sharing. We won't be considering cases that are so simple.

Let's write down the principal's problem of maximizing expected profit subject to those two constraints. Now, supposing that

- the revenue is either high ($\bar{y}$) or low ($\underline{y}$),
- if the manager works hard the company earns the high revenue with probability p, and
- the manager's compensation if the company earns the high revenue is $\bar{w}$ and the manager's compensation if the company earns the low revenue is $\underline{w}$,

then the expected value of the shareholders' profit, when the manager is induced to work hard, is given by

$$p(\bar{y} - \bar{w}) + (1 - p)(\underline{y} - \underline{w}). \tag{1}$$

Note that, since the shareholders are risk-neutral, they try to maximize (1). Next, if

- the manager could earn payoff U at another firm if she chooses to leave, and
- her cost of working hard is C,

then we can express condition ① (which ensures that the manager does not look for work at a different firm) as

$$pu(\bar{w}) + (1 - p)u(\underline{w}) - C \geq U. \tag{2}$$

This is called the **participation constraint**. Here, U represents the manager's utility function and captures the fact that she is risk-averse (i.e. its graph is bowed upward). Last, if

- the probability that the company earns the high revenue decreases to p' ($< p$) if the manager is lazy,

then the **incentive constraint** (condition ②), which ensures that the manager works diligently, can be expressed as

$$p\,u(\bar{w}) + (1 - p)u(\underline{w}) - C \geq p'u(\bar{w}) + (1 - p')u(\underline{w}). \tag{3}$$

That is, in order to incentivize the manager to work hard, the expected payoff from working diligently (the left-hand side) should be greater than (or equal to) the expected payoff from being lazy (the right-hand side). Note that the manager's cost of working diligently (C) is only on the left-hand side, because the agent need not pay C when she is lazy.

To summarize, given that there is a moral hazard problem in which the manager's effort level is not observable, it is optimal for the shareholders to design the manager's compensation, $\bar{w}$ or $\underline{w}$, in a way that

---

maximizes the expected profit (1) under

- the *participation constraint* (2), and
- the *incentive constraint* (3).

Figure 8.5 The shareholders' indifference curves (risk-neutral)

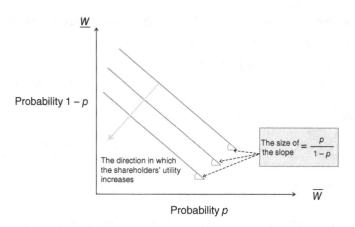

In other words, solving the moral hazard problem boils down to solving the constrained maximization problem whose constraints respect the agent's incentive to work hard and to participate. This is one of the most important messages in this chapter!

In what follows, we will solve this problem using a figure. Let's first draw the indifference curves of the shareholders and the manager. First, since the shareholders are risk-neutral, we can write their utility as

$$\underbrace{p\overline{y} + (1-p)\underline{y}}_{\text{expected revenue}} - \underbrace{p\overline{w} + (1-p)\underline{w}}_{\text{expected payment}}.$$

Note that only the expected payment changes when varying the manager's compensation, $\overline{w}$ and $\underline{w}$.[9] Since the shareholders' utility is constant if we hold the expected payment constant, the shareholder's indifference curves are downward-sloping straight lines that are given by the equation

$$\underbrace{p\overline{w} + (1-p)\underline{w}}_{\text{expected payment}} = \text{constant}$$

Take a look at Figure 8.5.

The size of the slope of the indifference curves is $p/(1-p)$, the ratio of the probability that the company earns the high revenue to the probability that the company earns the low revenue.[10] Recall that the shareholders' utility (and expected payment to the manager) is constant at any point along an indifference curve. Note that the shareholders' utility increases as we move toward the bottom-left indifferent curves (since the expected payment becomes smaller).

Let's consider the manager's indifference curves. Each of the manager's indifference curves is like that shown in Figure 8.6.

---

[9] Assuming the manager works diligently, the company's expected revenue is a constant value that does not depend on $\overline{w}$ or $\underline{w}$.

[10] We can rewrite the condition that expected payment = constant as $\underline{w} = -\frac{p}{1-p}\overline{w} + \text{constant}$, so the absolute value of the coefficient on $\overline{w}$, $p/(1-p)$, is the size of the slope.

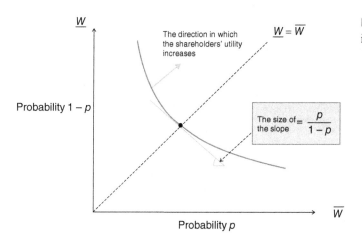

Figure 8.6 The manager's indifference curves (risk-averse)

While the shareholders' indifference curves are straight lines, the manager's indifference curves are *bowed toward the origin*. This is because the manager is *risk-averse*.

The Indifference Curves of a Risk-Averse Individual Are Bowed toward the Origin

Let me explain why a risk-averse individual's indifference curves are bowed toward the origin. Recall that the manager's utility is constant along any one of her indifference curves. That is,

$$\underbrace{pu(\overline{w}) + (1 - p)u(\underline{w})}_{\text{manager's utility}} - C = \text{constant.} \tag{4}$$

Let's calculate the slopes of these curves, $d\underline{w}/d\overline{w}$. In Chapter 1, Section 1.5, when I explained consumer behavior, we calculated the slopes of indifference curves using total differentiation. That method was meant to help you build intuition, but let me now introduce a more elegant method. We can express $\underline{w}$ as a function of $\overline{w}$ by writing $\underline{w} = \underline{w}(\overline{w})$. Plugging this into (4) and differentiating both sides with respect to $\overline{w}$, we obtain

$$pu'(\overline{w}) + (1 - p)u'(\underline{w})(d\underline{w}/d\overline{w}) = 0.^{11}$$

Solving this for $d\underline{w}/d\overline{w}$, we have

$$-d\underline{w}/d\overline{w} = \frac{p}{1 - p}\frac{u'(\overline{w})}{u'(\underline{w})}. \tag{5}$$

That is, the slope $(d\underline{w}/d\overline{w})$ is negative and its size is given by the right-hand side of Equation (5).

---

[11] If we use the "chain rule" and differentiate $u(\underline{w}(\bar{w}))$ by $\bar{w}$, we get $u'(\underline{w})(d\underline{w}/d\bar{w})$.

(cont.)

Figure 8.7 The meaning of an indifference curve being bowed toward the origin

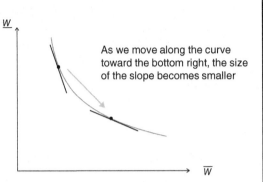

As we move along the curve toward the bottom right, the size of the slope becomes smaller

Now note that, since the indifference curves are bowed toward the origin, as we move along an indifference curve toward the bottom right, the size of the slope decreases (see Figure 8.7).

As shown in the figure, as we move toward the bottom right, we increase $\overline{w}$ and decrease $\underline{w}$. What happens if we increase $\overline{w}$ and decrease $\underline{w}$ in Equation (5), which expresses the size of the slope?

Since the graph of the utility function of a risk-averse individual is bowed upward, the marginal utility $u'(w)$ (= the slope of the graph) diminishes as income w increases. Consequently, if we increase $\overline{w}$, then $u'(\overline{w})$ decreases, and, if we decrease $\underline{w}$, then $u'(\underline{w})$ increases. Thus,

$$\text{the size of the slope of the indifference curve} = \frac{p}{1-p}\frac{u'(\overline{w})}{u'(\underline{w})}$$

indeed decreases as we move along an indifference curve toward the bottom right (as shown in Figure 8.7). Therefore, we have confirmed that *the risk-averse manager's indifference curves are bowed toward the origin*.

In addition, note that, when the manager receives the same compensation regardless of the company's revenue (that is, when the risk-averse manager bears no risk) and is paid $\underline{w} = \overline{w}$, we have that

$$\text{the size of the slope of the indifference curves} = \frac{p}{1-p}. \tag{6}$$

Looking at Equation (6), we can see that *this is the same as the size of the slope of the risk-neutral shareholders' indifference curves*. The importance of this point will become clear to you later.

Last, let's depict the range of values that satisfy the incentive constraint (3). Rearranging the terms in (3), we obtain

$$(p - p')(u(\overline{w}) - u(\underline{w})) \geq C.$$

The range of values that satisfy this equation is shown in Figure 8.8. Let me explain why.

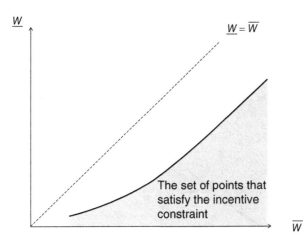

Figure 8.8 The range of compensation values that satisfy the incentive constraint

The boundary of the shaded region in Figure 8.8 is the curve given by

$$(p - p')(u(\overline{w}) - u(\underline{w})) = C. \tag{7}$$

That is, it is the set of points that satisfy the incentive constraint with equality. Since $(p - p') > 0$ and $C > 0$, it must be that $(u(\overline{w}) - u(\underline{w})) > 0$. This implies that $\overline{w} - \underline{w} > 0$, so we know that every point on the boundary of the shaded region lies below the dotted 45 degree line. This should not come as a surprise; it means that, in order to incentivize the manager to work diligently, her compensation should be higher when the company earns the high revenue than when the company earns the low revenue. Now, if we start from a point that satisfies Equation (7) and increase $\overline{w}$, the left-hand side of (7) becomes larger than the right-hand side. In order to maintain the equality, we need to increase $\underline{w}$ as well. This demonstrates that the curve given by Equation (7) (the boundary of the shaded region in Figure 8.8) is upward-sloping.[12]

Finally, we show that the optimal compensation values $\overline{w}$ and $\underline{w}$ that incentivize the manager to work hard under moral hazard coincide with point A in Figure 8.9.

In order to ensure that the manager receives a utility of at least U (her utility from working at a different company), the shareholders should pick values of $\overline{w}$ and $\underline{w}$ that are above the manager's indifference curve for utility equal to U, shown in Figure 8.9. Taking the intersection of this region and the region from Figure 8.8 that satisfies the incentive constraint, we have the gray region shown in Figure 8.9. The points in this gray region satisfy both the participation constraint and the incentive constraint. Within the region, the best point for the shareholders is point A, which is the point at which the grey region and the shareholders' indifference curve (the downward-sloping line in Figure 8.9) are tangent to each other. *Point A is the optimal*

---

[12] The precise shape of this curve depends on the utility function u. For the discussion that follows, it suffices to know that it is an upward-sloping curve below the 45 degree line.

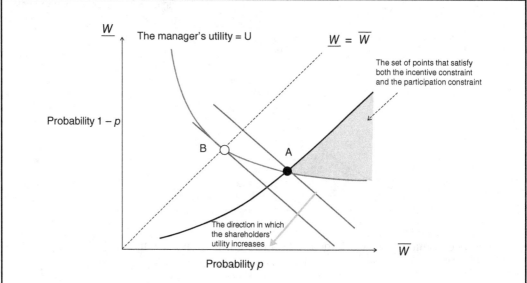

Figure 8.9 The optimal compensation when there is asymmetric information (A) and when there is not (B)

compensation package that balances both efficient risk-sharing and provision of proper incentives under moral hazard.

In order to deepen our understanding, let's consider the situation in which *there is no asymmetric information* and the shareholders can monitor the manager's effort. In this case, the shareholders can directly penalize the manager if the manager shirks. Therefore, there is no need to control the manager's incentives indirectly through $\overline{w}$ and $\underline{w}$ (i.e. we can ignore the incentive constraint (3)). Instead, the shareholders will choose the optimal point within the region that satisfies the participation constraint. Please take another look at Figure 8.9. The optimal point within this region is point B. As we verified in Equation (6), at point B, where $\overline{w} = \underline{w}$ and the manager bears no risk, the sizes of the slopes of the (risk-averse) manager's and (risk-neutral) shareholders' indifference curves are equal. In addition, the slopes of the manager's indifferences curves and the shareholders' indifference curves are the same $(= p/(1 - p))$, and, therefore, the two indifference curves are tangent to one another.

Observe that this implies that at point B, the optimal point *when there is no asymmetric information*, there is efficient risk-sharing, which we learned about in the previous section. That is, all the risk is borne by the shareholders and the manager is paid a fixed amount that is independent of the company's revenue. When the manager's effort can be directly observed, it suffices for the shareholders to provide an efficient, fixed compensation and to impose a huge fine on the manager if she is lazy.

Let me provide one case study that will illustrate the connection between the analysis above and the real world.

Case Study 8.1 The Role of Insurance "Deductibles"

If we alter the previous model so that

- manager = insurance customer
- effort = take precautions to prevent fires
- shareholders = insurance company

we can reinterpret this model as a model for moral hazard in the fire insurance market. (We can think of the value U that appeared in the participation constraint as the utility the customer would receive from purchasing insurance from a different company.) The insurance company wants people to take proper precautions to prevent fires in their homes ... but it cannot actually observe whether people take the precautions or are careless. The optimal solution to this moral hazard problem is point A in Figure 8.9, where the vertical axis gives the customer's income in the event of a fire and the horizontal axis gives the customer's income when there is not a fire. At the optimal point A, the customer has a low income when a fire breaks out. This means that, if the customer's losses from the fire are worth $20,000, *the insurance company does not cover the full amount; the customer must pay for some of the damage.*

In reality, many types of insurance have such arrangements. The amount that customers must pay for out of their own pockets is called an insurance **deductible**. For example, if a home fire insurance contract says "deductible: $300," it means that, if anything is damaged by a fire, the customer will pay for damages up to $300 and the insurance company will cover any remaining costs. One of the reasons that insurance companies do not cover the entire cost of the damages is that doing so might increase the likelihood of such accidents due to moral hazard (carelessness). Insurance policies that include deductibles can be thought of as achieving point A in Figure 8.9.

As we approach the conclusion of this chapter, I want to emphasize an important insight that we can take from Figure 8.9 and our analysis so far. If we compare point A (the optimal point when there is asymmetric information) to point B (the optimal point when there is not), we see that

① in both cases, the manager's utility is equal to U, which is the utility she could receive from working at a different company, but

② the shareholders' utility is higher at point B.

Therefore, for society as a whole (the manager and shareholders), point B (no information asymmetry) is a better outcome. We sometimes call

- point B, the optimal point when there is no asymmetric information, the **first-best** outcome, and
- point A, the optimal point when there is asymmetric information, the **second-best** outcome.

If we assume that the shareholders' expected profit is $48 million at point A and is $50 million at point B, then, if we move from a situation in which there is no asymmetric information to one in which there is, society as a whole suffers a loss of $2 million. In other words, it costs society $2 million due to moral hazard when there is asymmetric information and the manager's effort is unobservable.[13] Information economics teaches us why asymmetric information costs society, how much it costs society, and how we can design strategies and policies to minimize these costs.

Comment 8.2 Where Did the $2 Million Go?

The conclusion from the example above is that society loses $2 million if there is asymmetric information. But where on earth did these $2 million go? If we think about the answer to this question, we can deepen our understanding of the social cost of moral hazard.

When there is no asymmetric information, point B is optimal and risk is efficiently shared (the risk-averse manager is guaranteed to receive a fixed amount, say $5 million, regardless of the company's revenue). In this case, the manager receives as much satisfaction as she would if she worked for a different company.

On the other hand, if the manager's effort is not observable (i.e. there is moral hazard), then it is necessary for the manager to take some responsibility for the company's revenue. That is, in order to incentivize her to work hard, the manager should be paid less when the company earns the low revenue. When the manager's compensation depends on the company's performance, which has a random element to it, for the risk-averse manager to receive the same satisfaction as she gets from receiving $5 million for sure, it's necessary that she is paid more (in expectation). The reason is that

- if her expected payment is just $5 million, the risk-averse manager would prefer to work for a different company and be guaranteed to receive $5 million.
- Therefore, in order to be indifferent between being guaranteed $5 million and being paid depending on the risky outcome of the company's revenue, the manager needs to be paid more than $5 million in expectation.

The extra amount that the manager must be paid in expectation in order to be indifferent to receiving a guaranteed amount of $5 million is called the **risk premium** associated with the uncertain payment to the manager. The "missing" $2 million in the previous example is precisely equal to this risk premium!

Let's summarize the discussion above. If there is moral hazard due to the manager's effort being unobservable (asymmetric information), *it is necessary for the manager to bear some of the risk associated with the company's performance. The additional compensation the manager receives for bearing this risk (risk premium) is the social cost of asymmetric information.*

---

[13] This is sometimes called the **agency cost**.

9   Adverse Selection and Signaling

Let's continue studying the basics of economic analysis when there is asymmetric information. As I explained in Chapter 8, there are two main types of problems with asymmetric information:

- there are "**moral hazard**" problems, in which there is a *hidden action*; and
- there are "**adverse selection**" problems, in which there is *hidden information*.

In this chapter, we will study adverse selection problems. Specifically, I will explain

> how one can elicit others' private information (i.e. information that only they know).

9.1   What Is Adverse Selection?

The term "**adverse selection**," which we use in information economics to describe situations with hidden information, actually originated in the insurance industry. The basic problem with insurance markets is that there is asymmetric information (hidden information). To be precise, only the drivers (and not the insurance company) know how good they are at driving and how prone they are to getting into an accident. More accident-prone drivers are more likely to want insurance. In this case, if the insurance company does not think carefully about how to set its rates and chooses them naively, it may find itself in the following unfortunate chain of events.

- First, the insurance company calculates its insurance rates by looking at the average probability in society that someone gets into an accident.
- For people who are less prone to accidents than the average driver, the insurance rates are too high to be worth it. Therefore, these people won't buy the company's insurance. Only people who are more prone to accidents than the average driver will purchase the company's insurance.

- The insurance company then realizes that the average probability of an accident involving one of its customers is higher than expected (the societal average). Therefore, the insurance company raises its rates.
- The higher insurance rates mean that some of the people who bought the insurance previously, namely, the ones with relatively low risk of accidents, would stop buying the insurance. Only customers who are much more prone to accidents than the average customer will keep the company's insurance.
- This cycle continues, and eventually the insurance market collapses.

I can imagine that this type of scenario occurred in the early days of insurance industry and that people in the industry coined the phrase "adverse selection" to describe this phenomenon, while passing their wisdom on to their successors so that they could avoid making the same mistakes. It is called "adverse" selection because the "strongest" customers (i.e. the customers with the lowest probabilities of accidents) gradually disappear from a market, which is the opposite of what happens in the biological theory of natural selection, where the weakest animals disappear from an ecosystem over time.

A similar phenomenon can happen in the market for used cars. Oftentimes used cars have some issues, but these issues are known only to the seller and not to potential buyers. (Between you and me, when I was a graduate student, I sold a used car for $500 even though I had bought it for only $300!) If the buyer of the used car isn't aware of the possibility that the car may have undisclosed issues and makes an offer for the car, he may fall into the following vicious cycle.

- First, the buyer thinks of a price by looking at the average quality of used cars in society.
- Sellers whose cars are in good condition and worth more than the average used car won't sell at that price, so they don't put their cars on the market. In other words, only the low-quality used cars make it to the market.
- Looking at the quality of the used cars that are for sale, the buyer lowers the price he is willing to pay for a used car.
- Only sellers with even lower-quality cars stay in the market.
- In the worst case, the used car market collapses.

However, for a long time the field of microeconomics ignored problems of asymmetric information by modeling a situation like that above. The US economist George Akerlof (b. 1940) vividly showed how a market may become seriously dysfunctional if there is hidden information. Akerlof dubbed such a market a "**market for lemons**." A "lemon" is a slang term for a defective item, and I've heard it comes from the fact that we don't know if a lemon is good or rotten until we cut it open; we can't tell just by looking at it.

As the example above shows, in order for the insurance market or the used car market to function, *it is necessary to devise a way to elicit the private information of the customers and the sellers respectively*. That is, the insurance companies need to figure out how accident-prone a customer is, and the car buyers need to figure out whether the seller's car has any hidden issues. In this chapter, I will use a simple example to explain a basic method for eliciting private information.

Now we use the term "adverse selection" to describe general problems that involve private information, including but not limited to scenarios such as those we saw above in

Table 9.1 Examples of adverse selection (cases with hidden information)

	Holder of the private information	Private information
Used car market	Sellers	Quality
Bank loan	Borrowers	Risks associated with the project
Price regulation of utilities	Firms	Cost
Labor market	Workers	Productivity

which a market collapses. Table 9.1 shows other leading examples of adverse selection problems.

The last example in Table 9.1 concerns the labor market. A worker's ability (productivity) is known only to the worker and not his or her employer. In the following section, using this example we will consider the kinds of methods that can be used to elicit this private information.

9.2   Signaling

When someone with private information takes an observable action, we can provide rewards or penalties based on this action. If we do this properly, then

> people with different private information will take different actions, and we can therefore infer their private information.

In this case, the observable action signals the person's private information, so in economics we call this phenomenon "**signaling**."

In order to understand how signaling works, let's consider the following model of the labor market.

• Private information = the worker's ability (productivity).

Here, we express productivity by the Greek letter θ, and assume it is either high ($q = H$) or low ($\theta = L$). We call the private information (θ) the worker's "**type**."

• The action that reveals the private information to others (**signal**) = the level of education x.

For instance, we can take x to be the number of years the worker attended school. We assume that the worker's utility is given below:

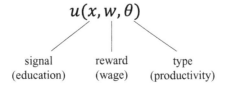

$$u(x, w, \theta)$$

signal (education)   reward (wage)   type (productivity)

Note that the worker's utility depends on his or her private information (type θ). This means that workers with different types will have different preferences. (I will explain why this is a reasonable assumption when we go over assumption 2.) Since people's actions are based on their preferences, this means that workers with different types should behave differently in certain situations. This is the theoretical reason that signaling works. In essence, signaling reveals private information because it combines the following two important economic insights:

1. we can infer a person's preferences from that person's actions (the idea of "revealed preferences"); and
2. people with different private information (typically) have different preferences.

By itself, condition 2 above is not sufficient to ensure that we can deduce a person's private information from his or her action (signal). In order for signaling to work, the signal (education level x) and reward (wage w) should be linked in a particular way.

To explain how this works, let me start by imposing several assumptions. First, let's suppose that a worker's utility increases as his or her wage increases. Let's also make this (realistic?) assumption.

Assumption 1: going to school is a pain (i.e. a worker's utility is decreasing in x).

Under these assumptions, a worker's indifference curves (various combinations of (education x, wage w) that provide the same level of utility) are upward-sloping curves, as shown in Figure 9.1.

Note that, on the indifference curve for $u = 10$, the utility is constant (and equal to 10) along the curve. If we move toward the top left of the figure, we decrease education x and increase wage w, both of which increase the worker's utility, as is indicated by the arrow in the figure. Now, suppose we start at the black dot shown in Figure 9.1, and increase the worker's education by one year without raising his or her wage. Since going to school is a pain (assumption 1), holding all else constant, the worker's utility decreases. In order to maintain

Figure 9.1 A worker's indifference curves

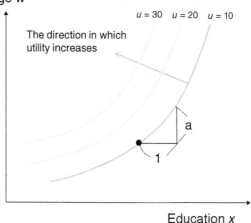

the original utility, we need to raise the worker's wage by a, as shown in the figure. This means that, for example, if $a = \$500$, then, to compensate the worker for attending one more year of school, we would need to increase his or her wage (monthly salary) by $500. This value a is just the slope of the indifference curve (the larger a is, the larger the slope is). Summarizing our work so far, we know

a(the slope of the indifference curve) = the increase in the wage needed to compensate the worker for an additional year of school

In plain English, this means the following.

The **slope of the indifference curve** = the psychological cost of studying (the **cost of signaling**).

We now impose another important assumption.

Assumption 2: as the worker's ability (type θ) increases, the cost of studying (signaling) decreases.

For people with high ability, attending an extra year of school is not that painful; however, for people with low ability, attending an additional year of school is very unpleasant and isn't worth it unless it increases their future wage a lot. Since the slope of the indifference curve captures the psychological cost of studying, we can depict assumption 2 graphically, as shown in Figure 9.2.

Figure 9.2 shows an indifference curve I_L for a worker with low ability (productivity) and an indifference curve I_H for a worker with high ability (productivity). In this figure, the slope of I_H is lower than the slope of I_L, which implies that the cost of studying (x) is lower for the high-ability worker. This is exactly what we stated in assumption 2. If assumption 2 holds, then the

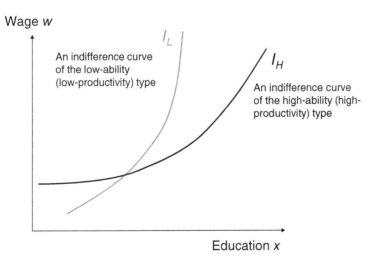

Wage w

An indifference curve of the low-ability (low-productivity) type

I_L

I_H

An indifference curve of the high-ability (high-productivity) type

Education x

Figure 9.2 As the type becomes higher, the cost of signaling becomes lower (single-crossing condition)

indifference curves of the various types of agents will intersect at most once, like those in Figure 9.2. For this reason, economists call assumption 2 the **single-crossing condition**. As we will see below, the single-crossing condition ensures we can incentivize high-type workers and low-type workers to send different signals.

Under these assumptions, suppose we give the workers a choice between the following two options:

A: high education, high wage;
B: low education, low wage.

If the workers with high productivity choose A and the workers with low productivity choose B, then,

> by looking at a worker's level of education, we can infer the worker's productivity (higher education signals higher productivity).

For this to work, there must be a certain relationship between alternatives A and B. Let's look at Figure 9.3.

Suppose that workers with low productivity choose point B of Figure 9.3 (a). What point will workers with high productivity choose? (We will call this "point A.") In order to determine the answer to this question, for each type of worker we draw an indifference curve passing through point B (see Figure 9.3 (b)). The curve I_L in the figure is the indifference curve containing point B for a worker with low productivity. Any point along this indifference curve gives a low-productivity worker the same utility as point B does. The points to the bottom right of this curve give a low-productivity worker less utility than point B does. Therefore, we have the following.

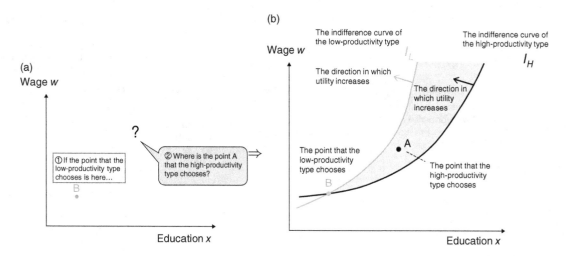

Figure 9.3 The condition for different types to choose different signals

Point A is to the bottom-right of the indifference curve I_L $\Rightarrow$ the low-productivity worker will prefer point B to point A.

On the other hand, I_H is an indifference curve for a high-productivity worker and contains point B, so the points in the top-left region relative to this curve give a high-productivity worker a higher level of utility than point B does. Therefore we have the following.

Point A is to the top left of the indifference curve I_H $\Rightarrow$ the high-productivity worker will prefer point A to point B.

In other words, *if point A lies somewhere in the gray region* of Figure 9.3 (b), then

- *a low-productivity worker will choose point B (low education, low wage);*
- *a high-productivity worker will choose point A (high education, high wage);* and,
- *as a consequence, if we look at a worker's educational background, we can deduce that worker's productivity.*

In information economics, when different types choose different observable actions, we call it **self-selection**. Figure 9.3 (b) shows the region in which self-selection occurs.

In order to improve our understanding, let's consider a concrete example and suppose that point B represents a high school graduate and point A represents a college graduate. I want you to look at Figure 9.4. If the wage for a college graduate is too high, as at point A' in the figure, then both the low-ability and high-ability types will choose to go to college. In this

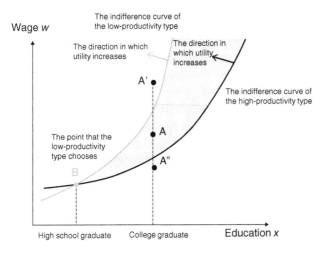

Figure 9.4 The wage of college graduates cannot be too high or too low

case, we can't use educational experience as a signal to differentiate between the types. Conversely, if the college graduate doesn't earn much more than the high school graduate, as at point A'' in the figure, then neither the low-ability nor the high-ability types will choose to go to college. Again, we can't use educational experience as a signal to differentiate between the types. For us to be able to look at a worker's educational experience and know his or her ability, it's necessary that the wage of college graduates be at an appropriate level that is neither too high nor too low. The range of acceptable wages is shown in the gray portion of Figure 9.4.

We can generalize the insights that we have obtained from this model in the following way.

Principle of Signaling

If someone can take an action (signal) that is

- beneficial for herself, but
- costly for people with a different type,

then she can reveal her type (private information) to others.

In the above example, the action of going to college (and as a result, receiving a high wage) is beneficial for people of the high-productivity type, but is costly for people of the other type. Therefore, the action of going to college works as a signal: people who go to college are, in effect, saying "I am a high-productivity type."

There is a wide range of examples in which we see the principle of signaling being used. Let me summarize some representative examples (see Table 9.2).

Table 9.2 Real examples of signaling

Private information (type)	Signal
Productivity	Educational background
A firm's solvency	Dividend
Quality of a new product	Expensive advertisements
Probability of an accident	Insurance deductible
Is he taking the job interview seriously?	Suit and tie
Is it a strong male?	Huge horns

Let's reiterate the basic mechanism through which signaling works.

The Mechanism through which Signaling Works

There is a cost for the action that functions as a signal.

- *The cost of signaling* (or the benefits that a person receives from sending a signal) *differs depending on* a person's private information (*type*).
- Therefore, only people of *the type for which the cost is low* (or the benefit is large) will *send a signal*. This means that, if a person sends a signal, we know his or her type.

Let's confirm this by looking at the examples in Table 9.2 one by one, starting at the top.

- **A firm's solvency**: a firm's financial status (sometimes called its solvency) depends on how much cash revenue it brings in. The firm knows its own revenue, but it is not directly observable to outside investors. Even a firm that is about to go bankrupt can sometimes hide this fact. In this example, dividends, which are cash payments to owners of the firm's stock, can function as a signal of the firm's solvency. Firms that are bringing in a lot of revenue can easily afford to pay dividends, but firms that aren't earning much money cannot.
- **Advertisements:** the next example provides an interesting insight into the question "What do advertisements communicate?" Oftentimes commercials and advertisements for new brands feature a popular celebrity, but what is the point of this? Since it lacks name recognition, when it introduces itself the brand wants to communicate that its product is high-quality, as well as to encourage people to give it a try. But, if that is the company's goal, wouldn't it be more effective to show experts' opinions on the product? An important point to note is that it costs a lot of money to have a celebrity appear in an advertisement, and most people understand this. Therefore, by hiring a celebrity to appear with its product, the company demonstrates that it is confident in its product. If it invests heavily in advertisements with celebrity appearances but the quality of the new product is bad and therefore people don't become repeat customers, the company stands to lose a lot of money. Knowing this, potential customers will think that celebrity appearances in advertisements signal that the new product has a good quality.[1]
- **Insurance deductibles**: the next example comes from the insurance industry. As I explained in Case Study 8.1 in Chapter 8, Section 8.2, insurance policies usually don't cover the entire cost of an accident but, instead, require the policyholders to pay some amount out of pocket. This amount is called the "deductible." For example, if the deductible is $300 and the cost of the

---

[1] In contrast, it doesn't cost a lot of money for a company to hire an expert to say "This brand's product is very good." Since such an advertisement is cheap, not only the firms with high-quality products but also those with low-quality products would want to use it, if it ever encouraged people to buy the new product. In other words, cheap advertisements do not work to signal high-quality. It may seem odd at first that we see very few commercials featuring experts who directly speak to the product's quality, while many commercials with popular celebrities who say almost nothing about the product's quality. But, according to the theory of signaling, the latter type of commercial would better communicate the quality of the product to consumers.

damage is $5,000, the policyholder will pay $300 and the insurance company will pay $4,700. If you look at an insurance company's pamphlet, you'll see several plans with different deductibles that people can choose from. Generally, less expensive policies have larger deductibles. Even though the customer knows (to some extent) how prone she is to having an accident, the insurance company has no idea. However, for safe drivers, it makes more sense to purchase a cheaper plan with higher deductibles, since accidents will probably be rare. Therefore, if we observe that someone purchases a plan with high deductibles, we can infer that she is likely to be a safe driver. In this way, the plan the customer chooses becomes a signal of how accident-prone she is.[2]

Table 9.2 also provides two non-market examples in which signaling occurs.

- **Suits and ties**: why do we wear a jacket and this funny string around our necks when we have a job interview? Actually, the fact that ties are uncomfortable to wear *might well be* the reason we wear them. Since a full suit is not comfortable, compared to T-shirts, for example, it can function as a signal that you are seriously interested in the job. I want you to look back at the box labeled "The Mechanism through which Signaling Works." The benefit of signaling is very high if you are keen to get the job offer. By wearing a suit and tie, you can communicate that you are taking the interview seriously.
- **Deer's huge antlers**: our final example is taken from biology. There are certain species of deer whose males grow very large antlers. For a long time people have been puzzled about the purpose the antlers serve. They don't seem to have any use, but, according to the theory of natural selection, they must offer some benefit. One interesting theory is that the antlers are actually not useful at all, just costly. The only function of the antlers is to signal the male deer's strengths, such as his immunity to viruses, to female deer. Female deer prefer to mate with strong males, but without antlers there would be little way for female deer to visually distinguish between a strong male and a weak male. Since having large antlers is just a hindrance, males that afford large antlers must be more fit and resilient than those without such large antlers. In biology, they call this idea of signaling the "**handicap principle**." Even in fields such as biology, we see interesting applications of game theory!

9.3   Signaling Equilibrium in the Labor Market

I want you to look back at Figure 9.3 (b) in the previous section. If the options "high education, high wage" (A) and "low education, low wage" (B) are judiciously positioned as in the figure, high-productivity workers will choose A and low-productivity workers will choose B. Consequently, we can deduce a worker's productivity (which is private information) by looking at his or her educational background. Now, how are points A and B determined?

---

[2] We saw in Chapter 8, Section 8.2, that insurance deductibles help to solve the problem of moral hazard. Since the policyholder bears some cost from an accident, she will make an effort to avoid getting into accidents. However, we've now seen that insurance deductibles also help to solve the problem of adverse selection, since they can help insurance companies elicit the probability of the policyholder having an accident.

In order to answer this question, we'll turn to a model of the labor market invented by the economist Michael Spence (b. 1943). Spence was a pioneer of analyzing economic problems involving asymmetric information and was the first to model the equilibria of a labor market with asymmetric information. For these contributions, he was awarded the Nobel Prize, which he shared with George Akerlof, whom I introduced in Section 9.1. Let me explain Spence's model using Figure 9.5. This is a two-stage model in which

(1) first, the worker observes her own type (ability or productivity) and then chooses her level of education; and,
(2) next, the firm offers the worker a wage after looking at her level of education.

Allow me to explain each phase in more detail.

First, when the worker is young, she learns her type (ability). Our model formulates the situation where people *share a common understanding of the relationship between education level and wage*. These expectations are modeled by the function that describes the relationship between level of education x and wage w,

$$w = w(x).$$

Figure 9.6 (a) shows an example of a curve that represents society's expectations about the wages corresponding to different levels of education. As you can see from the figure, a young person who is deciding on how many years of education to receive understands that high school graduates earn \$50,000 a year and college graduates earn \$75,000 a year. Knowing this, she will choose the level of education (and wage) that suits her best.

If a young person can freely choose any point along the curve shown in Figure 9.6 (a), which point would he or she choose? Figure 9.6 (b) shows the answer. The figure shows several indifference curves for a worker with high ability. Note that the indifference curves that are closer to the top left are associated with higher levels of utility, since the worker prefers less

Figure 9.5 Spence's signaling model of the labor market

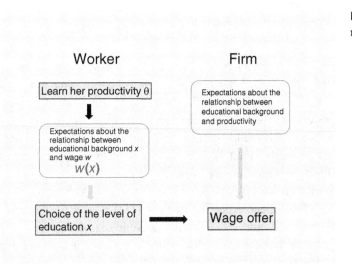

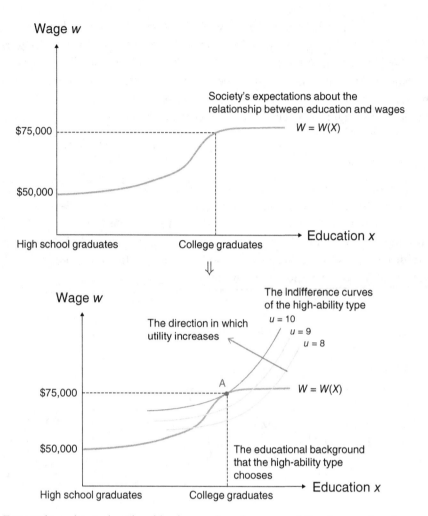

Figure 9.6 Expectations about educational backgrounds and wages, and the chosen education

studying (low x) and higher wages (high w). Along the curve $w = w(x)$ showing the relationship between education and wages, *the high-ability type likes point A most, since this is the point at which the curve $w = w(x)$ and the worker's indifference curve are tangent to one another.* Therefore, high-ability types choose the level of education corresponding to point A – i.e. they graduate from college. The point that the low-ability type chooses, although it is not shown in the figure, is determined analogously. That is, it is the point of tangency between the curve $w = w(x)$ and the low-ability type's indifference curve.

Now, let me make a remark that is a bit detailed, but is important. Although a young person with high ability chooses to go to college expecting to earn $75,000 after graduation, as shown in Figure 9.6 (b), when she graduates and gets a job it's possible that she doesn't actually earn $75,000 as expected. It's possible that she earns, for example, just $70,000. If her expectations turn out to be wrong, then she (and eventually society) will form new expectations about the relationship between education and wages. In other words, the original curve $w = w(x)$ in Figure 9.6 will be replaced by a new curve. Young people in the next generation will make their decisions about how much education to earn based on these new expectations. If this generation's expectations are proved wrong, then society once again adjusts its expectations. This process is repeated generation after generation. Eventually, the process may reach a point at which *society's expectations about the relationship between education and wages is stable from generation to generation*. At that time, young people's *expectations about their wages will be exactly correct*. We will now discuss such an "equilibrium" state in more detail.

Comment 9.1 Why Do We Care about an Equilibrium State?

From now on, we are going to *analyze* how the workers' private information about their ability can be communicated *using the equilibrium state*. (In what follows, I will give the precise condition for an equilibrium state.) You might doubt whether the actual outcome is always the equilibrium state in which everyone's expectations are proved correct. You might also be thinking that it makes more sense to analyze the adjustment process I described above in order to determine the sort of equilibrium that emerges.

Your point is well taken, but consider the following two situations:

- a situation in which people's expectations are always wrong, wages change frequently, and, consequently, people of the same type choose different levels of education from one generation to the next; and
- a situation in which people's expectations are correct most of the time, wages are fairly stable, and people of the same type choose the same levels of education from one generation to the next.

It seems that what we see in reality resembles the second situation. The equilibria that I am going to present are useful when describing and explaining this second kind of "stable" situation. You are right that we should also consider the adjustment process described by the first situation, but economists have not yet reached an agreement as to the kind of model that is suited to describing and analyzing the adjustment process, because it is much more complicated than the "stable" equilibrium state.

Next, let me explain how the wage is determined. What happens if some workers enter the labor market as college graduates, as in Figure 9.6? Since firms cannot directly observe the workers' true ability (asymmetric information), firms form expectations about how productive the average college graduate is. In general, we can assume that firms (and society in general) share the same *expectations about the productivity of the average college graduate*. As a concrete example, let's consider what happens if all firms share the belief that a college graduate's productivity is worth approximately $75,000 a year. What this means is that, if a firm hires a college graduate, it expects its annual profits to increase by $75,000. In this case, firms will

Figure 9.7 Signaling equilibrium in a labor market

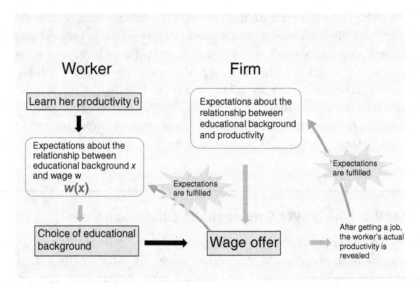

compete for the worker's services by offering as large a salary as possible (up to $75,000). The outcome of this competition between firms is that

$$wage = expected\,productivity.$$

That is, the salary for college graduates will be $75,000, which is equal to the expected productivity of a college graduate.[3]

Now, what does equilibrium in the labor market in the Spence model look like? Please take a look at Figure 9.7.

The equilibrium described in the figure works as follows. First, workers learn their own ability (productivity) when they are young. Then, given the prevailing expectations about the relationship between education and wages, they choose the level of education that suits them best. Here, note that, since the cost of studying differs depending on one's ability, it's possible that people with different abilities will choose different levels of education. Now, suppose that people with high ability choose to go to college expecting that, after they graduate, firms will offer them jobs paying $75,000. In the equilibrium, the workers' expectations about their wages are exactly correct, and the firms will indeed offer college graduates jobs paying $75,000. Why do firms offer that wage to college graduates? This is because, in the equilibrium, firms correctly anticipate that college graduates are worth $75,000 (= their productivity). After hiring workers, the firms can observe the workers' actual productivities, and, in the equilibrium, they find that their expectations were correct: it turns out that a worker's productivity is indeed worth

---

[3] If all firms offer a wage of $70,000 to college graduates, then each firm can hire college graduates and earn 75,000 − 70,000 = $5,000 of profit per worker. But, if one firm unilaterally offers a wage that is slightly more than $70,000, then all college graduates will choose to work for this firm, and the firm can (almost) monopolize the profit of $5,000 per worker that was spread among the other firms. The wage gradually increases in this manner, up until the point that all firms offer $75,000 to college graduates. This is the same reason that the price is equal to the marginal cost and firms earn zero profits in the Bertrand model.

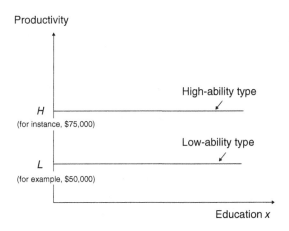

Figure 9.8 The relationship between productivity and education level

$75,000, as anticipated. This is the equilibrium state, in which both workers' and firms' expectations are fulfilled.

As I argued before in Comment 9.1, I think it's safe to say that, in the real world, we are in a state in which people's expectations are correct most of the time, wages are fairly stable, and people of the same type choose the same levels of education from one generation to the next. In this case, we can view society as being in the equilibrium state (called a signaling equilibrium) shown in Figure 9.7.

In what follows, I'll explain how such an equilibrium is determined. In order to make our analysis and conclusions as clear as possible, let's also impose the following assumption.

Assumption 3: education does not increase productivity at all. (See Figure 9.8.)

According to this assumption, education does not increase a worker's productivity at all. Education is just a pain in the neck, and all it does is to cause the students to suffer from studying difficult materials and completing demanding assignments. (Let me say one word here: how about a microeconomics class? Does this assumption make sense to you? And, if microeconomics does not really increase your productivity after finding a job, why do you study it? I'll explain this in greater detail in Comment 9.4.) Now that we've done the preparation, let's solve for the equilibria in this job market signaling model.

① Signaling Equilibrium where Workers' Types Are Revealed: Separating Equilibria

First, we consider a particular class of equilibria such that the following apply.

Workers with low productivity (the low type) choose the education level x_L and receive the wage w_L.
Workers with high productivity (the high type) choose a different education level x_H and receive the wage w_H.

Figure 9.9 How are the points, (x_L, w_L) and (x_H, w_H), that each type chooses in a separating equilibrium determined?

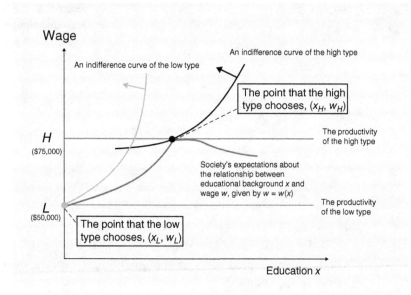

In other words, in these equilibria, since the different types choose different levels of education, which the firms can observe, *a worker's education level functions as a signal that communicates the worker's productivity (which initially only he or she knows) to the firms.* Equilibria in which private information is revealed because different types choose different actions (signals) are called **separating equilibria**.

The points that each type chooses under a separating equilibrium, (x_L, w_L) and (x_H, w_H), are determined as shown in Figure 9.9.

The following two conditions describe how the separating equilibrium outcomes, (x_L, w_L) and (x_H, w_H), are determined. Let's check by taking a closer look at Figure 9.9.

Conditions for a Separating Equilibrium

(I) Each type's indifference curves are tangent to the curve $w = w(x)$ (which expresses society's expectations about the wages corresponding to varying levels of education) at the distinct points (x_L, w_L) and (x_H, w_H).

(II) The point that the high types choose, (x_H, w_H), lies on the horizontal line that expresses the productivity of the high types; and, similarly, the point that the low types choose, (x_L, w_L), lies on the horizontal line that expresses the productivity of the low types.

Now I will show that conditions (I) and (II) imply that we have indeed obtained a signaling equilibrium as described in Figure 9.7. In what follows, I will explicitly state the equilibrium conditions that are informally described in Figure 9.7, and check those conditions one by one. In order to make my explanation more concrete, let's assume that the education level that the high types choose, x_H, is a college degree and the education level that the low types choose, x_L, is a high school diploma.

*Checking the Equilibrium Conditions described in Figure 9.7.

[1] The workers' optimal behavior: the workers of each type are choosing their optimal level of education based on their expectations about the relationship between education and wages given by the curve $w = w(x)$. (As explained in detail in Figure 9.6, for each type the optimal point is the point at which that type's indifference curve is tangent to the curve $w = w(x)$.)

That is, it's optimal for the low type to choose a high school diploma (x_L), which is expected to provide a wage of $50,000, while it is optimal for the high type to choose a college degree (x_H), which is expected to provide a wage of $75,000.

[2] The firms' optimal behavior: as a result of the decisions made in part [1], the workers in the labor market have one of two possible educational backgrounds: each worker is either a college graduate or a high school graduate. Note that, in Figure 9.9, the firms in the market offer a wage of $50,000 $(= w_L)$ to the high school graduates and offer a wage of $75,000 $(= w_H)$ to the college graduates. Although it is not depicted in Figure 9.9, the reason for this is that the *firms expect that the productivity of a high school graduate is worth $50,000 and the productivity of a college graduate is worth $75,000.* Under these expectations, the firms compete optimally for workers through their wage offers, and in the end their *wage offers are equal to the expected productivity.* (Give Footnote 3 another read if this is not clear to you.)

[3] The workers' and firm's expectations are fulfilled: the points (x_L, w_L) and (x_H, w_H) that are realized in the market *fulfill the expectations of the workers and the firms.* First, the workers' expectations that high school graduates will earn $50,000 and college graduates will earn $75,000 prove to be correct. The firms provide a wage of $50,000 for high school graduates, expecting that their productivity is equal to $50,000, which proves to be correct. The firms also provide a wage of $75,000 for college graduates, expecting that their productivity is equal to $75,000, which also proves to be correct.

You may find that the concept of a signaling equilibrium is more difficult to understand than the concept of a market equilibrium, in which price and quantity are determined simply by the intersection of demand and supply. If that is what you feel, please note that the equilibrium conditions (I) and (II) determine three things: the high type's choice (x_H, w_H), the low type's choice (x_L, w_L), and the society's expectations about the relationship between education level and wage, which is represented by function $w = w(x)$. Please read the comments that follow.

Comment 9.2 Where Does the Curve $w = w(x)$ Come From?

Isn't this one of the first thoughts you have when you look at the signaling equilibrium shown in Figure 9.9: *"The strangely-shaped curve $w = w(x)$ claims to show people's expectations about the relationship between education and wages, but where does it come from?"* The answer is that it is the result of the adjustment process described in Comment 9.1. That is, society has a rough idea of the salaries that are paid to high school graduates, junior college graduates, college graduates, graduate school graduates, and so on. If people take actions according to these expectations but the actual salaries that they receive are dramatically different, their expectations (and hence the curve $w = w(x)$) are going to be revised. The curve shown in Figure 9.9 emerges over time as *people's expectations and their actual salaries gradually get closer and closer together through these repeated adjustments.*

As you will see if you think about this a little, in an equilibrium, this curve (i.e. society's *equilibrium expectations* about the relationship between education and wages) *cannot be uniquely determined*. In fact, there are many possibilities. In short, there are many different curves $w = w(x)$ that satisfy conditions (I) and (II), and any of those curves could be society's expectations in some equilibrium (that is, *there are many equilibria* satisfying (I) and (II)).

To understand this idea, please take a look at Figure 9.10. In this figure, there are various possible expectations curves a, b, and c, which each result in the same outcomes, (x_L, w_L) and (x_H, w_H), that we saw previously in Figure 9.9. Each of these results in the same separating equilibrium. (You can check that conditions (I) and (II) for a separating equilibrium are satisfied.) The reason that there can be different expectations, each resulting in the same separating equilibrium, is that in this society *every person is either a high school graduate (x_L) or a college graduate (x_H), so there is no clear way for society to pin down the wage to expect for the educational level that nobody chooses.* For example, in a society that has expectations represented by the curve a shown in Figure 9.10, it may be that the expected wage for graduate school graduates is high because, before society settled in the equilibrium in which all people are either high school or college graduates, there were some people who went to graduate school, were extremely productive, and received very high wages. In contrast, in a society that has expectations

Figure 9.10 Various expectations a, b, and c, which all result in the same outcome: (x_L, w_L) and (x_H, w_H)

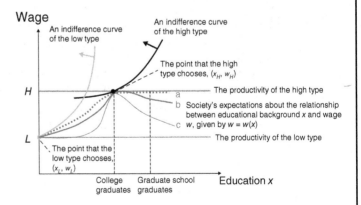

represented by the curves b and c shown in Figure 9.10, it may be that the wages for previous graduate school graduates were low or that society developed the stereotype that people who go to graduate school are "weirdos" and "useless" in the business world. When society settles in the equilibrium state in which nobody attends graduate school, there's no way to erase that stereotype.

Figure 9.10 shows that there can be multiple sets of expectations that result in the same outcome, but, if expectations change dramatically, the equilibrium outcomes that result also change. Please read the next comment.

Comment 9.3 There Are Many Outcomes that Can Result from Separating Equilibria

Even in otherwise identical societies, if people have different expectations they may settle on different equilibria. Please look at Figure 9.11.

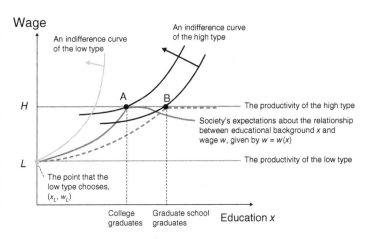

Figure 9.11 There are many outcomes that can result from separating equilibria

Point A in this figure is the point that the high-productivity types chose in the separating equilibrium that we saw before in Figure 9.9. Now, suppose that society's expectations about the relationship between education and wages changes to the dashed curve. In this case, the optimal point that the high-productivity types choose changes from A to A'. The resulting state is also a separating equilibrium. The reason is that this situation also satisfies conditions (I) and (II) for a separating equilibrium, as you saw previously.[4] Indeed, any situation that satisfies these two conditions is a separating equilibrium.[5]

---

[4] In order to further enhance your understanding, it would be good to check that the separating equilibrium conditions hold in this new state, just as we did for Figure 9.9.

[5] *A very detailed remark*: if it is well known that workers' productivity is either L ($50,000) or H ($75,000), then the expected wage of any worker should be between these two values. Therefore, in a rigorous game-theoretic analysis, we add the condition $L \le w(x) \le H$ for any x to conditions (I) and (II).

Comment 9.3 (cont.)

In a society with the expectations given by the dashed curve, in order for high-productivity people to demonstrate their ability to the firms, they need to go even further and attain a master's degree. The reason for this is that, since everyone expects that the wage for college graduates is not very high, all people with high productivity will continue on to master's degrees. In Japan, most students who study science, technology, engineering, and mathematics (STEM) fields continue on to master's degrees, while students who study the social sciences and humanities finish with a bachelor's degree. This could be due to the nature of these fields, but it could also be due to the fact that we have different equilibria for STEM students and social science/humanities students. In the social sciences and humanities, there are self-fulfilling expectations (equilibrium) that high-ability students stop after finishing college and those who continue to master's programs are "weirdos." (Note that the gray curve going through point A in Figure 9.11 slopes downward after the college graduate mark.) Similarly, in the STEM fields, there may be another self-fulfilling expectation that high-ability students continue to master's programs.

One of the most important lessons we should learn is that, in the "signaling model," in which people with private information take certain actions in order to signal their types to others, there can be many different equilibria. Which equilibrium is actually realized depends on the society's history – that is, what kinds of expectations people formed, and how those expectations were adjusted or revised over time.

There are *many possible equilibria* in the signaling model, and it is even possible that different equilibria are realized in otherwise identical societies.

This is one of the important insights from information economics.

Comment 9.4 Is It True that a Master's Degree in Economics Provides a High Income because Economics Is Useful?

Relative to other people, people with master's degrees in economics have higher incomes. In general, there is a positive correlation between education and wages. (*If we look at the data, people with more education earn higher wages.*) Since a worker's wage is determined by his or her productivity, we might be tempted to interpret this correlation as evidence that

"education increases productivity."

However, if we use the principles from information economics that we've learned in this section, we will discover the *truly surprising possibility* that this interpretation may be totally incorrect. Please look at Figure 9.8, which shows the relationship between education and productivity in the model that we analyzed previously.

In our model, education does not increase a worker's productivity at all. Nevertheless, we observe that, in the equilibrium outcome, the people with more education are more productive. The reason for this is that, in our model, there are people who were born with high productivities and people who were born with low productivities. *Education* does not affect people's productivity, but it does work to *sort out people with different levels of productivity*.

Do people with master's degrees in economics earn high incomes because they have learned valuable skills that raise their productivity, or is it the case that studying economics is inherently useless but acts as a *screening device* that separates students with different abilities? It is up to you to decide!

② Signaling Equilibrium where Workers' Types Are Hidden: Pooling Equilibria

In our analysis so far, we've seen that it's possible for the level of education that people choose to act as a signal that communicates their productivity (which only the workers themselves know) to the firms. However, in the signaling model of labor markets, there also exist equilibria in which everyone chooses the same education level regardless of their type, so the workers' private information (their productivity) is not communicated to firms. Such equilibria are called **pooling equilibria**.

Figure 9.12 shows how the educational background and wage (x^*, w^*) that every person picks is determined in a pooling equilibrium.

This figure conveys the two conditions for a pooling equilibrium.

Wage

Figure 9.12 Pooling equilibrium

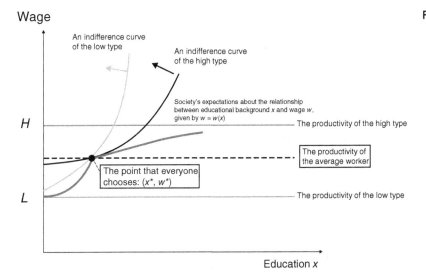

An indifference curve of the low type

An indifference curve of the high type

Society's expectations about the relationship between educational background x and wage w, given by $w = w(x)$

H — The productivity of the high type

The productivity of the average worker

The point that everyone chooses: (x^*, w^*)

L — The productivity of the low type

Education x

Conditions for a Pooling Equilibrium

(i)   Regardless of type, each person's indifference curve is tangent to the curve $w = w(x)$ (which expresses people's expectations about the relationship between education and wages) at the same point (x^*, w^*).

(ii) The point that every person chooses, (x^*, w^*), lies on the horizontal line that expresses the productivity of the average person in society.

Now, let's check why Figure 9.12 shows an equilibrium outcome. Let's assume that the productivity of a high type is worth $75,000, the productivity of a low type is worth $50,000, and that half of society are high types while the other half of society are low types. In this case, the productivity of the average worker is worth $62,500. In a pooling equilibrium, this is the wage that everyone receives.

*Checking the Equilibrium Conditions

[1] Workers' optimal behavior

The workers of each type choose their optimal level of education based on their expectations about the relationship between education and wages given by the curve $w = w(x)$. For each type, the optimal point is the point at which that type's indifference curve is tangent to the curve $w = w(x)$, which happens at the same point: (x^*, w^*).

[2] Firms' optimal behavior

As a result, everyone who enters the labor market has the same educational background. In Figure 9.12, the firms in the labor market offer a wage of $62,500 to the workers. Although it is not depicted in Figure 9.12, the reason for this is that the firms also expect that the average productivity of a junior college graduate is worth $62,500. Under these expectations, the firms compete optimally for workers through their wage offers, and in the end their wage offers are equal to the expected productivity: $62,500.

[3] The workers' and firm's expectations are fulfilled

The point (x^*, w^*) that is realized in the market *fulfills the expectations of the workers and the firms*. First, the workers' expectations to earn $62,500 proves to be correct. In addition, the firms' expectations that the average worker's productivity is worth $62,500 also proves to be correct. If firms look at the productivities of the workers that they hire, they will see that the productivities of half their workers are worth $75,000 and the productivities of the other half of their workers are worth $50,000. Therefore, the average productivity of one of their workers is worth $62,500, as expected.

Just as there can be many possible separating equilibria, *there can be many possible pooling equilibria*. In short, any outcome satisfying conditions (i) and (ii) is a pooling equilibrium. (You can deepen your understanding of this by drawing a figure depicting a pooling equilibrium that is different from the one shown in Figure 9.12.)

Case Study 9.1 MBAs

In the United States, people typically earn much higher salaries after earning a master's in business administration (MBA).

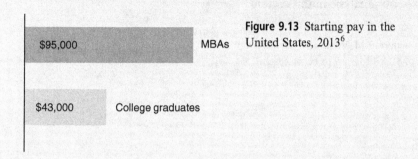

Figure 9.13 Starting pay in the United States, 2013[6]

In MBA programs there is a lot of reading and homework, and students need to study very hard over the course of the two years. Why do MBA graduates earn approximately $50,000 more than college graduates? Is it that an MBA education increases workers' productivities? Or, as we saw in Comment 9.4, is it that the rigor of MBA programs works as a mechanism to sort and identify people with inherently high ability, even though an MBA education does nothing to increase a worker's productivity?

Since it's difficult to imagine that just two years of education can increase a worker's productivity so substantially, it seems reasonable to believe that a significant reason for MBA graduates' high salaries is that MBA programs sort and identify people with inherently high ability. In contrast, although there has been a trend of establishing MBA programs in Japan, it's not the case that Japanese MBA graduates earn $50,000 more than Japanese college graduates. Why not? In order to come up with an answer, let's reinterpret the model we have just seen in this section by making the following changes:

- workers → people who go to college;
- high type → college students with especially high management ability;
- low type → ordinary college students.

In this context, we can think of the American situation as being a **separating equilibrium** in which having an MBA signals that a person is a high type and we can think of the Japanese situation as being a **pooling equilibrium** in which all people earn college degrees and (practically) nobody earns an MBA.

Once a society gets stuck in an equilibrium, it is difficult to change. In order to create a tradition of MBA programs in Japanese society, a virtuous cycle, as in Figure 9.14, needs to arise. To create

---

[6] Graduate Management Admission Council, "Corporate Recruiters Survey 2013," (Reston, VA: Graduate Management Admission Council, 2013).

Case Study 9.1 (cont.)

such a cycle, it's not sufficient for Japanese universities to establish MBA programs and to work hard to improve these programs. *Society's expectations must also change.* This is the major insight of our analysis in this section.

Figure 9.14 Virtuous cycle for an MBA program to be successful

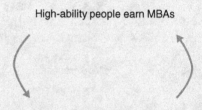

High-ability people earn MBAs

People with MBAs earn higher salaries

If MBA degrees had no signaling effect but an MBA education actually raised workers' productivities by as much as $50,000, then the MBA graduates' salaries would rise quickly in Japan; but this is not happening. The fact that it takes time for MBA programs to develop a reputation for sending out highly productive workers can be taken as evidence that the theory of signaling accurately captures the function of MBA degrees.

10   Last but Not Least: Let's Talk about Social Justice and Philosophy

It's been a long journey, but we have finally covered the basics of economic analysis. Now that you have learned the analytical tools (theoretical models) we use in economics, I believe that you have gained a strong understanding of how society allocates resources via the market mechanism. However, that is not the end of the story. The theoretical models you learned also give you deep insights into such questions as "Is our society doing the right things?" and "What should we do to make our society better?" Those are the questions about social justice and social philosophy. At the beginning of this book I promised that, after you learn the basic principles of economics, you will gain a new perspective on our society. In this final chapter, I am going to elaborate on this promise.

10.1   The Root of Our Disagreements about Social Justice: The Moral Standards of Community and the Moral Standards of Markets

First, please consider the following statements.

- Many problems in today's society are due to the fact that the only thing firms care about is earning higher profits. Society would be better off if firms cared about *the common good*.
- Society would be better off if people *worked for each other* and not just for themselves.
- We should abolish inequality between the rich and the poor; we ought to *share things equally*.

Don't you feel these statements resonate with you? These claims are based on **the moral standards of community**, which are principles about how we should treat people we are close to, such as family, friends, and neighbors. In the twentieth century almost a half of the world's countries attempted to use those principles to organize their economies. These socialist and communist countries used planned/command economies. Figure 10.1 shows a world map from the Cold War era during the 1960s.

The "aligned with West" corresponds to the capitalist countries that had market-based economies, such as the United States, nations in western Europe, and Japan. Conversely, the

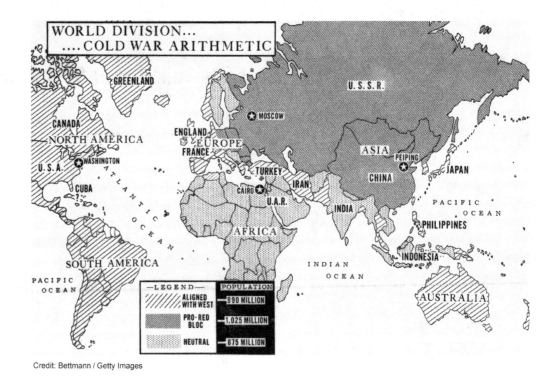

Credit: Bettmann / Getty Images

Figure 10.1 The world during the Cold War era (1960s)

"pro-red block" corresponds to the countries that had planned economies, such as the Soviet Union, China, and others in eastern Europe such as Poland and Hungary. The "aligned with West" was commonly referred to as the "West" and the "pro-red block" was commonly referred to as the "East." Although there was never a large-scale armed conflict, tensions were high and there was constant friction between the East and the West over economics, politics, and culture. For this reason, this period was known as **the Cold War**. During this time Germany was divided into "West Germany," which was aligned with the West, and "East Germany," which was aligned with the East. In fact, the capital city of Berlin, which was located in East Germany, was itself divided in two: West Berlin, belonging to West Germany, and East Berlin, belonging to East Germany. A large and heavily guarded wall divided the city and the movement of people was severely restricted.

Initially, the countries with planned economies achieved some remarkable success, but eventually their economies began to fail and the communist regimes collapsed. By the end of the twentieth century most of these countries had transitioned to capitalism. Figure 10.2 is a photo of the fall of the Berlin Wall on November 9, 1989. The fall of the wall was hugely significant and symbolized the fall of communism and illiberal government. We can see in the photo that Germans were enthusiastic about reunification.

An unmistakable lesson from this period is that the moral standards of community, when used as the principles that underpin an economy (communism), fare much worse than **the moral standards of markets** (capitalism).

Now, what exactly are the moral standards of community and the moral standards of markets that previously divided the whole world into two opposing groups? If we use the

Figure 10.2 The fall of the Berlin Wall.

Credit: Colin Campbell (Hulton Archive) / Getty Images

Table 10.1 It is often the case that helping in a community is like the prisoner's dilemma

	cooperation	selfish action
cooperation	3, 3	−1, 4
selfish action	4, −1	0, 0

Everyone is worse off if they pursue only their own self-interest

theoretical models of economics that we've learned so far, surprisingly, we can gain a clear understanding of the key differences between these competing philosophies. In what follows, allow me to explain in detail the kinds of insights into social philosophy that we can gather from the mathematical models we've studied.

(a)   What Are the Moral Standards of Community?

For much of the history of the human race, people lived in small communities. In these tight-knit communities, *helping close friends, relatives, and neighbors* was vital to the survival of the community. People knew each other well and were expected not to be lazy or selfish. Instead, they were supposed to work hard and freely share the fruits of their labor. Even in modern society, we know that we should behave like this around our family.

Table 10.1 captures an essential aspect of these pre-modern communities, where it is vital "not to be selfish."

You may notice that this is just a payoff matrix for the *prisoner's dilemma*.[1] The outcome that is best for the "community" is the state in which both players cooperate, and each earns a payoff of three. However, if one person unilaterally takes the selfish action, he or she increases her payoff from three to four. If we do not take any measures to eliminate that temptation, there is a risk that both players take the selfish action and, consequently, the two players – together and individually – earn very low payoffs (the Nash-equilibrium outcome that is circled is realized).

Table 10.1 is just a highly stylized example; in reality, working in a small community would be more complex and diverse. However, research in game theory has demonstrated that there are many real-life situations that are analogous to the prisoner's dilemma. Working together in a community involves a *small number of people whose payoff partly depends on what others will do*. This is exactly the type of situation that we study in game theory. In such a situation, *if each person takes the selfish action*, then society settles into *a Nash-equilibrium outcome*. We saw in Chapter 6 that Nash equilibrium outcomes are frequently *not socially (or Pareto-)efficient*. This is what we learned in detail when we initially studied game theory (please look back at Chapter 6, Section 6.2).

Why is it that Nash-equilibrium outcomes may not be socially efficient? If people pursue only their own self-interest, they don't take into account how their actions affect the well-being of others. People such as this will take any action that even marginally helps themselves, though it may be to the detriment of others. For instance, people might shirk group work or not return favors. If everyone takes these selfish actions, then everyone loses out. The major insight that we gain from applying game theory to various social and economic questions is that these sorts of situations (Nash equilibria brought about by self-interested behavior leading to a socially undesirable outcome) occur frequently.

Over time, communities must have figured out various ways to ensure that people cooperate and work for the common good. These are social norms or ethical obligations that:

- emphasize *compassion* for others and *public-mindedness*;
- *disapprove of* purely *self-interested behavior*; and
- promote *cooperation instead of competition*.

These social norms, which grew from the need to live harmoniously in small communities, form the basis for what I call **the moral standards of community**.

(b)   What Are the Moral Standards of Markets?

Over time, as economies have developed, a new set of moral standards – the moral standards of markets – has been introduced into our societies. The defining characteristic of modern society is that these new standards about markets govern so many aspects of our lives.

---

[1] In the table, player 1 chooses the top or bottom row, player 2 chooses the left or right column, and the numbers in each cell denote (player 1's payoff, player 2's payoff).

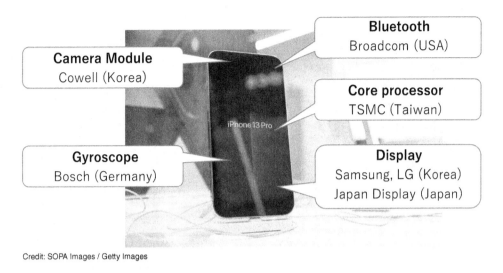

Credit: SOPA Images / Getty Images

Figure 10.3 Who produces smartphones (iPhone 13 Pro)?

Even in modern societies, *it is essential to help each other*, just as in primitive communities. However, today's society is built upon a network of help between an astronomical number of people who do not know each other. For example, if you stop reading and look around, almost every object you can see was produced by people whose names you don't know and whose faces you've never seen. Figure 10.3 shows how making a smartphone depends on different people around the world.

When you are using your smartphone, *you're enjoying the combined help* of a huge number of people from all around the world. Do you return the help to these faraway people who built your smartphone? If you are a part-time worker at a grocery store, you help the customers who shop there. Some of these customers might be bankers. If these bankers do a deal with Ford, Ford exports cars to Taiwan, and a Taiwanese worker who builds core processors for smartphones drives a Ford car to work, then your help at the grocery store eventually reaches one of the people who helped build your smartphone. In reality, the network of help would be much longer and more complicated. (In fact, we have no idea what the entire network looks like.) Nevertheless, there must be some way in which your work reaches the people who helped make your smartphone.

The market enables these kinds of network of help between an extraordinary number of people from all over with:

- dividing the chain of helping into small pieces (transactions in *many different markets* using the exchange of money); and
- *a clever use of "selfishness."*

As I explained in Chapter 3, consumers and producers pursue their own self-interest by considering the market price of different goods and deciding whether to buy or sell. They don't consider things such as "How can I give a hand to so-and-so?" or "Who needs help and where?" Still, through the market, society elegantly builds *a vast and complicated web of help* that brings together people who have never even heard of each other. With our theoretical models, we

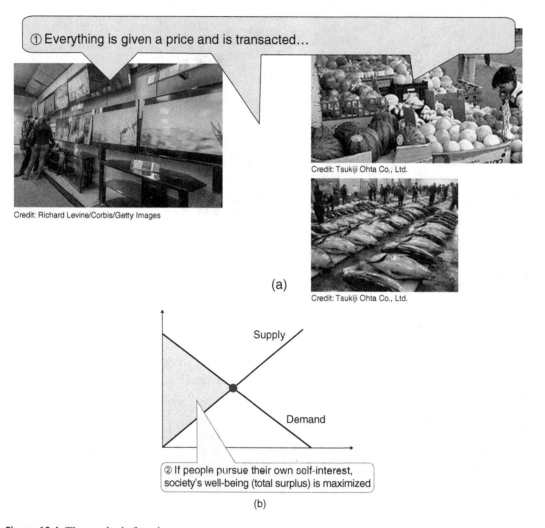

Figure 10.4 The market's function.
Source: Photo credit: Richard Levine/Corbis/Getty Images, Tsukiji Ohta Co., Ltd.

learned in detail about how this is achieved by the market mechanism, but Figure 10.4 gives a simple and concise summary.

For the market to be able to smoothly facilitate these interactions, it is important to

- allow for the *pursuit of one's own self-interest*;
- respect the *freedom of choice*, unrestricted by policy interventions or social conventions; and
- emphasize *fair competition*.

These are the values that form the basis for societies that extensively use market transactions.

What you've just read shows the **moral standards of markets**, which are quite different from the moral standards of community that emphasize compassion for others, disapprove of purely self-interested behavior, and promote cooperation over competition. In summary, we can say the following.

> Both the moral standards of community and the moral standards of markets suggest ways to *facilitate help* among members of society, but *the values that underpin these are in direct conflict.*

Our society is divided into groups that fight against each other about what is right and what is wrong, and the observation we have just made provides a sweeping way to understand why: the root of the disagreement is the *conflict between the moral standards of community, which reject self-interested behavior, and the moral standards of markets, which embrace self-interested behavior.* For example, the topics below, which are hotly debated in the media and on the Internet, can be seen as conflicts between the moral standards of community (the left-hand side) and the moral standards of markets (the right-hand side):

concerns about economic inequality	promotion of free market competition
anti-globalism	neoliberalism
conventional Asian social norms	American-style social norms

(c)   The Failure of Socialism and the Limits of the Moral Standards of Community

Let me summarize one of the main lessons from twentieth-century history. The basic idea of the communist regimes of the twentieth century was to *apply the moral standards of community* and its basic principles – compassion for others, disapproval of purely self-interested behavior, and cooperation over competition – *to governing the entire economy.* This was based on the highest standards of moral conscience and compassion for socially oppressed people, but in practice it failed. The centrally planned economies turned out to be hugely inefficient, and eventually stagnated. As we saw at the beginning of this chapter, many communist regimes had collapsed by the end of the century. This experience demonstrated that, perhaps surprisingly, *policies based on public-mindedness and working for the common good are not well suited for governing anything except for small, close-knit communities of people.*

Once again, recall the statements I put forward at the beginning of the chapter.

- Society would be better off if firms cared about *the common good*, not their profits.
- Society would be better off if people *worked for each other*, not just for themselves.

If you think those statements make sense but they are too idealistic to be true, you should realize that, all around you, there are places where these principles are actually put into action: government services! Recall your experiences with government services, and you'll immediately see the vast gap between reality and the ideals described above. Although there are many decent people who work in government (I will discuss this point in detail later), haven't you had a negative experience with a government service, such as at the post office or vehicle licencing agency, which you couldn't imagine happening at a private business? Please look at the following cartoon (Figure 10.5).

Figure 10.5 "Baito-kun" by Hasaichi Ishii (translation as provided by Author).
Source: Play Guide Journal Sha (1977); © Hisaichi Ishii.

This cartoon about buying prestigious super-express (*Shinkansen*) train tickets was published at a time when the Japan Railway Company, which was privatized in 1987, was still owned and operated by the government. Although it may be impossible for you to imagine, this is exactly what it was like to try and buy a Shinkansen ticket back then! That's why people such as me, who are old enough to remember those days, had a good laugh when we saw this cartoon.

Communism was an attempt to use the basic principles from the moral standards of community to govern entire nations, not just close-knit communities of people, and, unfortunately, it was a major failure. In the many failed communist regimes, we can observe the following pattern.

① Leaders assume that the principles of compassion and public-mindedness can be used to govern at a national scale. In reality, however, people do not uphold these values, causing *huge inefficiencies*.

② As a countermeasure, these leaders try to "discipline" or "correct" people by *limiting citizens' freedom* with *strict, overly-controlling laws,* brainwashing, state-run media, and mass surveillance, leading to a totalitarian society.

In countries with communist regimes, citizens monitored each other closely and reported people who they suspected of being anti-social and having anti-government opinions. People who fell under suspicion were harshly punished. This is exactly what happened during China's Cultural Revolution. *The Gulag Archipelago* by Aleksandr Solzhenitsyn, who won the Nobel Prize in Literature, describes a similar situation in the Soviet Union (Russia). Please take a look at the lazy person in the last frame of the cartoon in Figure 10.5 one more time. Isn't your reaction to think "This guy is outrageous!"? I can't help but think "Do something to sanction these arrogant guys!" whenever I'm annoyed by government services. However, if we react that way, it means we're in danger of falling into the same trap that people in the formerly communist countries fell into. In the same way that we get exasperated with workers at inefficient government offices, the communist regimes of the twentieth century were frustrated with people who they believed were not working according to the ideals of communism. (In fact, the communist regimes went so far as to send these workers to prison camps.) However, workers at notorious government offices such as vehicle licencing agencies and people such as hotel receptionists who provide friendly service are not actually that different. Sure, some people are naturally more friendly and suited to service jobs. But it's inconceivable that lazy, grumpy people choose to work in government services and industrious, friendly people choose to work for private companies. *The problem with the government agencies that especially aggravate us isn't the poor quality of the people who work there but the poorly designed system that promotes and perpetuates that kind of poor service.* The big failure of the communist regimes was that they did not recognize this simple fact.

In other words, people's demeanors at work depend on the design of the organizations where they work! For instance, someone might be lazy and rude when they work at a government agency because that attitude is tolerated there, but if that same person worked in the private sector they might act more professional and cheerful. Look back at the cartoon again. The lazy person in the last frame could be YOU, if you were placed in that workplace. When we get frustrated with government bureaucracies, we should *condemn the system, not the people*.

The lessons we should draw from the communist countries of the twentieth century, which devolved into illiberal police states, are as follows.

- A good society is one in which good outcomes can be obtained by *ordinary people acting in ordinary ways*.
- For this to happen, it's necessary to *design the system and institutions in a society very carefully*.

(d) The Roles of the Two Moral Standards

Let's summarize the discussion so far. There are different philosophies – the moral standards of community and the moral standards of markets – about how best to govern society, or, in other words, how to induce people to help each other. Figure 10.6 compares the two schools of thought.

The main lesson from twentieth-century history is that market economies are far better than planned economies at improving people's welfare. That isn't to say that markets are perfect;

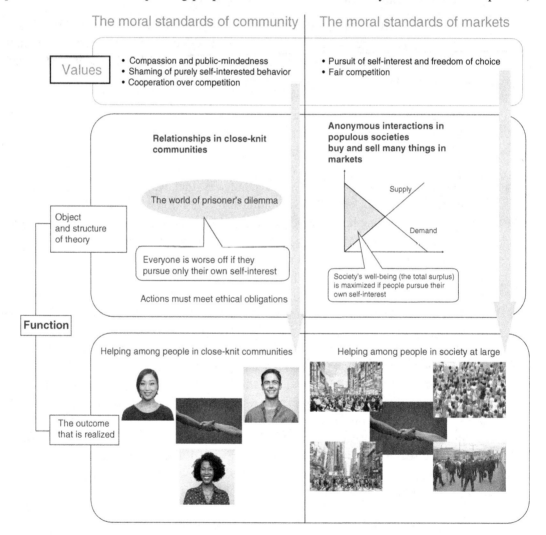

Figure 10.6 The moral standards of community and the moral standards of markets
Source: Helping among people in close-knit communities (from top left, clockwise): alvarez/E+/Getty Images; Kelvin Murray/DigitalVision/Getty Images; Morsa Images/DigitalVision/Getty Images; Morsa Images/DigitalVision/Getty Images
Source: Helping among people in society at large (from top left, clockwise): TommL/Getty Images; John Potter/Pixabay.com; Peter Roe/Pixabay.com; Alexander Spatari/Getty Images

they have serious problems as well. But, regardless of your political beliefs and stances, in order to make our society a good place to live in it's necessary that you use the market mechanism to some extent. This is the lesson we took from the events of the twentieth century.

On the other hand, there are many situations in which the moral standards of community have real value. In families, groups of friends, neighborhoods, organizations, or social movements to help the poor, minorities, and other vulnerable people, the governing principles from the moral standards of community are extremely important.

If we look at the major political disputes that bitterly divide our society from this viewpoint, we can see two main problems. The first problem is that people tend to be *far too fixated on arguments about the "values"* shown at the top of Figure 10.6. It's pointless to spend all our time disputing whether values such as public-mindedness or fair competition and freedom are superior. This only inflames passions and leads us to label and dismiss people who have different viewpoints as "greedy free-market fundamentalists" or "outdated leftist radicals." It doesn't help us determine what we should do to make our society better. In order to make these political disputes more constructive, we need to focus on the arrows in Figure 10.6, which show *how these values operate.* For example, Deng Xiaoping,[2] who led the Chinese economic reform and brought aspects of a market economy to China, used the saying "It doesn't matter whether a cat is black or white, only whether it catches mice" to express the idea that what is best for society should be determined not by values but by how these values function in reality. Without these reforms, China's current economic success would have been impossible. (Of course, these reforms also had negative aspects. It's important to consider whether or not the benefits of economic development are distributed equitably. We'll return to this idea in the next section.)

The second problem is that, due to the failure of communism, many of its associated principles, which are so critical to families, groups of friends, neighborhoods, organizations, or social movements to help the poor, minority, and other vulnerable people, have started to lose traction in society. For example, in Japan, many of the people who believed in the ideal of communism were instrumental in fighting against social injustice and worked on behalf of the poor. After World War II the Japanese Socialist Party (which was the second largest political party in Japan for a long time following the war) and many college students were driving forces behind those left-wing social justice movements. They earnestly believed that they could create a Japanese utopia through a socialist government based on values such as compassion and public-mindedness. Now that it's quite clear that such a utopian vision is unachievable, there are fewer and fewer people with the same level of commitment to social justice.

So, what should we do? A precocious student would say, "We should apply the moral standards of markets where it's necessary and we should apply the moral standards of community where it's suited." The basic idea here may be correct, but it is easier said than done. Research shows that, when monetary incentives and competition are introduced to people who are working together for the common good, the cooperative relationships unravel.[3]

---

[2] Although he modernized China's economy, politically he maintained single-party rule and suppressed the movement for democratization (Tiananmen Square protests).

[3] Juan Camilo Cardenas, John Stranlund, and Cleve Willis, "Local Environmental Control and Institutional Crowding-Out," *World Development*, 28(10) (2000): 1719–1733.

It appears that people are not able to easily switch from having cooperative mentalities in some situations and competitive mentalities in others. Then, how can we strike the right balance between the moral standards of community and the moral standards of markets? This is the serious challenge we face after seeing the events of the twentieth century. Try to think of your own ideas about what we should do.

10.2 Who Benefits from Markets? The Compensation Principle and Social Justice

The experiences of the twentieth century taught us that, in order to make our society a good place in which to live, it's more or less necessary that we utilize the market mechanism. But does everyone enjoy the benefits of markets, or are some people excluded? The key to understanding the relationship between markets and social justice is an idea that is usually buried in the back of traditional microeconomics textbooks: the "compensation principle." This fact will become clear to you from the discussion that follows.

Microeconomics does not make strong value judgments on what are the right things to do in our society. The only stance it takes is based on Pareto improvement and Pareto efficiency.

> If everyone in society agrees that state A is better than state B, then we should choose state A.

Microeconomics does not weigh in on what to do if there are disagreements; it is up to the people to decide.

However, in the real world, people always have disagreements. Once you graduate from school, you'll have to weigh different arguments and make tough decisions. So let's now depart from the traditional "value-judgment-free" microeconomic policy recommendations mentioned above, and *let's talk seriously about value judgments*.

If there are innovations in our society, such as a new product being invented or a new store launching, the market outcome changes. Moreover, the market outcome also changes when the government changes its regulatory policies and tariff measures. Any time the market outcome evolves in this way, there are usually people who gain and people who lose. Some examples follow.

- Consumers in the United States benefit from inexpensive imports from China. However, domestic producers in the United States were hurt by the lower prices.
- Smartphones made it much easier for people to take pictures and check the time. However, producers of cameras and watches, and local photo shops, were put out of business.

Regulating foreign trade or putting restrictions on new products are "market distortions" and result in an inefficient allocation of resources. If we were to abandon these regulations and bring about a state of perfect competition, then we could make *all people better off* by having those who benefit from the deregulation *pay compensation* to those who suffer from the deregulation. This is what we learned from the **(second) fundamental theorem of welfare economics**, which I explained in Chapter 3. This is the most important and surprising result that economics has produced. However, as you can see from the examples of trade with China and smartphones, in reality *life goes on without sufficient compensation being paid, if any compensation is paid at all*. This is the crux of the matter! The relationship between markets and social justice crucially hinges on this key point. How should we think about this?

The field of research known as "welfare economics" tries to inform our decisions when we must make value judgments. One idea from welfare economics is shown below.

> When there's a change in the market outcome (due to policy changes, innovations, etc.), if the people who benefit from the change can *compensate* those who suffer from the change in such a way that *everyone is left better off*, then *even if this compensation does not actually occur* it still must be allowed.

This is called the **compensation principle**. (This is sometimes called the "hypothetical" compensation principle, since this compensation may not actually occur.) Unless we interfere, markets naturally follow this principle.

However, if everyone could still be left better off if this compensation occurs, then shouldn't we just complete this compensation? How can it be *okay not to compensate* those who suffered from the change in the market? Thoughtful people used to laugh at the idea of the compensation principle and dismiss it as an *outrageous notion*. But the experiences of the twentieth century showed that the compensation principle can have surprising effects.

Applying the compensation principle in just one instance is difficult to justify. It doesn't seem right to just ignore those who are left behind by changes in the market. However, the experiences of the twentieth century taught us that, if we *adopt the compensation principle* and *apply it consistently, many people will be better off in the long run*. The British economist John Hicks (1904–1989) was the first to suggest that broad application of the compensation principle can have positive effects in the long run. For this reason, this idea is sometimes known as *"Hicks' optimism."* Figure 10.7 shows how this might work in practice.

Curve a in Figure 10.7 expresses the utility level that society can achieve given the government's regulatory policies. Society begins at point U on curve a. Since it expresses the maximum utility level that society can achieve, curve a is sometimes called the "utility (or possibility) frontier."

Now, suppose that the government deregulates the liquor industry. In this case, society can achieve a higher level of utility, represented by curve b. Society moves from point U to point V.

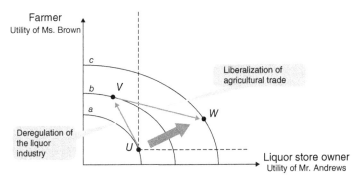

Figure 10.7 Broad application of the compensation principle can benefit everyone

The deregulation causes Mr. Andrews, who owns a liquor store, to lose money, but benefits Ms. Brown, who is a farmer. Hypothetically, if Ms. Brown (who benefited from the policy change) paid compensation to Mr. Andrews (who suffered losses from the policy change), then society would move from point V to a point on curve b that is in between the dotted lines, and both Mr. Andrews and Ms. Brown could be better off than they were at point U before the deregulation. However, the compensation principle says it's not mandatory for this compensation to occur.

Next, if the government liberalizes the trade of agricultural products, then this time the farmer, Ms. Brown, suffers losses and the liquor store owner, Mr. Andrews, benefits. Society moves from point V to point W. If we compare the current point W to the initial point U, *both Mr. Andrews and Ms. Brown are better off.* In other words, if the government consistently relaxes various regulations, sometimes people such as Mr. Andrews and Ms. Brown will benefit and sometimes they will suffer losses, but in the long run it's possible that everyone is better off.

You might be looking at the figure and wondering, "*This might be possible in theory, but does it really happen in reality?*" You may think that the situation shown in Figure 10.8 more accurately depicts what happens in the real world: deregulation and economic growth just keeps benefiting certain people and hurting the rest.

Whether Figure 10.7 or Figure 10.8 is more accurate is an empirical question. So let's look at some data and evidence to try and answer this question.

First, let's reexamine a figure that I first showed you in Chapter 1 (Figure 10.9). This chart shows the income per capita of South Korea and North Korea over time. We can see that there's a huge difference between the trend in South Korea, which adopted capitalism, and the trend in North Korea, which did not, even though these two countries have similar geographies and ethnic backgrounds. Over the course of South Korea's economic growth, there must have been many people who were put out of business by their competition and many others who prospered. It was probably rare that the people who gained from innovation and growth had to compensate those who suffered losses. That is, South Korea experienced rapid economic growth while it followed the "compensation principle."

When we compare the present to the 1970s, which is when the standards of living in North Korea and South Korea begin to diverge, is it the case that the benefits of South Korea's growing economy have accrued to just a handful of people, leaving many others worse off? And when we compare present-day North Korea (which has almost the same standard of living as South Korea did in the 1970s) to present-day South Korea, is it the case that lower-class and middle-class people have a higher standard of living in North Korea than in South Korea? Is South Korea better only for the wealthiest people? It doesn't appear so; the hypothetical scenario shown in Figure 10.8 doesn't seem to have occurred.

Figure 10.8 Won't deregulation and economic growth exacerbate inequality?

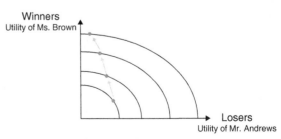

Dollars

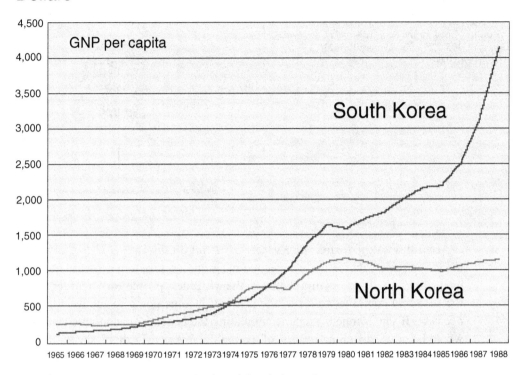

Figure 10.9 Capitalism and communism: the size of the pie for society
Source: Peter H. Lindert and Jeffrey G. Williamson (1985) "Growth, Equality, and History," *Explorations in Economic History*, 22, 341–377, Figure 1 (p.344). https://doi.org/10.1016/0014-4983(85)90001-4

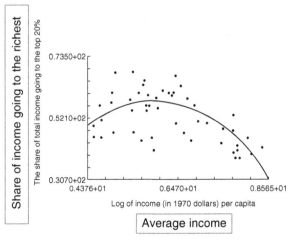

Figure 10.10 How much of the gains from economic growth do the "winners" receive (Kuznets curve)?
Source: Yasuyuki Sawada (2003) "Kokusai Keizaigaku" Kiso Kosu Keizaigaku 7, Shinseisha.

In order to think about things more carefully, let's look at another example to study who receives the benefits of economic development. The curve in Figure 10.10 shows the relationship between the average income in society and the percentage of total income earned by the wealthiest citizens. We call this the **Kuznets curve**.

Figure 10.11 Does economic growth help the lower class?
Source: David Dollar and Aart Kraay (2002) "Growth is Good for the Poor." *Journal of Economic Growth*, 7, 195–225. https://doi.org/10.1023/A:1020139631000

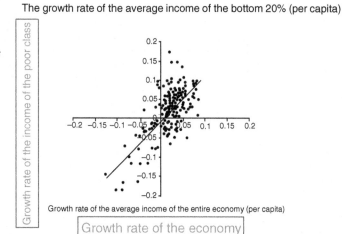

According to the figure, *the Kuznets curve has an inverted-U shape*. That is, as the average income in society increases due to economic growth (as we move toward the right in the graph), inequality initially grows more intense (the wealthiest people earn a larger share). However, as the economy continues to grow, the share of income going to the wealthiest people starts to decrease. If the "winners" kept accumulating the benefits of economic growth, then this curve would be upward-sloping instead of having the inverted-U shape shown in the figure.[4]

Now, let's turn to what happens with the "losers" from economic development. Figure 10.11 shows the relationship between the growth rate of the economy and the growth rate of lower-class incomes.[5] If we draw a trendline through the points in the figure, we will see that it's upward-sloping. This means that, as the economy grows, lower-class incomes also grow. If it were the case that the same people keep falling further and further behind as the economy grows, as in Figure 10.8, then the trendline should be downward-sloping.

Given these observations, what do you think? Some people are (understandably) skeptical when they first encounter the compensation principle and learn that it does not require redistribution from the so-called "winners" to "losers." They might also be unconvinced by the logic outlined in Figure 10.7, and say *"that is only a theoretical possibility"* or *"that's what the rich people are saying."* However, if we look at real-world data from the twentieth century, we see that the people with the lowest incomes also benefited from economic growth, even without redistributive policies by the government. In particular, as Figure 10.9 shows, if we compare market economies that follow the compensation principle and planned economies, we see huge differences in standards of living.

We can use additional back-of-the-envelope calculations to examine who benefits from the compensation principle. "Hicks' optimism" was that broad application of the compensation principle can have positive effects in the long run. The compensation principle may

---

[4] Thomas Piketty forcefully argues that the accepted idea about the Kuznets curve is outdated and that the curve is going to be N-shaped (that is, further economic development will increase inequality). Interested readers should consult his work, *Capital in the Twenty-First Century* (Cambridge, MA: Harvard University Press, 2014).

[5] I thank my colleague Professor Yasuyuki Sawada, who suggested that the data in Figures 10.10 and 10.11 are useful for studying who benefits from economic development and for allowing me to use the graph shown in Figure 10.10.

Table 10.2 The relationship between parents' occupations and their children's occupations

child / parent		professional	white collar			blue collar			Farmer
			large company	SME	self-employed	large company	SME	self-employed	
professional		0.47	0.20	0.13	0.04	0.05	0.08	0.02	0.02
white collar	large company	0.18	0.33	0.18	0.03	0.08	0.11	0.07	0.01
	SME	0.14	0.21	0.23	0.08	0.05	0.24	0.03	0.03
	self-employed	0.12	0.15	0.11	0.34	0.04	0.15	0.08	0.01
blue collar	large company	0.12	0.20	0.11	0.07	0.19	0.25	0.03	0.05
	SME	0.08	0.14	0.12	0.04	0.16	0.38	0.06	0.02
	self-employed	0.11	0.15	0.11	0.07	0.07	0.18	0.29	0.01
Farmer		0.05	0.13	0.09	0.06	0.06	0.31	0.09	0.21

not work within just one generation. The owner of the photo shop that went out of business when digital cameras became popular may think for the rest of his or her lifetime that things were better before digital cameras were invented. So, let us now examine *the extent to which children are affected by how their parents either benefited from or suffered from market changes.*

When they grow up, what kinds of jobs do the children of white-collar workers have? What about the children of farmers? Depending on how well your children fare, you may have different opinions about what society should look like. Fortunately, in Japan, sociology researchers periodically conduct detailed studies on the relationship between parents' occupations and their children's occupations.[6] Table 10.2 shows the results of one such study from 2005.[7]

If we look at the first row in the table, we can see that, among the children of professionals such as doctors or lawyers, 47 percent also become professionals, 20 percent get white-collar jobs, etc. On the other hand, the distribution of jobs among children of farmers is very different. You can see that it's quite likely that a farmer's child will also become a farmer. In general, children are quite likely to have the same jobs as their parents did. Considering this pattern, it seems natural that people will believe that a market change will affect their children in the same way it affects them.

What about if we consider the grandchildren's generation? Assuming that, even in the next generation, the ratios in Table 10.2 still represent the relationship between parents' occupations

---

[6] Satoshi Miwa and Hiroshi Ishida, "Fundamental Analysis of Japanese Stratification Structure and Social Mobility after World War II," in *Fundamental Analysis of 2005 SSM Japan Research: Structure, Trend, and Methods*, edited by Satoshi Miwa and Daisuke Kobayashi (Tokyo: SSM Research Association, 2008).

[7] This is a version in which the numbers (numbers of people) in appendix table 1 of the Miwa–Ishida paper, which appears in footnote 5, are changed to proportions. The original data are a cross-section of the males' current occupations and their fathers' occupations when they were 15 years old, in the 2005 SSM research. The data are from November 2005 and there are 1,924 pairs of fathers and sons in this sample.

Table 10.3 The distribution of occupations in the second generation

parent \ child		professional	white collar			blue collar			Farmer
			large company	SME	self-employed	large company	SME	self-employed	
professional		0.30	0.22	0.15	0.06	0.07	0.15	0.04	0.03
white collar	large company	0.20	0.23	0.16	0.06	0.08	0.17	0.07	0.02
	SME	0.17	0.21	0.16	0.07	0.09	0.22	0.06	0.03
	self-employed	0.17	0.19	0.14	0.15	0.07	0.18	0.08	0.02
blue collar	large company	0.16	0.20	0.14	0.07	0.11	0.22	0.06	0.03
	SME	0.14	0.19	0.14	0.06	0.12	0.25	0.07	0.03
	self-employed	0.16	0.19	0.14	0.07	0.09	0.20	0.12	0.02
Farmer		0.12	0.18	0.13	0.07	0.10	0.26	0.08	0.06

and their children's occupations, we can compute the distribution of occupations among grandchildren.[8] The results are shown in Table 10.3. (**Caveat**: what I am going to present is not a widely accepted view about the social mobility over generations. You should take it as a thought experiment about what would happen if Table 10.2 represented the transition probabilities of occupation from one generation to the next one.)

The grandchildren of professionals and the grandchildren of farmers still have different distributions of occupations, but you can see that the difference is getting smaller. Now let's look at the distribution of jobs among great-grandchildren (see Table 10.4).

At this point, great-grandchildren of professionals and great-grandchildren of farmers seem to get similar jobs. Looking at each row from top to bottom, we can see that, *regardless of people's occupations, the distribution of jobs among their great-grandchildren are almost the same*. If we keep computing the distributions of jobs in later generations, any differences that we initially saw in the first generation disappear entirely. Table 10.5 shows the distribution of occupations five generations ahead. Note that each row is practically identical.

This phenomenon is not specific to this particular data set. For any table like Table 10.2 that has only non-zero entries, if we compute the distribution of occupations in the second generation, third generation, fourth generation, and so on, the rows will quickly become identical.[9]

What we can see from the table above is that, regardless of people's occupations, their descendants several generations later will have almost identical distributions of occupations. In other words, *for a person of any occupation, the distribution of occupations of their*

[8] **A remark for mathematically inclined readers**: if we let Table 10.2 be a matrix P, the distribution of occupations in the nth generation can be computed as the product of matrices P^n.

[9] *A remark for mathematically inclined readers*: if we let Table 10.2, which expresses the transition probabilities of occupations, be the matrix P, then the unique probability vector x satisfying the equation $xP = x$ is called a stationary distribution. It is known that, when each entry of P is positive, each row of P^n rapidly converges (with exponential speed) to the stationary distribution x as n gets larger.

Table 10.4 The distribution of occupations in the third generation

parent \ child		professional	white collar			blue collar			Farmer
			large company	SME	self-employed	large company	SME	self-employed	
professional		0.23	0.21	0.15	0.07	0.08	0.1S	0.05	0.03
white collar	large company	0.20	0.21	0.15	0.07	0.09	0.19	0.06	0.03
	SME	0.19	0.21	0.15	0.07	0.09	0.21	0.06	0.03
	self-employed	0.18	0.20	0.14	0.09	0.09	0.20	0.07	0.02
blue collar	large company	0.18	0.20	0.14	0.07	0.10	0.21	0.06	0.03
	SME	0.17	0.20	0.14	0.07	0.10	0.22	0.07	0.03
	self-employed	0.18	0.20	0.14	0.07	0.09	0.20	0.08	0.03
Farmer		0.16	0.20	0.14	0.07	0.10	0.23	0.07	0.03

Table 10.5 The distribution of occupations in the fifth generation

parent \ child		professional	white collar			blue collar			Farmer
			large company	SME	self-employed	large company	SME	self-employed	
professional		0.20	0.21	0.15	0.07	0.09	0.20	0.06	0.03
white collar	large company	0.19	0.21	0.15	0.07	0.09	0.20	0.06	0.03
	SME	0.19	0.21	0.15	0.07	0.09	0.20	0.06	0.03
	self-employed	0.19	0.21	0.15	0.07	0.09	0.20	0.06	0.03
blue collar	large company	0.19	0.21	0.15	0.07	0.09	0.20	0.06	0.03
	SME	0.19	0.21	0.15	0.07	0.09	0.20	0.06	0.03
	self-employed	0.19	0.21	0.15	0.07	0.09	0.20	0.07	0.03
Fanner		0.19	0.21	0.15	0.07	0.09	0.20	0.07	0.03

descendants will be almost equal to the distribution of occupations in society. Therefore, it's possible that, in the not-so-distant future, *the benefits of markets will be shared equally among the descendants of today's citizens, irrespective of people's current occupations.*

This observation is related to the theory of justice of John Rawls (1921–2002), which promotes this idea.

> *We should try to make judgments about a society from the perspective of someone who does not yet know what socioeconomic class they will be born into.*

This is sometimes called making judgments from behind a "**veil of ignorance**." If we apply this principle, when we decide whether something is good or bad for society we should abstract from our own personal social status and consider the policy from the viewpoint of a hypothetical person who can be either a winner or a loser with some positive probabilities. The veil of ignorance is one of the most useful ways to think about social justice, because it is "operational," meaning that anyone can perform the aforementioned mental exercise to determine if a proposed social situation is good or bad.[10] The analysis we've done above shows that, when we consider what occupations our descendants will have, we are essentially behind a veil of ignorance.

When it follows the compensation principle, the market evolves without people who benefit from economic growth compensating those who suffer losses from economic growth. If we bear in mind our conclusion that, over time, the benefits of the market are likely to be shared by people of all different backgrounds, we may argue that application of the compensation principle *represents the interests of future generations.*

It's about time for us to wrap up. When the competitive market evolves due to new innovations, new companies, or new government policies, everyone can be left *better off if we redistribute some of the benefits from those who benefit to those who suffer losses.* In other words, economic growth is just like increasing the size of the pie for society, where everyone can be better off if we make sure to divide the larger pie and share it appropriately. However, in reality, *markets usually develop without such compensation being paid.* The idea that this is acceptable is called the **compensation principle**. This notion was previously dismissed as laughable and absurd, but in the twentieth century we saw

- big differences in the standard of living of citizens in societies that adopted this principle and societies that did not (Figure 10.9); and,
- if an economy develops according to the compensation principle, it won't necessarily be the case that a handful of people capture all the gains while the rest incur losses; the benefits of development are likely to be shared among many people (Figures 10.10 and 10.11, Table 10.4).

Based on the lesson we learned from the twentieth-century failure of communism, which is that, in order to make our society a better place to live in, it's necessary that we utilize the market mechanism to some extent, I think that the single most important point when considering social justice in the market economy is *how you judge the compensation principle.* We shouldn't just laugh off this idea, but ask ourselves how we can engage with it head-on.

How should we do this? It may help to consider a concrete example, such as the following.

- Although home printers and smartphones have made our lives easier in a lot of ways, print shops and telephone operators were hit hard.

---

[10] Rawls recommended that we make judgments from the perspective of *the worst-off in society.* In contrast, I've explained how to make value judgments based on how the average person in society is affected. Since at an abstract level it's not clear which approach is more reasonable, I would like you to look again at Figure 10.9, which compares North Korea and South Korea. If we consider average North Koreans and South Koreans, we can say that the situation in South Korea is better. Conversely, if we compare the poorest North Koreans and South Koreans, you can argue that the situation in North Korea is better. Which judgment makes more sense to you?

If we want to help these people, should we ban home printers and smartphones? A precocious student might say, "Instead of instituting a ban, we should have the people who profited from these inventions pay compensation to the people who lost their jobs." But, in reality, it's extremely difficult to decide who should pay compensation, how much they should pay, and who should receive compensation. Even if we are able to make these decisions, actually implementing these transfers would often be impossible. In other words, we can never hope to do this redistribution perfectly. So what should we do? Should we have banned home printers and smartphones? This is the key question every one of us needs to consider – a challenge for those who live in a market economy. If you are happy with your smartphone without thinking about those people who were hit hard by the introduction of smartphones, think about them. If you are against the market mechanism because market competition creates such people who are hit hard, do you really want to give up the fruits of the market mechanism, such as your smartphone? There is not a "correct" answer. I repeat, there is not a correct answer. And, I urge you to come to your own conclusions.

The market continues to evolve without necessarily compensating the people who suffer from these changes. But it is, somewhat surprisingly, possible that many people can benefit from a market economy that adheres to the compensation principle. This is what we learned from the experiences of the twentieth century. Nevertheless, we need safeguards or safety nets for people who are left behind by the market. What kinds of safety nets make the most sense? Will people accept the idea that it's fair if some people benefit from the market while others don't? There are tons of challenging questions that we need to ponder.

So far, I have explained my own insights from years of studying economics. These are just my personal opinions, and by no means represent well-established views in economics, so you shouldn't treat this chapter as a part of the "textbook." I do not intend to drill these ideas into you but, rather, I would like to encourage you to use your own critical thinking and reasoning to form your own opinions on how to improve society. Use the (rather provocative) ideas in this chapter as a stepping stone to formalize your own.

In my economics department, it is a tradition to give some of Alfred Marshall's words to our students who have just started to study economics. Marshall (1842–1924) was an English economist who clearly understood the fundamental function of markets, and the following words are from his inaugural lecture as a professor at the University of Cambridge.[11]

It will be my cherished ambition, my highest endeavour, to do what … I may, to increase the number of those, whom Cambridge … sends out into the world with *cool heads but warm hearts*, willing to give at least some of their best powers to grappling with the social suffering around them.

I too would like you to consider society's problems with "cool heads but warm hearts." That is what economics is all about. I wish you good luck!

---

[11] Alfred Marshall, *The Present Position of Economics* (London: Macmillan, 1885), from his inaugural lecture at the University of Cambridge.

APPENDIX A

Essential Mathematical Concepts: All You Need to Know to Read This Book

In the main text of this book, I explain things in ways that are intuitive and easy to understand if you vaguely remember mathematical concepts such as differentiation from high school. However, in case your math skills are very rusty or you have not learned this math before, I have written this appendix to explain the most basic and essential mathematical concepts needed to understand this text book. I leave the fine details and especially rigorous arguments to specialized books.[1] I have carefully selected only the content that is strictly necessary, which I will explain simply and intuitively. You may think, *"That's it? This section isn't very long; is this really all the math I need to know?"* Yes, that's it; this really is all you need to know.

A.1 Functions

A (single-variable) **function** assigns a number, denoted by $f(x)$, to any given number x.[2] For instance, we could consider the function $f(x) = x^2$. Analogously, a two-variable function assigns a number $f(x, y)$ to a pair of numbers (x, y). Similarly, we can define functions, called multivariable functions, with three or more variables.

Example A.1

The cost function, which assigns a cost $c(x)$ to a quantity x, is a single-variable function. If there are two products with prices p_1 and p_2, we can write the demand for the first product as a function of these prices and income I. The resulting function $x_1(p_1, p_2, I)$ is a three-variable function.

---

[1] For mathematics, I recommend referring to textbooks on real analysis (calculus) and linear algebra. For the basic microeconomics we study in this book, we primarily use calculus. However, linear algebra is useful in more advanced microeconomics and in the field of "econometrics," which deals with methods of studying economics using data.

There are certain mathematical concepts that are used frequently in economics but may not be fully covered in most mathematics textbooks. See Rangarajan Sundaram, *A First Course in Optimization Theory* (Cambridge: Cambridge University Press, 1996).

[2] To be a bit more precise, this is a function that assigns a real number $f(x)$ to a real number x. Real numbers are numbers, such as 1.025..., that can be expressed as a decimal.

A.2   The Slope of a Straight Line

The most basic single-variable functions are linear equations of the form $y = kx$. Linear equations can be expressed graphically as straight lines. Figure A.1 depicts the graph of the function $y = 2x$.

Make sure that you understand that *the **slope** of a straight line is expressed as b/a, the ratio of a and b*, as shown in Figure A.1. (We use this fact in Section A.3.) For more details, see the footnote below.[3]

A.3   Differentiation

Differentiation, which you may have studied in high school, is one of the main mathematical tools that we use in microeconomics.

> *The slope of the tangent line of the graph* of a function $f(x)$ is called the **derivative** of this function and is denoted by $f'(x)$ or $\frac{df}{dx}$ (Figure A.2).

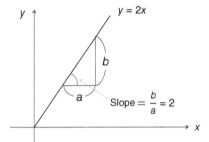

Figure A.1 The slope of a straight line (linear equation)

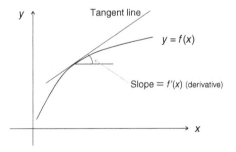

Figure A.2 The derivative of the function $f(x)$

[3] In this case, if the value of x increases by a, then since $y = 2x$ the value of y increases by $2a$. (That is, $b = 2a$.) Therefore, the slope of the line is $b/a = 2$. Note that the slope, 2, is the same as the coefficient on x in the equation $y = 2x$.

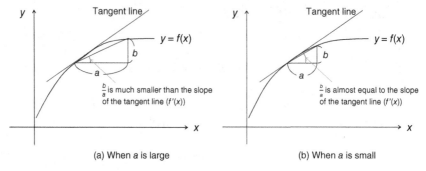

Figure A.3 Calculating the derivative

To understand how to calculate the slope of the tangent line (i.e. the derivative of the function), you can perform the following thought exercise.

First, look at the left-hand panel, Figure A.3 (a). As I explained in Section A.2, the ratio b/a of a and b is the slope of the angled edge (hypotenuse) of the triangle shown in the figure. You can see that, if x is increased by a large number a, then b/a (the slope of the hypotenuse of the triangle), which represents the ratio of the change in $f(x)$ to the change in x, is much smaller than the slope of the tangent line.

However, as we decrease a (the base of the triangle), you can see that the ratio b/a (the slope of the hypotenuse of the triangle) gradually approaches the slope of the tangent line. Figure A.3 (b) illustrates this fact. Therefore, *we can compute the derivative as the value that b/a (the slope of the triangle in the figure) approaches as we get close to zero.*

Now, note that, since b is the amount by which $f(x)$ increases when we increase x by a, we have

$$b = f(x+a) - f(x).$$

Therefore, the derivative of the function $f(x)$ can be calculated as

$$\frac{f(x+a) - f(x)}{a}$$

when a gets infinitely close to zero.[4] This thought exercise should give you an intuitive understanding of derivatives (which are very important in microeconomics) and how we compute them.

The meaning of derivatives: The derivative of a function $f(x)$ represents *how much the function $f(x)$ changes when x increases slightly*. (More precisely, it is the ratio of the change in $f(x)$ to a small change in x.)

---

[4] If we use mathematical notation, $f'(x) = \lim_{a \to 0} \frac{f(x+a)-f(x)}{a}$.

Here's a helpful example of how we can calculate a derivative.

Example A.2

Let's calculate the derivative $f'(x)$ of $f(x) = x^2$. Since

$$\frac{f(x+a) - f(x)}{a} = \frac{(x+a)^2 - x^2}{a}$$

$$= \frac{(x^2 + 2ax + a^2) - x^2}{a} = 2x + a,$$

if we make a infinitely close to zero we have $2x$. That is, *the derivative of $f(x) = x^2$ is $2x$.*

As you can see, the derivatives of simple functions are generally easy to calculate. *Derivatives are useful because they can help us understand how a function behaves.* For example, if $f'(x) > 0$, then the function $f(x)$ is increasing at x (see Figure A.4 (a)). There is also an important relationship between derivatives and the maximums/minimums of functions. Figure A.4 (b) illustrates this relationship, which plays a very important role in microeconomics.

Derivatives and maximums: *For points at which f is maximized, $f'(x) = 0$ holds.*

For example, if x represents quantity and $f(x)$ represents profits in Figure A.4 (b), *by differentiating $f(x)$ and setting $f'(x)$ equal to 0 we can compute the quantities at which profits are maximized.*

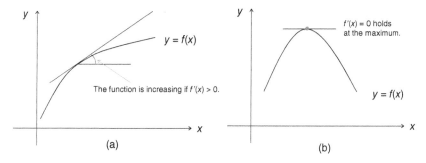

Figure A.4 Derivatives and the function's movement

A.4   Differentiation of a Multi-Variable Function

From here on, I will go over concepts that you may not have seen in high school.

In microeconomics we frequently deal with problems with many variables, such as quantities and prices of different goods. Therefore, it's helpful to understand differentiation of multivariable functions. Using what we know from differentiation of single-variable functions, let's explore how to differentiate multivariable functions such as $f(x,y)$.

> **Partial derivative**: If we fix y and differentiate $f(x, y)$ as a single-variable function of x, we obtain the partial derivative of f with respect to x, denoted by
>
> $$\frac{\partial f}{\partial x}.$$

We use the "round d" symbol ∂ in $\frac{\partial f}{\partial x}$ to indicate that this is the partial derivative of a multivariable function, as opposed to the derivative $\frac{df}{dx}$ of a single-variable function. We can define the partial derivative $\frac{\partial f}{\partial y}$ of f with respect to y analogously.

Don't let phrases such as "partial derivative" or strange notation such as $\frac{\partial f}{\partial x}$ intimidate you; *this isn't very different from what you learned in high school!*

> When you study microeconomics, there will be times when you are intimidated by the mathematical formula and think, *"There's absolutely no way I can comprehend this! It's too advanced!"* However, *I assure you that you can understand the material if things are explained to you clearly.*

So don't give in to those feelings, and keep trying! Let me use an example to explain how to calculate partial derivatives and show you that it's not very difficult.

Example A.3

Let's partially differentiate the function $f(x,y) = x^2 y$. To do so, we can just differentiate it by treating y as a constant. As we saw in Example A.2, the derivative of x^2 is $2x$, so we have

$$\frac{\partial f}{\partial x} = 2x\boxed{y}.$$

↑
Treat this part as a constant

If you understand how to differentiate single-variable functions, you can easily calculate partial derivatives of multi-variable functions. See? Partial derivatives are nothing to be scared of!

If you recall the "meaning of derivatives" that I explained in Section A.3, it is easy to grasp the meaning of partial derivatives.

> ## The Meaning of Partial Derivatives
>
> The partial derivative $\frac{\partial f}{\partial x}$ of a function $f(x,y)$ with respect to x represents, for a fixed value of y, *how much the function $f(x,y)$ changes when x increases slightly.* (More precisely, it is the ratio of the change in $f(x,y)$ to a small change in x.)

In microeconomics textbooks, you will rarely need to numerically compute derivatives or partial derivatives, but it's important to understand the meaning of derivatives and partial derivatives and to remember the formulas that we can use to differentiate common types of functions in economic models. One of the formulas that you will use the most is the following:[5]

$$\boxed{\text{The derivative of } f(x) = x^a \text{ is } f'(x) = ax^{a-1}.}$$

What we saw in Example A.2 was just the case of $a = 2$ in this formula.

Example A.4

The derivative of $f(x) = x^3$ is $f'(x) = \frac{df}{dx} = 3x^2$.

Next, let's consider the case in which there is a function $f(x)$ and, moreover, x is a function of another variable z (i.e. $x = x(z)$). In this case, $g(z) = f(x(z))$ is called the **composite function** of $f(x)$ and $x(z)$. In microeconomics, we often analyze situations in which a change in one variable changes the object we are interested in indirectly through a change in another variable. For example, you might imagine a scenario in which a change in quantity changes the price, and the change in price changes profits. How can we determine the effect of the change in quantity on profits? The following formula, sometimes called the chain rule, plays an important role.

The Chain Rule

The derivative of $g(z) = f(x(z))$ is $g'(z) = \frac{df}{dx}\frac{dx}{dz}$.

Intuitively, the reason that this formula holds is as follows.

① First, if we *increase z slightly*, then x changes by $\frac{dx}{dz}$.
② Next, if x *changes* in this way, then f changes by $\frac{df}{dx}$.

Therefore, $g(z) = f(x(z))$ changes according to the combined effects of ① and ② $\left(\frac{df}{dx}\frac{dx}{dz}\right)$. This is the formula above.

---

[5] Just between you and me… If you know only this formula and the fact that the derivative of the function $y = \log(x)$ is $1/x$, then you can understand most economics textbooks.

Example A.5

In the case in which $f(x) = x^3$ and x is a function of another variable z, then we can express $f(x(z))$ as a function of z only. Let's denote this by $g(z)$. Using the chain rule to differentiate $g(z)$ with respect to z, we have

$$g'(z) = \frac{df}{dx}\frac{dx}{dz} = 3x^2 \frac{dx}{dz}.$$

(I calculated this using the fact that the derivative of $f(x) = x^3$ is $3x^2$, as we saw in Example A.4.)

Next, let's consider the case in which

- there is a function $f(x,y)$; and, moreover,
- x and y are functions of a third variable z (i.e. $x = x(z)$ and $y = y(z)$).

In this case, how does the value of f change if we change z? The answer is given by the derivative of the composite function $g(z) = f(x(z), y(z))$ with respect to z. It is calculated as follows.

Formula for the Derivative of a Composite Function

The derivative of $g(z) = f(x(z), y(z))$ is $g'(z) = \frac{\partial f}{\partial x}\frac{dx}{dz} + \frac{\partial f}{\partial y}\frac{dy}{dz}$.

This may look complicated at first, but it is easy to understand intuitively why this holds. If we increase z slightly, it generates an effect on f, through the change of x as follows.

$$g'(z) = \boxed{\frac{\partial f}{\partial x}}\boxed{\frac{dx}{dz}} + \frac{\partial f}{\partial y}\frac{dy}{dz}$$

① First, if z increases marginally, x changes this much

② Next, if x changes, f changes this much

Example A.6

For $f(x, y) = x^3 y$, if x and y are functions of another variable z (i.e. $x = x(z)$ and $y = y(z)$), then we can write $f(x(z), y(z))$ as a single-variable function of z, which we'll denote by $g(z)$. Differentiating g with respect to z using the formula above, we see that

$$g'(z) = \frac{\partial f}{\partial x}\frac{dx}{dz} + \frac{\partial f}{\partial y}\frac{dy}{dz} = 3x^2 y \frac{dx}{dz} + x^3 \frac{dy}{dz}$$

differentiate $f = x^3 y$ with respect to x differentiate $f = x^3 y$ with respect to y

holds.

That is, $\frac{\partial f}{\partial x}\frac{dx}{dz}$ represents z's *effect on f through x*. Analogously, the right-most term $\frac{\partial f}{\partial y}\frac{dy}{dz}$ in the above equation represents z's *effect on f through y*. A change in z changes f through these two channels, so, as a whole, f changes according to the formula above.

Next, allow me to explain one more formula that you will use frequently. If

$$f(x(z), y(z)) = x(z)y(z)$$

and we apply the formula given above, we obtain the "**product rule**," which describes how to differentiate the product of functions.

The Product Rule

The derivative of $x(z)y(z)$ with respect to z is $x'y + xy'$.

Just to be clear, x' and y' are, respectively, the derivatives of $x(z)$ and $y(z)$ with respect to z.

Note also that, if we differentiate $f(z, y(z))$ with respect to z when $y = y(z)$, we find the following.

The derivative of $g(z) = f(z, y(z))$ is $g'(z) = \frac{\partial f}{\partial z} + \frac{\partial f}{\partial y}\frac{dy}{dz}$.

This is the case in which we set $x(z) = z$ in the formula for the derivative of a composite function. You don't need to remember this formula separately from the other one, but we use it when I explain the "Slutsky decomposition" in Chapter 1 of this book, so I've included it here for your convenience.

A.5   Practice Problem

If you are worried about whether you have enough familiarity with the mathematical concepts we've reviewed, try doing the practice problems below. If you can solve these problems easily, you are all set!

(1) If $f(x) = x^a$, then $f'(x) = \boxed{A}$
(2) If $f(x,y) = x^4y^2$, then $\frac{\partial f}{\partial x} = \boxed{B}$
(3) If we differentiate $f(x)g(x)$ with respect to x, we have $\boxed{C}$
(4) If we differentiate $f(g(x))$ with respect to x, we have $\boxed{D}$
(5) If we differentiate $f(x(z),y(z))$ with respect to z, we have $\boxed{E}$

You can compare your answers to the solutions in the footnote.[6]

---

[6] A: ax^{a-1}, B: $4x^3y^2$, C: $f'g + fg'$, D: $f'g'$, E: $\frac{\partial f}{\partial x}\frac{\partial x}{\partial z} + \frac{\partial f}{\partial y}\frac{\partial y}{\partial z}$

Constrained Maximization Problems and the Method of Lagrange Multipliers

This section should be read after Chapter 1, Sections 1.1 through 1.5, which cover basic consumer theory.

B.1   Interior Solutions

In economics, we often deal with constrained maximization problems – problems related to maximizing a function under a set of constraints – so let me explain how to solve them. My goals are for you to:

- *master the procedure* to solve for the optimal solution;
- *understand the precise conditions* under which we can use that procedure; and
- *gain an intuition* for why this procedure gives us the optimal solution.

I will leave rigorous proofs to mathematics textbooks.[1]

First, a few remarks. Many of the constraints we encounter in economics problems, such as the budget constraint $p_1 x_1 + \cdots + p_N x_N = I$, are equalities. However, in many cases these equality conditions can alternatively be formulated as inequality conditions. For instance, we can take the budget constraint to be

$$p_1 x_1 + \cdots + p_N x_N \leq I \quad \text{(expenditure} \leq \text{income).}$$

Moreover, although I did not explicitly state this in the main part of the textbook, in many economics problems the variables cannot take negative values. That is, we implicitly impose the additional constraints that

$$x_i \geq 0, i = 1, \ldots, N.$$

For example, if x_i is consumption of good i, then x_i must either be zero or a positive value, since it is nonsensical to consider negative consumption. Bearing in mind these two points, let's consider the constrained maximization problem.

---

[1] For example, Sundaram, *A First Course in Optimization Theory*, contains a proof of proposition B.1 (sufficiency), which I will state below.

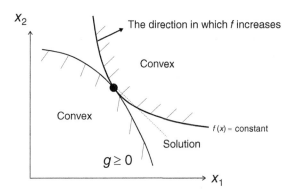

Figure B.1 Quasi-concave programming

The Constrained Maximization Problem M

$$\max_{x} f(x)$$

$$\text{s.t.} \quad g(x) \geq 0$$

$$x_i \geq 0, i = 1, \ldots, N$$

---

where $x = (x_1, \ldots, x_N)$

In this problem, we want to maximize $f(x_1, \ldots, x_N)$ given the constraints $g(x_1, \ldots, x_N) \geq 0$ and $x_i \geq 0$, $i = 1, \ldots, N$. We call f, the function that we are maximizing, the **objective function**.

In many models that we encounter in microeconomics, the objective function and constraints take forms that are convenient and easy to work with. For example, recall the utility function $u(x)$. In consumer theory, we mainly analyze the case where *the areas above the contour lines (i.e. indifference curves) are convex sets. Such a function is called a **quasi-concave function**.*[2]

We are now going to review constrained optimization problems in which both the objective function f and the constraint g are quasi-concave functions. Figure B.1 gives a visual representation of this type of constrained maximization problem, which we call **quasi-concave programming**.

Example B.1

Determining optimal consumption is a quasi-concave programming problem, as shown in Figure B.2. Likewise, the expenditure minimization problem (minimizing expenditure while achieving or exceeding some given level of utility $\bar{u}$) is also a quasi-concave programming problem. In the expenditure minimization problem, the objective function is $f(x) = -p_1x_1 + p_2x_2$ and the constraint is $g(x) = u(x) - \bar{u} \geq 0$ (I want you to try drawing a depiction of the expenditure minimization problem on your own.)

---

[2] More precisely, for a function h, if for any constant c the set of all x that satisfy $h(x) \geq c$ (which we can write in mathematical notation as the set $\{ x \mid h(x) \geq c \}$) is a convex set, then h is a quasi-concave function.

Example B.1 (cont.)

Figure B.2 Optimal consumption

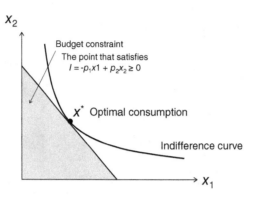

In the earlier example of optimal consumption, at the solution x^*,

(i) the constraint is satisfied with equality (i.e. $g(x^*) = 0$); and
(ii) all variables have positive values (i.e. $x_i^* > 0$, $i = 1,\ldots,N$).

It is often the case that the solution to microeconomics problems satisfies conditions (i) and (ii). (A solution in which all variables have strictly positive values and therefore satisfies condition (ii) is called an **interior solution**.) How can we find a solution that satisfies both conditions? It suffices to follow the simple procedure described below.

---

① First, construct the function $L = f(x) + \lambda g(x)$ where $\lambda \geq 0$ is an unknown.
② Next, differentiate L with respect to each variable x_i and set the derivative equal to zero ($\partial L/\partial x_i = 0$).

We call the function L a **Lagrangian** and we call the variable λ a **Lagrange multiplier**. To understand exactly how this procedure works, consider the following conditions:

$$\frac{\partial L}{\partial x_i} = 0, \quad i = 1, \ldots N. \tag{B.1}$$

$$\lambda \geq 0. \tag{B.2}$$

The proposition below says that an interior point that satisfies the constraints with equality and satisfies Conditions (B.1) and (B.2) is an interior solution. Conversely, if there is an interior solution that satisfies the constraints with equality, it must satisfy Conditions (B.1) and (B.2). In other words, Conditions (B.1) and (B.2) are necessary and sufficient conditions for a point satisfying the constraints with equality to be an interior solution. (To be precise, there are additional conditions that are satisfied in most cases. The precise statement is the following.)

Proposition B.1: in a constrained maximization problem M, suppose that the objective function f and constraint g are differentiable quasi-concave functions. Let x^* be an interior point that satisfies the constraint with equality. Then the following are true.

Sufficiency: if, for at least one i, $\frac{\partial f}{\partial x_i}(x^*) \neq 0$, then, if x^* satisfies Conditions (B.1) and (B.2), it is a solution.

Necessity: if, for at least one i, $\frac{\partial g}{\partial x_i}(x^*) \neq 0$, then, if x^* is a solution, it satisfies Conditions (B.1) and (B.2).

For those who are interested, I'll later explain the extra condition that appears above ("for at least one i..."). For now, please continue reading and try not to get too hung up on the small details.

This procedure for solving a constrained maximization problem is called **the method of Lagrange multipliers**. (To be precise, the method of Lagrange multipliers is for problems with constraints that can be written as $g(x) = 0$. The Karush–Kuhn–Tucker conditions allow us to solve problems with constraints involving inequalities. There are many theorems that state the relationship between the Karush–Kuhn–Tucker conditions and solutions to constrained maximization problems. I've included the version related to quasi-concave programming since it best fits the theory of consumption.[3])

Let's try to build some intuition about *why the method of Lagrange multipliers finds solutions to constrained maximization problems*. If we compute the equation shown in condition (B.1), we have

$$\left(\frac{\partial f}{\partial x_1}, \ldots, \frac{\partial f}{\partial x_N}\right) = -\lambda\left(\frac{\partial g}{\partial x_1}, \ldots, \frac{\partial g}{\partial x_N}\right).$$

How should we interpret the left- and right-hand sides?

We can think of the left-hand side as giving *"the direction in which f increases most steeply."* To be more precise, it is a vector that points in the direction orthogonal to f's contour line (indifference curve) and in which f increases (see Figure B.3). We denote this using the notation

$$\nabla f = \left(\frac{\partial f}{\partial x_1}, \ldots, \frac{\partial f}{\partial x_N}\right)$$

and call it f's **gradient**. (The symbol ∇ is called "nabla.")

---

[3] Refer to Kenneth J. Arrow and Alain C. Enthoven, "Quasi-Concave Programming," *Econometrica*, 29(4) (1961), 779–800. In this section, I have reorganized and stated the Arrow–Enthoven condition for problems with a single constraint that is satisfied with equality at an interior solution. The "necessity" part of proposition B.1 is slightly different from the version that appears in this paper, but it is relatively easy to directly prove it.

Figure B.3 Gradient of a function

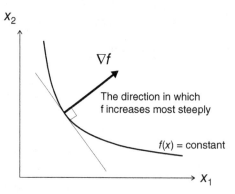

Example B.2

If $f = x_1 + x_2$, its contour lines are straight lines with slope -1. Indeed, $\nabla f = (1, 1)$ is orthogonal to these contour lines and gives the direction in which f increases most steeply (see Figure B.4).

Figure B.4 Gradient of the function $f = x_1 + x_2$

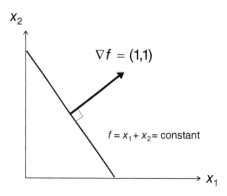

Note that we can now rewrite the optimality condition (B.1) from the method of Lagrange multipliers as

$$\nabla f = -\lambda \nabla g.$$

This equation holds when *the gradients of the objective function f and the constraint g face in exactly opposite directions.* Looking at a picture may help you build intuition as to how the method of Lagrange multipliers solves constrained maximization problems (see Figure B.5).

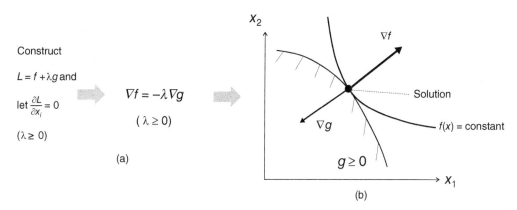

Construct

$L = f + \lambda g$ and

let $\frac{\partial L}{\partial x_i} = 0$

$(\lambda \geq 0)$

$\nabla f = -\lambda \nabla g$

$(\lambda \geq 0)$

(a)

(b)

Figure B.5 How the method of Lagrange multipliers solves constrained maximization problems

Comment B.1 Why Are the Additional Conditions Necessary?

There may be readers who are concerned about the additional conditions beginning with "for at least one i…" that appear in Proposition B.1. Let me explain why these extra conditions are needed, starting with the one in the "Sufficiency" portion. (This is a very technical discussion, and readers who are not interested need not read it.)

Let's consider an objective function such as the function f shown in Figure B.6 (a). Note that f is a quasi-concave function, since the areas above the contour lines are convex.

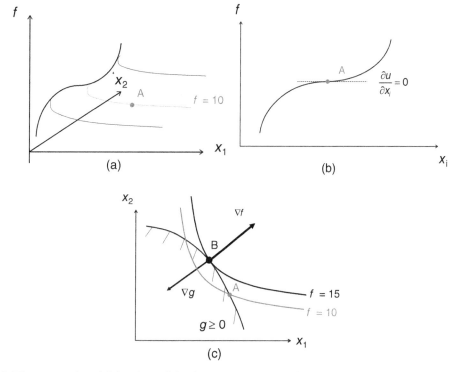

Figure B.6 The reason the additional condition is necessary

However, the slope of f is zero at the points on the contour line where $f = 10$. For instance, if you look at Figure B.6 (b), which shows the cross-section of the graph through point A, you can see that the slope of f with respect to both x_1 and x_2. $(\partial f / \partial x_i (i = 1, 2))$ is zero. In other words, the gradient ∇f is zero at point A. Now, examine Figure B.6 (c). Point A is clearly not a solution, even though the conditions

$$\nabla f = -\lambda \nabla g \tag{B.1}$$

$$\lambda \geq 0 \tag{B.2}$$

hold at $\lambda = 0$ (since $\nabla f = 0$). Of course, Conditions (B.1) and (B.2) also hold at point B, the true solution. But, without the additional condition "if for at least one i, $c \frac{\partial f}{\partial x_i} (x^*) \neq 0$" in Proposition B.1, there may exist points that satisfy (B.1) and (B.2) but are not solutions.

A similar additional condition appears in the "Necessity" portion of Proposition B.1, and the reason it is needed is analogous.

B.2   Corner Solutions

Not all solutions will be interior solutions (i.e. $x_i^* > 0, i = 1, \ldots, N$). For example, in Figure B.7, the optimal consumption of the second good is zero, so the solution x^* is not an interior solution.

When a solution is not an interior solution, it is called a **corner solution**. Recall that we previously used the condition

slope of the indifference curve = price ratio

to solve for optimal consumption when there is an interior solution. However, at the corner solution shown in Figure B.7, this condition does not hold; the slope of the indifference

Figure B.7 Corner solution

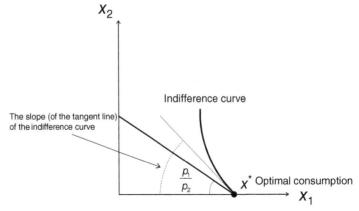

curve is greater than the price ratio. At the corner solution with $x_2{}^* = 0$, the optimality condition is

$$\underbrace{\frac{\partial u/\partial x_1}{\partial u/\partial x_2}}_{\substack{\text{slope of the indifference curve} \\ \text{(marginal rate of substitution)}}} \geq \underbrace{\frac{p_1}{p_2}}_{\text{price ratio}}.$$

We can rewrite the optimality condition of a constrained maximization problem (Proposition B.1) to include the case when a corner solution is optimal. For that, it suffices to *replace* condition (B.1) of "$\partial L/\partial x_i = 0$" *with* the condition

$$\partial L/\partial x_i \leq 0$$

only for the case in which the optimal solution is $x_i{}^* = 0$. In the earlier example, supposing

$$\begin{cases} \dfrac{\partial L}{\partial x_1} = \dfrac{\partial u}{\partial x_1} - \lambda p_1 = 0 \\[2mm] \dfrac{\partial L}{\partial x_2} = \dfrac{\partial u}{\partial x_2} - \lambda p_2 \leq 0 \end{cases}$$

we can reorganize the terms to derive the optimality condition of a corner solution (B.3).

B.3 Concave Functions and Quasi-Concave Functions

In the constrained maximization problem described in Section B.1, we assumed that the areas above the contour lines (which correspond to indifference curves) of the objective function f and constraint g are convex sets. Determining the optimal consumption bundle is one example of this type of problem. However, in other problems, the objective function f and constraint g may satisfy a slightly different, and stronger, condition: the region below the graph of the function is a convex set. Figure B.8 (a) depicts a function satisfying this condition.

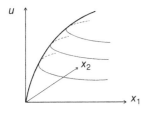

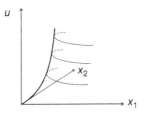

Concave function

$$u = x_1^{1/3} x_2^{1/3}$$

(a)

Quasi-concave function

$$u = x_1 x_2$$

(b)

Figure B.8 Concave function and quasi-concave function

If the region below the graph of a function is a convex set, we call that function a **concave function**.[4] As you can see in the figure, the (two-dimensional) area above any contour line (indifference curve) of a concave function is a convex set, so *any concave function is also a quasi-concave function. However, the converse is not necessarily true.* Figure B.8 (b) depicts a function that is quasi-concave, but not concave.

If the objective function f and constraint g are both concave, and not just quasi-concave, then we can use a simplified version of Proposition B.1.

Proposition B.2: in a constrained maximization problem M, suppose that the objective function f and constraint g are differentiable concave functions. Let x^* be an interior point that satisfies the constraint with equality. Then, the following are true.

Sufficiency: if x^* satisfies Conditions (B.1) and (B.2), it is a solution.

Necessity: if there is a point x such that $g(x) > 0$, then, if x^* is a solution, it satisfies Conditions (B.1) and (B.2).

Comment B.2 The Relationship between Quasi-Concave Functions and Concave Functions

In mathematics textbooks that cover constrained maximization problems, you might learn "non-linear programming" or "concave programming," and you will usually see a version of Proposition B.2. Since, in consumer theory, the utility function to be maximized is quasi-concave but not necessarily concave, I have first stated Proposition B.1, which is especially useful in economic analysis.

Remember, a utility function is just a way of expressing people's preferences, and any function that assigns larger numbers to more preferred things is a valid utility function representing someone's preferences (refer to Chapter 1, Section 1.1). Therefore, the new function $f(u)$ that we obtain by transforming a utility function u with a monotonically increasing function f,[5]

$$v(x) = f(u(x))$$

is also a utility function that represents that same person's preferences (because it still assigns larger numbers to more preferred things).

In many cases, the (quasi-concave) utility functions used in economic models become concave functions when transformed by an appropriate monotonically increasing function. For example, the

---

[4] Therefore, a function u such that the set $\{\,(x,y)\mid y \leq u(x)\,\} =$ (the area below the graph of u) is a convex set is called a concave function.

[5] That is, f is a function such that $u < u'$ implies $f(u) < f(u')$.

non-concave utility function shown in Figure B.8 (b) becomes the concave function shown in Figure B.8 (a),

$$v(x_1, x_2) = x_1^{1/3} x_2^{1/3},$$

when we transform it using the monotonically increasing function $f(u) = u^{1/3}$. Since the result is the same regardless of whether we use u or v (we will still find the consumer's most preferred bundle), *it suffices to use the utility function that makes the calculations easier.*

If you look at this example, you may be tempted to think that any quasi-concave function can be transformed into a concave function by a monotonically increasing function, and therefore that you need to know only the concave programming problem (Proposition B.2). In fact, this is not true; there are quasi-concave functions that cannot become a concave function by any monotone transformation.[6] In this sense, it is a theoretical necessity to consider concave programming and quasi-concave programming separately.

---

[6] A simple example appears in David M. Kreps, *A Course in Microeconomic Theory* (Princeton, NJ: Princeton University Press, 1990), 2.6.7, so refer to this book if you are interested. In reality, it's unlikely that such a strange utility function would be needed for economic analysis.

APPENDIX C

Compensating Variation and Equivalent Variation

Using Demand Curves to Estimate the Gains and Losses that Consumers Experience due to Price Changes

C.1 Compensating Variation

How much does a consumer lose from a price increase and how much does a consumer gain from a price drop? These are very important questions that are relevant to many economic problems. Fortunately, we can estimate the effects of price changes using the demand curves that we can observe in the markets. The Slutsky decomposition will be key to this analysis, and this is one of the reasons why we should be interested in the Slutsky decomposition. Let me explain why.[1]

Recall the story I used to explain the Slutsky decomposition (Chapter 1, Section 9, part (c)). A power plant collapsed due to an earthquake, causing a power shortage. Therefore, the electricity company raised the price of electricity. However, people were unhappy with the higher prices, since the power plant's collapse was due to the electricity company's faulty architectural plans. The customers demanded that the electricity company compensate them for the losses they experienced from the price increase. If the electrical company were to pay compensation, how much would they owe the customers?

The expenditure function (Chapter 1, Section 1.8) can answer this question. Recall that the expenditure function $I(p,u)$ returns the expenditure needed to achieve utility level u under the price profile p. Letting electricity be the first good, suppose that the price of electricity increases from $p_1 = a$ to $p_1 = b$. Then the price profile before the price increase is $p = (a, p_2, \ldots, p_N)$ and the price profile after the price increase is $p' = (b, p_2, \ldots, p_N)$. Let u be the utility level that consumers received prior to the price increase. To achieve utility level u after the price increase, the consumers would need to spend exactly

$$I(p', u) - I(p, u) \tag{C.1}$$

---

[1] In introductory textbooks, the benefit consumers receive from market transactions is captured by consumer surplus. However, for this to be true, the consumers' utility functions must have a special property: quasilinearity. If the consumers' utility functions are quasilinear, then price changes have no income effect (see Chapter 3, Section 3.1, part (c)). In this appendix, I will explain how to accurately measure consumers' gains without imposing such a strong assumption.

more dollars. This is the amount of compensation that the electricity company would need to pay its customers to ensure that they are just as happy after the power plant's collapse as they were beforehand. If you look closely at Expression (C.1), you'll see that the only difference between the two terms $I(p',u)$ and $I(p,u)$ is the price profile. Moreover, the only difference between the price profiles p and p' is the value of p_1, the price of electricity. Therefore, the value of (C.1) can be computed as[2]

$$\int_a^b \frac{\partial I}{\partial p_1} dp_1. \tag{C.2}$$

Due to Shephard's lemma (Chapter 1, Section 1.8), we know that $\frac{\partial I}{\partial p_1}$ (the slope of the expenditure function) is equal to the value of the compensated demand function $\overline{x}_1(p,u)$. Consequently, the amount the electricity company owes its customers can be written as

$$I(p',u) - I(p,u) = \int_a^b \overline{x}_1(p,u)dp_1.$$

This change in the expenditure that is necessary *to maintain the original utility u (i.e., the utility before the price change)* after a price change is called the **compensating variation**. Just as with the story of the electricity company, the compensating variation represents the amount of money needed *to compensate the consumers for the losses they suffer from the price increase.* (This is why it is called "compensating" variation.) Figure C.1 shows this graphically.

To calculate the grey region in Figure C.1, we need to know the compensated demand function $\overline{x}_1(p,u)$ (i.e. the consumption that achieves utility u under the price profile p as cheaply as possible). Unfortunately, the compensated demand function is not directly observable. However, we can directly observe the demand function $x_1(p,I)$. Fortunately, there is a special relationship between the compensated demand function and the demand function. The Slutsky decomposition describes exactly how the two are related.

Figure C.2 (a) shows how the effect of the price increase on consumption (demand) can be decomposed into the substitution effect and the income effect. The arrows on the X axis show how much the substitution and income effects contribute to the total change in the quantity demanded. Recall that the substitution effect in panel (a) represents the movement along an indifference curve, which (by definition) is the change in compensated demand. In panel (b), these two effects are depicted in a graph with the price of electricity on the Y axis and electricity consumption on the X axis.

Let's review the Slutsky decomposition once again. The change in demand for electricity when the price of electricity increases can be decomposed into the substitution effect (change in

---

[2] Note that, if we fix all other variables and treat $I(p,u)$ as a function only of p_1, which we will denote by $f(p_1)$, then we can write (C.1) as

$$f(b) - f(a) = \int_a^b f'(x)dx.$$

(This is a formula you may have learned in high school.) Next, since f is just $I(p,u)$ as a function of only p_1, the derivative f' is equal to the partial derivative $\frac{\partial I}{\partial p_1}$. This is why (C.1) can be calculated as (C.2).

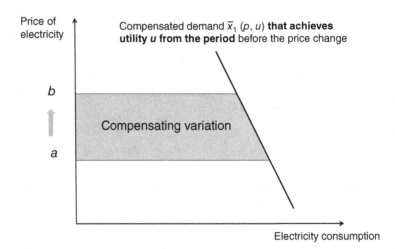

Figure C.1 The amount of money needed to compensate the consumers for the losses they suffer from the price increase

compensated demand = movement along an indifference curve; consumers consume more gas and less electricity) and the income effect (the change due to the fact that consumers' incomes have effectively decreased due to the price increase). If electricity is a normal good (consumption of the good increases if income increases), then consumption of electricity decreases when the consumers' incomes effectively decrease. Therefore, *the income effect is negative.* Figure C.2 depicts this scenario.

Thus, if electricity is a normal good, then, when the price of electricity increases, compensated demand for electricity decreases due to the substitution effect, but demand for electricity decreases even more due to the additional income effect. You can verify this by looking at Figure C.2 (b): *the demand curve has a flatter slope than the compensated demand curve (by the amount of the income effect).*

Given those observations, let's finally consider how to use observable data to estimate the amount of money needed to compensate the consumers for the losses they suffer from the price increase (i.e. the compensating variation). The compensating variation is the combination of the grey and slanted-line regions (to the left of the compensated demand curve). The area of the slanted-line region cannot be computed without knowing the compensated demand curve, which isn't directly observable. However, we can compute the area of the grey region shown in Figure C.2 (b) using the demand curve, which is observable in the market. The grey region to the left of the demand curve represents the change in consumer surplus. Note that this grey region (the change in consumer surplus) is slightly smaller (by the amount of the slanted-line region in Figure C.2 (b)) than what is needed to compensate consumers for the losses they suffer from the price increase (compensating variation). The difference between the demand curve and compensated demand curve is due to the income effect, so, if the income effect is small, then the difference between the change in consumer surplus and the compensating variation (the slanted-lined region) is small. In addition, as you can see in Figure C.2 (b), if the price

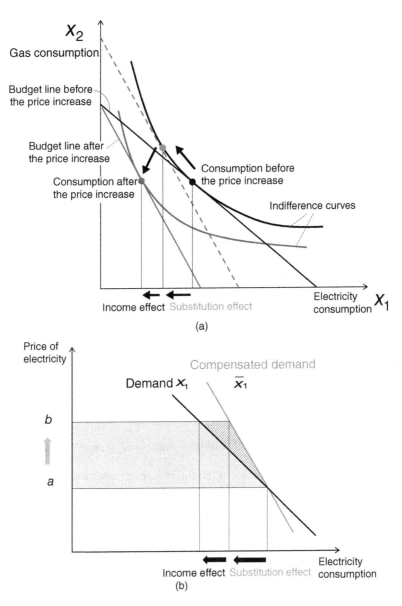

Figure C.2 The relationship between demand and compensated demand, from the Slutsky decomposition

change is small, then this difference is also small (relative to the size of the compensating variation).[3] Let me summarize the discussion so far.

---

[3] The change in consumer surplus is a *lower bound of the compensating variation*, but we can also calculate an *upper bound of the compensating variation* from observable data. It's simple: *(electricity consumption before the price increase)* × *(the change in the price of electricity)*. If the consumer receives this much money, she can consume the same amount of electricity as she did before the price increase. Therefore, she can achieve at least as much utility as before the price

When the price of a normal good (consumption of the good increases if income increases) increases, then we know the following about the amount of money needed to compensate consumers for the losses they suffer from the price increase (compensating variation):

- compensating variation $\geq$ the change in consumer surplus;
- when the income effect is small or when the price increase is small, the compensating variation and change in consumer surplus are approximately equal.

In Chapter 3, Section 3.1, part (c) (consumer surplus), I give a detailed explanation of the special case when the change in consumer surplus and compensating variation are exactly equal (i.e. when there is no income effect).

C.2   Equivalent Variation

Last, let me explain "equivalent variation," a concept that is very similar to compensating variation. Let p be the original price profile and let p' be the new price profile after a price change. Here, we consider the case in which *income $\bar{I}$ does not change before or after the price change*. Let u and u' be the utilities before and after the price change respectively. Recall that compensating variation is the difference in how much money is needed to achieve *the original utility u* under the new and old price profiles, and can be computed using the expenditure function as

$$\text{Compensating variation} = I(p', u) - I(p, u).$$

In contrast, **equivalent variation** is the difference in how much money is needed to achieve *the new utility u'* under the new and old price profiles, and can be computed using the expenditure function as

$$\text{Equivalent variation} = I(p', u') - I(p, u').$$

Comment C.1 The Meaning of Equivalent Variation

In our example with the price of electricity, what does equivalent variation represent? When thinking about this, it's important to be careful about one thing. Since u' is the maximum utility that can be achieved under the new price profile p' and income $\bar{I}$, the minimum amount of

---

increase. (There is a possibility that she could achieve an even higher level of utility than beforehand if she changes her consumption pattern to account for the new prices.) This means that the compensating variation, which is the amount of money needed to compensate consumers for the losses they suffer from the price increase, is at most this much.

money needed to achieve utility u' under the price profile p' (i.e. $I(p', u')$ must be $\overline{I}$.[4] Therefore, we have that

$$\text{Equivalent variation} = \underset{\substack{\text{income} \\ \textit{after} \text{ the price increase}}}{\overline{I}} - I(p, u').$$

However, since we are considering a scenario in which income does not change after the price change, we can rearrange this equation to get

$$\underset{\substack{\text{income} \\ \textit{before} \text{ the price increase}}}{\overline{I}} - \text{equivalent variation} = I(p, u').$$

This equation implies that, under the original price profile p, if the consumer's income were to decrease by the equivalent variation (the left-hand side of the equation), her income (the right-hand side of the equation) would be just enough to achieve the lower utility level u' that arises after the price increase.[5] In other words, *the equivalent valuation measures the damage caused by the price increase in terms of the reduction of income before the price change.* Since this is equivalent to the damage the price increase inflicts on the consumer, it is called the "equivalent" variation.

Using a calculation analogous to the one we used when studying compensating variation, the equivalent variation when the price of the first good changes from a to b can be written as

$$I(p', u') - I(p, u') = \int_a^b \overline{x}_1(p, u') dp_1.$$

This expression is different from the expression we derived for compensating variation in that the compensated demand $\overline{x}_1(p, u')$ is *with respect to utility u', the consumer's utility after the price change.* Graphically, this is the region to the left of the compensated demand curve *with respect to utility u', the consumer's utility after the price change* (see Figure C.3).[6]

---

[4] This fact isn't trivial, and requires a proof. See Chapter 1, Section 1.9, part (a) (duality), for a discussion of this property.

[5] This property is also called "duality" (see Chapter 1, Section 1.9, part (a)).

[6] The bundle the consumer chooses after the price increase must be the cheapest way of achieving utility u', her maximum possible utility under the new prices, and is equal to her compensated demand $\overline{x}_1(p, u')$. For this reason, at the new price b, the compensated demand curve with respect to the new price profile and the demand curve exactly coincide. That is, they intersect at point A in Figure C.3. (This too is a property called "duality." See Chapter 1, Section 1.9, part (a).) Figure C.3, like Figure C.2 previously, assumes that electricity is a normal good. According to the Slutsky decomposition, the compensated demand curve relative to the post-price-increase utility u' has a steeper slope than the demand curve (by the amount of the absent income effect).

Figure C.3 The decrease in income that is equivalent to the damage inflicted on the consumer by the price increase (equivalent variation)

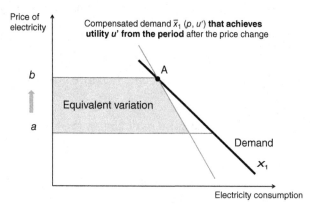

Figure C.4 Equivalent variation, consumer surplus change, and compensating variation

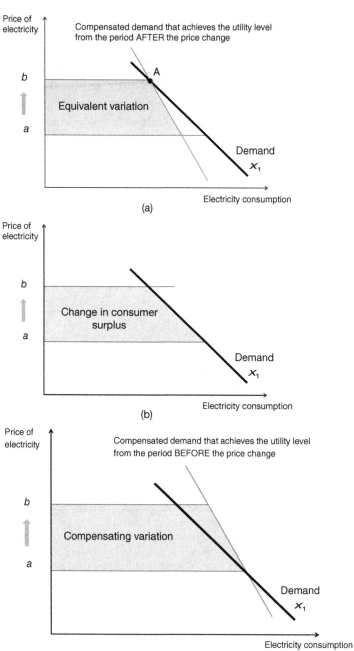

C.3   Summary

Let's recap everything we've learned. Suppose the price of one good increases tomorrow, and therefore your utility will decrease. *If tomorrow you get a subsidy that is equal to the compensating variation, you could maintain today's higher utility level. If your income today is reduced by the amount that is equal to the equivalent variation, you will achieve tomorrow's lower utility level today.* Figure C.4 depicts the relationship between the equivalent variation, the change in consumer surplus, and the compensating variation after the price of a normal good increases.

If the price of a normal good increases, we have

Equivalent variation < consumer surplus < compensating variation.

When the income effect is small or when the price change is small, these three quantities are almost equal. If the income effect is zero, these three quantities are exactly equal.

A Step-by-Step Guide to Proving the Second Welfare Theorem[1]

The second fundamental theorem of welfare economics, which states that any (Pareto-)efficient resource allocation can be achieved as a competitive market equilibrium using appropriate lump-sum transfers, is one of *the most important results in economics*. It illustrates an important advantage of the market economy and reveals the scope and limits of economic policies. Here is a detailed proof of the second fundamental theorem of welfare economics.

You may wonder, *"Why should I bother to learn the proof of this theorem?"* There are several reasons.

- By studying the proof, you will learn the key to achieving efficient resource allocation and that efficient allocation of resources is always associated with "prices" that can theoretically be computed, even when the efficient allocation is not achieved by the market mechanism. In short, you will develop a *deeper understanding* of two key concepts in economics: efficiency and prices. The conditions of the second fundamental theorem of welfare economics are somewhat complicated, but by studying the proof of the theorem you will get a sense of which conditions are truly essential. Additionally, you will see how we can weaken certain conditions, which will help you *understand when the theorem is applicable and how to use it*.

It is particularly important that policy-makers have a strong grasp of these points, so *I strongly encourage businesspeople, government officials, and economists in the private sector, as well as journalists who want to understand economics, to look at this proof*. The second fundamental theorem demonstrates that, when there are many buyers and sellers in a competitive market, *government intervention in the economy can be minimal* (since any desirable outcome can be achieved by income redistribution and does not require manipulating the market). For this reason, *this theorem is sometimes criticized – often by people who are skeptical of the market mechanism – for relying on "unrealistic" assumptions. However, if we examine the proof of this theorem, we can see that many of its assumptions are reasonable descriptions of reality.*

The final reason to study the proof of this theorem is that

- apart from some minor details, the logic of the proof is unexpectedly simple.

---

[1] I thank Professor Daisuke Oyama of the Graduate School of Economics at University of Tokyo for valuable suggestions.

This proof is often omitted from microeconomics textbooks because it is too "advanced" and "difficult." I will show you that it is not.

D.1   First, Some Preparation

The proof of the theorem is composed of (relatively simple) facts that come together to form the larger proof. Let me explain the facts we will make use of.

Preparation 1: "How Much Can the Economy Produce?" and Set Addition

How much of each good can the economy produce, making full use of current resources and production technology? Answering this question sounds like a formidable task, but, using a theoretical model, we can very easily get the answer using "set addition."

First, recall that each firm's activity is represented by a *production plan*. When there are N goods, firm j's production plan can be expressed as

$$y^j = \left(y^j_1, y^j_2, \ldots, y^j_N \right),$$

where the positive elements in this vector represent output quantities and the negative elements represent input quantities.

Example D.1

Suppose there are two firms, a bakery ($j = 1$) and a mill ($j = 2$), and suppose there are three types of goods: bread ($n = 1$), flour ($n = 2$), and wheat ($n = 3$).

Bakery $y^1 = (20, \ -1, \ \ 0)$ (produces 20 loaves of bread from 1 kg of flour).
Mill $y^2 = (0, \ \ -1, \ \ -1.5)$ (produces 1 kg of flour from 1.5 kg of wheat).

In this example, if the two companies are combined, the economy can produce 20 loaves of bread from 1.5 kg of wheat. That is, it can implement the following production plan:

$$y^1 + y^2 = (20, \quad 0, \quad -1.5).$$

Recall that we denoted the set of all production plans that firm j can feasibly implement by

$$Y^j = firm\ j's\ \textbf{\textit{production possibility set}}.$$

Using this notation, an economy-wide production plan in the example can be written as $y^1 + y^2$, where $y^1 \in Y^1$ and $y^2 \in Y^2$. Let's denote the set of all such $y^1 + y^2$ by the sum of the sets Y^1 and Y^2,

$$Y^1 + Y^2.$$

This kind of "set addition" is used later in a slightly different manner, so I'll state a formal definition here.

A Math Toolkit for Economists: Addition of Sets $A + B$

In general, *we denote by $A + B$ the set of all elements $a + b$*, where a is an element in set A and b is an element in set B. In mathematical notation, the sum of two sets A and B is

$$A + B = \{a + b | a \in A, b \in B\}.^2$$

Using this notation, if there are J firms in the economy, we can say:

the set of production plans that the economy can feasibly implement $= Y^1 + \cdots + Y^J.$

If we denote the initial quantities of the various goods by

initial endowment $w = (w_1, \ldots, w_N),$

then, after each firm $j = 1, \ldots, J$ implements production plan y^j, the subsequent quantities of the various goods are represented by

$$y^1 + \cdots + y^J + w.$$

At the beginning of this section, we asked how much of each good the economy could produce, making full use of current resources and production technologies. The answer: the set of all $y^1 + \cdots + y^J + w$. Denote by $\{w\}$ the set consisting only of the initial endowment. Now we can rewrite the answer to our question as

$$Y^1 + \cdots + Y^J + \{w\}.$$

Let's summarize the discussion above.

Denoting each firm j's production possibility set by Y^j and the initial endowment by w, the set of all possible production plans the economy as a whole could feasibly implement is

$$Y = Y^1 + \cdots + Y^J + \{w\}.$$

We call Y the **economy-wide production possibility set**.

---

2 $\{a + b | a \in A, b \in B\}$ is notation that signifies "the set of all $a + b$ such that $a \in A, b \in B$."

Preparation 2: If the Entire Economy Is Maximizing Profit, then Each Individual Firm Is Also Maximizing Its Profit

The reason for this is simple: since the economy-wide profit is just the sum of each firm's profit, if the profit of the economy is maximized, then each firm's profit must also be maximized. Let's rewrite this important fact using mathematical notation. Recall that, under the price profile p, if firm j has production plan y^j, its profit is equal to py^j.[3]

Profit Maximization of the Economy Implies Profit Maximization of the Firms

If, among the economy-wide production plans $y \in Y^1 + \ldots + Y^J$, the production plan

$$\bar{y} = \bar{y}^1 + \ldots + \bar{y}^J \ \left(\text{where } \bar{y}^j \in Y^j \text{ for each firm } j\right)$$

maximizes profit py, then, among firm j's production plans $y^j \in Y^j$, $\bar{y}^j$ is a production plan that maximizes firm j's profit py^j.

Why is this so? If $\bar{y}^j$ does not maximize firm j's profit py^j, then, by replacing $\bar{y}^j$ with the production plan that maximizes firm j's profit, we can increase the economy-wide profit above $p\bar{y}$.[4]

For the same reason, the following more general statement regarding maximization and minimization on sums of sets holds.

Maximization/Minimization of the Whole Implies Maximization/Minimization of Each Part

If, among the elements a in $A^1 + \ldots + A^K$, the element

$$\bar{a} = \bar{a}^1 + \ldots + \bar{a}^K \left(\text{where } \bar{a}^k \in A^k \text{ for each } k\right)$$

maximizes pa, then among the elements $a^k \in A^k$, $\bar{a}^k$ is an element that maximizes pa^k.

Preparation 3: Separating Hyperplane Theorem

The mathematical heart of the proof of the second fundamental theorem of welfare economics is the following simple geometric fact. Please look at Figure D.1.

If sets X and Y are tangent to each other, as shown in Figure D.1 (a), then we can draw *a straight line that separates the two*. The reason that we can draw this straight line is that X and Y are *convex sets* – that is, they do not have any "dents." If either set is not convex, such

---

[3] A remark about notation: for $p = (p_1, \ldots, p_N)$ and $y^j = \left(y_1^j, \ldots, y_N^j\right)$, $py^j = p_1 y_1^j + \cdots + p_N y_N^j$.

[4] This is the contraposition of the statement that we need to prove.

as the set Y' in Figure D.1 (b), it is not necessarily true that we can draw a straight line that separates the two sets.

Since convex sets are important in this step, let's remind ourselves of the precise definition of a *convex set*. A convex set is a set such that, for any two points a and b in the set, the set contains every point on the straight line segment connecting points a and b. (In other words, for any t such that $0 \leq t \leq 1$, the weighted average $ta + (1 - t)b$ is contained in the set.) Figure D.2 (a) shows a convex set, whereas Figure D.2 (b) shows a set that is not convex.

Next, let's look more closely at the straight line that separates the two convex sets X and Y. Figure D.3 shows the same sets as those in Figure D.1 (a).

In this example, the straight line that separates X and Y is given by $px = p_1x_2 + p_2x_2 = 8$. Moreover, the following statements are true.

① For $\bar{x}$, the point at which X and Y are tangent to each other, $p\bar{x} = 8$.
② For any point x in X, $px \geq 8$. (For example, for $x' \in X$, $px' = 9$.)
③ For any point y in Y, $py \leq 8$. (For example, for $y' \in Y$, $py' = 7$.)

Figure D.1 Separation of convex sets

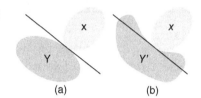

Figure D.2 What is a convex set?

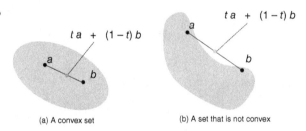

Figure D.3 The straight line $px = 8$ separates X and Y

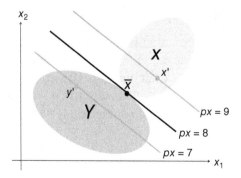

That is, the existence of a straight line that separates X and Y means that

$$\text{if } x \in X, y \in Y, \text{then } px \geq py, \qquad (*)$$

for some $p \neq 0$. Please confirm this by looking at Figure D.3.

Figure D.3 shows an example in two dimensions, but this fact can be generalized to convex sets in N dimensions. If convex sets X and Y in an N-dimensional space are tangent to each other, then there exists some non-zero coefficient vector $p = (p_1, \dots, p_N) \neq 0$ satisfying (*). If $N = 2$, as in Figure D.3, then the shape given by the equation $px = p_1 x_1 + \cdots + p_N x_N =$ constant (where $p \neq 0$) is a straight line. If $N = 3$, then px is a plane. In general, for larger N, we call the shape given by $px = p_1 x_1 + \cdots + p_N x_N =$ constant a **hyperplane**. So, if two convex sets X and Y in an N-dimensional space are tangent to each other, there exists a hyperplane given by $px =$ constant that separates the two sets (so as to satisfy (*)). This fact is known as the **separating hyperplane theorem**.

In Section D.4, "Detailed Remarks," I will define more precisely what it means for X and Y to be "tangent to each other" and I will give a more formal statement of the separating hyperplane theorem. I recommend that you skip these remarks at first and continue reading so that you understand the outline of the proof.

Preparation 4: An Expenditure-Minimizing Point Is a Utility-Maximizing Point (Duality)

Using Figure D.4, let's review duality, the fact that an expenditure-minimizing point is a utility-maximizing point. We saw this previously when we studied consumer theory (Chapter 1, Section 1.9, part (a)).

- Among the consumption bundles that yield no less than utility U, the bundle that minimizes expenditure (Figure D.4 (a)) is

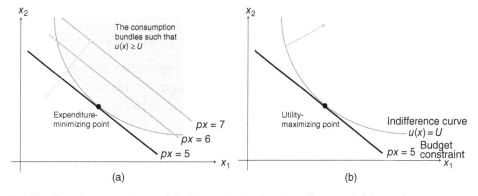

Figure D.4 Duality: the expenditure-minimizing point is also the utility-maximizing point

- the utility-maximizing consumption bundle (Figure D.4 (b)), among those that are affordable given income equal to the minimized expenditure (equal to 5 in this figure).

For duality to hold like this, we require a certain condition, which I will explain later.

D.2   Outline of the Proof

Now that we've prepared, let's prove the second fundamental theorem of welfare economics. I this section I sketch an outline of the proof, and in Section D.4 I will explain some of the finer details.

First, let's choose an arbitrary resource allocation that is Pareto-efficient, and denote it by

$$\left(\overline{x}^1, \ldots, \overline{x}^I, \overline{y}^1, \ldots, \overline{y}^J\right).$$
$$\underbrace{\qquad\qquad}_{\text{consumption bundle}} \quad \underbrace{\qquad\qquad}_{\text{production plan}}$$

We are going to prove that this allocation can be achieved as *a competitive market equilibrium after reallocating income*.

To begin, I carefully define the feasibility of the Pareto-efficient resource allocation that we have chosen. In Section 3.3 (g), we said that the allocation is feasible if

$$\underbrace{\overline{x}^1 + \cdots + \overline{x}^I}_{\text{consumption bundle}} \leq \underbrace{\overline{y}^1 + \cdots + \overline{y}^J}_{\text{production plan}} + \underbrace{w}_{\text{initial endowments}}$$

holds. When this does *not* hold with equality, it means that some goods are not consumed and are left over. In this case, who disposes of the leftover goods? In this section, we define feasibility more precisely by answering this question. Concretely, we will assume that producers dispose of the leftover goods.

Condition 1: the producers can dispose of unnecessary goods.[5]

So, supposing that the producers dispose of the unused goods, the condition for feasibility of a resource allocation is given by the following equality:

$$\overline{x}^1 + \cdots + \overline{x}^I = \overline{y}^1 + \cdots + \overline{y}^J + w.$$

Note that, since any efficient resource allocation is (by definition) feasible, the above equality (balance of consumption and production) holds for any efficient allocation.

Now, let's consider *what it means for a resource allocation to be Pareto-efficient*. Roughly speaking, a resource allocation is Pareto-efficient if there is no feasible allocation that would

---

[5] We can restate Condition 1 more precisely: *if y belongs to the economy-wide production possibility set Y, then any y' such that y ≥ y' belongs to Y.* This means that, starting from any feasible allocation, the producers can dispose of any amount of goods that they choose to. For this reason, we sometimes call this assumption "**free disposal**."

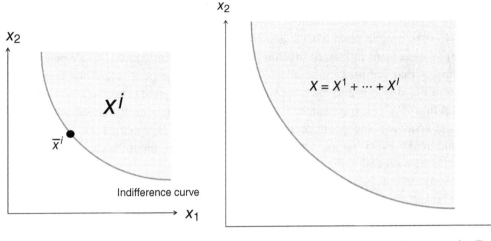

(a) The bundles that give consumer i at least as much utility as the current bundle $\overline{x}^i$ gives

(b) The bundles that give everyone at least as much utility as they have under their current bundles

Figure D.5 Constructing the set X of goods that would make everyone happier

make everyone better off. Suppose that we somehow calculated all the consumption bundles that make every person happier. The Pareto-optimality condition can be restated as the following:

> The set X of goods that would make everyone happier and the set Y of goods that are feasible do not overlap.

It may seem impossible to calculate the goods that would make every person happier, but in fact it's fairly easy if we use the concept of set addition that we saw before. Let me explain.

Step 1 Construct the Set X of Goods That Would Make Everyone Happier

At a Pareto-efficient allocation, each consumer i receives utility $u^i(\overline{x}^i)$. Then the set of bundles that give consumer i at least as much utility as $u^i(\overline{x}^i)$ is $X^i = \{x | u^i(x) \geq u^i(\overline{x}^i)\}$, the set of points above consumer i's indifference curve containing the point $\overline{x}^i$ (see Figure D.5. (a)).

The set of bundles that would make everyone happier compared to the current (Pareto-efficient) allocation can be represented by

$$X = X^1 + \cdots + X^{I}.^6$$

---

[6] Since an allocation is Pareto-efficient if it is not possible to raise at least one person's utility without lowering anyone else's utility (i.e. there are no Pareto improvements), it may seem more natural to you to define X as the set of consumption bundles where at least one person is happier and no person is worse off than beforehand. However, the proof turns out to be simpler if we define X as it is here.

Here we have made use of "set addition," which we saw in Preparation 1. (Conveniently, the set X is convex; I'll explain the reason later.)

Now, bearing in mind what a sum of sets represents, let's confirm that X is the set of bundles that give everyone at least as much utility as they currently have. An element x in X is a sum of elements that are in $X^1, \ldots, X^I$ (i.e. $x = x^1 + \cdots + x^I, x^i \in X^i$). Therefore, if x is a feasible allocation of goods and each consumer receives the goods specified by $x^i \in X^i$, then, by the definition of X^i, each consumer will have at least as much utility as beforehand. Put differently, if the economy can produce the quantities of goods specified by some x in X, then we could make every consumer (weakly) happier than beforehand. For this reason, in this textbook, we'll call X the "**improvement set**."[7]

What kind of shape does the improvement set X have? If each consumer's indifference curves are bowed toward the origin, like those in Figure D.5, then each set X^i is convex. In this case, since X is the sum of convex sets, *X is also a convex set*. This is easy to verify if you review the definition of a convex set (see Section D.1) and think carefully. (I've included an explanation in the footnotes.[8])

Step 2 | By Efficiency, the Improvement Set *X* and Production Possibility Set *Y* Are Tangent to Each Other

If you think for a moment about what the improvement set X represents, you will see that the improvement set X and the economy-wide production possibility set Y are tangent to each other at

$$\text{current total consumption point} = \overline{x} = \overline{x}^1 + \cdots + \overline{x}^I,$$

as shown in Figure D.6. The reason for this is that, roughly speaking, if there is some intersection between the two sets, then we will be able to make every consumer happier than they currently are. In other words, we could execute a Pareto improvement. However, this contradicts our assumption that the original allocation is Pareto-efficient. (A more precise explanation is given in Section D.4, "Detailed Remarks.")

This figure *captures the essence of what it means for a resource allocation to be efficient*, so please try to memorize this picture.

---

[7] The boundary of X is sometimes called **Scitovsky's social indifference curve** and X is sometimes called Scitovsky's upper contour set. They are named for the inventor of these concepts, Hungarian-American economist Tibor de Scitovsky (1910–2002).

[8] The proof that *X, the sum of convex sets $X^1, \ldots X^I$, is a convex set*. In order to show that X is convex, it suffices to show that, for $a, b \in X$,

$$ta + (1 - t)b \in X$$

holds for all $0 \leq t \leq 1$. By the definition of X, we can write $a = a^1 + \cdots + a^I$ and $b = b^1 + \cdots + b^I$ where $a^i, b^i \in X^i$, so we have that

$$ta + (1 - t)b = \sum_{i=1}^{I} (ta^i + (1 - t)b^i).$$

But, since each X^i is a convex set, we know that each term $(ta^i + (1 - t)b^i)$ on the right-hand side belongs to X^i. Therefore, $ta + (1 - t)b$ is a sum of elements from each X^i, and therefore belongs to $X = X^1 + \cdots + X^I$. Thus, X is a convex set.

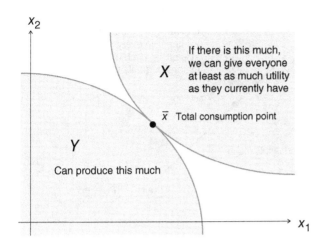

Figure D.6 Pareto efficiency implies that the improvement set X and production possibility set Y are tangent to each other

Step 3 | There Exist "Theoretical Prices" that Separate the Improvement Set X and the Production Possibility Set Y

As we saw in Step 1, if the set of points above each consumer's indifference curve is a convex set, *then the sum of these sets, the improvement set X, is a convex set.* Likewise, if each firm's production possibility set Y^j is a convex set (as they were when we studied producer theory), *then the economy-wide production possibility set Y is also a convex set.*[9]

By the separating hyperplane theorem, which we learned in Preparation 3, we know that there exists a coefficient vector $p = (p_1, \ldots, p_N) \neq 0$ that separates X and Y (see Figure D.7).

This vector p represents the "theoretical prices" (or shadow prices) accompanying the Pareto-efficient allocation. Keep in mind that the efficient allocation

$$\big(\overline{x}^1, \ldots, \overline{x}^I, \overline{y}^1, \ldots, \overline{y}^J\big),$$

consumption bundle   production plan

which has been the reference point for our discussion, could be achieved in many ways. For instance, it might not be the outcome of a competitive market; instead, it might be an allocation determined by a supercomputer and implemented in a planned economy. *Even if an allocation is not determined by the market and we therefore don't observe prices of goods, there are still theoretical prices[10] for the goods in this allocation.* This is what Figure D.7 illustrates.

---

[9] Recall that $Y = Y^1 + \cdots + Y^J + \{w\}$. Since the singleton set $\{w\}$ is convex (it trivially satisfies the definition of a convex set), Y is the sum of convex sets and, therefore, is convex.

[10] You should think of "theoretical prices" as what the price of the goods and services would be if this allocation were realized as a market outcome.

Figure D.7 There exist theoretical prices $p = (p_1, \ldots, p_N) \neq 0$ that separate X and Y

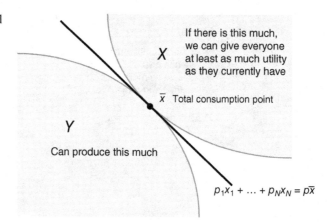

Comment D.1

Does the discussion above really reveal the true essence of prices? My explanation was very abstract, so you might think that this is just an academic exercise with no relation to reality. But is that really the case? Nobody has ever calculated *the economy-wide production possibility set Y,* but, if you think about it, it *must exist*, since there has to be a limit to what the economy can produce. Likewise, nobody has calculated *the improvement set X*, but, since every single person could tell you the goods that would make them happier, it too *must exist*. Last, if an efficient resource allocation is achieved, the improvement set X and economy-wide production possibility set Y must be tangent to each other, so, by the mathematical fact called the separating hyperplane theorem, we know that "theoretical prices" must exist as well. In this context, *we can think of the market economy as an ingenious mechanism that solves the incredibly difficult problem of determining the point at which the sets X and Y (which nobody has measured) are tangent to each other and the accompanying prices for each good. How does it do this? Well, it's done in a "decentralized" way. The market divides this huge computational problem into smaller problems that the firms and the consumers solve as profit maximization problems and utility maximization problems. This is what computer scientists would call "parallel computing."*

In a market economy, goods and services are assigned some number we call a "price," and people use these numbers to decide how much they consume and produce. If you pause to think about it, it is a bit weird, isn't it? And this weird mechanism has been used by human beings for a very long time. Why is that, and what is a "price," anyway? Since the time of Adam Smith, people have proposed various theories about what prices are and how they are determined. Some have said that a price reflects the cost of producing a good (the cost/labor theory of value). Others have suggested that a price measures how "useful" a good or service is (the utility theory of value). Figure D.7 depicts a very general, final answer that the field of economics has eventually settled on. I ask you to examine once again *what "prices" are by looking at this figure.* As you can see, the proof of the second fundamental theorem of welfare economics is at the heart of microeconomics and reveals the essential nature of prices, markets, and the efficiency of resource allocation!

Step 4 Under Theoretical Prices, the Consumption Bundle and Production Plan Are Optimal

Let's look again at Figure D.7. Among the points in X, the total consumption point $\bar{x}$ minimizes economy-wide expenditure under the price profile $p = (p_1, \ldots, p_N)$ (see Figure D.8 (a)). In addition, among the points in Y, $\bar{x}$ maximizes economy-wide profit py (see Figure D.8 (b)).[11]

Before I explain what we can learn from Figure D.8, let's remind ourselves why we're doing this in the first place. In general, there may be many different efficient resource allocations. We want to show that any one of these allocations, say

$$(\bar{x}^1, \ldots, \bar{x}^I, \bar{y}^1, \ldots, \bar{y}^J),$$
consumption bundle   production plan

can be achieved as a market equilibrium after the government reallocates income. Note that, since total consumption $\bar{x} = \bar{x}^1 + \cdots + \bar{x}^I$ must be equal to the sum of each firm's output and the initial endowment of goods w, we have that

$$\bar{x} = \bar{y}^1 + \cdots + \bar{y}^J + w.$$

Let's now consider Figure D.8. Take a look at Figure D.8 (b). If, among the points in $Y = Y^1 + \cdots + Y^J + \{w\}$, the point $\bar{x} = \bar{y}^1 + \cdots + \bar{y}^J + w$ maximizes the economy-wide profit (as shown in the figure), then from Preparation 2 we know that each individual firm's profit $p\bar{y}^j$ is the maximum profit that can be attained from any of the production plans in Y^j. That is, *each firm's production plan $\bar{y}^j$ that is specified in the efficient resource allocation*

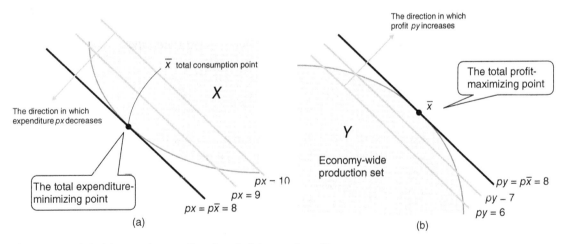

Figure D.8 Minimizing total expenditure/maximizing total profit

---

[11] An element y of the set Y can be written as $y = y^1 + \cdots + y^J + w$, where y^j is firm j's production plan and w is the initial endowment. Therefore, $py = py^1 + \cdots + py^J + pw$ *is the economy-wide profit $py^1 + \cdots + py^J$ plus the constant pw* (the value of the initial endowment).

$(\overline{x}^1, \ldots, \overline{x}^I, \overline{y}^1, \ldots, \overline{y}^J)$ *is the production plan in Y^j that maximizes that firm's profit under the price profile p, which we obtained in Step 3.*

Next, turn your attention to Figure D.8 (a). If, among the points in $X = X^1 + \cdots + X^I$, the point $\overline{x} = \overline{x}^1 + \cdots + \overline{x}^I$ minimizes economy-wide expenditure (as shown in the figure), then – for the same reason as previously – we know that each individual consumer's expenditure $p\overline{x}^i$ is the minimum expenditure that can be achieved from any of the consumption bundles in X^i. In other words, each consumer's consumption bundle $\overline{x}^i$ that is specified in the efficient resource allocation $(\overline{x}^1, \ldots, \overline{x}^I, \overline{y}^1, \ldots, \overline{y}^J)$ is the consumption bundle in $X^i = \{x | u^i(x) \geq u^i(\overline{x}^i)\}$ (= the set of consumption bundles that provide at least as much utility as the current consumption bundle) that minimizes that consumer's expenditure under the price profile p, which we solved for in Step 3. By "duality," which we saw in Preparation 4, we know that each consumer's expenditure-minimizing consumption bundle $\overline{x}^i$ is also *the consumer's utility-maximizing consumption bundle if his or her income is equal to the minimized expenditure $p\overline{x}^i$*. (Reviewing Figure D.4 may help you understand this.)

Therefore, if we give every consumer i exactly $p\overline{x}^i$ of income, then we could realize the consumption bundle $\overline{x}^i$ specified in the efficient resource allocation as the market outcome of utility maximization under a budget constraint. Is it possible to give each consumer i exactly $p\overline{x}^i$ of income? How would we accomplish that? Recall that, since $\overline{x}^1 + \cdots + \overline{x}^I = \overline{y}^1 + \cdots + \overline{y}^J + w$ (i.e. consumption = production + initial endowment of goods), we know that

$$p\overline{x}^1 + \cdots + p\overline{x}^I = p\overline{y}^1 + \cdots + p\overline{y}^J + pw.$$

Consequently, *if the government appropriately redistributes* the total income in the economy, which is equal to the total profit $p\overline{y}^1 + \cdots + p\overline{y}^J$ plus the value of the initial endowment pw, then *it is possible to give income $p\overline{x}^i$ to each consumer i.*[12]

This is the reason that, if the government redistributes income, any efficient resource allocation

$$(\overline{x}^1, \ldots, \overline{x}^I, \overline{y}^1, \ldots, \overline{y}^J)$$
consumption bundle   production plan

can be realized as both a utility maximization and profit maximization point (i.e. a perfectly competitive equilibrium) under the price profile p that we solved for in Step 3. This wraps up the overview of the proof of the second fundamental theorem of welfare economics.

---

[12] I want to make sure you understand this part, so let me give you a concrete example of a lump-sum transfer. Let p be the price profile accompanying a given efficient resource allocation. Suppose that consumer's i's expenditure $(p\overline{x}^i)$ is $50,000, but consumer i's income (the sum of the value of his or her initial endowment, pw^i, and his or her share of each firm j's profit, $\theta_{ij}p\overline{y}^j$) is only $40,000. In this case, the government can increase consumer i's income to the necessary $50,000 by collecting $10,000 from the other consumers and giving it to consumer i. A transfer of money that does not depend on production or consumption choices, such as the transfer the government makes in this example, is called a "lump-sum transfer."

D.3 The Proof at a Glance

The discussion up to this point has been rather long, so let me *give you a concise overview of the proof that you can absorb at a glance.* If we ignore the more detailed aspects, we can distill the logic of the proof of the second fundamental theorem of welfare economics down to a few logical steps, as below.

- First, take an arbitrary Pareto-efficient resource allocation:

$$\left(\overline{x}^1, \ldots, \overline{x}^I, \overline{y}^1, \ldots, \overline{y}^J\right).$$

$$\underbrace{\phantom{\left(\overline{x}^1, \ldots, \overline{x}^I\right)}}_{\text{consumption bundle}} \quad \underbrace{\phantom{\left(\overline{y}^1, \ldots, \overline{y}^J\right)}}_{\text{production plan}}$$

- Construct the set Y (the economy-wide production possibility set), which shows how much the economy can produce in total, using set addition:

$$Y = \underbrace{Y^1 + \cdots + Y^J}_{\substack{\text{firm's production} \\ \text{possibility sets}}} + \underbrace{\{w\}}_{\substack{\text{initial} \\ \text{endowments}}}.$$

- Construct the set X, which shows what quantities of goods are needed to give the consumers at least as much utility as they had under the efficient allocation, by adding together each set

$$X^i = \left\{x^i \mid u^i\left(x^i\right) \geq u^i\left(\overline{x}^i\right)\right\} = \text{the region above each person's indifference curve,}$$

resulting in

$$X = X^1 + \cdots + X^I.$$

- Since the given resource allocation was assumed to be efficient, we know that the sets X and Y are tangent to each other. Moreover, by the **separating hyperplane theorem**, we know that there exists a price profile $p = (p_1, \ldots, p_N)$ that separates the two sets. (This is the core part of the proof.) Therefore, as we can see in Figure D.9, the production point and consumption point for the given allocation are, in fact, the profit-maximizing point and the utility-maximizing point under this price profile. The arrows labeled ① represent the basic property of set addition that "maximization/minimization of the whole implies maximization/minimization of each part" (see Preparation 2 in Section D.1). Arrow ② represents "duality," the fact that "an expenditure-minimizing point is also a utility-maximizing point."
- Finally, if we give each consumer i income $p\overline{x}^i$, the given efficient allocation can be realized as a market equilibrium under the price profile p. (Consumers maximize their utility given their incomes and the firms maximize their profits.) We know that $\overline{x}^1 + \cdots + \overline{x}^I = \overline{y}^1 + \cdots + \overline{y}^J + w$, since total consumption and total production must be equal, so

$$p\overline{x}^1 + \cdots + p\overline{x}^I = p\overline{y}^1 + \cdots + p\overline{y}^J + pw.$$

This means that, if the government appropriately redistributes the right-hand side of this equation (the total profit $p\overline{y}^1 + \cdots + p\overline{y}^J$ and the value of the initial endowment pw) which is equal to total income in society, then we can indeed make each consumer i's income $p\overline{x}^i$. **(Q.E.D.)**

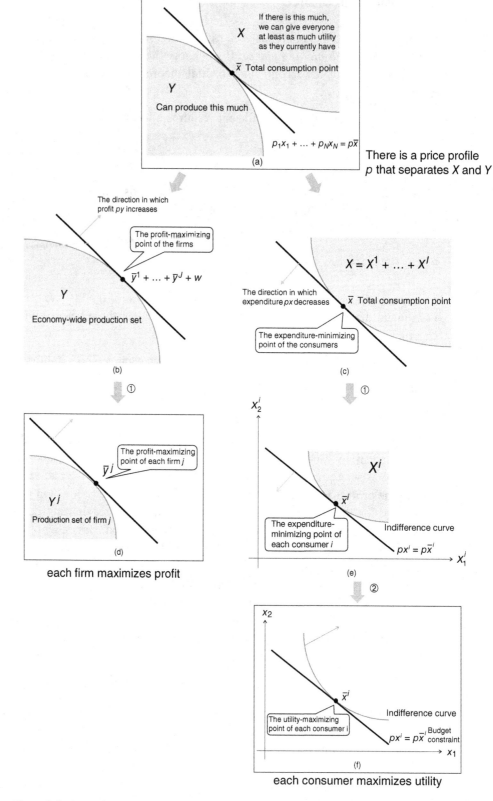

Figure D.9 A concise overview of the proof of the second fundamental theorem of welfare economics

D.4   Detailed Remarks

Let me finish my explanation of the proof by reviewing the detailed parts that *I* initially brushed over.

① **An Explanation of Why the Improvement Set *X* and Production Possibility Set *Y* Are Tangent to Each Other**

I am going to give a more precise explanation of Step 2 in Section D.2, where I said that, beginning from an efficient resource allocation, the improvement set *X* and production possibility set *Y* are tangent to each other.

First, I want you to look back at Figure D.9 (a). The set *Y*, in the bottom left, is tangent to the set *X*, in the top right. You can see from the figure that the prices that separate the two sets cannot be negative.[13] Allow me to explain more precisely why this must be true.

Please look at Figure D.10. The set *X*, located in the top right, and the set *Y*, located in the bottom left, are not tangent to each other, but overlap.

In that case, we can take two points *x* and *y*, as in Figure D.10. Note that point $x = (x_1, \ldots, x_N)$ belongs to the improvement set *X*. However, note that at the point *y*, which belongs to the production possibility set *Y*, the quantity of every good is higher than at *x*. (That is, $y_n > x_n$ for all *n*; we can write this more succinctly as $y > x$.) To say that "*X* in the top right and *Y* in the bottom left are *tangent* to each other" means precisely that this cannot happen. To summarize:[14]

If $x \in X$ and $y > x$ then $y \notin Y$. (*)

Now, I claim that, if we construct the improvement set *X* based on an efficient resource allocation, the above condition (*) is necessarily satisfied. To prove this claim, it suffices to show that the following condition holds.

Condition 2: at any feasible resource allocation, there is at least one consumer whose utility increases if her consumption (of some good or goods) increases.[15]

Let's prove that the improvement set *X* in the top right and the production possibility set *Y* in the bottom left are indeed tangent to each other (i.e. condition (*) holds). Toward a

---

[13]   Look at Figure D.9 (a), which shows an example with only two goods ($N = 2$). If $p_1 < 0$ and $p_2 > 0$, then the straight line $p_1 x_1 + p_2 x_2 = p\overline{x}$ is *upward-sloping*. Since the straight line $p_1 x_1 + p_2 x_2 = p\overline{x}$ that separates *X* in the top right from *Y* in the bottom left must be downward-sloping, we know that the price of each good must be non-negative.

[14]   Condition (*) also holds when *X* and *Y* do not overlap at all. So, precisely speaking, when *X* and *Y* share at least one point, (*) is the condition that the set *X* in the top right and the set *Y* in the bottom left are tangent to each other. (Note that, in this context, *X* and *Y* share the total consumption point $\overline{x}$).

[15]   When does Condition 2 fail to hold? Condition 2 does not hold in the near-impossible case that, at some efficient resource allocation, there is not a single consumer who could achieve a higher utility by consuming more. Since this case is so uncommon, this condition is almost always assumed to hold.

Figure D.10 The case in which the improvement set X and the production possibility set Y overlap (and so are not tangent to each other)

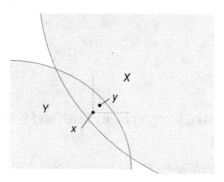

contradiction, suppose that condition (*) does not hold, and there exists some $y \in Y$ and $x \in X$ and such that $y > x$. Then, the following are true.

(1) From the definition of X, if we appropriately distribute the goods in x, we can ensure that all consumers have at least as much utility as they did under the efficient resource allocation.

(2) Starting from the efficient resource allocation, from Condition 2 we know that there is some consumer whose utility we can increase by offering that consumer more of a certain good. To simplify things, we'll call that good "good 1." Consider another point y' at which only the quantity of good 1 has increased relative to x ($x_1 < y_1$):

$$y' = (y_1, x_2, \ldots, x_N).$$

We assumed that the point $y = (y_1, \ldots y_N)$ belongs to the production possibility set Y, so the point y' must be feasible since it contains less of goods 2 through N than y contains, and, by Condition 1, producers can dispose of unnecessary goods. But, if the economy produces y', then we can distribute the goods in such a way that all consumers have at least as much utility as they did beforehand, and at least one consumer has strictly higher utility. But this contradicts our assumption that the initial resource allocation is efficient. Therefore, it must be that condition (*) indeed holds.

② A Precise Statement of the Separating Hyperplane Theorem

There are several versions of the separating hyperplane theorem, but we will use the following form.[16] Note that, since we use condition (*), which applies when X in the top right and Y in the bottom left are tangent to each other, we know that the prices separating the two sets are positive or zero.

---

[16] I adapted the following version of the theorem into the version you see in the text, which is more convenient for our discussion:

   If Z is a convex set in an N-dimensional space and Z does not include any point with only positive coordinates, then there exists some $p = (p_1, \ldots, p_N) \neq 0, p_n \geq 0, n = 1, \ldots, N$ such that for all $z \in Z$, $0 \geq pz$ holds.

   If we apply this to $Z = Y - X$, then we obtain the version of the separating hyperplane theorem that I stated in the main text.

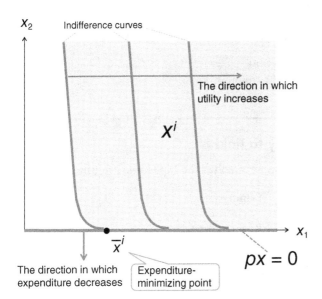

Figure D.11 An example in which expenditure is zero and duality does not hold

---

Separating Hyperplane Theorem

If X and Y are convex sets in an N-dimensional space and condition (*) holds, then, for any $x \in X$ and $y \in Y$, there exists $p = (p_1, \ldots, p_N) \neq 0, p_n \geq 0, \; n = 1, \ldots, N$ such that

$$px \geq py.$$

---

③ **If Expenditure Is Zero, then Duality May Not Hold**

Duality (Chapter 1 and Preparation 4 in Appendix D.1), the property that an expenditure-minimizing point is also a utility-maximizing point, *may not hold if expenditure is zero.* Suppose that the expenditure-minimizing point is $\overline{x}^i$, as shown in Figure D.11.

The grey region is the set X^i of points that give consumer i at least as much utility as he or she has under the current consumption point $\overline{x}^i$. Under the price profile p shown in the figure, the price of good 1 is zero and the price of good 2 is greater than zero. As you can see, from among the points in the grey region, the current consumption point $\overline{x}^i$ indeed minimizes expenditure px.

I want you to note that the minimized expenditure is equal to zero. The budget line under the income equal to this minimized expenditure ($= 0$) is the horizontal black line shown in Figure D.11. However, *this expenditure-minimizing point $\overline{x}^i$ is not a utility-maximizing point* on this budget line. This is because, as we move along the budget line toward the right, utility increases. Therefore, duality, the property that an expenditure-minimizing point is a utility-maximizing point, is not satisfied.

To show the last part (Step 4) of the proof of the second fundamental theorem of welfare economics, we need to exclude these weird examples.[17] For that, it suffices to require that

- the minimized expenditure is not zero; and
- the utility function $u^i(x)$ is a continuous function.[18]

Lemma D.1 Condition for Duality to Hold

Under a price profile $p \geq 0, p \neq 0$, suppose $\bar{x}^i$ solves the expenditure minimization problem

$$\min_{x^i} px^i$$

$$\text{s.t. } u^i\left(x^i\right) \geq u^i\left(\bar{x}^i\right)$$

If condition (i), *the minimized expenditure, is not zero* ($p\bar{x}^i \neq 0$) and condition (ii), *the utility function $u^i(x)$, is a continuous function* are satisfied, then $\bar{x}^i$ also solves the utility maximization problem

$$\max_{x^i} u^i\left(x^i\right)$$

$$\text{s.t. } px^i \leq p\bar{x}^i.$$

The proof of this lemma is simple but contains some tricky details, so I will explain it in the Supplementary Appendix. Note that the following condition was used to ensure duality holds.

Condition 3: the utility function of each consumer is a continuous function.

D.5   A Precise Statement of the Theorem

Now I am ready to rigorously state the second fundamental theorem of welfare economics, along with the conditions that ensure it holds. To simplify the statement of the theorem, I will define some terminology.

Definition: a **theoretical price profile** p for a resource allocation $\left(\bar{x}^1, \ldots, \bar{x}^I, \bar{y}^1, \ldots, \bar{y}^J\right)$ satisfies the following two conditions.

   Profit maximization: each firm j's production plan $\bar{y}^j$ maximizes profit under the price profile p.

---

[17] Figure D.11 illustrates an example in which the second fundamental theorem of welfare economics does not hold. Concretely, what type of scenario could this graph describe? Consider an economy in which there is no firm and just one consumer i. Suppose that the initial endowment is $w = \bar{x}^i$, the improvement set is $X = X^i$, and the production possibility set is $Y = \{\bar{x}^i\}$. The only straight line that separates X and Y is $px = 0$, as shown in Figure D.11 (note that the indifference curves are tangent to the x axis). But, under this price profile, $\bar{x}^i$ is not a utility-maximizing point.

[18] For readers who are not mathematically inclined: if a utility function is *continuous*, it means that, when consumption changes, utility responds continuously (i.e. it doesn't jump).

Expenditure minimization: each consumer i's consumption bundle $\bar{x}^i$ minimizes expenditure among the consumption bundles that provide at least $u^i(\bar{x}^i)$, the utility of the current bundle.

Now that we have defined theoretical price profiles, I will state the second fundamental theorem of welfare economics.

Second Fundamental Theorem of Welfare Economics

Condition 0 (convexity): for each consumer, the region above any indifference curve is a convex set. In addition, each firm's production possibility set is a convex set.

Condition 1: the producers can dispose of unnecessary goods.

Condition 2: at any feasible resource allocation, there is at least one consumer whose utility increases if her consumption (of some good or goods) increases.

If Conditions 0 to 2 are satisfied, then there exists a theoretical price profile $p \geq 0$,[19] $p \neq 0$, that satisfies the profit maximization/expenditure minimization condition for any Pareto-efficient resource allocation $(\bar{x}^1, \ldots, \bar{x}^I, \bar{y}^1, \ldots, \bar{y}^J)$. Moreover, if

Condition 3: the utility function of each consumer is a continuous function; and

Condition 4: each consumer's expenditure under price profile p is not zero ($p\bar{x}^i > 0$)

hold, then the Pareto-efficient resource allocation $(\bar{x}^1, \ldots, \bar{x}^I, \bar{y}^1, \ldots, \bar{y}^J)$ can be realized as a perfectly competitive market equilibrium if the government conducts a lump-sum income redistribution policy.

If Condition 4 is not satisfied, it means that there is a consumer who consumes only goods for which the theoretical price is zero, and therefore has zero expenditure. Intuitively, such a strange thing should not usually happen, and in almost all cases Condition 4 "should" hold. Here are some (relatively realistic) conditions that ensure that Condition 4 is satisfied.[20]

Lemma D.2

If the following conditions hold, then each consumer's expenditure under the theoretical price vector is not zero (i.e. Condition 4 holds).

Condition 4a: there exists a feasible production plan such that the quantity of every good is positive.

Condition 4b: for each consumer, there is at least one good that satisfies the following conditions:

---

[19] For inequalities of vectors, refer to p. 181.

[20] It was quite difficult for me to come up with relatively realistic and easy-to-understand conditions on consumers' utility functions and firms' production technologies to ensure that Condition 4 holds, but after some effort I was able to come up with Conditions 4a to 4c. You can read about the more general "resource relationship" condition in Kenneth Arrow and Frank Hahn, *General Competitive Analysis* (San Francisco: Holden-Day, 1971), chap. 5, sect. 1.

- if consumption of that good increases, then utility increases; and
- there is some firm that can increase production of that good if it uses more labor.

Condition 4c: there is no consumer who works 24 hours every day and has zero time for leisure.

Since the proof of this lemma is a little involved, I have put it in the Supplementary Appendix.

D.6   If There Are Many Consumers and Producers, the Second Fundamental Theorem of Welfare Economics Holds Even Without the Strong Assumptions

From the preceding discussion, you probably understand that the most *important assumption* for the proof of the second fundamental theorem of welfare economics is the assumption that *the economy-wide production possibility set Y and improvement set X are both convex*. As I explained previously, this assumption holds if each firm's production possibility set is convex and each consumer's indifference curves are bowed toward the origin. However, it is quite possible that these conditions imposed on each individual firm and consumer do not hold in the real world. Anyone who questions whether these conditions actually hold may *naturally wonder whether the second fundamental theorem is just a theoretical construct that has no bearing on reality*.

In fact, if there are many consumers and producers in the economy, then, even if individual firms' production possibility sets and the regions above the consumers' indifference curves are not convex, the economy-wide production possibility set Y and improvement set X are approximately convex, and therefore the second fundamental theorem would still hold. Please look at Figure D.12.

For this firm in the figure, when the labor input is small, production efficiency increases as labor increases (i.e. the slope of the curve, which gives the marginal productivity of labor, increases), so the production possibility set is not convex. There may be many firms like this in the real world.

Figure D.12 A firm with a non-convex production possibility set

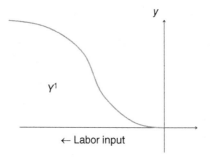

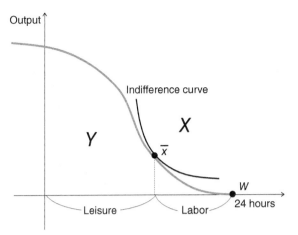

Figure D.13 An economy in which the second fundamental theorem does not hold because Y is not convex

If this were the only firm in the economy, then the economy-wide production possibility set Y would have the same (non-convex) shape as the one shown in Figure D.12, so the conclusion of the second fundamental theorem may not hold. For example, in the economy shown in Figure D.13, with just one consumer and a single firm with a non-convex production possibility set, at the efficient allocation $\bar{x}$ there does not exist a price profile that separates X and Y. In this case, the conclusion of the second fundamental theorem does not hold.

Let's consider what happens if there are many consumers and many firms whose production possibility sets are not convex. Suppose there are K consumers and K firms, each with the non-convex production possibility set shown in Figure D.13. What is the shape of the economy-wide production possibility set $Y = Y^1 + \cdots + Y^K$ (where $Y^1 = \cdots = Y^K$)? This set becomes larger and larger as K increases, so, when we depict these sets, it is better to adjust the scale of the axes. What matters to us is the production possibility set that each individual consumer faces, so let's draw $\frac{1}{K}(Y^1 + \cdots + Y^K)$, *which converts the economy-wide production possibility set to the one that an individual consumer faces* (see Figure D.14).[21]

As you can see from the figure, *as the number of firms grows large, the economy-wide production possibility set becomes approximately convex*. Why does this happen? Please look at Figure D.15.

Consider the case in which there are two firms and there is one unit of labor per each firm (and therefore there are two units of labor altogether). (Figure D.14 (a)). If each firm uses one unit in the exact same way, then both firms' production will be at point a in Figure D.15, so the average of the firms' production is also point a. Therefore, there is no difference between an individual firm's production and the economy-wide average of the firms' production. However, suppose that we assigned both units of labor input to one of the two firms, and gave the other firm no units of labor input. In this case, the firm with two units of labor input will achieve

---

[21] Kenji Tsukada, a student in the PhD program at the Graduate School of Economics at University of Tokyo, created the original figure. I thank Mr. Tsukada.

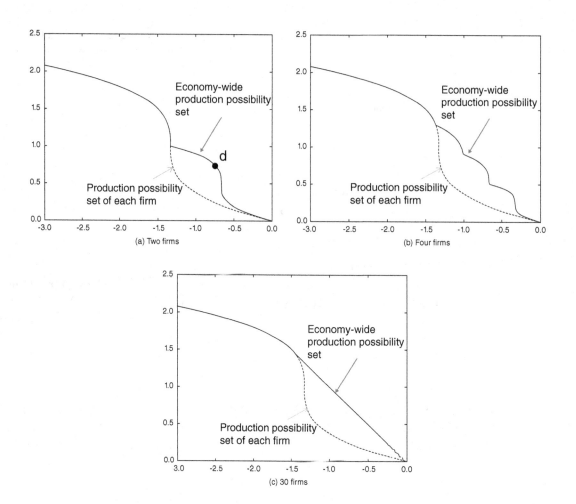

Figure D.14 As the number of firms grows large, the economy-wide production possibility set becomes approximately convex

point b and the firm without any units of labor input will achieve point c, which means that the economy-wide average of the firms' production is now point d. This is exactly how point d in Figure D.14 (a), which we saw earlier, was achieved. As the number of firms becomes large, many points along the straight line L in Figure D.15 become achievable, by designating some fraction of the firms to produce point b and the others to produce point c. For instance, if there are 30 firms, then using this strategy we can achieve any point from among the set of points that divides L into 30 equal parts. As Figure D.14 (c) shows, if there are as many as 30 firms, then the economy-wide production possibility set is extremely close to being perfectly convex.

We can show analogous properties for consumers too. Even if the regions above each consumer's indifference curves are not convex, if the number of consumers is large the economy-wide improvement set will be nearly convex. Consequently, *if there are sufficiently many consumers and producers in the economy*, we can think of the economy-wide production

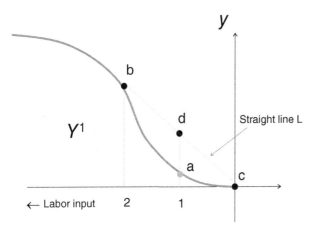

Figure D.15 The reason the economy-wide production possibility set becomes approximately convex

possibility set Y and improvement set X as being approximately convex, so *there is a basis for thinking that the second fundamental theorem of welfare economics still holds.*[22]

Comment D.2

Congratulations. Thank you for your patience. How was that? After reading this entire Appendix, don't you have a much deeper understanding of the market mechanism and the role of prices? Those of you who have carefully read this book up to this point have a solid grasp of economics. Now you will be able to look at the world with an economic perspective, analyze different kinds of economic problems, and weigh the advantages and disadvantages of various economic policies. In other words, you are now ready to think like an economist – I'm giving you your honorary diploma!

Supplementary Appendix: Proof of the Lemmas

① Proof of Lemma D.1

Toward a contradiction, suppose that the conclusion is not correct and there exists a consumption bundle x' that satisfies the budget constraint and gives a higher utility than $\bar{x}^i$ gives. Note that, since x' satisfies the budget constraint,

---

[22] What I have explained here is an introduction to an area of economic theory that deals with "**large**" **economies** in which there are many consumers and firms. If you are interested in learning more about this field, you can consult a resource such as Werner Hildenbrand, *Core and Equilibria of a Large Economy* (Princeton, NJ: Princeton University Press, 1974). The relationship between set addition and convexity that I explained is based on the Shapley–Folkman lemma (see Wikipedia: https://en.wikipedia.org/wiki/Shapley%E2%80%93Folkman_lemma).

$$px' \leq p\bar{x}^i \tag{1}$$
$$\text{expenditure} \quad \text{income}$$

and x' is chosen to satisfy

$$u^i(\bar{x}^i) < u^i(x'). \tag{2}$$

If (1) holds with inequality ($<$), then point x' gives a utility no less than the current bundle ($\bar{x}^i$) and is also cheaper than $\bar{x}^i$, contradicting our assumption that $\bar{x}^i$ is the cheapest bundle that gives at least as much utility as $\bar{x}^i$. Therefore, (1) must hold with equality. From condition (i), we know that $0 < p\bar{x}^i$, so combining these two conditions we have that

$$0 < px'.$$

Now, let t be a number slightly less than one. If we consider a new consumption bundle tx', we can see that $p(tx') < px'$. Why? Since $0 < px'$, we know $0 < (1-t)px' < px' - p(tx')$. From this and (1), we get

$$p(tx') < p\bar{x}^i.$$

That is, the expenditure at tx' is lower than the expenditure at the current consumption bundle $\bar{x}^i$. Moreover, since the utility function u is continuous, if t is sufficiently close to one, then $u^i(tx')$ is almost equal to $u^i(x')$. Using this fact and (2), we get

$$u^i(\bar{x}^i) < u^i(tx').$$

So consumption bundle tx' gives a higher utility than the current consumption bundle $\bar{x}^i$ gives. However, this contradicts our assumption that, from among the consumption bundles that give at least as much utility as $\bar{x}^i$, $\bar{x}^i$ is the cheapest.

Since we have reached this contradiction, it must be that our assumption that there exists a consumption bundle x' that satisfies the budget constraint and gives a higher utility than $\bar{x}^i$ gives is false. Therefore, among the consumption bundles that satisfy the budget constraint, $\bar{x}^i$ must maximize utility. **(Q.E.D.)**

② Proof of Lemma D.2

After implementing the production plan $\hat{y}^1, \ldots, \hat{y}^J$ as in Condition 4a, there are $w + \hat{y}^1 + \cdots + \hat{y}^J$ units of goods in the economy, and the quantity of each good is positive. The theoretical prices are given by $p \geq 0$, $p \neq 0$, so we have

$$p(w + \hat{y}^1 + \cdots + \hat{y}^J) > 0. \tag{3}$$

Each firm j's production plan $\bar{y}^j$ at the efficient allocation in the second fundamental theorem of welfare economics is a profit-maximizing point under the theoretical price profile, so we have $p\bar{y}^j \geq p\hat{y}^j$. From this and (3), we have that

$$p(w + \bar{y}^1 + \cdots + \bar{y}^J) > 0. \tag{4}$$

Since total consumption and production must be equal, we know that $\bar{x}^1 + \cdots + \bar{x}^I = \bar{y}^1 + \cdots + \bar{y}^J + w$. Substituting the left-hand side into Expression (4), we obtain

$$p(\bar{x}^1 + \cdots + \bar{x}^I) > 0.$$

In other words, there is at least one consumer whose expenditure is positive. Then, from Lemma D.1, duality holds. Therefore, this person's consumption bundle $\bar{x}^i$ is a utility-maximizing point under the price profile p. If, for this consumer, the price of the good specified in Condition 4b is zero, then his or her utility can be increased if he or she consumes more of this good for free. This contradicts our assumption that $\bar{x}^i$ is a utility-maximizing point. Therefore, the price of this good must be positive. Now, if the wage is zero, then the firm can increase its labor input and produce more of this good, which would increase its profit under the price profile p. But this contradicts our assumption that each firm's production plan is a profit-maximizing point under the price profile p, so the wage must be positive.

As I explained in Chapter 3, Section 3.3, part (b), if we let good 1 be leisure, each consumer's expenditure toward good 1 is "wage × leisure consumed," which is positive by Condition 4c. Thus, since each consumer's expenditure on leisure is positive, each consumer's total expenditure is positive. **(Q.E.D.)**

Index

Printed in the United States
by Baker & Taylor Publisher Services